This copy of

BEHOLD JERUSALEM!

is number

793

*in a
limited edition
of 1000 copies*

GRAHAM K. GRIFFITHS

★ BEHOLD ★
JERUSALEM!

FOUND! - THE ZODIACAL MIRACLE
IN THE MAP OF BRITAIN & N. IRELAND
AND ITS MESSAGE FOR OUR TIME

★

• A ~~LONGINUS~~ Publication •

Published by:
Longinus Publications
27 Old Gloucester Street, London WC1N 3XX
e-mail: longinuspublications@emjaygee.fsnet.co.uk

ISBN 0 9543519 0 8

British Library Cataloguing in Publication Data.

Dedication

To my parents Gwen and Bryce,
my wife Linda and daughters Morwenna and Holly
who unwaveringly believed in me when I myself didn't.
God bless you.

★

Dedicated too
to you tides and winds,
you frosts, rains, rivers, streams and worms,
and all those folk who have either knowingly or not
aided and abetted the miracle underfoot.

★ ★ ★

Tabula Smaragdina - The Emerald Tablet

"Heaven above, Heaven below;
Stars above, Stars below;
All that is over, under shall show.
Happy thou who the riddle readest."

(Cited by Katherine Maltwood in her book
A GUIDE TO GLASTONBURY'S TEMPLE OF THE STARS)

Acknowledgements

First and foremost to my wife *Linda*
whose bread-winning, unfailing love and support,
even in the darkest of days, allowed me to stay at home and play amongst the stars.
Without her this book would not be in your hands.

To *Gag* whose gift of iron from heaven
gave me the backbone to finally open my mouth
and tell all who would care to hear of this miracle in the landscape.

JF, the first outside my family who heard and
answered "Put it down on paper" - thank you for your camaraderie
and wise council in those early days.

MM, for her courage in editing this epic ramble
and yet still keeping a cheery tone whenever I phoned.

Alan Sinden, for that gesture of confidence - you never knew it,
but what you said proved a major turning point
in my wavering as to whether to
give the whole thing up or go for the final hurdle.

Especial thanks to my old friend *Steve Tatler* (aka *Boromir*),
who waited patiently until called for,
and then came quickly and unflinchingly into the fray.
His design and computer skills giving the strange child
clothes fit to walk out into the world in.

Last, but not least, a deep bow of gratitude to the gifted sight and intuition
of *Mary Caine* and the late *Katherine Maltwood*.
Without you I would have remained blind to this life enhancing miracle.

★

Thank you all from the bottom of my heart.

Contents

★

IT BEGAN
WITH
A BOY
WHO READ
CLOUDS

★

An Introduction you shouldn't skip!

To the peoples of antiquity the Isle of Britain was the very home and environment of mystery, a sacred territory, to enter which was to encroach upon a region of enchantment, the dwelling of gods, the shrine and habitation of a cult of peculiar sanctity and mystical power. Britain was, indeed, the insula sacra of the West, an island veiled and esoteric, the Egypt of the Occident. Legends of its strange and perilous marvels were current among the semi-civilised races who dwelt over against its ghostly white cliffs; it was regarded as the haunt and refuge of giants, demons and spirits; by not a few, even as the paradise and resort of the dead"

THE MYSTERIES OF BRITAIN, Lewis Spence

Glastonbury Road

I think it was Christmas morning 1962. At a council house in Glastonbury Road (although 100 miles away from that Somerset town) a boy sat up in bed and pulled out of his bulging pillowcase full of gifts, one which, when unwrapped, hadn't the glitter of the boxed model Spitfire, the Lone Star Colt 45, or the shiny leather football which lay already opened at his side; he held now the rather educational-looking *Readers' Digest Great World Atlas*. Nevertheless, and so as not to seem ungrateful to his mom and dad who were watching him open his presents, he made a gesture of interest by turning to the page illustrating the British Isles to find the town where he lived. However, he was to see on that page something he'd never noticed before.

Sure, the shape of the British Isles was already familiar to the 11-year-old, but on this magical morning that distinctive green slab was to magically transform itself, for he saw in a flash, silhouetted out of the coast of north Wales, a cackling old hag, with the entire island of Anglesey forming her bonneted head, and she, seemingly, pointing with outstretched arm at the tiny speck which was Bardsey Island. Then in quick-fire succession he saw outlined just below her, a snarling beast lashing a barbed claw out of the coastline of southwest Wales, followed by the whole of England's southwest peninsula flipping itself into the shape of a gigantic fish - its head buried somewhere deep inland. Finally, on the other side of the country he showed his parents how that east coast held the colossal profile of a bald-headed man who was pointing a stubby finger towards Europe. The lad laughed with his parents at these almost cartoon figures, although a moment later the atlas was closed and put aside because more presents still were jostling to get out of that pillowcase.

The truth was, that that 60-second interlude of spotting giants profiled in Britain's coastline was no big deal to either him or his parents, for his imagination had always run wild. Indeed, it could be said that some days he went to school only to list the procession of giants and all manner of other fabulous things which would, weather conditions permitting, file past his classroom window in the form of clouds. That said, those four giants in the atlas were to prove a case of 'once seen never forgotten'. From that day on he'd always see them just behind the TV weather forecaster's shoulder, though never did he associate them with those characters of the zodiac. Another 17 years would have to pass before he'd make that connection and to realise that that big boring atlas had contained the most wondrous gift imaginable.

Glastonbury High Street

And so the child who saw fabulous things in the clouds was now 28 years old and his eye keener than ever, having become a professional illustrator. 'Chance' then found him one day idly thumbing the artist Mary Caine's book *The Glastonbury Zodiac - Key to the Mysteries of Britain* in a book shop in that Somerset town, where he was making his first-ever visit.

Until that moment he'd never heard of this so-called Glastonbury zodiac but soon found that Caine's book was based upon the discovery made by another artist, Katherine Maltwood, back in the 1930s. She claimed to have found the 12 signs of the zodiac gigantically formed and outlined by the hills, streams, lanes and hedgerows in a ten-mile diameter circle around Glastonbury itself. However, to most who have come across her theory which she published in her own book *A guide to Glastonbury's Temple of the Stars*, she'd found nothing but a coincidental freak of nature, if that.

Freak of nature or not, listen to this. When I opened Caine's book I found almost perfect outline replicas of those four giants I'd found animating Britain's coastline on that Christmas morning all those years ago,

although my versions were hundreds of times larger. Moreover, I could also see that my 120-mile-tall cackling crone was in fact a rendering of the Earth Mother aspect of Virgo. There, too, were Leo, my 117-mile-long snarling beast, Pisces, my 155-mile-long fish, and the head of her Sagittarius was that profile I'd spied looking out of the east coast!

Without a second thought I bought Caine's book, ran across the road to the sanctuary of the ruins of Glastonbury Abbey, and in the peace of a roofless chapel spent the warm afternoon avidly reading the print from off its pages.

The gist of what I read went like this: Maltwood had received a commission to illustrate an itinerary for the then newly-translated medieval manuscript *The High History of the Holy Grail*, purportedly written at Glastonbury Abbey. In following the tale's knights as they quested for the Grail and their confrontations with giants and ferocious beasts, she formed a hunch that the vividly described locations for these adventures seemed familiar to certain areas around Glastonbury itself.

Prompted by her hunch she was soon scanning a map of the area. It was then, without, I would imagine, any thoughts whatsoever of those giants and beasts existing as part of the actual landscape, that her sculptor's eye was confronted by what seemed a vast lion, shaped in the landscape by streams and ancient country lanes. Even the way the fields were laid out seemed to accentuate its feline stretch, while an expansive beech wood gave it a perfect mane - and just imagine the effect of that in autumn! But that wasn't all, close by this lion she then discerned, by the same topographical means, a giant human figure with one arm upraised above its head - a head perfectly formed by a prominent hill. She was obviously intrigued by this, but it was only when later mentioning her curious finds to an astrologer friend, that the names Leo and Gemini were tentatively attached to those two figures. A casual enough connection, but, boy, was it to let the zodiacal cat out of the bag. In next to no time the full complement of zodiacal figures revealed themselves to her, and remarkably all in correct astrological sequence, in an enormous circle upon that Somerset landscape.

Her amazing discovery was, of course, to greatly inspire her. After years of further research, her mapped giants augmented by aerial photographs, she settled on the theory that the *High History of the Holy Grail* was revealing that the adventures of those Grail-questing knights were being played out amongst the astrological giants and beasts of the constellations - albeit those as mirrored upon Somerset's pastures! And an interesting theory too, especially when read alongside current opinion that, encoded between the lines of another medieval Grail romance, namely *Parzival*, there are further strong hints that the 'way' to the Grail was, at least for those in the know, always an astrologically signposted one.

Fascinating stuff, but, by the time the shadows from that romantic ruin of an arch were lengthening and I was leaving the abbey grounds for my journey home, I'd come to the conclusion that my own childhood discovery of giants on a map, no matter how startlingly similar in shape to Maltwood's own giants, couldn't possibly be zodiacal, for I'd found but four characters and thus 'coincidence' had to have the final say.

For mile after M5 mile, however, the whole thing nagged me and upon arriving home I reached again for that big old atlas, and guess what? Upon the page bearing the map of Britain, my eye was instantly beguiled by the sight of two more virtual carbon copies of Maltwood's giants, though again massively enlarged. I saw Libra represented as a white dove (as at Glastonbury) suddenly filling every bird-like inch of the Isle of Wight, whilst directly in her flight path Capricorn was bucking in the mainland's south coast! As for Maltwood's six remaining figures, these would become the virtual templates for the six extra figures that I would eventually find over the next 13 years cut out of the rest of Britain's coastline. Maltwood's own 10-mile-diameter circle of star giants were becoming so dwarfed in the process, yet so wonderfully placed, that I'd find it in the end to be prescribing exactly the starry eye of the whopping fish the 11-year-old caught on that Christmas morning!

Coincidence or an artistic imagination running riot again? Read on.

In 1972 members of the Pendragon Society discovered another landscaped zodiac, although only partially complete, in the Preseli mountains of Wales. These figures, too, were miniature mirror images of the coastal set I would later find. Taking all these discoveries into account, I submit to you evidence in triplicate of the heavens come down to earth, indicating that something absolutely astonishing is going on beneath our feet. And for a taster of this triplicated phenomena just check out the following.

Katherine Maltwood

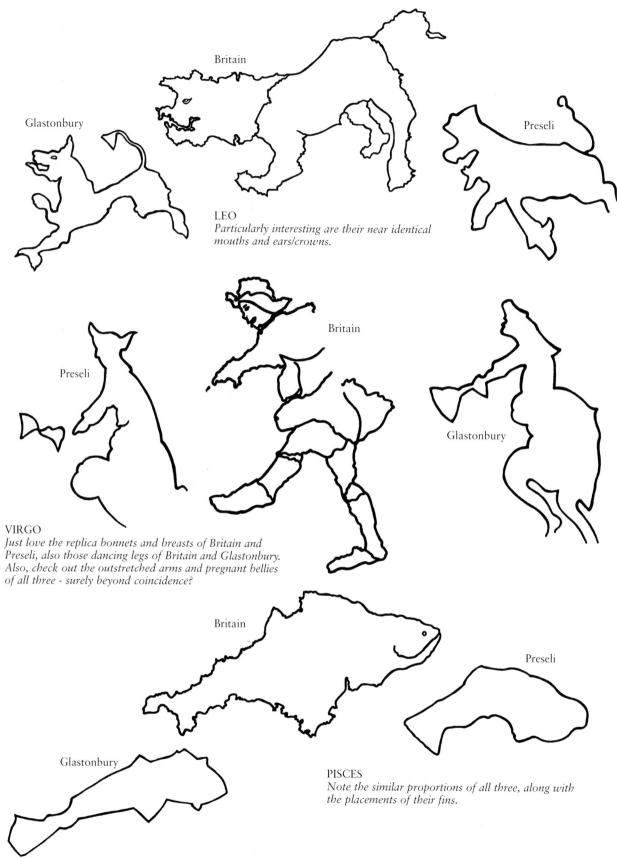

Britain

Glastonbury

Preseli

LEO
Particularly interesting are their near identical mouths and ears/crowns.

Preseli

Britain

Glastonbury

VIRGO
Just love the replica bonnets and breasts of Britain and Preseli, also those dancing legs of Britain and Glastonbury. Also, check out the outstretched arms and pregnant bellies of all three - surely beyond coincidence?

Britain

Preseli

Glastonbury

PISCES
Note the similar proportions of all three, along with the placements of their fins.

So if it's not all but a coincidental fluke, who or what could be behind it?

Are they the work of cat-eyed extra-terrestrials with a penchant for enormous landing pads fashioned after the signs of the zodiac, super-technologically-advanced Atlantians armed with cliff cutting lasers, or what? Well, neither, for the truth behind its creation could be even more dumbfounding. I believe these terrestrial star giants can only be the product of what must be an unsung intelligence working through, in this case, the not-so-random chiselling of tide, wind, rain and frost; prompting the slips and slides of sediment and rock, and dictating both the way rivers cut their courses and worms contour their hills. Indeed, even in the mundane doings of man, from his tramping out of ancient trackways to his later canal cuttings, it seems he has unknowingly aided and abetted the inland contours of this aeons-in-the-making wonder work. Why, I have found, just as Maltwood did, that sometimes even place names seemed to verify the giants I have discovered lying beneath their given spot!

Thus, I put it to you that there can be no other cause behind these gargantuan figures than an aware and articulate God/cosmic mind/metaphysical force, call it what you will, more beautifully *everywhere* and *in everything* than most of us over the past 2000 years have ever conceived. And if so, my, how our earth has proved once and for all, through this masterpiece of communicative landscaping that she is, just as the shaman always said she was, a sacred living, thinking and articulate Being.

But you ain't heard nothing yet!

Agreed, it's all sounding pretty wacky, but even this preposterous sighting of giants in a landscape is but the tip of what may prove to be an almighty iceberg, one coming out of a fog

of forgotten knowledge. It's on course to challenge every damn thing we think of as watertight fact regarding this planet and our fleeting lives on it. If this artist's eye is true, the implications will be staggering.

You see, what's on the front cover of this book is far more than just a pretty picture. I'm going to show that this starry miracle now arrived upon the doorstep of the world also contains, via its cunning rearrangement of the astrological sign sequence, both a terrible warning to people living now and yet word, too, of a fabulous future beyond our wildest dreams. And if I am correct in thinking this to be some extraordinary landscaped message, we shouldn't be surprised by the earth's way of conveying it. The 12 characters of the zodiac, those mythologised star clusters, have, since the dawn of civilisation, strangely compelled folk around the globe to look up in the hope of distilling guidance from their nightly alignments. Is it not apt, then, that those constellations, wherein men intuitively sensed they could read their fate, should become a prophetic pictorial sign language. Remember, too, that myths were our ancestors' favourite way of preserving and passing on essential truths to future generations. Taking these things together then, it seems our not-so-mute planet has commandeered the past's classical sign language in order to speak to us all, as universally as possible, at a time that must be so in need of urgent guidance that the fate of the entire creation may hang upon its interpretation.

I can think of no other reason for this almighty materialisation of mythical star pictures upon the face of our planet.

The writing on the walls of Britain and Ireland

Therefore, and without having to leave your armchair, I invite you upon an incredible clockwise journey through these topographical constellations, in an effort to decipher what our earth might be trying to tell us in this picture sign-language. And the pictures are so graphic that one doesn't need to be an astrologer to work them out. But be warned, we'll be venturing over strange ground indeed, and some passages of the pictorial land-poetry we'll visit have the power to trigger such a strange sense of recognition of something infinitely remote, yet so acutely intimate, that a peculiarly poignant tug of the emotions can become a regular occurrence - but don't ask me why. At other points on our journey, though, we'll have no choice but to laugh our socks off at the disarming down-to-earth humour sprinkling our path, presumably as a sign that we're neither lost nor insane!

Laugh, I hope you will, when finding out that when we are gathered in the corner of Sagittarius' right eye we'll actually be in a place called Eye! Then again, if you love this planet, a smile might be hard to summon when I demonstrate how, by striking straight lines around a selection of Britain's coastal extremities, one can erect the all-enveloping shape of an almighty ark (*see Cancer*). This, too, is a dazzling replica of the distinctively shaped ark that Maltwood found imprinted on Somerset's pastures. And do arks not appear when all life is threatened, especially by rising seas?

"What we cannot deny is that the sea levels are rising…We cannot ignore the situation."
Elliot Morley, Environmental Minister - November 2001

It is unnerving, then, to learn that if global warming is a fact, current scientific estimates are that, within a century or less, a one-metre rise in global sea levels, due to the melting of the polar ice caps, will cause catastrophic flooding worldwide. This news is especially worrying when, upon our journey of interpretation over these prophetic star giants, we see graphically illustrated on the map, via both their pertinent positioning and the mythological voices invested in them by our ancestors, the precise areas where Britain, this vast ark, may herself be inundated. What's more, these places, although deciphered by me as bearing pictorial warnings of major flooding, long before any talk of global warming and rising seas, are exactly where today's experts predict they will be. I'll take you to these screaming areas of concern and you can make up your own mind.

To add to this sense of warning we'll also see that although our ark safely envelopes all the land-dwelling giants stationed on English and Welsh soil, ingeniously making them its very cargo or passengers, Northern Ireland's Scorpion (and God how I wished that particular sign had appeared anywhere else but there!) is ominously cast adrift. We will try to understand why, particularly when we visit the place where Scorpio's sting sinks alarmingly into its own back; and where the land-poetry will demand we ask questions so discomfiting that we may not want to hear answers. Likewise, when I take you to the ground-sign that is representative of our presently dawning astrological age of Aquarius which, at Glastonbury is landscaped as a phoenix, (and the reasons why water is replaced by fire will be made astonishingly clear upon our arrival there) we will stand aghast at the clamouring signs on the map. These signs, when aligned to certain myths, seem to scream out the reasons this miracle might have chosen this present time to breach our perception. In short, we'll see how, via mankind's negligence of the sanctity of planet earth and the laws of life, we have arrived upon the terrible brink (albeit one we're oblivious to) of a seemingly irreversible environmental disaster; hence the arrival of this ark upon our doorsteps.

This perilously dangerous time is succinctly summed up by the actual pose of this phoenix, for let me tell you in advance that *Aquarius is the only sign the land has seen fit to turn completely upside down!* When we walk round her flaming wings and find Britain's nuclear sore of Sellafield smouldering there, the land-poetry will take your breath away.

But there'll be hearteningly hopeful signs too, for via this mythological picture sign-language I believe that this planet of ours could be offering us one last chance to recognise that *heaven is on earth* if only we can open our eyes before it's too late.

In walking these green constellations we may even be following in famous footsteps

I'm also going to show that the child who read clouds may not have been the first to spot wisdom-bearing giants in Britain's foundations. Take the enigmatic sixth-century Welsh bard Taliesin, who is judged by some scholars to be the flesh and blood truth behind the legendary figure of Merlin. He will accompany us upon our wondrous way, for 1,500 years ago this old seer seemed to know what the cover of this book tells now. For a tidbit of what we'll be hearing from him, listen to him here tease the unaware of his own time about the colossal lion that he, too, knew to be concealed within the landscape:

> *There is a load of nine hundred wagons*
> *in the hair of his two paws.*
> *Three springs arise in the nape of his neck;*
> ***Sea roughs thereon.***

Sea, let me tell you, *is*, even as you read this, roughing the neck of the catlike creature the boy found lashing out of the coast of Wales - the riddler Taliesin's own homeland!

Intriguing to us too will be the ancient Egyptian idea of where their heaven (Duat) was, for this place had dual locations. One occupied an area of the starry night sky, the other, a *mirror* of the same, but located *somewhere on Earth*. This 'Lower Sky',

however, was deemed to be an underworld frequented by monsters and through which their god, Osiris, grappling in turn with each monster (star giant?), would quest in union with the sun-god in an effort to win knowledge and with it illuminate the dark places, bringing bliss, even resurrection, to the dead, who resided there. Maybe the 'dead' were just those who couldn't see the true wonder of their own existence: the uninitiated.

Anyway, this Egyptian belief in an earthly reflection of the heavens will certainly grab our attention as we, Osiris-like, hike through the starry monsters embedded in Britain's foundation, especially when we learn that this underworld of theirs had 12 sections to pass through, and how the words *"To the West!"* were always inscribed on the underside of ancient Egyptian coffin lids. This was the direction the soul of the deceased would have to fly in order to find its way to Osiris' blissful realm in the '*Lower Sky*'. Hearing all this, I think, even this early, a small low-key 'Wow!' might be in order.

On the strength of the above and other curiously Egyptian-sounding clues we'll find scattered over these western fields, we'll find it ever-so-tempting to kick around the idea that the deep seated catalyst behind their whole concept of that 'Lower Sky' was an actual subconscious sensing of Britain's own mirror of the night sky, which was, even then, being burnished just beyond their western horizon. Or, then again, did their priests, those scribes of Osiris' quest through that 'Lower Sky', have intimate first-hand knowledge of the place? Either way, and at 12 o'clock high on this prophetic star-clock, I will point out enough stunning evidence on the ground to suggest that Osiris *is himself* pictorially nailed, along with other mythological deities, to the very cross that bears the landscaped Christ - indeed, their overlapping right hands even pierced by the same nail! But more of this in the chapter, *'The Dark Twin'*.

I should also tell you now that, once confronted by this visually stunning amalgam of 50-mile-tall God-Men crucified upon Cumbria's towering cross (itself 180 miles tall), you will be presented with a startling new insight into what may have been going on behind the scenes at Golgotha. This, for me anyway, was so much more beautifully meaningful than the Bible's account, that one may feel that something vital has hitherto been censored, even robbed, from those last pages of the New Testament. Certainly, when we climb Britain's own Golgotha in the stars the landscape will prompt us to witness a replay of the crucifixion like no one has ever envisaged before, and the potential ramifications will be explosive.

Needless to say, then, that not everything is shown on the front cover artwork, for when I painted it eight years ago I had neither the guts nor the understanding to include more than the one figure on that cross, even though the map insisted there were more. Although everything is now illustrated (confessed, if you like) within the chapters themselves, that cover artwork will forever bear witness to my own censoring of what I thought was too controversial for you to see. Indeed, because of my cowardice, you will have to wait until the last chapter to see the stupendous masterstroke, which at the culmination of our journey the genius within the landscape uses to graphically animate that crucified Christ, to the point where he visibly dances off his cross in a starburst jig of joy! This mesmeric piece of land-craft just has to be seen to be believed, but I beg you not to rush to that last chapter to see this miracle within the miracle until you've trod what I feel is the preparatory step-by-step path which leads there.

And speaking of paths, we may also find ourselves following in the footsteps of Jesus himself, and, if so, a tantalising endorsement, perhaps, of the old tale that still insists today that Jesus as a youth visited Britain. "*But why would he have come here?*" has always been the question to stem the rumour. "*To personally experience the miracle that his God was crafting even then beneath his feet.*" will be the potential bombshell of an answer we'll ponder on along the way.

Outlandish, then, will be our food for thought as the map leads us into the shocking prospect that Jesus may have walked this same star-signposted path to ultimate wisdom. Not only this, though, for we shall find scintillating evidence on the ground that this extraordinary landscape has, for whatever reason, recorded and reanimated excerpts from so many metaphysical mariners' adventures: Noah's sojourn in the ark in order to preserve life; Jason's sailing in the Argo to seek the golden fleece of starry Aries; the Sumerian hero Gilgamesh's voyage to the far western Island of the Blessed in search of immortality; Jonah's tumble from his ship into the jaws of a great fish; Sir Galahad's mystic sleep aboard the so called Miraculous Ship of Solomon in the hope of dreaming guidance to achieve the Holy Grail; King Arthur's own sailing upon a glass ship to secure the Grail-like Cauldron of Rebirth from out of the bowels of the earth; the Celt's Hu the Mighty, the Egyptian's Osiris and Isis, and the Hindu's Isi and Iswara, all Noah-like riders out of other versions of the flood. And because one thought will rapidly lead to another upon our own adventure, it will be compelling for us to further consider whether Britain's own vast green star-ship was, in fact, the original deck on which some of these global myths were played out for the tutelage of mankind.

With each passing mile, and by our simple overlaying of an ordinary road map with constellations, we will do our best to fathom the fantastic.

And speaking of Christ...

Even eight years on from the day I plucked up enough courage to put pen to paper on this literally stumbled-over discovery, I still have days of tormenting doubt, for what I've found I know just shouldn't be.

I am also aware that, after the sight of that front cover and these equally hard-to-believe introductory paragraphs you, too, may have already grave doubts as to whether to go another step with me. So let me share with you a moment which I always recall whenever a fit of doubt harangues my own reason and insists I too go no further. It is something so disarmingly beautiful that doubts tend to melt into ripples of goose bumps. It goes like this: *"So what the bloody hell has the crucified Christ got to do with the zodiac anyway?"*.

That's how my one-line rant went in the bewildering moments following his sudden and totally unlooked for 50-mile-tall arrival out of a bog-standard Michelin road map. Simply, I was appalled by this blatant Christian hijacking of what I thought should be the non-religiously dogmatic stars.

I remember nervously phoning a friend who knew what I was working on and telling him of my latest find, almost willing him to say, *"Graham, take a holiday!"*, for surely star giants filling the map of Britain was absurd enough without capping them with Christ. But to my surprise he only asked: *"Has he a side wound?"*

OK, I knew all about that spear thrust into Jesus' side and how his uncle, Joseph of Arimathea, was supposed to have collected a few drops of the Messiah's blood in the cup that Jesus had used at the Last Supper. This act had inaugurated the whole Grail epic - and because Joseph had then brought that cup to Britain the quest for it was primarily focused upon these isles. Anyway, like some modern day Doubting Thomas, I wedged the phone in my neck and jabbed a digit into the spot on the map where such a wound would be, I found beneath it, in the wilderness of northern England, a solitary high peak which someone sometime had named High Cup Nick so as to

completely freak me out a few days before Good Friday 1994.

High Cup = Grail! Nick = Wound! - the wound which bleeds its knowledge of Christ consciousness into the cup which is, in reality, this whole magical landscape - King Arthur's entire realm? Is this what it meant?

Is this the spellbinding reason behind Joseph's bringing of the Holy Grail, the symbol of experiencing the God within oneself, from the Old Jerusalem to this, the New, in the shape of an almighty picture of heaven on earth emerging out of the fabric of Britain and Ireland? If so, and if we can successfully decode the message in this landscape, will we also come to intimately, and to an incredibly intense degree, experience the God within ourselves and within every grain of sand - as intensely beautiful as even Christ himself experienced it? Is this, the hidden truth of the whereabouts of the Holy Grail, now finally and spectacularly unveiled beneath our very noses? A truth so enormous that it can now be seen for what it is, even from the window of an orbiting space station? The further you go on this weird and wonderful journey the more impetus I hope you will have to answer, *"Yes"* - even though reason, schooled by today's standards, will be yelling, *"Ridiculous!"*.

After we've visited High Cup Nick, I'll then take you to look into the river which, like a charm, delineates that Cumbrian Christ's closed eyes, and if you still come away from that spectacularly named wound in his side with doubts, then the movingly explicit name of this river should finally allay them, for it remembers, would you believe, the last person Jesus himself looked upon before closing his eyes on that scene at Golgotha.

Fantastic questions - fabulous answers

And when you've looked into those enchanting, watery eyes you'll have to struggle to decide whether this same hauntingly beautiful face on England's high hills is itself a disarming affirmation of the artist William Blake's own vision of the New Jerusalem that he, also, saw rising on the backs of giants through the rocky foundations of Britain. Is it also an affirmation, in particular, of his now intensely provocative question: "*And did the countenance Divine shine forth upon our clouded hills?*"

Even this question, also from his famous hymn *Jerusalem*: "*And was the Holy Lamb of God on England's pleasant pastures seen*", may now also receive the answer, "*Yes*" when seeing the lamb of starry Aries spanning the distance from the east to the west coast. A lamb measuring an astonishing 245 miles from nose to tail and fit perhaps to overlap the lamb which has a throne in the midst of the New Jerusalem as described in St John's *Revelation*. Even that visionary New Jerusalem itself had 12 gates of entry!

But that image on the front cover of this book is not a vision just for mystic eyes, for here's a rock-solid New Jerusalem for all to see, and with it surely word that such a place can spread over the entire globe if we can only work in harmony with, rather than against, the incredibly creative force which here has proved itself to be inherent throughout all nature. Imagine, then, what wonders we'd create with that same force, when having already seen how inanimate bedrock, via a soft word whispered at its core, has patiently shape-shifted itself, with the help of the elements, into this 189 x 290-mile ark. In its hold is a message of hope from the stars; upon its mast the Christ crucified who, on behalf of every master teacher, from Osiris onwards, has touched the lives of men and women in an effort to help them embrace the divinity inherent within every atom of the creation. However, judging by our current misuse of both our planet and fellow men, their efforts may have ultimately failed. So, then, is this one last beautiful and monumental plea from

the depths of a hurting planet?

And was Maltwood's discovery of Glastonbury's zodiac the earth's way of priming us to the language it would use 70 years on to create the last-ditch message that now confronts us?

Think about it. At Glastonbury the zodiacal characters are all in the correct astrological sequence and we are, of course, being told that this is no fluke. Thus logically, when those same signs are perfectly replicated hundreds of times larger, and yet this time pointedly rearranged, surely we're being asked to read from that new alignment the reason behind the whole shocking spectacle? A spectacle which must, at this very moment, be at its pinnacle of completion, for the truth is that owing to perpetual coastal erosion it will never again be seen so figuratively perfect. Therefore, logically it must be that this writing on the wall of Britain and Northern Ireland is specifically spelling out a message *both for us now and perhaps for the next few generations still to come.*

The mind-boggling hoops that this audacious appearance on the face of the planet will demand we pass through, in order to define its meaning, may be impossible for some, but, I hope, enthralling for many.

But come on, surely anyone, artist or not, could conjure any damn shape they like out of a map, be it of China or Cheltenham?

I hear the valid point and agree totally. Out of Britain's spaghetti tangle of roads, rivers and contours I wouldn't bet against anyone unravelling anything from Mickey Mouse to a half-decent Morris Minor!

That said, I must emphasise that the most important point of my own discovery is that these zodiacal giants have formed their key profiles, not from any inland trickery of roads and rivers, but almost exclusively from the tamper-proof coastline; and these coastal-cut figures mirror those Glastonbury and Preseli templates so uncannily closely that 'coincidence' just isn't a viable answer. Indeed, I happily set out to write this book on the strength of those coastal clues alone, and it was only when I was halfway through the writing of the manuscript that I noticed that there was an inland completion to each of those profiled clues in the cliffs (*see Gemini*). Only then was some artistic skill needed in the unravelling of them from out of the spaghetti, and, let's face it, until then a three-year-old could have traced around those figures which the coast had already made so plain.

Nevertheless, and as wonderful as these inland promptings are to the completion of hands, feet, hooves and wings etc, I must stress that you can discount all my inland creativity, for what the coast has done of its own magical accord speaks mightily for itself: not one inch of it, to the east, west or south of Hadrian's Wall, has been left unused in its own breathtaking artistry.

You might go on to argue that the shapes in the coastline itself can be suggestive of any number of alternative images. I do recollect some years ago a TV documentary which in doing its best to demolish the whole Glastonbury zodiac theory, and making the point that anyone could make anything out of the shapes in a map, had some guy armed with a felt tip pen turn the entire Welsh coastline into a pig's head - and pretty good it was too!

Even so, and now you've seen that front cover, I'll gladly challenge anyone to turn that south-western peninsular into anything more harmonious to its distinctive sea-sculpted shape than a great fish. Likewise can you find anything that would fit more snugly into the area from where Sagittarius stares out than his own enormous profile, or is there something better tailored to either that corner of Wales, where I see a snarling beast with one lashing paw, or where that bonneted woman points out to sea? What's more, I'll even show how, in

1795 and 1862, two other artists saw and illustrated the 11-year-old's hag, fish and bald man, although, like him, they never realised they'd spotted three out of the 12 characters of the zodiac - because they hadn't the luxury of Maltwood's 'Key to the Secret' templates, either!

No, once you've seen the coastal edge of the puzzle slot together, and its pieces checked off against those on Somerset's pastures and Preseli's mountains, the miracle underfoot cannot be side-stepped, no matter how science, history, religion and even commonsense will scramble to do so, in order to ward off the undermining of the foundations upon which they're built.

All aboard!

Away now, to the English Channel where, against all reason a gigantic wave-skimming dove with white geological wings, *really does wait* to lead us aboard an ark that shouldn't be, but which stubbornly is. An ark whose pastured planks must have been embedded upon this dot of land at the beginning of time in order to become visible to an era when the end of all time threatens. A time when man must be further away than ever from acknowledging the divinity within every cell, and thus it is hell rather than heaven that he is about to set into irreversible motion. Hence this ark, this survival time-capsule, full of the archetypal imagery of love and the glory of life has arrived in the backyard of mankind as both a warning and a lifeline - a gift, no less, containing the forgotten wisdom of the past in the hope that it may, in the nick of time, preserve the future; cleverly encoded in the mythology our ancestors devised so as to withstand the passage of time.

It is time then, if you have the nerve, to challenge all you've ever believed in, to mentally board her and recklessly rummage amongst her starry cargo for the whys and wherefores behind her outrageous docking in the face of this new millennium. In our delving we will, of course, be lifting lids and latches on things judged impossible by today's yardstick of what can and can't be. However, as you journey through her sparkling holds, you will have to surmount all the protests and rejections your adult mind will assuredly stack up as a barricade to what you'll see and hear. Thus you will need to adventure as though you were a child again, seeing everything fresh and full of wonder. The open-minded might then return with a perception of their existence upon this magnificent blue-marbled orb, rejuvenated and enriched beyond compare - and perhaps that's all that's expected of any of us, so as to make the difference needed to bring about a new and globe-spanning Jerusalem.

Or then again, maybe you'll jump ship early and return wishing for a title better suited to your opinion of what you've seen than *Behold Jerusalem!* So may I venture to suggest instead *Behold the Lie of the Land!*, a title I've dallied with many times myself, until, that is, I remember High Cup Nick along with a few dozen other name-dropped gems in the map -

all of them admittedly absurd yet at the same time devastatingly disarming, all of them preposterous yet physically proving a miracle has occurred. So, amid the goose bumps, I end up generally shaking my head and laughing my socks off at it all, because if I didn't laugh I know that this, the most painfully beautiful and innocent thing I have ever laid eyes upon, could literally break my heart. But that's me.

★ ★ ★ ★ ★

Today I heard that glaciologists on the British Antarctic Survey had announced that the 670-feet-thick, 500-billon-ton Larsen B ice shelf, covering an area of 1,255 square miles and the size of Luxembourg, after being in existence for an estimated 1,800+ years, has, in less than a month, totally disintegrated due to an obviously unnatural rise in temperature. Following this dramatic announcement, I say you can go make of that silently screaming front cover what the hell you like - but just do it quickly.

SPRING EQUINOX 2002

*"It's an indication of global warming which is extremely stark...
I think it's a wake-up call to the whole world that when an ice
shelf of such enormous proportions can break up, that shows
the effect we are having on the planet"*

(Michael Meacher, Environmental Minister,
in response to the above announcement
Daily Mail 20.3.2002)

*NB: re sections headed **Defining the body**

Within most of the coming chapters there will be a section headed by the above title and noticeable by its change of type style. This is for those members of our party with a passion for map reading and who'd like to know the nitty-gritty of every river, footpath and bump in the road that delineates the particular giant underfoot. These sections, however, can be skipped by those in a hurry, **although do look out for any paragraphs highlighted in bold text for these are further gems which just shouldn't be bypassed**.

Acknowledgement of main sources of reference

*The major source in plotting the inland forms of the giants was the series of Michelin Road Maps of Great Britain and Ireland, numbers 402, 403, 404 and 405, scale 1/4000000 - 1 inch:6.30 miles.

*The Glastonbury Zodiac figures, found by Katherine Maltwood, are reproduced by courtesy of the Somerset Archaeological and Natural History Society.

*Mary Caine's variations of Maltwood's figures are taken from her book **The Glastonbury Zodiac - Key to the Mysteries of Britain** and are reproduced by courtesy of Mary Caine.

*The figures of the Preseli Zodiac are my own copies of those that are printed in the book **Glastonbury, Ancient Avalon, New Jerusalem**, edited by Anthony Roberts and published by Rider and Company 1978.

*All geological maps are reproduced by kind permission of the British Geological Survey, IPR/26-11C.
©NERC. All rights reserved.

*The black and white line drawings of the Glastonbury and Preseli figures have in some cases been reversed so as to simplify comparison.

CHAPTER 1

LIBRA

• *The Dove* •

★

The first giant along the way

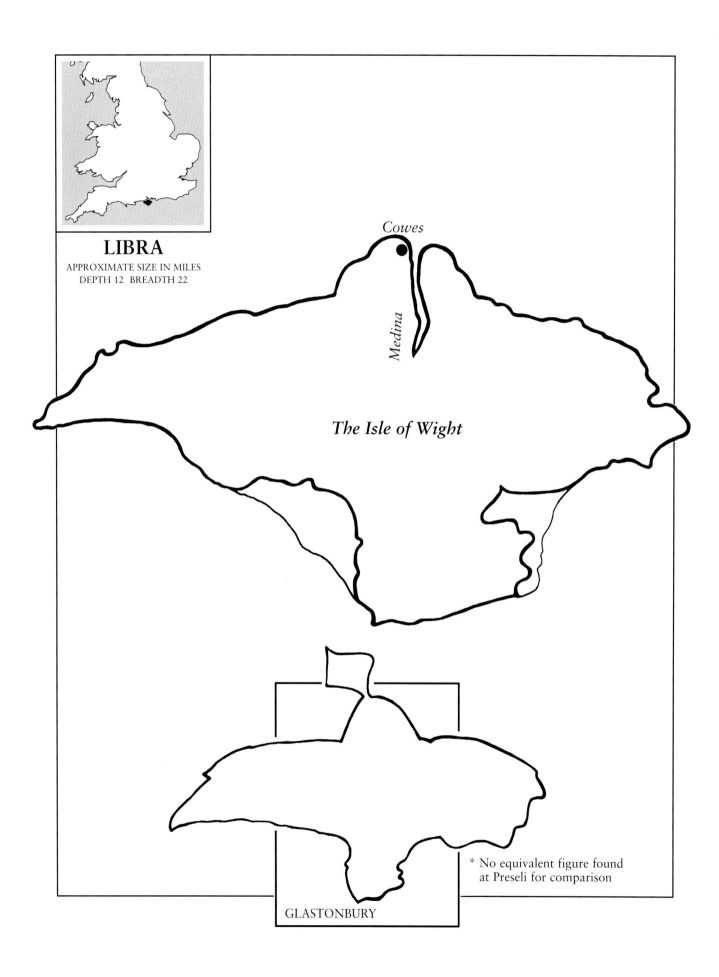

LIBRA

APPROXIMATE SIZE IN MILES
DEPTH 12 BREADTH 22

Cowes

Medina

The Isle of Wight

GLASTONBURY

* No equivalent figure found
at Preseli for comparison

Our journey begins with the Bible's help

"I give you the end of a golden string;
Only wind it into a ball,
It will lead you in at Heaven's gate,
Built in Jerusalem's wall."

JERUSALEM, William Blake

GENERAL AREA: THE ISLE OF WIGHT IN ITS ENTIRETY. THE DOVE IS FLYING DIRECTLY TOWARDS THE MAINLAND.

o why begin our incredible journey around Britain's star giants by first heading to Libra? And why, if this is Libra, are the scales replaced by a dove?

At the time I found the last piece of the zodiacal puzzle hiding in Britain's coastline, and had finally acknowledged the miracle I had stumbled upon, the artist in me could still see nothing much beyond the tip of his paint brush, pictures were his forte. He thus surmised that once the thing was painted and, he hoped, hung upon a gallery wall, his work would be done. He was wrong.

Having painted it nearly six feet tall (by far the largest painting I had ever undertaken) I then, literally with the last dab of colour, stood back and I guess for the first time really questioned the thing before me. Just what exactly had I painted? '*A map*' I replied. '*And aren't maps guides - things to be followed?*'

As map and guide sank in, I remember hearing somewhere over my shoulder Ireland's 'troubles' again disturbing the 1 o'clock news. Instinctively I glanced at the separate panel upon which I had reluctantly painted that Scorpion-haunted country, a pairing that had concerned me ever since first laying eyes upon it. I guess that the very real pain of that place, along with the probable stemming of the adrenalin which had surfed me through many weeks of fevered work on the painting, was making me inexplicably anxious and deflated, when I should have been experiencing excitement at the prospect of now being in a position to show off my 'find' to the world. I was swamped by a feeling that in my rush to paint all I'd found I had been insensitive to *something*; blind to *something* still yet to step from behind that magic curtain of fields.

As the artist, I was mortified by the prospect that I'd not been as perceptive as I thought I had, while the businessman in me was equally appalled to think that if I had missed something, then I had worked five solid weeks for nothing, because the method in which I had painted the picture rendered it impossible to correct. Besides, I really couldn't give it any more unpaid time for I'd a living to make as a freelance graphic designer; indeed, I'd already turned down several commissions to allow me unbroken time on the painting.

Fatigued, I sat down on the floor beneath that weight of giants. Were my sudden misgivings in reality symptomatic of a massive attack of 'cold feet'? Here at the finishing post was I simply 'losing my bottle' at the thought of the ridicule the work would undoubtedly attract? But no, those shapes in the coastline still looked so convincing to me, I knew I hadn't deceived myself - so why this avalanche of doubt? And then I think I knew. The whole thing lacked a *reason*; as it stood it was no more than a pretty picture, albeit remarkable and yet in that provocative placement of Scorpio, in tandem with the one o'clock news, a blatant affirmation of the sectarian poison it had for so long harboured upon its back seemed to scream out. So, was the picture trying to tell a story too?

I turned off the radio and replaced it with Durufle's *Requiem*. I needed to think.

But where, if it was a map, would it lead?

Surely if this was a map that was meant to be followed to some prescribed end, the reason behind it must be profound. Why, perhaps even some treasure awaited - the treasure of what has become this real life Treasure Island of Britain! But because I had always felt that whatever forces had shaped this land must themselves be under the influence of something intrinsically holy, though far removed from any Christian doctrine, my mental image of Long John Silver's casket of doubloons was, nevertheless, immediately transposed by a Holy Grail - that enigmatic cup of supposed spiritual wisdom and healing which had fuelled so many legendary quests.

Intrigued, I then mused that if one could follow this map would it, in turn, lead to a translation of the message behind the picture, and, if heard, would such insight be tantamount to the achieving of the Grail itself? Answers then to why it is Scorpio who straddles Northern Ireland, why the zodiac has

bulged Britain, and maybe even a reason why man hurtles through time and space upon this beautiful blue-marbled orb.

Admittedly both Maltwood and Caine were convinced that a journey around Glastonbury's zodiac in its prime was, in effect, an allegorical way to the Grail. This, added to the 300-mile-tall cross held aloft by Britain's lamb of Aries, must have sparked my thought of a Grail map. However, my hunch would have redoubled its attraction if I'd have known that, without even looking, I would eventually find the actual figure of the Christ perfectly placed upon that same land cross, and he bearing the most mind-bogglingly wonderful Grail clues possible - even though I was initially repulsed by the sight of this Christian hijacking of something which the Church itself would condemn as hocus-pocus!

For now, though, the word 'ludicrous' was the inner response to my hunch. "No more ludicrous than the prospect of the 12 zodiac signs being found in Britain's profile," I countered.

Although no more than a throwaway thought, that idea of a map to lead one to the Grail was in hindsight to become, for me, the magical key to this whole conundrum. Without my knowing it, the magnitude of the apparently silly concept had, there and then, sold me a ticket to an astonishing nine-year journey that was to begin whilst still sitting cross-legged on my studio floor! Neither did I know that the cost of that ticket would be the scrapping, not only of that newly-completed painting, for it showed only the features cut into the coastline but so, too, everything I ever thought was fact about this earth and my existence upon it. As I have said, at the time of doing that first painting, I was unaware that each zodiac giant's body was wonderfully completed inland by features in the landscape.

My career, too, was to be sacrificed for the duration of the trip, for the intensity of the discoveries to come and my writing of them demanded it. Thus I was to write the book on no pay, my wife Linda, an SRN, having to become the family's main breadwinner. It was to be a bumpy ride and if I had known all this that lunchtime I would have torn that ticket in two. But, believe me, that was the best thing I never did!

So still sitting cross-legged and unaware of being shanghaied, one thought quickly led to another and in answer to my next question, "But where exactly on the map would one set out in search of the Grail?" my intuition was to throw into the air, like a magician's dove, the early medieval book of *Le Conte del Graal*, even though I'd never read it! Let me explain.

At that time in my life I had never read an actual Grail romance (between you and me I always imagined them to be utterly boring!) but what I did have to hand was Malcolm Goodwin's reference work of the whole Grail legend entitled *The Holy Grail - Its Origins, Secrets & Meaning Revealed*. Though again, I had never properly read it, buying it primarily as a source of picture reference material.

My whim gets encouragement!

Anyway, I was soon lying on my belly randomly dipping into that book's richly illustrated pages, though, I guess, with no more conviction than to casually titillate my boyish notion of a Grail map before it would inevitably melt away in the cause of adult commonsense. Finding shapes of giants in the coastline was one thing, but the last people to seek the Holy Grail were, I believe, the team from Monty Python. Say no more! However, hooked by those few dips, I soon learnt that the earliest written Grail romance, and probably based upon a far earlier Celtic tale, was by Chretien de Troyes, a 12th-century French poet. Although his *Le Conte del Graal* was left unfinished it seems that a whole spate of continuations of it were carried out by a succession of anonymous authors between 1190 and 1225, such was its popularity.

Reading on, it was to be a snippet from one of these so-called 'continuations' that unexpectedly massaged my whim with a very logical answer as to where a journey in search of the Grail should begin. Indeed, it was the very place where, in legend, the Holy Grail was said to have first made landfall on British soil after supposedly journeying from Jerusalem. Perhaps from one Jerusalem to another?

In it we are told how, after the crucifixion, Joseph of Arimathea, the uncle of Jesus, accompanied by Nicodemus and the Virgin Mary, fleeing persecution in their own land, journeyed to Britain and brought with them that Holy Cup used by Jesus at the Last Supper. It was also said that Joseph held it to catch a few drops of the Christ's blood spilt while upon the cross. It then describes how before the travellers arrived on mainland Britain they landed first upon '*The White Isle, which is a part of Britain*'. With this came the irresistible clue that would, in less than an hour, lead me through heaven's door and on course for the Grail!

You see, with that sighting of a White Isle my eye went to where on my artwork the world-renowned white cliffs of the Isle of Wight defined Libra's white dove - an island which, although not part of the mainland body of star signs, '*is a part of Britain*'!

Thus, could that White Isle and the Isle of Wight be one and the same place? If so, what better place for a modern seeker of the Grail to begin his journey than where Joseph and the Grail began theirs on western soil! And could we, by starting off on our own journey from this small white-washed ante-chamber to Albion's secret, be in poetical step with some lost wisdom of the ages which was perhaps now coming to light in this extraordinary map of heaven overlaid upon earth? My adrenalin was back and urging me to suck it and see!

*Note: the dove, by the way, as a sign to guide one to the Grail, was to gain even more

strength over the course of the next few days when, from my new-found love of Grail romances (would you believe!), I learnt that it was always a dove that heralded the imminent arrival of the Grail into the sight of those who sought it!

Discounting, then, the above bonus of the significance of a dove in answering my question as to where to begin a Grail quest, that lunchtime's seemingly obvious name-play of the White Isle with England's conspicuously snow-white Isle of Wight, was, for my childlike self, as magical as it was comical. Indeed, even the adult side of me couldn't help but smile at the disarming audacity of the double connection.

Disarming maybe, though I grant you a seemingly frivolous set of coordinates by which to start any journey! That said, I aim to prove that through the eyes of someone who is brave enough to see as a child, the whole experience can become an enchanting revelation. Though you may need to be able to apply a little adult logic and reason to the new shapes and sounds that this extraordinary landscape has reworked into a picture of heaven on earth, this namely by relating what the land has done to episodes from a near global mythology of the quest for enlightenment. Through such eyes and understanding the land, the past, the present, and indeed the future will come alive in a way we never expected, a catalyst to a whole new perception of existence.

But let us stay with that lunchtime

OK, I'd got what seemed an intriguing place from where to start out upon a Grail quest, but would it pan out in the long term, for the pressing question now was "Where to next?" The options were going to be enormous, for if the dove was to lead the eye to the next destination in the scheme of things, assuming there was a scheme, it had now a choice of the

whole of England, Wales, and Northern Ireland upon which to perch next!

The dilemma had the adult in me warning that the dove was a wild goose in disguise and only an infantile chase would ensue. But the boy reminded me that this miracle in the map had first peeped out to an 11-year-old and thus might only ever be visible to an unencumbered child. I'm talking about those of us, of whatever age, who are still free-minded enough to chase a rainbow against all the 'sensible' reasons that the adult side of us will invariably throw up so as to persuade us to stay at home.

So, an object that is only visible to the child-like? A nice thought, but even after chasing this rainbow on and off for 31 years it was alas the adult in me who was still, for the most part, captain of my ship. Instead of trying to gag him I decided to placate him by allowing him to apply his own logic to what the laughing cabin boy was urging him to do - to follow where the dove would next fly.

The easy answer to this was to see her alighting upon the figure of Capricorn, directly in front of her present flight path. Nevertheless, I was, for some reason, not entirely satisfied with that seemingly entirely logical solution - probably because there was an even more logical answer just moments away!

Slowly, and again with a sense of fun, the answer I needed started to rise from out of the flood, for staring me in the face was not only the Isle of Wight's geological white dove, but in front of her was that great Cancerian ark (*see Cancer*) whose hull I had found to encompass every star sign except Scorpio - and the only story I'd ever heard that featured an ark and a dove was Genesis!

Within moments my fingers were scrolling through the Bible's onion-skin pages, my eyes rapidly trawling verses for that word dove. Then out she flew:

'Also he sent forth a dove from him, to see if the waters were abated from off the face of

the ground; but the dove found no rest for the sole of her foot...'
Genesis, Chapter 8, Verses 8-9

In another moment I was back on the floor with my trusty Michelin map spread out and my eye and finger tip coming down together on that channel of water which separates the Isle of Wight from the mainland figure of Capricorn, and known as The Solent. Such a useless name as far as solving my quandary of 'Where to next?' but one which was again to have the 11-year-old in fits of giggles, though even the muddled expression of the captain was soon to pucker even more as my intuition connected *sole* from the above verse with the *Sole* in *Solent*. Mad or what?

"If I am digging a pit for myself with that one," I thought, "then why this deliciously exciting feeling as I make the link?" With an imagination being now directed by the Bible, I watched the dove replay her abortive flight directly over The Solent, but didn't find that dry ground to rest the sole of her foot, so relentless was and still is the water's grasp there. But on her second flight, so the Bible continues, she did at last find dry land (perhaps even on the Isle of Wight itself?) after which she sped back with a token olive branch to where Noah was anxiously waiting aboard the ark.

Of course Noah! I drowned the background *Requiem* with a shout of "Bingo!"

Now the only star *man*, so to speak, on this zodiac-bearing ark of Albion is Sagittarius, he whose great head and shoulders fill that whole southeast corner of England. Indeed, the placement of his head seems to give the ark its very own figurehead and thus a poetic pointer perhaps to the overlapping of Noah, he being the head of the ark. Valid reason then to look to the dove to fly directly back to his hand just as the Bible told?

But now my game was getting serious. Now my boyish whim of the dove winging its way back to old Noah in the shape of Sagittarius seemed not too unreasonable. However, it needed something physical upon which the adult could feel he was again on safe, albeit strange, ground. In short, if this dove idea was to really take flight I needed more of that disarming magic that had happened a few moments ago with that White Isle. I needed something visual on the map to jump out again and shout, "See! you're on the right track." If, on the other hand, there was no signpost to back up my hunch, whether of tantalising name-play or geological feature, then I would again be sitting before nothing but a pretty picture.

Heart-rate noticeably increasing, my finger tip now traced the most plausible and direct route east that a homing dove could take to the awaiting hand of that Sagittarian Noah - along the English Channel. As my finger slowed near his hand, the hairs upon my own prickled - the proof that my finger was bang on a dove's course was already indelibly remembered on every atlas the world over. Yet until reading it anew, through eyes now willing to see just a fraction beyond the mundane, I had never raised so much as a passing query as to what might lie behind the spelling of that narrowest stretch of sea between England and France.

Imagine, then, my thrill when, within moments of laughing at my own stupidity at wondering whether Solent had any relationship to the sole of a dove's foot, I saw that my finger was in fact flying along the now astonishingly named *Strait of Dover - straight as a dove's flight* to the outstretched hand of this zodiac's own Noah in disguise! Here laughing in my face was guidance to where the dove wished to lead our eye next. Although this was as humorous as my adding White Isle to the dove-shaped Isle of Wight, there was now an element of quiet awe creeping into the game - just what was I now uncovering?

The thrill of the chase

This growing sense of awe apart, it still seemed that the only criterion needed for the following of this star map was a sense of fun and a trust that rainbows could be caught! Up until that lunchtime I had seen the picture as a miracle, perceptible only from a vantage point many miles above Britain. However, exploring these giants at ground level seemed to be giving the thing another dimension of proof. In this new light, place names and geographical features were not only conspiring to underline the giants' presence, but they were encouraging in this viewer an astonishingly new perception. It was, though, not a perception raised, but in a sense 'lowered' or 'slowed down'; tuned perhaps to how rocks may perceive their own existence; a way of seeing just a fraction beyond the everyday and into a magic that must pervade the entire environment - only we may be living too fast to register it.

At the same time, and from even these first two steps on the map, I was overwhelmed with a sense that I was being led by the *knowing* land along a preordained route through these terrestrial constellations - and for a *reason*. My lunch break had become a walk through an enchanted forest, where the path was already marked with brightly coloured ribbons purposefully left upon the branches, and I needed only to carry on collecting them to reach some final goal. That ribbon which bore the name Solent meant nothing at all to me

(except, I think, it being an old brand of menthol cigarettes and, as in *Wolf Solent*, a novel by John Cowper Powys!) but it was nevertheless a vital gambit in getting the happy-go-lucky traveller to follow where the dove *really* wanted to lead next.

I wasn't there yet, though, for one more strip of fluttering white ribbon had to be collected before the dove had underlined its legendary flight back into the reality of this wonder map. She had still to land upon Noah's hand and I tingled with anticipation as to whether on that hand of Sagittarius there would be another signpost - or was I pushing the luck of the hour too far? Or then again, was I going mad?

The best laugh yet!

Still smiling with a schoolboy grin at what I had already found, I allowed my finger to thud down upon the knuckle of Noah's little finger, and again I lifted it to see what, if anything, marked the spot. My grin then turned into out-and-out laughter and the slapping of thighs, boy and man together, as another swipe of the land's magic wand had again made the 'impossible' seem plausible. There, singing off the map, (and again I had never previously made the connection) was *Dover*, the alighting place of the dove, ancient white-cliffed portal into this realm of no longer concealed star signs; one could call it heaven's door!

Oh what divine foolishness! The only thing 'goosey' about this journey were the constantly rippling bumps upon my neck! That glorious knuckle where once upon a time someone did what can only be God's humorous bidding in underlining this miracle underfoot for us living now, when he stood up and named that place Dover. Or perhaps it was some totally different name that, in the fullness of time, would, nevertheless, evolve along with this divine land poetry into the sound of dove. Whatever, I was, I hope like you now, simply enchanted by the prospect of Noah's hand being for all time poetically and geographically stained by dove droppings!

And please don't think my above suggestion is flippant, because it is this same innocent joy that pervades this whole down-to-earth miracle. I will repeat many times that this beautifully outlandish journey will make you laugh as much as it will, in parts, touch a few to the point of tears. Though to do this my fellow travellers must have the courage to allow their inner child to rise above the cynicism that growing-up can bring and seek again the magic behind the ordinary. You may have walled up your child-like self, but delve deep, it is still there.

More clues - and even a coo?

'Coincidence' will of course be the word most used against something that just shouldn't be. That said, coincidence may well be all that's behind a little historical note from 1663 and as such perhaps not worth recounting here. However, because it makes me smile nearly as much as the *sole of a dove's foot* did, I'll mention it anyway.

Recorded on a plaque screwed to the beak of this great coincidence-defying dove is the fact that two ships left the quay at Cowes (the town upon its beak) and set sail, with God speed, to colonise and take the Word to Maryland in the New World. It pleases me no end to tell you that these two vessels were blessed with the names *The Ark* and *The Dove*. Agreed, no more than a nugget of nothingness but my, how it again 'coos' in poetic harmony with the ridiculously wonderful thing that has dropped in our lap! But ward it off as 'coincidental' if it pleases you, along with Wight/white, Strait/straight, Dover/dove, and indeed the twelve signs of the zodiac cut out of Britain's coastline. I should tell you, however, that come the last chapter that 'cop-out' will have worn very thin indeed!

But returning to the beak of Albion's dove, I'd just like to indulge my younger self for a moment or two longer, as he'd love to have a play with that name Cowes, totally at the expense of adult reasoning!

Eyes twinkling, he now weighs Cowes, just for the fun of it, mind, alongside *coos* and wonders whether our dove could be delightfully *cooing* as well? Some may say that in no way can the boy legitimately squeeze a 'coo' out of a cow (as in Cowes) on the grounds of pronunciation alone, as Cowes is pronounced exactly as it is written. And yes, it does sound stupid to consider otherwise, but, in defence of the fantastic, let me mention the author John Cowper Powys again and the fact that his Cowper is pronounced as Cooper. So cows *can* coo after all!

With that possible cooing still in our ears, I am reminded by Mary Caine that for the Welsh Druids, God's creative Word could be sensed, at times, as divine inspiration - via a dialogue with the Muse, and to this force of inner illumination they gave the name *Awen*. They symbolised the vehicle of this inspiration as three bars of light in the formation of an arrowhead around a centre shaft, and which Mary quite rightly sees as echoing a dove in its bird-like shape, thus the spirit of God, encapsulated in the form of a dove, would mirror perfectly the imagery of that one which, in the Bible, hovered above the baptism of Jesus and which, in a sense, inaugurated Jesus' own Grail journey from the wilderness to the cross.

Interestingly, when looking at Britain's dove as a stylised arrowhead, its centre shaft would be most accurately lined by the River Medina which issues from its heart, symbolising the poetical flow of the Word of God, or the Awen, issuing via that cooing Cowes beak. Lovely imagery once more, especially so when Mary also informs us that the Druids pronounced Awen as *A-hoowen* - perfect mimic of a dove's call!

Note: peculiar name 'Medina' for an English river, Medina being the Arabian city where another messenger of God, the Lord Mohammed, fled from Mecca and where, upon his death, he was laid to rest.

However, one of my favourite clues, in spurring me on to think that there is a dove locked into this white walled isle, is the place name which shines upon the tip of its right wing. This is Culver Cliff, and *Culver*, I was accidentally to discover, was once old English for *dove*. Poetic justice or what!

Weights or Wings?

Remarkably, in the Glastonbury zodiac, too, Libra has also been sculpted as a dove and argued as such by both Maltwood and Caine. For my own part though, if it were not for their astute insight I would never have seen through the dove to Libra. Indeed, I actually doubted even their findings until I made my own enquiries into the characteristics of Libra.

Compare, too, the stunning similarity in shape of both birds. In particular, notice how one wing seems to be fully unfurled, whereas the other seems slightly folded or perhaps even injured. Note, also, their underlying proportions; how they seem so similarly weighted, as though drawn one after the other and by the same hand, though again, the Isle of Wight dove dwarfs its Somerset twin many times over.

Librans, however, may still be smarting over Messrs Maltwood, Caine, and Griffiths' presumptuous scrapping of your traditional scales, but surely the mere fact that Libra has always been astrologically classed as an *air sign* must question those scales, which were, of course, introduced by the Romans?

But listen to what my own look into Libra brought to light before deciding whether it's weights or wings you Librans would rather have upon your back.

Ariel Guttman and Kenneth Johnson in their book *Mythic Astrology* seem to further Messrs Maltwood, Caine and Griffith's case when inadvertently underlining some exquisitely dove-like attributes to Libra and Librans, even though they at no time mention a dove directly, or question the validity of the scales: '*Thus Libra's traditional attribute as the Sign of Love and Marriage is well founded and entirely harmonious with a sign ruled by Venus - this is why Libran types are believed to be such skilled diplomats and why Libra is the sign of Peace*'.

Now can you find a better symbol for love and peace than the dove? Scales to my knowledge have never decorated wedding cards, nor do they, for all their balancing imagery, get used very often as logos of peace; rather, in both cases, it is a dove that more often than not finds a way in to grace the message.

Changing tack slightly, someone mentioned something else which may help a dove's case, especially in the context of the zodiac stowed within an ark. It seems that in the Welsh tongue, the oldest language still in use on this island, the nearest words, in visual appearance, to the word Libra are *Lli Bras*. However, as close as the two versions look when written side by side the translation of the Welsh, at least at first glance, has nothing to do with astrology, let alone scales... or does it? *Lli Bras* translated into English, (and I double checked this with the National Welsh Library) can translate, albeit a little awkwardly, into "*of the great flood*". Intriguing, or is this just more coincidental silliness?

But whatever your views, please remember that it was neither Maltwood, nor Caine, nor I who caused a dove to perhaps sign Libra in these two earthly zodiacs: it was Mother Earth herself - and I guess again for some good and mighty reason!

And with her begin the reasons

If you remember, that revelatory lunchtime

began with me feeling that this landscape had created more than just a pretty picture, but carried with it too a reason; a message, even. So, before we bid the dove farewell and prepare to join Noah aboard his safe house upon the waves, let me give you one possible reason to ponder on, born only from what we have already found. A reason, however, that, as we journey deeper into this miracle that is in the map, will demand more and more attention.

It goes something like this - perhaps the underlying reality of Noah's ark is that it was never a vessel of planks but an ark-shaped *island*, an unsinkable island or vessel upon which all those 'two by two' species would more sensibly fit and where ample grazing would be found upon its grassy 'deck'! So, is it *this* green-pastured ark of Britain that has somehow always been behind every deluge and ark story ever written - versions of which are to be found in many cultures? Or, more bewildering still, is it that this 'remembering' land has chosen to copy, in colossal fashion, a moment from a very real event from the deep past as a warning of an imminent repeat - and clamouring for our acceptance of the coming of this vast lifeboat?

Time to fly

And so with Dover's entry into the magic, Durufle's *Requiem* spun to an end, and in the space of its own enchantment I had risen from deflation to exhilaration. My crazy notion of a Grail map had been encouraged by what seemed the most wonderful evidence on the ground. But again, would this wacky brand of magical guidance continue throughout the rest of the journey, and even lead to some all-

enveloping reason for the whole dumbfounding thing? In answer, and nine years on, I can only say Yes! Yes! Yes! The land will be seen to confirm time after time at grass roots level what can only be seen in its entirety from space, namely the earth trying to commune to all mankind the beautiful secret of his own existence - before it is too late. But most will write it off as 'coincidence' - and they must, for, if not, the beliefs of a lifetime would be shredded in an instant.

Now to board the ark!

Notes: the elements alone are responsible for the shaping of the Isle of Wight's dove. However, I hope nature will excuse the artist in me, who, at the risk of overdoing a job already so well done, would like to suggest what might be a shapelier tail. This can be achieved by taking the B3399 from Brighstone in the west and heading inland, continuing through Shorwell to where this road touches the coast at Chale. This painless plucking of an acre or two of land from the dove's side can be repeated in the east. Here you should head inland from Sandown on the A3056 but soon go south on the unmarked road to join the A3020 to Ventnor.

I should also like to draw your attention to the not-widely-known constellation of Columba that is depicted as a dove bearing an olive branch. The engraving of the night sky, as reproduced under the chapter on Sagittarius, stunningly portrays this heaven-sent bird flying directly to the legendary 'talking figurehead' of the great ship of the constellation of Argo Navis. This is a strikingly similar flight path to the one our dove of Albion is now to embark upon.

CHAPTER 2

SAGITTARIUS

• *Layer upon layer of giants* •

★

The second giant
along the way

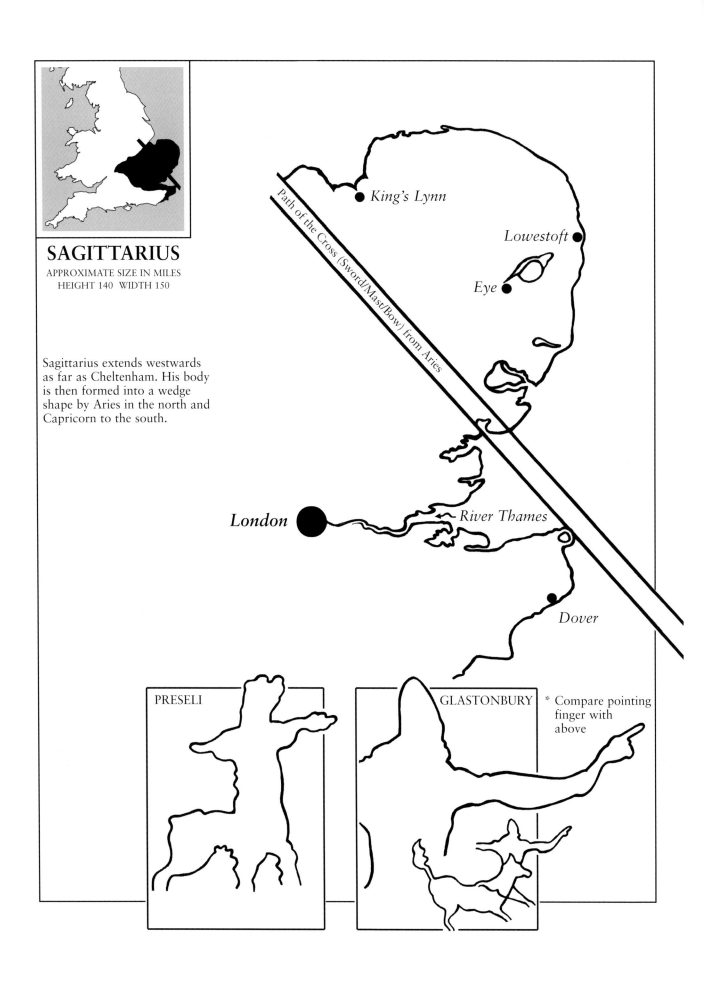

SAGITTARIUS

APPROXIMATE SIZE IN MILES
HEIGHT 140 WIDTH 150

Sagittarius extends westwards
as far as Cheltenham. His body
is then formed into a wedge
shape by Aries in the north and
Capricorn to the south.

King's Lynn

Lowestoft

Eye

Path of the Cross (Sword/Mast/Bow) from Aries

London

River Thames

Dover

PRESELI

GLASTONBURY

* Compare pointing
finger with
above

Straight as a dove to Noah's hand ... so threat of flooding?

"And Albion fell into Furrow; and The Plough went over him."

JERUSALEM, William Blake

GENERAL AREA: SOUTHEAST ENGLAND - FROM FOSDYKE ON THE WASH AT HIS FURTHEST NORTHERN POINT, TO DUNGENESS IN THE SOUTH. LONDON IS HIS HEART.

fter our intriguing findings on Libra, and with the beginnings of perhaps a new way of seeing beyond the everyday, our questing group of wide-eyed children, albeit perhaps still dragging the cynical baggage of an adult, now set foot upon the terrestrial constellation of Sagittarius, in order to seek more proof that something extraordinarily magical *really has* taken place beneath our feet - beneath all our stuck-up-in-air adult noses! So let's continue our journey in the way that we seemed to be led by the dove, with a twinkle in our eye, a happy-go-lucky attitude, and a will to attempt to relate whatever we do find to a legend that would seem to mirror the same; a recipe which just might continue to aid the unravelling of what our earth may be trying to say through this miracle in a map.

So picture our band of sky-walkers now upon the hand of Sagittarius and looking up into his almighty face, 80 miles from his chin to his bald pate!

Always an abode of giants

'Giant!' A long time ago the word must have made the boy's eyes as big as saucers when, on page 31 of his Christmas atlas, he saw in that bald-headed bulging of the east coast, the epitome of every giant who'd ever stomped earth. More recently the boy-become-man was to raise his eyebrows again upon discovering that the first recorded name of this island rang of giants; and logged by that Carthaginian sea captain as *'The island of the Albiones'* - even Aristotle referred to the place by the same name. That philosopher presumably also knew that the name came from the giant who was rumoured to hold sway there.

"Albion!" William Blake knew him too; and made him the actual psyche of Britain in his visionary poem *Jerusalem*. Indeed, he saw him as one with the very fabric of its physical foundations; a giant who, like King Arthur on awakening from an eternal slumber, causes a golden age, a New Jerusalem, to blossom once more *'on England's green and pleasant land'* upon Albion's own earthy limbs. Surely then, at least to this still wide-eyed child, the giant whom he spied all those years ago occupying this ancient portal corner of Britain must be *he*, Albion himself - even if his adult self still finds it hard to believe. Indeed, the deeper we journey through these constellations that have fallen to earth in the shape of Britain, the more we shall become aware of Blake's prophecy of a Jerusalem upon British soil building into an astonishing reality, to such an extent that it has become second nature to me to simply refer to this whole miracle as *Albion*.

And so with 'Giant' further exciting some jangle of intuition I never knew I had, it was to the vaults of mythology that both young dreamer and old cynic alike went to hunt a colossus or two. This was done in the hope that they could either help understand the child's vision as to exactly why this giant of giants, in the guise of Sagittarius, was pointing out of this particular corner of Britain, or else confirm the adult's fear that, since the Isle of Wight, it really is a wild goose chase the pair of us, and *you*, are on.

Anyway, the first bellow we heard in defence of the impossible came from the Celts' own Bran the Blessed, so large, they said, that *no house nor ship could hold him*. We shall hear his astonishingly relevant tale shortly. However, the deeper man and boy dug, the more other giants moaned for equally valid returns, and they were not only of British rootstock. So welcome along with Albion, Bran and Noah (whom we already suspected), the likes of Jupiter, Atlas, the giant Sumerian god Ea, and, I fancy, even St Christopher; all, I believe, now returning as one voice from out of the mythological memory stored in this almighty head of Sagittarius. And that voice bears a startlingly graphic warning - a warning coming to tell anyone with eyes willing to *see* just how our hitherto blindness to the full wonder of this planet has brought us all to a looming day of chaos.

Though it also has to be said that in this alarming pictorial prophesy, there is as much hope to be found, as there is doom. Indeed, if we do not turn these newly-opening eyes away from that which, in our present ignorance, we could easily laugh away as 'absurd', we will also learn that, just beyond that awful day, a

state of heaven, even Blake's New Jerusalem, really will be found on earth. Indeed, if I have read this landscape correctly we shall find that it has never been anywhere else!

Hard to swallow I know, and yet for some, I fancy, that just one look at the front cover of this book will have already sparked a genealogically remembered *something*; a returning burst of memory of *something* as frightening as it is paradoxically enormously hopeful - yet this a thing perhaps just a fraction beyond full intellectual comprehension. As we journey on, goosebumps may on many occasions confirm such a vibe. To these few I say I bring nothing new, just maybe the deciphering of a wonder map which has always belonged to you - a map to bring you home to the long unseen truth in yourself, via the stars; whatever the obstacles.

But let's get digging.

Layer upon layer of giants - beginning with Noah

OK, let's exhume those aforementioned giants one by one, let them shake the dust of ages from their awesome limbs and let us hear what they have to say for themselves in the context of their possible overlapping of this gigantic earthen effigy of Sagittarius/Albion - again, maybe the embodiment of them all. And since the dove brought us first to his Dover-marked hand, we'll allow the larger-than-life figure of Noah to speak first. Although Noah was not recorded as a giant in physical stature, he nevertheless had a gigantic life span of five centuries!

So what does Noah bring to the overall *reason* for this astonishment upon our doorstep this morning? Simply, his ark remains the ultimate symbol of refuge, strength and safety for all living things at those times when the sea level rises dangerously, and so it is the universal symbol of the preservation of the seed of life, when life itself is threatened.

When the sea level rises dangerously - isn't that exactly what ecological experts are predicting right now? It is an unnerving fact that, even as I write, vast areas of the Antarctic ice cap are breaking up and melting into the sea, due to a general global warming. Researchers have said that, if the present trend continues, within the next ten generations the global sea level may have risen by 200 feet! Even the most conservative predictions calculate a metre rise over the next century, constituting a major redrawing of the map of the world. Needless to say, the consequences would be devastating.

And so, the timing of this vessel's arrival upon our doorsteps and the sense of urgency it must warrant are equally devastating.

Jupiter

Since we are digging into Sagittarius, sooner or later our spades must make contact with the Roman god Jupiter, ruler of this astrological House of Sagittarius; though in esoteric astrology his role was even grander, being seen as the *Protector of the entire Horoscope.* What worthier head then to be placed at the very prow of this ark of star signs! Just look at the artwork and see for yourselves the apparent genius of the earth in allotting this figurehead position to Sagittarius - no other sign could occupy it either as forcibly or as logically. Simply brilliant!

The land must surely be shouting, *"Yes!"* to this mythic line of thought being the key to the unravelling of its message.

Thus in terms of the overall message, the placement of Sagittarius/Jupiter, this protectorate head of the horoscope, here at the head of the ark is perfect underpinning to the way the land is guiding our thoughts.

Atlas

Now from Greek mythology comes a giant of giants, Atlas, and how perfectly we shall find him too overlaid upon this station of Sagittarius.

To the Greeks, his home, The Hesperides, which was a veritable garden of the Earth Mother, was to be found somewhere on the far western horizon, a land referred to as 'The Isle of the Blest'. So I ask, was Britain this mythic land - certainly the coordinates would be correct; and was the giant Atlas who there guarded the golden apples of wisdom (translated by Sesti in *The Glorious Constellations* as the stars Atlas supported upon his shoulders) really *this* landlocked giant of Sagittarius/Albion?

Putting all this to one side let's touch lightly upon the tale of Atlas, for in Britain's land mirror we will find a most dazzling reflection.

First of all, in his legendary holding up of the heavens upon his awesome back, do we not have the perfect duplication in this figure of Sagittarius? Again just look at the cover to see the myth come so graphically alive. Sagittarius really does seem to be visually carrying the majority of the other star signs upon his back! But let us hear the rest of his story because the twinning gets even better.

One day the hero Perseus arrived in that wondrous garden of the Earth Mother wishing to pick those wisdom-filled apples (or stars) for himself. Atlas refused the hero's wishes, so Perseus thrust the head of snake-haired Medusa into the giant's face - the consequences of which are pure earth zodiac. I will let Thomas Bulfinch describe the moment from his book *The Golden Age of Myth and Legend:* "*Atlas, with all his bulk, changed to stone. His beard and hair became forests, his arms and shoulders cliffs, his head a summit and his bones rocks. Each part increased in bulk until he became a mountain (and such the pleasure of the gods) heaven and all its stars rests upon his shoulders.*"

OK, it's a myth - a child's bedtime story, but suddenly with this miraculously graphic map of Britain before us the event takes upon itself an amazing new light - suddenly we are watching a dream come spectacularly alive!

True, the Atlas mountains in Morocco were always thought to be the location of the giant's subterranean imprisonment, but doesn't this great zodiac of Albion now bear the full flowering truth to the tale's hidden message? A land upon the Greek's western horizon where the Earth Mother's own special garden was, and in whose foundations Atlas was cast to hold up the constellations upon his back for all time. Think about it! See it for yourself written hundreds of miles high; Britain *is* the Earth Mother's Garden of Delights seeded with the very constellations and all quite visibly carried, as was told, upon the back of a giant - this Sagittarius/Albion/Atlas! Thus we are shown that in Britain's starry fields are grown the apples of wisdom (the Word carried by these terrestrial constellations) that could save us yet - the golden apple or star wisdom is what fills the holds of this green ark to the preservation of life beyond the cataclysm.

Neither am I alone in twinning Atlas with Albion, indeed I am in wonderful company. From an introduction to his now lost painting of *The Ancient Britains*, Blake wrote *"The giant Albion, was Patriarch of the Atlantic; he is the Atlas of the Greeks."* He even goes on to suggest that, *"The stories of Arthur are the acts of Albion."*

Apart from the blatantly obvious tying-up of this myth of Atlas to the oh-so-clear pictorial evidence on the ground, I also wonder whether there is here an allegorical picture of the state of mankind today. Have we before us an image of what happens to men when we have lost that star wisdom, the wisdom of our true selves? If so, are we also,

like Atlas poetically turned to cold stone?

St Christopher

When looking at Atlas holding up that awesome weight of star signs, how alike he becomes to St Christopher, another giant from the East. Remember how he carried the Christ child, a symbol of the world's ills, upon his back across a flood? Again, look at the cover and see how easily this act too is replayed. See how this saint, now cast in rock, poetically carries not only all Britain upon his back, but in particular the lamb of Aries, and, in the shape of Gemini, a divine child - a babe which we shall discover later to be the unborn Christ child no less! Just look how his neck visibly buckles under the strain. And what about the flood? Equate it with Antarctica's continuing melt down!

Consider, too, whether those same 'ills' are now symbolically focused by the state of Britain today - she and the world's sociological and spiritual millstones only able to be lifted by the inner birth of that Child of Gemini, who, we shall find, is representative of a new perception of the God, who must now be proved to be *aware*, even in stone.

Bran the Blessed

The land's voice, mythologically keyed, now urges us to remember especially the homegrown giant, Bran the Blessed, once king of this land. We find his wondrous life recorded in the ancient *Mabinogion*, though the episode that should interest us here comes as he lay dying from a poisoned dart received in Ireland (Scorpio!), and how he commanded that his head should be severed from his

poisoned body. His head, he promised, would not decay but would continue to give verbal succour to his people.

It is said that for those who listened to his speech, time stood still for 87 years, which were enraptured in bird song - such was the aura of bliss that hung upon Bran's soothsaying.

Bran afterwards ordered his head to be taken from Wales and buried at the White Mount (Tower Hill) in London, which, uncannily, is the location of the very heart of Sagittarius in this, Britain's last resting place of giants! Moreover, he made a prophesy that while his head lay buried no invader would despoil this so-called Island of the Mighty - mighty, perhaps not so much for feats of arms, but for the giants that even then bulged its pastures?

They buried Bran's head facing Gaul as he instructed (exactly as is this great head of Sagittarius), Gaul then being the present day France, Switzerland, Belgium and the Netherlands.

So what does Bran himself bring to this developing message? I think we are once more being given a massive 'thumbs up' to our line of our thought because of the similarities with Sagittarius. Bran's giant head is buried here, of all places, and facing exactly the same way as the head of Sagittarius; then there is that promise that while his head remains in that position no harm will come to his land (this ark). So, he is again confirming why it is Sagittarius/Jupiter/Noah, those protectors of horoscopes and arks, whom the earth has willed to bulge the ground at the head of this ark. However, Bran has more to say than even this, for remember that this was once his kingdom - and we shall hear from him again shortly.

Ea

And still they come! Another giant of a demigod whose myth can be graphically re-read upon this home of Sagittarius is the Sumerian god Ea. Ea was the king of primordial waters and protector of both fishermen and sailors, remembered too for guiding the Ark of Utnapishtim (the Sumerian Noah) through another time when the seas had dangerously risen.

Sesti says of Ea that he "...*directed through his pilot, the Ark of Utnapishtim while the elements raged. Similarly he guided the ship of Gilgamesh during his pilgrimage to the Island of the Blessed. It was believed Ea swam in front of the ship in the form of a human bust.*"

How interesting that mention of the *Island of the Blessed* is. Is it one and the same place with the Greek's Isle of the Blest on that far western horizon where Atlas held up the stars? And when we read *Blessed* does not Bran the Blessed ring bells again? I think it does and not only in name connection, for Bran, too, was known to wade in deep waters before the boats of his warriors - another talking head above the waters.

Again we find that one giant's tale supports another until they all merge to give the one picture.

So off with their heads!

Noah, Jupiter, Atlas, St Christopher, Bran, and Ea have, I think, already spoken for themselves by six times graphically underlining the strength gathered in this station of Sagittarius. That said, the beheaded Bran, however, demands a fresh hearing.

He first asks us to begin by noting on the artwork how the down shaft of the cross lays provocatively across the combined necks of these guiding giants when extended southwards. Now when you look at this, doesn't that cross become suggestive of a sword - a sword which has the Christ upon its hilt? Indeed, see how old Sagittarius seems to be actually thumbing the edge of that blade, as though testing its keenness.

So what, if suddenly we see it as a blade,

does it imply?

As mentioned earlier, some of the mythology related to this figure seems to will us to see him as being weighed down and turned to stone. This is, perhaps, descriptive of the human race that is bereft of the wisdom of its true place amongst the stars - not knowing, nor wanting to know, that what the stars sing has turned the intended gift, man's inheritance, into a terrible burden. This is a burden of ignorance that has robbed him of the knowledge that he *is* God - along with every gnat and seaside pebble! He is blind to the new beginning that awaits him - the magic he has forever overlooked in the cause of his own perceived greatness.

So what cheer for Sagittarius or mankind if by some miracle the scales could fall from his and our eyes? When painting him I felt compelled to show his eye as blind, though at the time there seemed to be no reason for this. If suddenly he could see clearly, he could look up from his position of ignorance and see that the sword that threatens decapitation of that old crippling perception bears no malice, for it is held by the Christ. It can, therefore, only be a blade of truth; though still able to bring awful pain to those who do not want to hear or see it.

"Think not that I am come to send peace on earth: I came not to send peace, but a sword."
MATTHEW, Chapter 10, Verse 34

The above quote, however, is but one man's spiritual unravelling of what this corner of the wonder may portray. For a more 'slap you in the face' and physically down-to-earth reason for placing a sword across a neck I advise again pondering the very real fact of a rising sea, alongside what mythology has told us of Bran and St Christopher, and, in a symbolic sense, of Ea too.

Before I offer up this next interpretation,

you should know that although it sounds prophetic I certainly do not claim to be a prophet. I am an artist, I read pictures, not ephemeral visions narrated by angelic voices, and, in this case, pictures hundreds of miles tall, formed of granite, rivers, cliffs, and even honest-to-goodness road systems, so you don't have to be an Ezekiel to get an eye full of it all!

Now I don't know about you, but when I see a sword crossing the neck of a giant, and he being one whose brothers are Bran and St Christopher (who were *both* beheaded), I cannot but think of actual physical decapitation. I then see that broad nape of his sea-washed neck and know that that particular area of land is some of the lowest-lying in all Britain. My prying eye then looks to the other side of his neck from where that same blade re-emerges and where the river Thames flows out as though from a sliced jugular. It is no secret either that this area, too, is prone to any abnormal advance of the tides, hence the millions of pounds already spent on the Thames flood-prevention barrier.

This all-too-graphic picture in the landscape, mingled as it is with my reasonable concerns that a day of chaos looms, leaves me to suspect that, whatever elemental fury slams into this colossal lifeboat, the sea at these two obvious weak points may make inroads in an attempt to actually sever that great head, true to its entwined myths. To warn us, the earth has selected out of mythology's universal storehouse of wisdom a 140-mile-high clear-cut picture!

If it were not for the serious implications of what I feel the land is trying to warn us here, the artist in me would admit to wanting to stand back entranced, imagining the sight of the risen sea waters, like streams of blood, graphically seeking to re-enact that beheading of Bran the Blessed, his head then becoming a virtual speaking Grail of sorts - seeking too perhaps, to replay the moment when that ship

of Gilgamesh (another who sought the Grail of his time) was safely led through the waves by the god Ea. The myth tells us that Ea swam, as a bust, a little way off in front of the ark - just as this head of Sagittarius would look if severed from the rest of the ark!

But remember, too, that myth tells us that Bran gave good council to those who would listen, even after decapitation, and Ea still guided his sailors, though he was no more than a head above the waves. Even in terrible circumstances there then seems a picture of hope too.

Myth is the key to the code

Without doubt myth in the western world carries little currency today, therefore we must thank the late Joseph Campbell, the world's foremost authority on mythology, for inspiring a few to see its true worth. He saw myth as the key to the experience of *'the rapture of being alive'*. On the back cover of his book *The Power of Myth* and under a sub-heading of, *How mythology illumines our lives* it is said about Campbell, *"To him, mythology was the song of the universe, the music of the spheres."*

Who cannot now, with *Behold Jerusalem!* in their hand, begin to suspect that such a theory may well have some foundation, especially when, after just these first two steps on this myth-singing landscape, we have witnessed several global myths come dancing back out of this mirror as solid realities. If we suspect that even the rocks and elements are tuned to these universal myths, the shorthand of life's preservation and glorification, then surely we must have even more reason to feel the rapture of a life in the midst of it all - suddenly we have a whole new dimension to play in!

Under the banner of mythology many throughout the ages have set out in search of this same enrapturing of their being. These quests have had many names: 'The Search for the Holy Grail' is how many have seen theirs, but whether looking for a golden cup, apples, a fleece, something won at the end of 12 (zodiacal?) Herculean labours, or, as in the case of that Mesopotamian hero-king Gilgamesh, a herb of life, I wonder, as I did in Libra, whether all were originally looked for within *this* magical star-filled cargo of Albion's ark, even though it would have then been still within its own evolutionary infancy.

Throughout our *Grand Tour* through green constellations we will dog what seems many a hero's still-warm trail. But if I am wrong and Perseus, Jason, Hercules, Gilgamesh, or even Jesus never did set sandal upon these shores in search of their ultimate wisdom, then the equally fantastic fact must be that wherever those heroes first acted out these global lessons to mankind, this magnetised land was somehow aware of their every move. And so, in honour of the universal truths they sought, the essence of their adventures has somehow graphically been recorded in a picture sign language. These then reassembled in a montage of film cuts allied to the mythology of the stars and laid out in the joint form of a clock and map. All was then bound in an ark shape for safe keeping through the centuries, thus constructing a monumental message for an age when there would be nearly no time left at all for a mankind bent on self-destruction to find a way back to an inner truth and thus the true *rapture* of a life on this holy earth. Mythology is then the vehicle of God's word to us who must be on the brink, the wise language of antiquity that has weathered the aeons and arrived intact into this new millennium where it is needed most.

Even the boy within me winces at the absurdity of what I have just written, but by the end of our journey you may be more sympathetic to such fantastic thinking.

Now to pace him out.

Defining the body

With our heads into the wind, the North Sea to our left will be our guide.

In and out of his great buckled neck we go - this bay charmingly named The Wash. Waves polish his great bald head, Cromer being its crown. Turning down his forehead, we'll pass through Great Yarmouth and Lowestoft. Orford Ness perches on the tip of his nose.

His open mouth has lips of Felixstowe and Harwich, while his tongue is licked into shape by the rivers Orwell and Stour, leaving Shotley Gate on its tip.

Sounds plausible?

Clacton-on-Sea marks his rugged chin and with it I can't help wondering if, from here, one could hear that monstrous tongue slop and rattle within its cavernous mouth? I wonder because my dictionary certainly suggests so: "clack: noise or clatter of human tongues".

The River Thames then traces his forearm out to that so graphic stub of a thumb, tipped by North Foreland. Christian Canterbury rests on the back of his pagan hand. White-capped waves complete that fist to Dover, that returning place of the dove - and what a powerful profile he has. Though we cannot complete him without giving mention to a string of hills whose name is a tattoo upon his cheek, in case anyone should ever forget that they walk upon a giant, these the **Gog Magog Hills. According to homegrown mythology, Gog and Magog were giants on a par in size, strength and bad temper with Albion himself; the pair remembered even to this day in effigy upon London's Guildhall.**

Bull's-eye!

But what of that blind eye? Well, there it is, just a little to the east of the town of *Eye* in Suffolk!

That laughing name-play magic that we found in Libra is at it again!

While writing this chapter I began reading *The Sun and the Serpent* by Hamish Miller and Paul Broadhurst. It describes their dowsing and mapping of the famous ley line from Cornwall's St Michael's Mount to Glastonbury. From there, it led them across the entire width of the country to a point where it leaves Britain's east coast at a little place called Hopton, which, unknown to them, lies upon this giant's forehead; indeed, the position of his mystic 'third eye'. According to them, this is a charmed spot marked by a burnt-out tower of an ancient church now wreathed in ivy and home to a flock of doves. A lovely and poetic touch to this head of old Noah!

However, and for me even more enchanting, the authors mentioned that before the ley line had shot out to sea they had followed it through the place of Eye. Eye! I had never until then heard of the place, let alone known that it was almost in the corner of my giant Sagittarius' own eye! How those goosebumps returned!

I was to further learn that in ancient times there was a large barrow mound surrounded by water at this same spot - what a magnificently gleaming eyeball it must have made from the air! This original barrow was later heightened so as to hold up the weight of a Norman fort, or should I say "lookout"?

Unfortunately, though, the actual location of Eye is sadly just a little too far southwest to be exactly in this giant's eyeball, and this may be the reason I never noticed it before. As far as my own artist's eye can judge, it is about six miles away from where I have felt impressed to locate

it. I placed it in and around the vicinity of Fressingfield, Metford, Halesworth and Walpole, with the river Waveney perhaps giving it an eye brow, while the river Blyth may denote a tear trickling out of one corner. All these are six miles from Eye but close enough, I believe, because, on a head approximately 80 miles high by 55 wide, six miles is no distance at all, between friends. And what a lovely line of vision this giant will have once his sight returns, from Eye to Hopton's tower of doves, again no finer sight for the sore eyes of any Noah.

*__Note:__ *many years after finding Eye in Sagittarius' own eye I decided to take another quick look at the map of this area before finally going to press. Anyway, it seems that the magician in the landscape had one last dove up his sleeve by which to make a marvellous end of my schooling in a miracle, for through that town of Eye flows a river I'd never noticed before, and with it I have the belated pleasure to tell you that it's called the DOVE - unbelievable but true! And as a friend said, with this surely the last 'eye' has been well and truly dotted!*

With a Dove (Dover) on his hand, and that Dove now seen to be astonishingly reflected in his Eye, we are being told in the most beautiful language ever devised that the memory of Noah is, for a fact, embedded in this singing landscape - presumably for an almighty reason.

But others nearly got here before me!

Now let us cool our heels in The British Library's map department there in the very heart of him whom we have just hiked back into reality.

Here's a good place to learn that I was certainly not the first to spy a great head with an eye at Eye, nor was I the first to see fins bristling out of that south-western peninsular where Pisces swims. Let me explain.

The introduction to Miller and Broadhurst's book is written by the acknowledged guru of

earth mysteries, John Michell. In his piece, Michell reminisces about a 'crude' mural he once painted on a Glastonbury café wall and which he designed around the passage of that famous ley line. He goes on to describe that his picture took its form from the shape given by the entire southern half of England where that line ran. This resulted in the creation of a fantastical serpent-like creature whose eye he

Geography Bewitched! - England and Wales.
By Richard Dighton, 1795. The British Library.

planted on top of Eye (where else!) while its feet he placed near Land's End.

Without ever having had egg and chips at this establishment, I can only assume that Michell's creature, having an eye where Eye is, must have had a head pretty well occupying the bulged area where the mighty skull of old Sagittarius now clothes itself in fens and fields. Pity though, about those feet being where *fins* should have been!

Michell's very near miss was, however, both pre-empted and maybe even bettered in 1795 by the artist Robert Dighton, who saw fit to produce a six-penny whimsical map of Britain where he, too, sniffed the implant of a giant, though one *with* fins!

Dighton, was one of many 'jobbing' artists of that time who, just for fun, joined in an apparent craze for plonking gigantic pictorial images on every map they could lay their hands on; from Britain to the Baltic all manner of figures suddenly began to animate whole countries. These coastal and border-hugging pieces of whimsy ranged from the humorous to the absolute fantastic, and even a few were of a political bent. Indeed the entire atlas was their creative oyster! From what I have seen of them, most did try their best to gain their initial form from the coastlines, although, if you think I've used 'artistic licence' in cobbling this map of star signs together, well you should see theirs running riot! Simply, if a piece of coastline didn't fit in with their plans it was chopped off or else ignored. Having said that, I also came across a rendition of North Wales, which, for those of us who will soon plot the same area, will be an absolute delight - we shall meet her in a few hundred miles time in the chapter on Virgo.

But to return to Dighton's effort: he was, without knowing it, definitely on the right scent, for, although like Michell he saw the whole of southern England as one enormous monster, he had let the nitty-gritty of the coastline govern his pen. In so doing he saw what anyone looking just a little beyond the obvious can see superimposed upon that south-western peninsular - namely *fins a-plenty* on a perfectly proportioned fishy body. Neither could he resist placing a dreadful eye in that vicinity of Eye, with the rest of its head occupying exactly the same area as my Sagittarius, albeit with a much larger mouth.

Unfortunately Dighton saw no fish's head buried inland and so was robbed of seeing Pisces, and, perhaps, as a consequence, all the other star giants too. Thus, having no clue either of Capricorn splashing around in between that fish tail and that great Sagittarian head, he simply grafted the fish's body to the head and thereby created a 'serpenty thing', just as Michell did. His map of whimsy, intriguingly entitled *Geography Bewitched*, can still be seen in The British Library, but please turn a blind eye to the jolly Toby jug-like man who sits astride the serpent with a tankard of beer in his fist!

In Dighton's defence, remember that, 200 years ago, he didn't have the luxury of working from a *Michelin* map, or, more importantly, the vital template of Katherine Maltwood's Glastonbury zodiac.

OK - *if you think you've found Sagittarius then where's the rest of him?*

At this point, some of you may be champing at the bit to ask where the rest of this giant's body is, namely that majestic centaur lower half, as is clearly depicted on both the Glastonbury and Preseli zodiacs.

The answer is that Albion's Sagittarius is totally minus his horsy lower half, unless it's buried somewhere deep below the depths of the English Channel and the fields of France - but I doubt it. Personally, I feel that the rest of his body has been found surplus to the land's specific requirements. Simply, we are being directed to focus upon the significance of his head and pointing hand.

Examine him now alongside the classical 1690 portrayal of Sagittarius. Yes, I have cropped off this one's lower half and have even stolen his bow, but only to prove that Albion's giant really *is* him; indeed, I know it's him by that stub of a pointing thumb alone! Look, too, at the line drawings of the other two earthly zodiacs and see this same give-away characteristic.

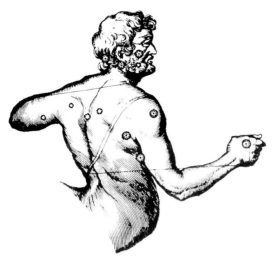

Sagittarius. From Hevelius, Uranographia totum coelum stellatum, 1690. The British Library

As for the missing bow - curiously in all three earth zodiacs Sagittarius seems to be minus this, yet could those pointing fingers or thumbs be aiding the holding of a bow or arrow? So, has that bow been taken away from him for some reason, or is it still to be placed in his hand? Blake may be suggesting an answer in *Jerusalem: "Then Albion stretch'd his hand into Infinitude; and took his bow."*

Another clue may be found in the Bible. Remember how, when we were pacing out this giant, we found upon his cheek a line of moderate hills yet indelibly branded as 'gigantic' by the infamous title of The Gog Magog Hills. Well, Ezekiel knew a Gog too - and this is what he heard God threaten he would do to him:

"And I will smite thy bow out of thy left hand, and will cause thine arrows to fall out of thy right hand."
EZEKIEL, Chapter 39 Verse 3

More cryptic still we find in verse 6 of the same Chapter this warning to the equally troublesome Magog:

"And I will send a fire on Magog, and among them that dwell carelessly in the isles: and

they shall know that I am Lord."

Again, if these pictures on the ground are meant to convey something, then is the above quotation a warning to both the giants and unwary peoples of *these* British Isles of a catastrophe either long past or still to come?

But if you don't agree with arks having figureheads - especially ones that can talk...

We have now seen how perhaps the mythological strength of many giants has been gathered and compacted into the soil sinews of this prodigious station of Sagittarius. And it makes sense, for he is truly the figurehead of this ark and therefore designed to take a terrible battering in whatever storms are to come. Likewise mythology seems to be telling us that this same head is vastly intelligent, a virtual Grail in itself, thus we are advised to cling to its every word, even though it may become visually severed at the storm's height.

But if a 'talking figurehead', especially one upon Noah's ark, is beyond your patience, then allow your inner child to direct your stare back into the mirror of all this - the one up there in the night sky.

Heavens above - can you see her? Up there, deep within the Milky Way and in a section of sky known to the ancients as The Sea: there she sails - the perfect sister ship to this ark of Britain. We are gazing at the constellation of Argo Navis, the Ship. I will have more to say about this, the original ark in the chapter on Cancer, for now, though, I will only touch upon men's earliest myths of this star ship, myths that may be of vital use to us, their descendants, who have since forgotten how to sail with the harmonic tides of the universe.

This ship was made from the wood of a talking oak or Tree of Life that, in turn, endowed its giant figurehead with the *gift of speech* so that it could warn its crew of impending dangers! *Now* do you hear the voice of this land ark's own figurehead roar from off the face of the planet? Once more, see how the images of myth are finding a new voice in this looking-glass landscape - *so listen to this ark!*

Take a look now at the 300-year-old engraving of the heavenly Argo Navis. Do you wonder at the sight of its great figurehead? Have you an idea that you've seen this picture somewhere before? Of course you have - the essence of it is plastered all over the cover of this book! Marvel, then, at the land's own mind-blowing replica: see two doves flying directly towards two talking figureheads; with a smile also check those fishes, one of stars, the

other of granite, both swimming towards the stern. We are looking at sister ships in sister seas: as above, so below!

Again, I found this engraving only when I was nearly at the end of writing this book and I was, and for that matter I still am, delightfully devastated by it.

So let us now put these Sagittarian finds in our knapsack and make our way to the next star sign - and although this land zodiac is out of traditional sequence, our step, from Sagittarius into Capricorn, *is* perfectly in step with the mirror above. Thus clock*wise* is the way we travel from now on.

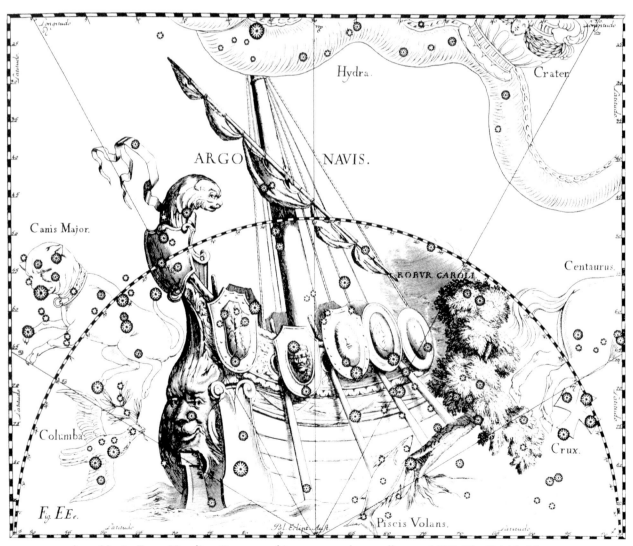

Argo Navis. From Hevelius, Uranographia totum coelum stellatum, 1690. The British Library

CHAPTER 3

CAPRICORN

• *The Sea Unicorn* •

★

*The third giant
along the way*

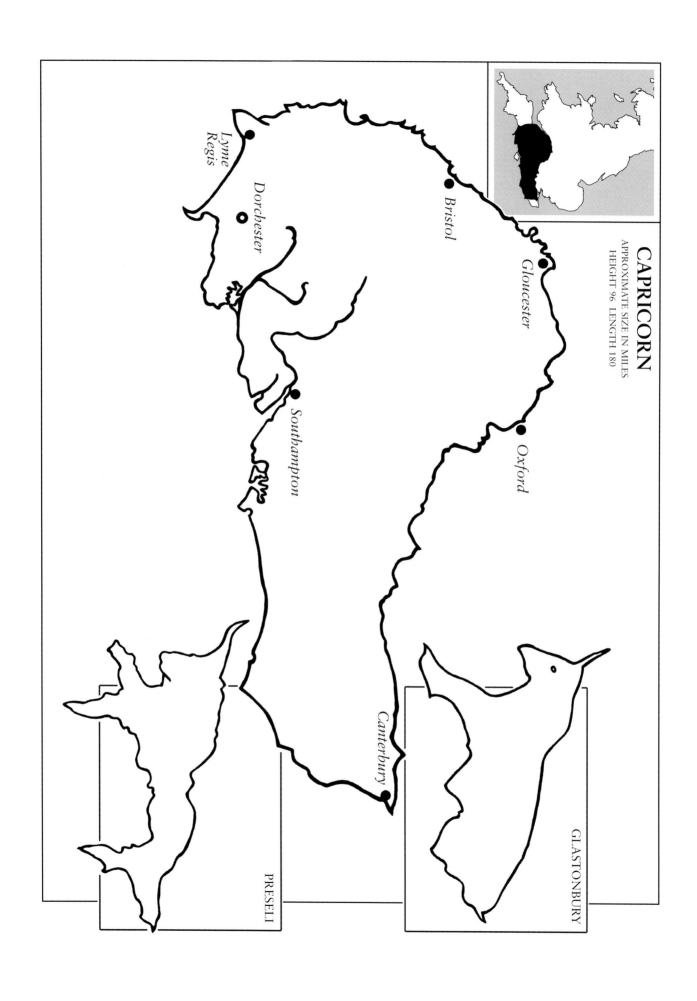

CAPRICORN
APPROXIMATE SIZE IN MILES
HEIGHT 96 LENGTH 180

Lyme Regis

Dorchester

Bristol

Gloucester

Southampton

Oxford

Canterbury

PRESELI

GLASTONBURY

The Broken Horn of Plenty?

"What's Poetry if it isn't something that has to fight for the unseen against the seen, for the dead against the living, for the mysterious against the obvious? It's the only Lost Cause we've got left! It fights for the ... for the ... for the Impossible!"

A GLASTONBURY ROMANCE, John Cowper Powys

GENERAL AREA: FROM ITS FISH TAIL, MARKED BY CANTERBURY IN THE EAST, TO AS FAR WEST AS THE BRISTOL CHANNEL. STOW-IN-THE-WOLD MARKS THE MOST NORTHERLY POINT OF HER ARCHED BACK.

To my eyes the Capricorn figures at both Glastonbury and Preseli are more akin to unicorn-fish than goat-fish and I see Albion's version as no different. Thus, and for what must be a good reason, Capricorn is stamped three times upon the face of the planet as a splendid mythological unicorn, though one born of the waves and of all psychological and spiritual deep waters - a moonlit Night Mare! Witness a creature fetched from the Dreamtime and which, for age upon age, represented the height of purity. To glimpse a unicorn was always a sign that one was near the very borders of paradise itself, those pastures of primordial bliss; and I think its meaning is no less so here, seen bucking the foundations of these southern counties of Albion. For you to see her now is confirmation that you and your 'child within' are already three giant strides over that same fabled border and ready now to chase, not only rainbows, but a unicorn too!

Hunting the not-so-impossible

Just observe the dynamics of her; how her great back arches as she frolics in the waves alongside the hull of the ark; her bold head tucked upside down as though thrusting that mystic horn into the foaming English Channel. Sure, a fabulous sight, but remember we are hunters; a reported sighting of her is no good to us; we want the scent of her; want to know where she's been and where she might be wanting to lead our thoughts; we certainly want to know whether she has any geological markings, or any of those disarming name-plays, like we found on the first two signs, that could again confirm the impossible. We need all this to track down the reason for her sudden arrival in our very own backyards, where we thought the border of paradise could never be.

Being fairly well acquainted with this part of the country, I needed no research to find my first half-clue: upon her back she carries the aptly named Vale of the White Horse where a gigantic image of a white horse has been beautifully cut out of the turf to expose the underlying white chalk. Of course I instantly wondered whether like that same geological whiteness, which so brilliantly paints that dove of Libra, there was here, too, poetic confirmation of this wonder-horse's own milk-white flesh rippling but an inch or two under the green?

Spurred on, my research into this ancient art

form of exposing white figures by cutting away the turf was itself to reveal that, although practised in other parts of the country, it was very much concentrated in this unicorned area where the local speciality was to cut images of white horses! Indeed, I was to learn that another 14 such horses of differing ages strode over this same mystic beast, each of them still filling us with the same awe as that first one at Uffington did when it shone out clean and new beneath an Iron Age moon.

More uncanny still, however, was my further discovery that all but one of these 15 white horses are in the half of this sign which is the horse, its fish tail, I believe, only giving a home to one! Why? My inner voice offers up a tantalising reason of its own. For instance, were the people who cut these white horses subconsciously prompted by that force which was at work shaping the greater white horse beneath their feet? And was this part and parcel of that same sympathetic magic which inspired someone to come up with the name Dover to emphasise where a dove perched on the hand of Noah; or another to name Eye almost exactly where an eye should be on the face of Sagittarius?

And what sympathy! Even geologically speaking (with the emphasis on the *logical*, and this only the third giant into our journey through 16), this uncanny land poetry seems so tailored to each giant that at least two out of the 16 who could rightfully demand to be painted white, Libra and Capricorn, just so happen to be located where the underlying whiteness of the land is a renowned feature. Indeed, from this Unicorn's ear eastwards (thus taking in all her body) the cliffs themselves begin to acquire an increasing whiteness until going solid white at the Isle of Wight and Dover. However, from that same ear tip westwards, and therefore along the under belly of Pisces, one would return with the equivalent of only a few bucketsful of whiteness, and this only from the area of Beer and but an ear twitch west of Seaton which tips the ear. (We shall later see how, delightfully, the ear tip of the lamb of Aries is also white.)

Thus, whether by suggestive earth colourings or place-name clues, it all seems cunningly manoeuvred not only to embellish the giant in question, but also to bolster its actual presence so that by the end of our journey it will be hard to waive it all aside as the coincidental slips and slides of tongues and sedimentary deposits. Rather we will see it as being intelligently orchestrated by what must be one vast and loving mind; a mind that has for aeons harnessed everything from the minuscule works of worms to the thunderous movements of landslides to shape this dazzling picture message, to the effect that everything, but everything, is *aware* like we never knew, and what is more is trying urgently to communicate with Man via this same picture sign language.

Yesterday, I know, we could easily have turned away from this with a deaf ear and a condescending chuckle; we could have waived away the whole absurd proposition as New Ageist pie in the sky. This morning, however, especially with the growing signs that our planet is being pushed out of balance, I propose that the pie is in our faces! Look at the map - to deny it is to deny the nose on your face. Something extraordinary has happened and the disarming poetry of it will not go away - poetry, which may or may not include these 15 white horses cut into the head and shoulders of a 180-mile-long wonder-horse. Imagine, however, if these same white mares were, say, dotted over the figure of Taurus, or Leo - a poetic disaster! That said, and having just put forward a case perhaps for the poetic input of these chalk horses, I have to admit that not one of them has a horn or fish tail. And so, with tail slightly edging between my own legs, the still amused and undeterred 11-year-old dared me to see whether there were any place names on this mare that could, like Eye, Strait/Straight of Dover/Dove, Isle of

Wight/White, give me my goosebumps back!

By taking up the challenge, I knew that here was going to be another defining moment of either my madness or this miracle's reality. I also knew only too well the kind of guy I was: in a word 'fickle', and if nothing breathtaking was waiting for me out there to confirm 'Big Time' that I was walking upon a fabulous creature with a mythological tale to tell, then no matter what wonderful finds I'd already stashed in my knapsack, I would tip its contents over the nearest cliff and get the hell back to my studio, for what was already hanging on my wall was madness enough for any man! In short, I needed one hell of a confidence booster to keep me going - otherwise I'd think the kid within really had been kidding me!

With adrenalin pumping again, and in less than five minutes, both dreamer and fickle graphic designer had raced 180 miles from tail to head and, having found nothing, were in danger of falling off the last curls of her frothy mane and into the Bristol Channel, with an accompanying damping of my spirits. And yet somewhere deep within me I just knew that even at this seemingly dead end the land would present me with something marvellous. I felt that I was being toyed with, my renowned fickleness being laughingly teased as though by some clever magician, who would take me to the very edge of disappointment purely to make the result of the final circle of his wand the more spectacularly rewarding.

And so it was to be, for just as I was to tumble, doubting, off the cliff I was grabbed by my neck and hoisted firmly upon her great mane, for there upon the last western curl of this flicking mane was a place name fit to rid this graphic designer's fickleness for the rest of his journey into a new way of perceiving this planet, for there laughing in his face was the astonishing confirmation of **Weston-Super-Mare!**

I laughed until I cried - if this was madness

it was too beautiful for me to want to return to sanity.

Again I sat back and imagined if such a graphic label had been found upon the head of Aries or Pisces - disappointment guaranteed! But no, all these clues have been dropped exactly where they should be in order to both spur on and delight a traveller with new eyes.

Many weeks later I was to stumble over another wonderful place name upon the very horn itself and which was to be the icing on this particular cake, but I'll leave that one waiting to the end of this chapter and a final flourish of my own wand regarding this Super Mare.

Goat or unicorn? Two horns or one?

And so with such an incredibly precise signpost indicating exactly what we travellers now stand upon, let us once more prepare to delve into mythology in an effort not only to decipher just what this creature has to add to the overall message, but maybe, too, why a unicorn *Super Mare* has taken the place of Capricorn's traditional goat, for our final mythological interpretation will depend upon it. So first, let's see her true breed.

Yet again the resemblance of Albion's Capricorn to that of Glastonbury and Preseli is tantalisingly close, although to be perfectly honest, I rate this figure, along with Scorpio, as the two least like their counterparts in those other two zodiacs. Having said that, and again to my eyes, all three versions seem far more unicorn/fish than goat/fish. Why? Well count their horns for yourself - one each I take it? In my book that makes them all unicorns!

Admittedly, in the mythology of the stars my push for a single-horned unicorn over a double-horned goat would seem to be on somewhat dodgy ground; a unicorn has never ever been mentioned as having anything to do with Capricorn. Indeed, its goatish claims are amplified by the Greeks who saw Capricornus as the star cluster which Zeus gave as a gift to the she-goat/nymph Amalthaea for having nursed the god when he was a baby, along with her own son Pan.

Is this a massive vote in favour of two horns over one, then? Seems so, but first hear the rest of the myth. It seems Amalthaea had fed both babies from her celestial horn, her *Cornucopia* from which flowed inexhaustible nourishment and wisdom. Her magic horn was only ever spoken of in the singular - so scope for a unicorn after all?

So, I say again it's Capricorn the single-horned cornucopian sea unicorn for me – although I have noticed that whenever Mary Caine sniffs the scent of a unicorn drifting in and out of Glastonbury's fields, she too locates one as possibly hiding in Capricorn's pastures, though I feel she'd always side with the goat over the unicorn ...but I could be wrong. In only her second paragraph she refers to the horn of Glastonbury's own Capricorn as: *"Single, long and straight, it makes a unicorn out of Capricorn..."*

Nor do I in any way wish to challenge the vision of the first star seer, who joined up those starry dots that form heaven's Capricorn and proclaimed its head to be double-horned and thus a goat. However, that seemingly *single* line of stars that sprout from Capricorn's starry head in the examples I have found in books on astrology (see below) give the distinct impression that there's only one horn up there too.

But then again, perhaps that ancient astrologer will turn around and advise me to better gauge the stars on earth and to leave those in heaven to him, for the land obviously has its own evolving tale to tell. Well said!

However, before you

decide which of us is right, it is as well to remember that in the days when men still believed in unicorns and claimed sightings of them when stalking in twilit woods, their description was often to the effect that the wonder horse had of all things a *goatish* head, albeit single-horned. What is more, its front feet were sometimes even reported as being cloven. Apparently then, unicorns seem always to have been shifting amalgams of both horse and goat. As for Capricorn, though, all schools of thought may now examine at first hand the fabulous creature that we've found grazing in the rising mist of Albion along with the following theory of Sesti. After relating another reason that the form of a goat occupies one half of Capricorn, he then seems to query whether there may yet be more mystery behind its pedigree: *"However, our Capricornus is much more ancient and the explanation of this figure is perhaps lost in the mists of time."*

So shame about the horn!

Having then canvassed for a unicorn over a goat, I must confess that the only physical disappointment with Albion's magical beast is that unfortunately it has a horn that is less than perfectly straight and not very long either! How hard it strives to take its form out of Chesil Beach and Portland Bill but fails to make a straight and sharp job of it. In fact it seems almost chiselled in half. Or was it perhaps once majestically formed, but now that it has a message to bring, the earth needs us to see it as damaged?

We shall look into this most i m p o r t a n t question shortly, but for now I'd like us to take our first look at the wonderfully interesting *Geological Map of the United Kingdom (South)*, produced by the Institute of Geological Sciences, 3rd Edition, 1979. This is a map that shows, in graphic blocks of colour, the actual rock and sedimentary make up of Britain. However, for us who now try to see beyond the ordinary, these same once fluid rivers of rock will be seen, time and again, almost to animate these giant figures of Albion. Indeed, in the case of Gemini's Griffin, it was solely this map that gave birth to him!

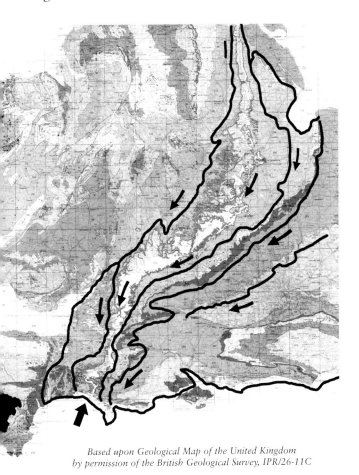

Based upon Geological Map of the United Kingdom by permission of the British Geological Survey, IPR/26-11C

In the case of our sea unicorn see how, from the far north and east of Britain, the differing sedimentary deposits seem pulled southwestwards and funnelled, with what

seems focused intent, directly into the very forehead and horn of this vibrant mare in the region of Lyme Regis. Moreover, the overall shape of this flow itself seems like a great inverted horn, a tornado of unicorn magic!

It is also interesting that these same solidified flows seem especially to connect the heads of the lamb of Aries and Sagittarius to this head of Capricorn. I didn't at first latch onto the possible purpose of this, but then I wondered if, instead of those frozen rivers of force being 'pulled' towards the head of Capricorn, they were, on the contrary, being symbolically transmitted outwards *from* it towards those other two signs, as though they were perhaps 'feeding' from the unicorn's fount of wisdom, that Horn of Plenty. And with that thought I remembered Amalthaea!

From our dissection of Sagittarius, remember how we found the Roman god Jupiter also embedded there? Well, the Greek equivalent of Jupiter was Zeus - yes, he who was suckled from the she-goat Amalthaea's funnel-shaped Cornucopia! That's not all. If this sedimentary tide really does strive to become a subtle subterranean retelling of that Greek myth, then we must find a Pan too, that other infant who suckled alongside Zeus, and so make the picture not just complete, but marvellously so. Well, we shall eventually find him, and startlingly so, within the shadow of the Christ on the cross in the station of Aries. Proudly cloven-footed he joyfully awaits us with others who, likewise, prepare to shock us rigid at the end of our journey. For now, though, just put in your knapsack the image of a unicorn horn being an agent of nourishment - an image perhaps now backed up by the poetic retelling of an archaic myth, remarkably spelt out in the sedimentary ebb tide that in the beginning gave rise to the extraordinary shape of this land - for a *reason*.

But I digress - easy to do when walking in wonderland! No matter then how intriguing that subterranean artistry, we must still come back to the glaring fact that the Glastonbury and Preseli horns are very much more complete than this weird little stump of Albion's mare. And because the rest of this lovely figure is so clearly and faultlessly sculpted, as indeed are all the other signs to come, I can only feel that this damaged horn may yet have some significant message of its own to impart in aid of the greater picture - nothing appears for nothing upon this prophetic landscape.

Its injury is our injury - its healing will be our healing

Does its deformity, for instance, portray a now damaged Cornucopia, a sign of today's many injurious acts against the land, and consequently against ourselves, resulting in a spiritual starvation of sorts? If so, can we again look towards finding verification of this in myth, or, dare I say, in myth wrapped up as religion? Let us look to religion first.

Without doubt, the arrival of Christianity, coming as it did with the Age of Pisces, although perhaps not at the outset, nevertheless signalled the rise of God the Father to the demise of God the Mother. And with that shift, nature, and the divinity once attached to it, was to be branded evil, thus communion between man, beast, and the land became outlawed. The feminine Yin set against the masculine Yang, the positive male polarity more valued than the negative female and the father's white thought more holy than the mother's black. This unbalancing resulted, especially for us in the west, in our mass divorce from the environment, and with it the fount of any prospect of paradise on earth capped, left to sour, and become overgrown to the point where barely anyone could remember that it ever existed. Indeed, if it were not for the legacy of mythology we today would have no conception of a state of paradise - not even of a thing called a unicorn!

So, with this in mind, take another look at the cover, and suspecting this unicorn to be a creature perhaps with more affinity to the goddess and femininity, can we now see her actually *charging* into that next sign of Christianity-loaded Pisces? Such a clash would leave the wonder horn of the goddess's most wonderful beast broken, and men consequently blinded to the full magic of their spiritual kinship with nature - and so would it also leave the cornucopia broken?

I don't know. I might be out of my ground; some would suggest even 'out of my tree', but confronted by such an overall miracle suddenly arrived upon our doorstep we must all strive to find both rhyme and reason for it, however intellectually aggravating. For my own part, I have found that the deeper we go into the reason for the earth's incredible shaping of Britain, the more this 'bridging of sundered opposites' will take up our picture-prompted thoughts - becoming indeed the fundamental issue behind this whole conundrum. So does Albion illustrate a way to the bridging or rebalancing, a harmonious bringing together of the so-called female Yin and male Yang, the material and the spiritual - and is this the chemistry behind the Grail itself, indeed even the key to its actual attainment?

Moving on, though still with the thought that her broken horn is the prime focus of what this sign wishes us most to muse upon, I recommend that we should again dip into myth. Indeed I think we should put a replica of her damaged horn into our knapsacks and carry it with us throughout the rest of our journey; wrap it in a soft cloth and, in doing so, have a will to try and mend it. Carry with it, too, a vital piece of ancestral belief regarding the magical properties of such a wonder horn when unbroken and spiralling proud - a belief that it was both a magical detector and cleanser of poison, especially in water.

Keeping in mind the actual pose of Albion's unicorn, let's now glean more of this beast's 'water-conning' capabilities.

Our ancestors evoked an aura of purity and chastity around the unicorn, more than any other creature. This was perhaps crystallised in the folk memory from that moment when, either in dream or reality, someone somewhere watched a unicorn step down to a poisoned lake, where all the more mundane beasts waited thirstily on the banks, as though expectant of her coming. On arrival, she was seen to dip her horn into the polluted waters, which were immediately purified, enabling the rest of the animals to safely drink their fill.

Visualise that scene whilst casting another look at the cover. Is not that tale being played out now by all the wondrous creatures of Albion? Just look how Capricorn in a powerful gesture dips her horn into the poisonous seas of our polluted planet! From this imagery, my own fathoming suggests that until men can believe in unicorns again, in the inherent holiness of every atom of this planet and in the belief that our dreams really can be made to get up and walk this beautiful planet (for our nightmares already do), then that broken horn/cornucopia will remain as a curse upon creation.

But how can we bring about a healing? I even wonder whether simply to acknowledge her pitiful horn, indeed, this whole miracle underfoot, may be to begin to mend it? For surely to see and believe in this miracle is to change overnight one's own perception of this earth, and then to perhaps awaken and demand more strongly than ever before the cleansing of the seas and the air, to passionately fight against the raping of the rain forests, and for God's sake plead for a halt to our scientists playing at God by the tampering with the gene. Such feelings were sparked for me, and I hope for you too, via the sight of what the land has done, and with it by the sudden and painful acknowledgement of the God that must always have been aware and singing out of everything, including ourselves - just like our ancestors believed. And I wonder too if we could mend our rift with nature, rejoin in our hearts the Yin and Yang, whether a paradise would begin to magically return all over the planet - is not this wonder of Albion the very proof that it could!

But getting back to the tale of the unicorn dipping its horn in water, I found a starry slant on it in my excellent source book *The Lore of the Unicorn* by Odell Shepard. The author refers to the unicorn as being implicated with the moon and femininity and informs how, in ancient times, this union was seen as especially apparent in the similarity of that beast's single horn to that of the singular horned appearance of a new moon: *"The animal is most readily associated with the new or crescent moon, which might indeed seem to dwellers by the sea to be leading the stars down to the water and to dip its horn therein before they descend."*

For a second time I ask you, is not the entirety of Albion the exact pictorial portrayal of this scene? See Capricorn now justifiably leading down the very constellations to the sea - to earth!

But there is yet more potential medicine to swallow. Wherever that Unicorn was first glimpsed cleansing the lake, whether in some virgin forest at the time when all the world was young, or in a dream remembered and recounted by one enlightened to its portent, it was nevertheless a strong enough sighting to prompt many a paranoid petty prince and duke in 14th century Europe to have such a horn (albeit more often than not a fraudulent tusk of the narwhale) on their dining table in order to detect the poison in the goblet. To dip it in the spiked wine would cause the horn to perspire beads of a dew-like substance, would you believe!

This healing horn did not just excel in the purification of water and wine, for it had other miraculous medicinal attributes too, though all antidotal in some characteristic. One of these beliefs, stemming from at least the 4th century BC, states how the horn was a deterrent against scorpions and therefore of particular value to travellers of Albion who will eventually have to confront one in Northern Ireland! Indeed, one David de Pomis in 1587 proclaimed that for a horn to protect against scorpions, *"there is not money enough in the world to pay for it."*

Of course, I'm not advocating that we should all now run out and hunt high and low for a wand of this magical stuff. What I am trying to suggest, however, is that we travellers into a newer perception must hang on to the symbolic grain of wisdom, which may have prompted that belief into the cleansing and healing properties of the unicorn's horn in the first place. I recommend that these scraps of archaic lore, albeit at first glance seemingly foolish, should be also popped into your knapsack and kept for a rainy day, along with

other fragments we shall collect along this same anciently trod way, for their eventual collective effect upon our understanding of this shocking sight of Albion might, in the end, prove again *"not money enough in the world to pay for it."*

However, the best medicine of all is laughter!

This admittedly off-beat and quirky wisdom, hidden away in rhymes and fireside tales, has always been as free as wild berries, and hung just as juicily right in front of our mostly upturned noses; ignored because it was free; too outlandishly coloured; and seemingly the staple of old wives and peasants. More often than not, it was bypassed as not being serious food for thought. And so here are four more wild berries of unicorn lore, from out of whose juice we may be able to ferment both reason and cure for that broken horn.

The first taste will, I know, add confusion to my earlier musings which tended to view our unicorn as having feminine qualities, giving her an excuse for her wayward charge into the sign of Pisces and its Christian/masculine connotations, yet I must include it and leave you to press out whatever liquor it may hold.

From the 13th to the 16th centuries, representation of the unicorn in ecclesiastic decoration was widespread throughout Europe and often depicted in a scene of the so-called Holy Hunt - the capture of the beast being only possible via the gentle hand of a virgin, a lady often represented as the Virgin Mary. For the first taste of this particular berry I will let St Ambrose provide both the question and answer: *"Who is this Unicorn, but the only begotten Son of God."*

Then there is a unicorn of oriental belief, the Ki-lin, and thought of as no less holy. From ancient China, Shephard brings us a luscious fruit to the effect that the Ki-lin *"is to come in the shape of an incomparable man, a revealer of the mysteries, supernatural and divine, and a great lover of all mankind."* He is also supposedly expected to arrive in conjunction with the coming of a particular constellation. Interesting.

Strangely then, in both East and West the unicorn has come to represent a messiah figure, and I can but venture the question whether that constellation is Aquarius, which is not only the epitome of clear water, but, even as I write, is swinging into final position to inaugurate the new astrological age arriving with this new millennium.

But I said the best medicine was laughter - so let me tell you that my young inner self and I giggled for an hour when sampling the next couple of berries. And their taste? Just pure unadulterated fun!

Our first smile comes via a charming piece of old French prose romance called *Le Chevalier du Papegau*. In it we hear that King Arthur's ship (which could only be this ark of Albion - *see Cancer*) was once stranded high and dry and that it took a giant and a unicorn to drag it off the sandbank and back into deep water. Look then to the cover - doesn't that overall picture laughingly fit the prose? Mentally tie a rope around her neck while attaching the other end around the Ark's figurehead and see how she too could be seen, without too much imagination, to be dragging the ship backwards off an imagined sandbank. She's certainly putting enough back into it!

However, being not very practical, perhaps I've got myself in a wee bit of a tangle by suggesting that we tie a rope around the neck of the beast, for surely that would strangle her? So let's seek further advice on such matters with a dip into the Hebrew Talmudic writings for the last berry and the best giggle.

Now as odd as this suggestion may sound I would ask you to bear with me, for I'll show you something that may give both rhyme and amusing reason for the awkward sight of a unicorn with a poor damaged horn and a slopping fish tail. It goes something like this:

we are taken back to the day the ark set sail and, in particular, to the trouble with one of its passengers, a mysterious single-horned creature called a re'em, which, whether unicorn or not was later (and with divine providence for me!) officially classified as such.

Hear, then, the map of Albion laugh under the beautiful and comical weight of the following description. It tells us that the size of this re'em/unicorn was out of all reasonable compass, indeed, so tall was she that clouds rolled along her back! Well then, if Albion's re'em stood up we'd see her tower some 96 miles high - more than tall enough to cause havoc with air traffic control!

Though the best bit is when we are told that she was too large to be got into the ark (as is Albion's re'em!) and so (wait for it!) *she had to be towed along behind by a cord tied to her horn!*

If you can't believe in this yarn, step back and see the truth as hammered into these walls of Albion. See how easy it is to visualise Capricorn being awkwardly dragged by the ark (and boy what a massive ark it would have been), and so little wonder why the middle part of her horn seems rope-burned away, as the ark tugged her colossal weight through the mountainous waves of the deluge - and may do so again! From this news can we also deduce a reason for her fish tail, for in those deep waters surely such would be far more use than hind legs?

For me, I think we are witnessing mythology get up and dance, and this is surely for one hell of a *reason*! And although we are only three steps into forming a picture of that *reason*, the first three pictographs, it must be said, all spell FLOOD! And there the laughter stops.

But whether you see true mythological cause for that damaged horn in the above scraps of ancestral lore, or take on board my own hunch that it may be injured as a pointer towards our own lost sense of spirituality and kinship towards the land, I think that that less-than-perfect horn is meant to be the absolute focus point of Capricorn's message to us. To reflect on this defect will, however, give credence to her wonderful presence in Albion's south, which, in turn might give her back her magic and you the opportunity of being nourished as the god you are from that single-horned cornucopia of forgotten wisdom.

The deeper we ponder the mythology of the unicorn, the quicker she may lead us through the thicket of our ignorance to the realization that our Holy Hunt is not to capture her, but to get just a glimpse, for in such a sighting is to win the release of the entangled child within, the one who dreamt this fabulous creature in the first place; a dream which the planet has now glorified as no dream at all, but a universal truth - a medicine, a salve, to a wounded mankind and a poisoned planet.

Defining the body

We shall now unravel that which our adult sensibilities tell us cannot be.

We'll begin with her great head, so, start at Seaton in Devon, which is the tip of her ear. Now follow the whitening coast eastwards. Chesil Beach and Lyme Bay between them give her that long and straight forehead, but do not continue so as to furnish her with an equally long and straight horn. This becomes stunted and deformed at Portland Bill, a place where man's own works strangely echo the imagery to which the land here seems to be drawing our attention. **This poetically broken horn is physically underlined by the major quarrying taking place here for its famous yellowish-white Portland stone, which is extensively used in buildings throughout Britain.**

Further signs of damage?

Sense, too, another echo of that underlying spiritual damage when hearing how for many years her horn was not only home to Her Majesty's war ships but to one of her prisons too. A wound then poetically pointing to the damage we have done not only to the planet, but to ourselves?

We now go around the horn's tip, past Weymouth to Swanage on the end of her snorting nose, which curls round into a fabulous sea-foamed mouth. Hamworthy is on her tongue - a place from where you can almost hear her jubilant whinny!

From Poole on her chin, head inland to Sturminster Marshall and follow the river Stour to Sturminster Newton. This line gives us the lower jaw contour and completes her head. Even where her mane must flick over her broad rocking horse forehead seems clued into the scheme of things - **Broadmayne** is the village that marks it. Her eye is Dorchester.

Now to draw what is for me one of the subtlest yet most powerful parts of this entire zodiac: her bent-up foreleg, so splendidly characteristic of early depictions of the heavenly Capricorn (see following engraving). Start 50 miles inland at Marlborough, heading south on the A346 and A338 to Salisbury, then continue alongside the river Avon down to Ringwood. Here curve east on the A31 to junction 2 on the M27; this is the lower tip of her hoof. Now go south again via Totton and follow Southampton Water into the Solent. Curl west and you will see just how perfectly the river Beaulieu draws the top of the hoof.

Still with the leg, go west now along the coast, but at Boscombe turn inland and pick up the A338, A35, and A350 to draw a lovely bent knee. At Sturminster Marshall take the unmarked road northeast to Bradbury Rings. Unfortunately these rings and the Roman road we are to follow next are not marked on the *Michelin* map. When my eye first took this line I thought it was a touch of artistic licence as there was absolutely nothing there to guide me. Imagine my delight in finding later, on another map, the old Bradbury Rings as a focal point to some Roman roads - the one we take to complete this fore leg contour heads towards Sixpenny Handley. My thanks to the Romans!

And just compare those legs!

Take a break now to compare the 1603 engraving below to this creature of Albion. I know it's stubbornly double-horned but just compare those tucked-up forelegs! That tail isn't a bad copy either.

As we gaze at such land wizardry, however, never forget that, as in the case of all Albion's giants, it is the actual coastline which initially begets the immovable profile, thus there is absolutely no artistry from yours truly, I only held a pencil and traced what was there - and let's face it, a child could do that! So with that

leg, this fabulous beast is, for me, quite finished - I've seen enough to know what the land requires me to know. However, for the purists let us now complete her by heading deep inland.

Return to the tip of her ear at Seaton and there pick up the river Axe inland to Axminster. Here take the unmarked road to Membury and beyond so as to cross over the A30 and meet up with the A303. The river Yarty follows a similar path. Once on the A303, head southwest but soon pick up the B3170 to Taunton. Take now the A358 to Williton, skirting the Quantock Hills. At Williton it's the A39 back to Bridgwater where we can take the river Parrett into Bridgwater Bay. Flow northwards now with the river Severn all the way to Gloucester; but do look over your shoulder at her lovely flowing mane drawn by the coastline, especially those

Capricorn. Bayers Capricornus, 1603.
The British Library

flicking curls at **Weston-Super-Mare** - and I still can't believe that name! Brean Down and Sand Point mark other curly tips.

At Gloucester take the A436 to Andoversford, then the B4068 to Stow-on-the-Wold. The A436 to Oddington and the river Evenlode then jointly take us to the river Thames at Oxford; the old man himself floating us leisurely down to Reading.

Back on the road again we're off the A329 to junction 3 of the M3 hoping to join the M25 near Chertsey. Follow this to Maidstone where we need the A249 to junction 5 on the M2 and onto Canterbury. This marks the top tip of the fish tail from where you may take either the A28 or the Great Stour river down to Ashford. All that's left now is the A2070 and A259 to Hastings where it's over to that master template cutter of the coastline west to Southampton and thus completion.

The place of her heart

Magnificent Stonehenge could well be her heart, but in my own heart of hearts I believe that this honour lies with the equally impressive circle of Avebury, where stones were hoisted far earlier than Stonehenge and, at the time of writing, are all still touchable!

My preference for a heart at Avebury, however, is based only upon a snippet I saw in *The Acorn Book of Birthing the Cosmic Child*, and I quote: *"If AVE-BURY means 'buried heart' perhaps this is a place where our hearts will awaken and we can once again feel and breathe with the whole universe"* Interesting too, the same piece goes on to say: *"Grace Cooke, a well-known clairvoyant, sensed that the place on Earth which receives the greatest concentration of incoming energies from the stars is Avebury."*

With that I think there is a very beautiful end to any debate as to where the heart might be, but before I leave the issue altogether I have another snippet, which pertains to the magic that may be found here. In Wolfram von Eschenbach's *Parzifal*, the story of Sir Perceval's quest for the Grail, we are told that the wound of Anfotas, the Grail King, could only be cured by several strange medicines, one of which being the heart of a unicorn. This wound is sometimes translated as being at one and the same time the very land itself. Thus, if that which lies buried at Avebury can cure the injured land in the shape of the Grail King, it may at the same time, too, perhaps help heal that mirrored and consequential wound in us all.

Lastly that icing on the cake, or in this case the icing on the horn!

Remember my rush to find a place name on this creature fit to blow my mind and thus keep me on the trail? Well I missed one! And if you have any lingering doubts about what we've just hiked over, then this one should finally blow them away. Let me, then, twirl my wand and tell you that upon the horn itself there are only three place-names marked, the most prominent being **Fortuneswell**. And if its breakdown of *Well of Fortune* doesn't excite you, especially after all we've talked about, then let me tell you that the mystic Cabalists assigned to Capricorn the tenth trump of the tarot, the **Wheel of Fortune!** I take it that man's future fortune really is well and truly tied up with this horn!

On we go now, westwards into Pisces.

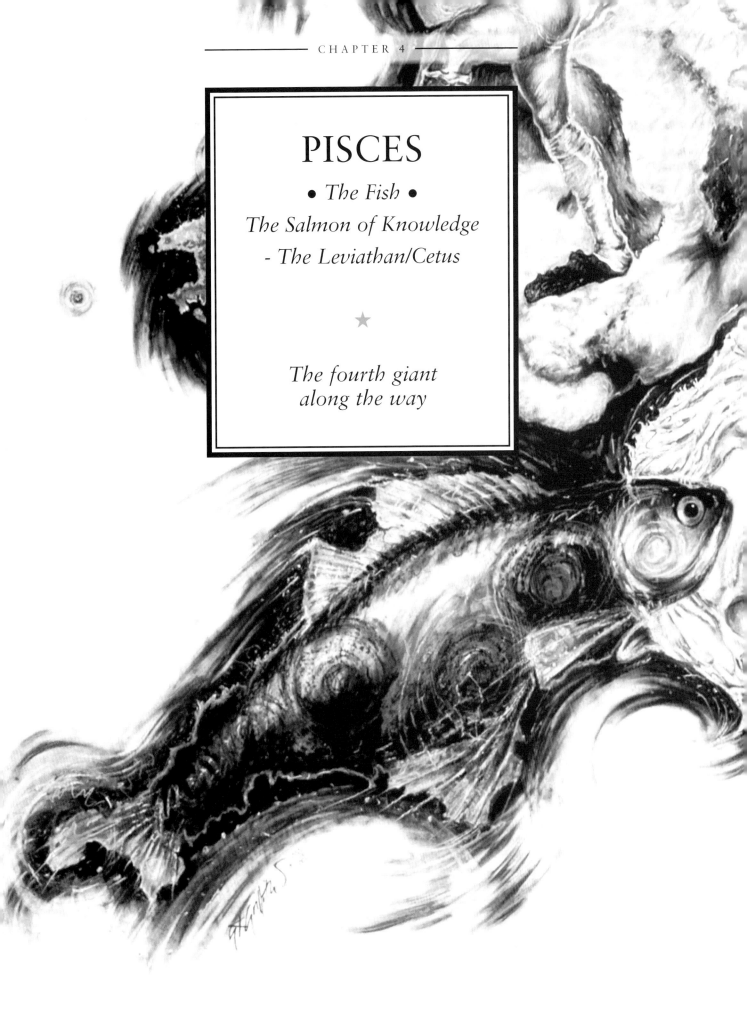

CHAPTER 4

PISCES

• *The Fish* •
The Salmon of Knowledge
- The Leviathan/Cetus

★

The fourth giant
along the way

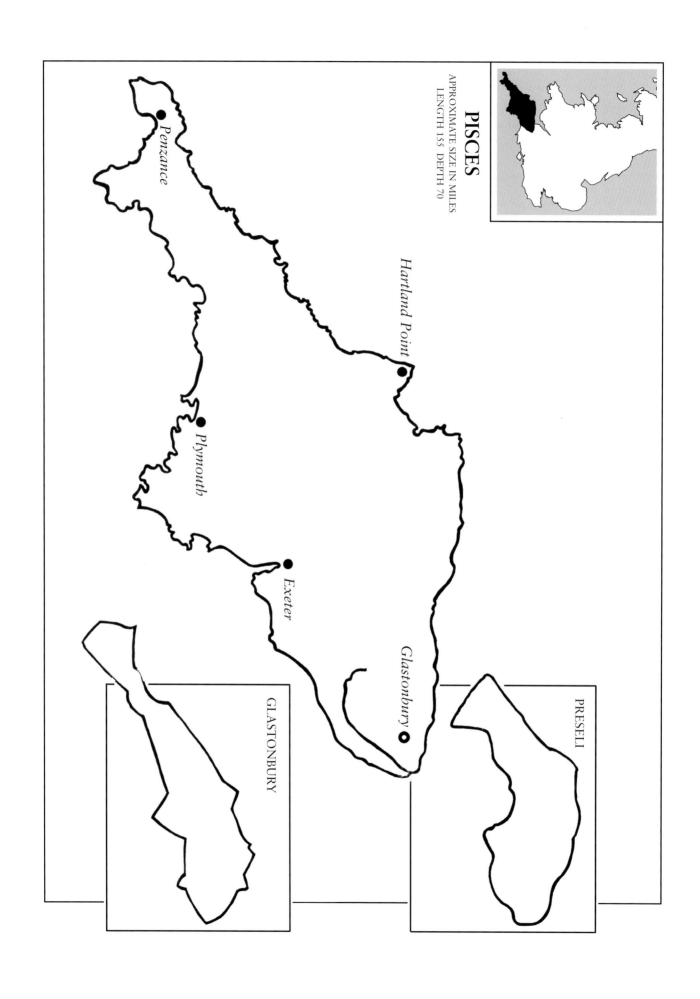

PISCES

APPROXIMATE SIZE IN MILES
LENGTH 155 DEPTH 70

Penzance

Hartland Point

Plymouth

Exeter

Glastonbury

GLASTONBURY

PRESELI

Tracking the boy Jesus into the eye of Pisces

"Keltic tradition held that 'the salmon of knowledge was the oldest living thing, whoso ate of him would enjoy all the wisdom of the ages' He was said to haunt the Severn River."

THE ENCHANTMENTS OF BRITAIN, Katherine Maltwood

GENERAL AREA: THE ENTIRE SOUTHWEST PENINSULA - ITS NOSE NUDGES AS FAR NORTH AS SHEPTON MALLET.

This great fish, with its every fin so perfectly sea nibbled from out of that peninsula, was one of the first four giants that jumped out at me as a boy, and although its head was more cunningly disguised inland, I always knew it was there, in the former wetlands of Somerset, waiting to be dug out.

But come on - who *hasn't*, in an idle moment, with an atlas open on a map of the southwest, suspected this peninsular of looking decidedly fishy? If so, don't let the adult in you ever let him off the hook again as being but a day dream, for this monster of both deep space, and even deeper memory, is real enough!

Here, then, glides the legendary Salmon of Knowledge, that, true to Celtic belief, has the river Severn uncannily flowing over his back. For the time being, though, see him only as taking the role of Pisces on this terrestrial zodiac's stage.

Let's land the catch

Before we delve into this great fish's many sunken secrets, and there is more to this fish than initially meets the eye, let us haul him aboard to prevent him from slipping out of sight.

Defining the body

Let's start with his head, which, although not as instantly apparent as the rest of its sea-cut body, is nevertheless, not too difficult to catch sight of once you know where to look. From Highbridge near Burnham-on-Sea on the Bristol Channel, head inland on the B3139 to Shepton Mallet which dots its nose-come-upper lip – now turn around that nose to Cannards Grave which denotes the mouth. Take the A371 down to Castle Cary from where the rest of him is easy to net. All we need do now is follow the old railway cutting all the way to Axminster – although if you wished to soften the line you may cut the same shape from Yeovil to Forde Abbey by treading the course of the county border which separates Somerset and Devon from Dorset. After that, from the abbey to Axminster and the sea at Seaton (which marks the ear tip of that neighbouring unicorn) the river Axe will be the only guide you need.

The line of the mouth itself is shown heading southwest from Cannards Grave as the A37 and A303. However, near Stoke-sub-Hamdon watch its delightful gill-like curve through Illminster and on to the outskirts of Taunton.

Because the rest of this vast fish is so deftly

defined by that sea-scaped peninsula, there is little need to give further co-ordinates except to name Hartland Point and Morte Point as the tips of its back fins, whilst Prawle Point and Exmouth tip the underbelly fins. Land's End marks the tip of the tail.

The line that I think defines its spine is one we can't actually see. It's a ley line, an invisible river of earth energy charted by dowsers and already mentioned in this book. This ley line gives our fish its backbone from St Michael's Mount (a tiny island just off this fish's tail) to Glastonbury.

The coming of the boy Jesus

Now we shall really see if you have the staying power to see this journey of Albion through. Or will the adult in you, when confronted by the prospect of Jesus having come to Britain to walk these star signs for himself, cap the source of this fountain of new things in which you have been happily splashing for three chapters? Certainly the mere mention of the name Jesus will be for many, and for a variety of good reasons, one hell of a turn off. I have to confess, it was for me too, but let's just say I'm now glad I stayed on to listen to what he had to say for himself. And for what it's worth, he seems to speak like never before.

And so with the rock-solid reality of this all-too-obvious fish shape now securely netted, I would ask you to romance with me a while. I want to put it to you that some 2000 years ago, when this fish's ley line of a spine was perhaps still used by the wise in ways we have today forgotten, it was this same ribbon of force that marked the tingling path from tail to fish's head which *those feet in ancient times* once passed along (see William Blake's *Jerusalem* at the end of this book). At that time, according to a still stubbornly smouldering West Country legend, Joseph of Arimathea and his young nephew Jesus passed this way en route to Glastonbury.

I for one believe that there is more truth than romance in this strange goose-bumpy tale that has been retold beneath the thatch of West Country cottages for generations, especially when we now replay it upon this new soundingboard of the map that is Albion.

Certainly the legend of Joseph bringing Jesus with him to this southwest corner of Britain has persisted against all the scholarly scoffing. Indeed, its plausibility finds strength in the fact that Cornwall has for thousands of years been world renowned for its tin deposits, and Joseph, presumed to have been a wealthy trader, would have assuredly known the sense in making such a trip, if only for a little wheeling and dealing in that rare commodity.

That said, the legend insists that Joseph and Jesus did not tarry long in Cornwall for they had larger fish to fry at Glastonbury. But why Glastonbury? It was no thriving centre of world commerce, only a scattering of houses built on stilts at the edge of a swamp that just so happened to have 12 hills jutting out of it, and those in the shape of the 12 signs of the zodiac, indeed a microcosm of the miracle that was budding throughout Britain! So was this why they headed to this otherwise empty spot? If so, and they wished to 'take-in' the entire experience of it all, then Glastonbury would have been the perfect place to head for. A stumbling block to this theory, however, is the fact that in none of the recorded rumours of their visit here were earth zodiacs ever mentioned as the 'pull' that brought them. Though, in defence of the theory, remember that this phenomenal secret underfoot has come down to us in a sort of poetic code within the land. For the unenlightened tellers of the tale at the time, their visit was wonder enough to pass on, whereas for us, now armed with the incredible speaking map of Albion, the true reason behind their visit might now have become startlingly apparent. In short, we shall be told in no uncertain terms that when Jesus

and Joseph came here they knew damn well what was going on beneath their feet!

Clues to back this up begin with an appreciation of their landing in Cornwall, making this almighty fish of Pisces their first, and perhaps mystically pre-ordained, footfall upon this zodiac. Certainly, as sea travellers from the south, they would have had Libra, Sagittarius, and Capricorn as equally obvious first landfalls. But no, Pisces was their choice, and one, I'm going to suggest, that had nothing to do with Cornish tin! But have patience, again allow the picture sign language on the map to drip-feed its message.

Anyway, once upon Cornwall's fish tail we know that by means of either following its magical ley line spine or by some other route, their real destination was Glastonbury, some 150 miles to the north. And once at Glastonbury the significance of choosing Pisces as their landing place upon Albion's zodiacal wheel starts to become clear. Why? Because it is recorded that they had their first sight of Glastonbury's own miracle from the top of Wearyall Hill and which just so happens to be Glastonbury's own Piscean fish! And which, incidentally, is reached by first walking up Fisher's Hill! I trust you are going along with me on this one!

However, you've heard nothing yet, for this particular verse of land poetry is only just beginning. Indeed, allow me the most delicious pleasure of beginning it by telling you that Glastonbury's fish, along with the rest of those Somerset star giants, who form that perfect circle there, are, at one and the same time, exactly prescribing the 30-mile round and glassy eye belonging to Albion's greater fish! As beautiful as it is stunning, isn't it?

Thus, it is another zodiac that is revolving in the starry all-seeing eye of Albion's Pisces, the very sign that the birth of Jesus had marked as the new astrological age. Indeed, that sign of the fish would itself become synonymous with the Christ, and one that would almost compete

with the cross as his personal mark. Poetically stupendous then, to realise that when that boy stood upon Glastonbury's fish he was in all truth a fish within a fish within a fish - he was the very pupil in the eye of the sign that had heralded his own birth - he, the apprentice Messiah, who would be remembered as the ultimate Fisher of Men! Wonderful!

Surely Albion's Piscean placements now exude more than a hint of being a spectacularly prearranged stage setting, devised not only to receive *those feet* but also to direct them to a poetically profound landmark, a mark that again shouts to the high heavens that if Jesus and Joseph ever came here they KNEW EXACTLY WHAT THEY STOOD UPON - and it is high time *we* did too! This must be the message that is trying to cross over two millennia to reach us in the 21st century. We, who, at this very moment, are crossing over into the next astrological new age of Aquarius, which is marked at both Glastonbury and upon this greater stage of Albion as a phoenix in flames. When we reach Aquarius on the map we shall be made to know why.

For now, you enquiring travellers, who still have the desire to continue on this hike back into the memory that is oozing out of this mesmeric landscape, have a treat awaiting on that night when Jesus and Joseph arrived in that starry fish's eye.

Starry, starry night

It is, then, a moonlit and frosty night 2000 or so years ago and you are on top of Wearyall Hill. And weary too are those two visitors from the east, as the name of this hill still charmingly implies today. Yet they are joyful too, knowing that they stand on a fish, that is itself swimming in the revolving eye of one far greater, and along whose great green ley lined spine they may have just journeyed to get here.

But watch Joseph, for, so the legend goes, he commemorates the profound moment by thrusting his staff into that hill top where it instantly bursts into a hawthorn tree in a froth of blossom. This, in itself, is a miracle that has come down to us today as a remarkable reality, for a direct descendant of that wondrous little tree, and for me the most magical tree in the world, still bends upon that windy fish-sculpted hill today. Curiously, it blossoms each year, astonishingly out of season, preferring to bedeck itself in a cloud of white stars at Christmastime no less! It is fact that this is the only thorn tree in all Britain (except for one or two others budded from the original) to flower at this extraordinary time of year and people, drawn from all over the world, still come to witness this winter maypole blooming amid the earth's reflection of heaven as they have done for hundreds of years. In the larger picture we can also see it as the very twinkle in the eye of Albion's greater monster of the deep.

Note: traditionally, each Christmastime, a few sprigs of its blossom are ceremoniously cut and sent to the royal family; such is its magic even in these cynical times. Tests, too, have been carried out to determine just what species of thorn tree it is; the results, I believe, came back with the news that it was possibly of a Levantine variety!

Albion, like that little thorn, is also preposterously flowering out of bounds and thus will be bypassed by many as a freak of nature. To a few, however, it will be a sight of spring in the depths of an otherwise progressively darkening winter of global decay and unbalance. But with this book in your hand, may I suggest you have a sprig of the early flowers of a coming paradise, whether you are yet ready to acknowledge it or not. Indeed, should you be living on Albion, these same rare blooms are pushing up through the floorboards of your very own lounge!

Thus I believe it was Britain's double zodiac that was the magnet that drew the youthful Jesus to our shores in his own quest to find the Grail within himself, and one can only imagine what visions of eternity were revealed to him in Albion's starry gardens. One thing only is certain, though, and that is if he was aware of these wondrous works of his Mother, the Earth, he would also have been aware of that picture of his own destiny, the 300-mile high cross upon which his star-burst figure soars at the very apex of all these rabbit-warrened, sheep-grazed, chemical-dumped constellations of Albion. As we journey deeper we'll find that his destiny has now become ours. But more of this when we reach Cumbria.

Note: after targeting this great fish's eye of Glastonbury, that ley line continues another 180 miles across country to perfectly pierce the town of Eye - that very eye of Sagittarius. Once more it's as though we're being asked to LOOK again - urged to perceive like never before.

Oh, and if Jesus and Joseph did follow this same flowing line of force to Glastonbury's zodiacal eye, guess where it would eventually lead them out of this sign, should they have wished to journey on? Well, if Miller and Broadhurst have down their job well (and they had no idea they were here journeying over the form of this fish of Albion) it eventually spouts directly out of its Shepton Mallet/Cannards Grave mouth!

Fish within fish

As mentioned at the beginning of this

chapter, I felt that lurking in the depths of this earthly star-fish was another fish, though not born of stars, but in a mystic pool which but mirrored them each night - this that Celt-revered Salmon of Knowledge.

Their belief stated that this salmon lived in a deep well below the Tree of Life and ate of the nuts of knowledge that fell from it, and whosoever ate of that salmon would likewise be fed on the knowledge of the universe - the true knowledge of themselves. And because I'd heard it said that, to the Druids, the Tree of Life and mystery was an oak, I, of course, assumed those nuts of wisdom to be acorns. No big deal in that - but I thought I'd better check it out anyway.

Note: it is thought that the Druids believed Jesus to have been crucified upon this same revered tree. With this in mind, see how Albion's fish seems placed to swim directly beneath the overhanging branches of that cross/tree, which, incidentally, seems to be purposefully leaning his way to make sure its fruits drop towards him.

However, taking off the shelf a book on Irish mythology, I was soon corrected as it stated that their Salmon of Knowledge ate not acorns but the hazel nuts that had freshly fallen from the Tree of Life.

Now the hazel is a lovely *bush*, and its nuts, when covered in chocolate, are wonderful - but *Tree of Life* it certainly ain't!

Confused, I read on. I then found that the Irish had a legend that once upon a time a strange giant from the east visited Ireland. He came clutching a mighty branch that he had torn off a wondrous tree that he said grew in the Lebanon; the branch bore three fruits: hazel nuts, apples and *edible acorns*, and these magical fruits had sustained him upon his long march west. I even discovered that Ireland's very own Tree of Life, the great tree of Mugna, also bore those same three fruits that had hung

upon the giant's branch, again giving an edible acorn equal status with the apple and hazel nut as mythological wisdom food. Thus my assumption of an acorn-eating Salmon of Knowledge wasn't a case of me barking up the wrong tree after all!

But so what? And who cares? These were my thoughts as I, beer in hand, revolved aimlessly in my chair. Earlier that evening I'd already put the chapter on Pisces to bed, so why start grubbing around the Tree of Life for fish food? Answering myself I said: "Well, because both Maltwood and Caine suspected that this same fabled salmon lurked in the shape of Glastonbury's own fish, and because I feel that the land's greater mythologically-based message to the world comes in the unique layout of Albion's super giants, I think a quick cast of a fly, or better still an acorn, over that southwest peninsular would do no harm." So out again came the maps.

Yawning, I let my tired eye trawl its body but found nothing that specifically shouted "fresh salmon!" That is until I reached its mouth.

The precise placing of its mouth is, I'd say, at Cannards Grave, a weird name. I tried to find some secret significance there, but found nothing except the site of a chieftain, buried long ago. Then, almost on the point of letting my curiosity off the hook, I suddenly noticed on the map a conspicuously straight and dotted line protruding right out of its Cannards Grave mouth, just like a fishing line! Or rather, perhaps, I should refer to it as a cord?

"Canst Thou draw out a leviathan with an hook? or his tongue with a cord which thou lettest down?"
JOB, Chapter 41, Verse 1

Instantly, and with a fisherman's expectation, I decided to trace that same fishing line back to the rod, or even to the bait - the map almost screamed out at me to do it.

I soon found that this dotted line was part of

that long overgrown road once pounded by Rome's legions, the famous Fosse Way. Alas, no more than three green field-miles of its once former glory were still here dotting the map before it abruptly ended - where? Nowhere in particular, except for us, the wide-eyed, opened-mouthed, anglers of Albion. Rome had paced out this three mile long fishing line straight to, and precisely ending on, the sweetest bait ever to tempt a mythic salmon to rise, there on top of **Oakhill!**

Was this coincidental, or stunningly evidential? These are questions for all of us to wrestle with individually. For myself, I know this must be more land poetry of divine conception for the simple reason that it had me again laughing my socks off.

When my laughter, however, tapered off into just a big daft grin, another thought came to me as my eyes lingered upon that mouth; and I ask who could not, when faced with such an almighty fish's mouth, think of Jonah!

We're out, but was Jonah once in?

So let's leave the innards of this fish by the route Jesus and Joseph may have done, along that ley-lined way so that we travellers poetically, and most charmingly, are burped out of this Leviathan's Shepton Mallet/Cannards Grave mouth. And what a *grave warning* of a sign to stick here of all places. Lucky, then, we got in through the rear door at Land's End!

Poor Jonah was not so lucky, though, his trip down the gullet of gullets was filled not with laughter but with terror. So let's see how it was for him through his own panic-filled eyes:

*"The **waters encompassed me about***
(*a peninsular location?),
*even to the soul: the depth closed me round about, the **weeds*** (*an allusion to seaweed - entrails of a fish or exactly what he says - weeds, the dense trees and undergrowth of an Albion 2000+ years ago?)

were wrapped about my head.
I went down to the bottoms of the
mountains: *the earth with her **bars***
(*tree trunks?)
was about me for ever: yet hast thou brought up my life from corruption,
O Lord my God."
JONAH, Chapter 2 Verses 5 and 6
(*Brackets mine)

Now even if we put the matter of Albion to one side for a moment, Jonah's description surely tempts one to see his ordeal as being suspiciously upon dry land. If so, and you, like me, are now putting two and two together by thinking it was maybe Albion's land-locked whopper which really (mythologically speaking) swallowed poor Jonah, try to think of a reason to back the suspicion up. For instance, could it be that this topographical Leviathan was some kind of initiatory enclosure upon this star clock of Albion, wherein enlightenment might be won - and to succeed would this be seen in another sense as partaking of the flesh of that Salmon of Knowledge? Seems ever so logical doesn't it. Indeed, it gets better.

It is interesting to know that, from the 17th century, it was officially agreed that it was Cetus, the biggest fish in the heavens, which was responsible for swallowing Jonah. Thus, is this star-born Cetus another fish within this star-copied whopper of Albion? If so, it is another fabulously logical reason why Jonah may have tumbled down this 155-mile long land-crafted throat!

Such an event would be monumental on Albion's Piscean soil. Monumental, though perhaps not so surprising, to Comyns Beaumont, who back in the 1940s wrote his book *Britain, the Key to World History* - arguably a book with even wilder notions than are contained in this one! Anyway, he firmly believed that the bulk of Biblical events were originally played out on sites within the British

Isles, and that it was only after the deluge that these places and events were relocated in the next Holy Land: Palestine. As we journey on, his bizarre theory will several times quietly tug your sleeve and ask to be at least thought about under Albion's new and astonishing light.

Though it may not have been only Jonah who went down into this place to find himself in God, for there have been many heroes who descended into these same topographical entrails in search of that ultimate wisdom - King Arthur among them. According to Layamon's *Brut*, he, too, was three days in the belly of a whale, presumably here in the house of Pisces - this part of his own Round Table realm of the zodiac!

*Note: in my old Bible there's a section in the back entitled Reptiles and Amphibia of the Bible, where, in brackets and written next to the category of whale, is this: **some land-monster.**

Intriguingly too, especially for us who have just followed the possible tracks of Jesus through the belly of this land whale, could these following words be in memory of his own sojourn within this Piscean giant - or a prediction of a deed he must yet perform? If so, and assuming that initiatory Salmon of all Knowledge is here, have we also found another reason why Pisces was his first port of call?

This is how Jesus answered the scribes of the Pharisees with a prophesy aimed possibly at us in this giant fish-finding time. He had been talking to them about the Day of Judgment and they had asked him for a sign to let them know when it would come. So listen to how Jesus provocatively relates the experience of being within a whale to that of being *"in the heart of the earth"*.

"But he answered and said unto them, an evil and adulterous generation seeketh after a sign: and there shall be no sign be given to it, but the sign of the prophet Jonas:
For Jonas was three days and three nights in the whale's belly: so shall the son of man be three days and three nights in the heart of the earth."
MATTHEW, Chapter 12, Verses 39 and 40

Rightly or wrongly I again sniffed from between these lines the scent of peaty Albion rather than salt sea. And I ask, what better place to wear that title of *"the heart of the earth"* than here, on this pictorial outpouring of the earth? Put your hand to the ground and feel its giant pounding!

With that let us leave the land of Pisces by hopping over the River Severn, which separates this whale from the land of Wales, making sure you don't step on the tail of a lamb, and land within earshot of a lion's roar. In Albion's realm, you see, the lion and the lamb really do lie peacefully side by side.

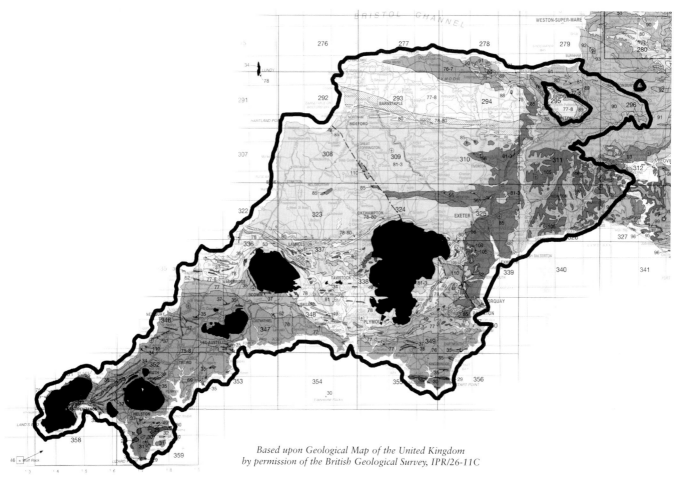

Based upon Geological Map of the United Kingdom by permission of the British Geological Survey, IPR/26-11C

PISCES

Here is the South West peninsula as depicted upon the *Geological Map of the United Kingdom*. Pay special attention to the area of where the head of Pisces/Cetus should be, for although shaping it slightly differently to my version cut by roads and rivers, it still gives us a most marvellous profile of a monster from the deep. Indeed it looks somewhat better than my version! See how the flow of those sedimentary layers has produced what seems a terribly gaping and tooth filled mouth via what must have been an inspired inflow of Jurassic Low Lias. Different, yes, but surely between the intelligences of mineral and water, and man's own stumbling variety, a fish was ever the one wish in this area of Albion.

The eye on this one would seem a little further to the south west making Glastonbury become as though a tempting morsel floating before its nose.

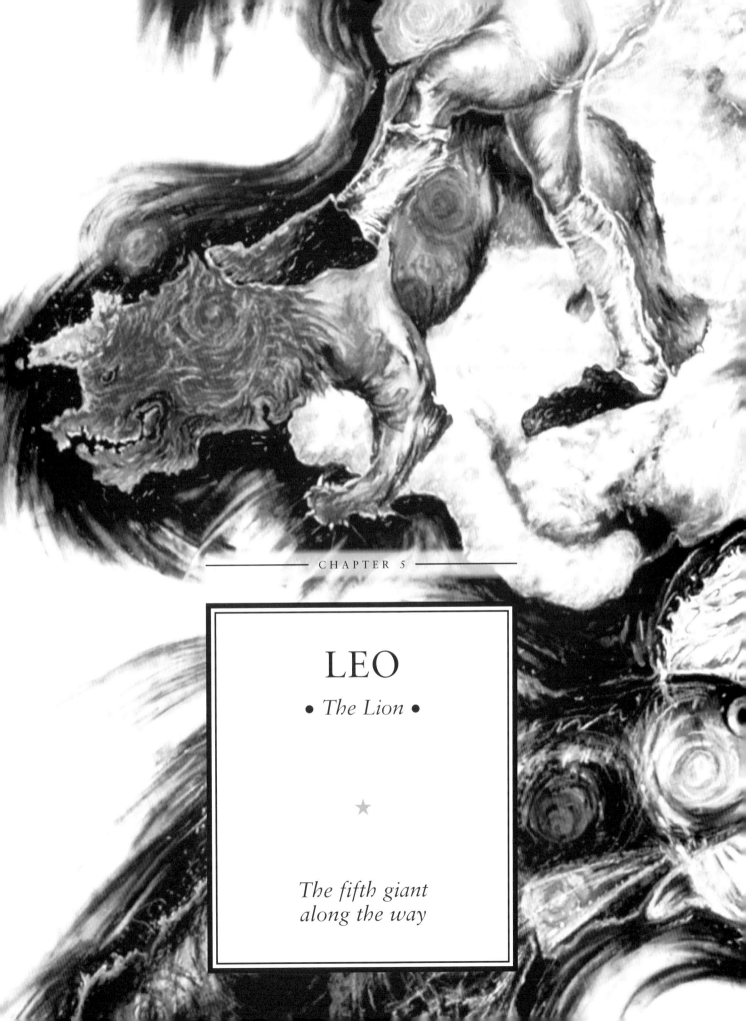

CHAPTER 5

LEO

• *The Lion* •

★

*The fifth giant
along the way*

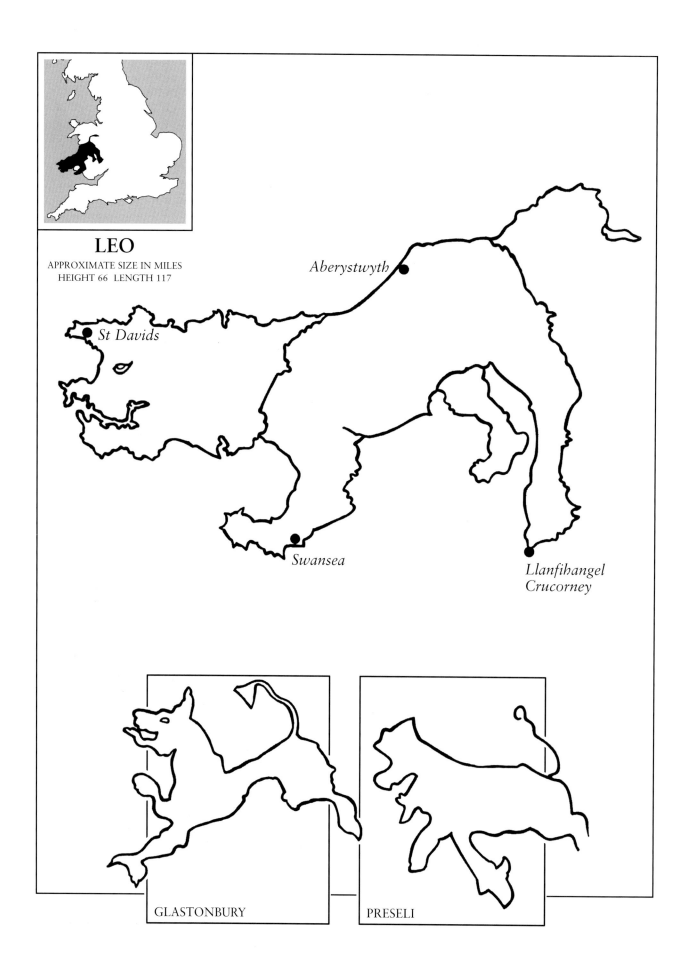

LEO

APPROXIMATE SIZE IN MILES
HEIGHT 66 LENGTH 117

Aberystwyth

St Davids

Swansea

Llanfihangel Crucorney

GLASTONBURY

PRESELI

Lion, Lioness or Lyonesse?

"There is a noxious creature,
From the rampart of Santanas,
Which has overcome all
Between the deep and the shallow;
Equally wide are his jaws
As the mountains of the Alps;
Him death will not subdue,
Nor hand or blades;
There is a load of nine hundred wagons
In the hair of his two paws;
There is in his head an eye
Green as the limpid sheet of icicle;
Three springs arise
In the nape of his neck;
Sea-roughs thereon..."

Taliesin

GENERAL AREA: THE SOUTHWEST CORNER OF WALES.

his was one of the original four giants that leapt out at me as a boy, and again one that I feel, in its coastal tracery alone, is blatantly obvious.

Roland Smith must have seen this creature in the coastline while writing his book *Wildest Britain*. Sadly, though his insight was urging him to spot it, he pursues it no further than the opening line in his chapter on Pembrokeshire, the county which gives birth to the lion's head and menacing paw: *"Pembrokeshire thrusts out its clawed hand into the blue, storm-wracked Celtic Sea..."*

Many must have seen this coastal cat, but only a few happy-go-lucky fools have allowed their eyes to tarry longer upon the land's initial enticement. But we can now, thanks to Katherine Maltwood, take up its invitation to hunt deeper, to look for the rest of that creature whose clawed hand gives the cat away - although a creature that no sane person would ever dream of looking for amongst the headlands of Wales. Happy perseverance, however, will, at the end of this seemingly impossible hunt, be both rewarded and confronted by the rest of such a gigantic beast, one coming in at over 100 miles in length and nearly 70 miles tall! This, the snarling constellation of Leo, spread for thousands of years upon the land and for all the world to see... but few ever have, even though Taliesin, the famous Welsh bard and wise man gave a big enough hint - as you can read in his riddle at the beginning of this chapter. Some see Taliesin as the physical truth behind the myth of Merlin himself, but we'll hear more of him in the next chapter.

Defining the body

So without further ado go hunt this lion for yourselves through this land of intellectual nightmares!

See how it shows its claws as it lashes out that splendidly obvious foreleg from Swansea into the Bristol Channel. You can easily follow this coast as it strikes past Mumbles Head on the elbow to that barbed paw. Count the claws, picked out and spiked by Oxwich Castle, Porteynon Point, Worms Head, Burry Holmes and Whiteford Point. Thorn-like in the middle of the paw is the standing stone known as King Arthur's Stone.

The coast along Llanrhidian Sands gives a contour line to his upper foreleg until the river Loughor takes over and finishes the job where it crosses the M4. Then the river, together with the A48 to Carmarthen, delineates the proud chest.

Carmarthen marks the start of the neck, which is to be drawn by the River Tywi and the coast of Carmarthen Bay; the place name of Red Roses charmingly marks the throat. The start of the lower jaw begins at Tenby, and again we need only follow the coastline to its chin at St Govan's Head, from where we tumble through those curled-back lips of St Ann's Head and Sheep Island, and into that mother and father of all snarls - that gaping tooth filled mouth of Milford Haven Water.

From St Ann's Head it's still the coastline which defines him, so around the nose of Wooltack Point we go and onto the rolled up skin of that snarling muzzle, from St Brides to Broad Haven; his forehead is well lined by St Brides Bay. His eye, by the way, I would guess is around Roch/Dudwell Mountain, although on my map, this place unfortunately lacks

Taliesin's "Green limpid sheet of icicle" (frozen pool?), which may have glinted in the sun in his own time. That said, perhaps in winter there is still some well or pool here that freezes over in honour of the Bard's song.

As with the Glastonbury and Preseli zodiacs, this lion seems to wear a crown of sorts and the overall likeness to these other two is, I think you will agree, quite remarkable. The crown of Albion's Leo is tipped at two points, at the front by St David's Head and at the rear by Stumble Head. St David's Cathedral must be the jewel within it.

From Fishguard, in Taliesin's "Sea-roughed nape" of his neck, (do three springs arise here too?) the coast northwards cleanly cuts his back until it curls into the River Dyfi to start drawing his hindquarters and rear left leg.

As we pace out the neck - an interesting observation

It seems that those famous blue stones of Stonehenge were originally quarried in the Preseli Mountains, here on the nape of his neck. Indeed, the location for these stones, which were thought to be magical, is at the very end of Virgo's/the Earth Mother's big toe. It's as though she's saying "Look, here they are - your mystic blue stones!" Likewise, she may be alerting our attention to Preseli's own zodiac which these same mountains have wrought for an equally mystical purpose.

Follow now the Dyfi to Cemmaes Road where we'll pick up the A470 to Caersws. From here follow the river Montgomery through Newtown to Dolfor where the B4355 will take us around Cilfaesty Hill to Felindre.

At Felindre head south on the unmarked road to join the B4356; follow this southeast to Knighton. Here allow Offa's Dyke to lead you, for it admirably digs out the rest of the leg down to Kington. Now take the A4111 to

Willersley where we then zig-zag down on the B4352 to Kingstone; the underside of that left hind paw begins here.

From Kingstone, cut across country to Pontrilas where the A465 takes us to Llanfihangel Crucorney on the front of the paw. Most interestingly this same place marks the heel of Virgo's foot.

From here it is again good old Offa's Dyke which draws the front of this left hind leg and which at the same time draws the calf muscle of the Earth Mother's right leg - deft economy of line! Stay in Offa's Dyke to Hay-on-Wye. Here (a little artistic licence) take a line northwest through Newchurch and head across country until you run into the junction of the A44 and A481.

Now go to Crossgates on the A44. (I feel it should be Crosslegs, for it is here that the Earth Mother's leg actually crosses the lion's!) Stay on the A44 to Rhayader where we'll use the unmarked road past the Craig Coch reservoir to pick up the Dyfed/Powys border line as far as Pant Mawr. This completes the left hind leg, but before we move on it is worth noting that the river Dove runs down this rear leg through the aptly named Golden Valley, not a bad name on this most golden of sun signs.

Let's now do the underside of his belly. Starting at Rhayader, follow the River Wye southwards to where it shortly connects to the stream that flows into, or out of, the Caban Coch reservoir via Elan village. Follow this stream to the reservoir and curl with its shape to where the river Claerwen meets it. But from here another little cheat, for we must go as the crow flies over the mountain of Drygarn Fawr to the village of Abergwesyn.

At Abergwesyn follow the unmarked road along with the river Irfon down to Llanwrtyd Wells, taking the A483 to Llandovery, followed by the A4069 to Llangadog and Brynamman. Then it's the A4068 to Gurno and the Swansea valley where the river Tawe will glide us all the way to the sea and that lashing foreleg.

Finally the right hind leg: start at Abergwesyn where we'll travel down the country road to Beulah. The A483 to Builth Wells, and A470 to Erwood gets us to the paw. We then take country roads from Erwood to Crickadarn and curving on round to Felinfach on its toe. We continue the underside of the paw by heading to Llyswen where it's more unmarked country roads to Painscastle, (Is there an injury to this paw too?) Bryngwyn, Glascwm, Hundred House, Newbridge-on-Wye, and finally to Rhayader and a pint of best bitter!

But have we dug out a Lion or a Lioness?

Lion, Lioness, or even Lyonesse?

In all three earth zodiacs, Leo seems to lack a prominent mane, indeed, is it a lion at all? To add a touch of eastern spice to such a thought, we find that the Babylonians knew this same constellation as the Great Dog, so could that strange crown shape upon all three lions of Albion be no more than a pair of large flapping dog's ears? Thus Leo becomes deciphered, through the Babylonian way of seeing things, as a large hound.

For me, though, this lack of a prominent mane prompted first a thought of a lioness, which then slipped off my tongue as *Lyonesse*. Now there's a thought! The disappeared realm of Lyonesse has, for generations, tempted men to wonder where it might have been prior to that terrible night when the waters submerged it. Could this corner of Wales be that sunken legendary land - sunken not beneath the waves after all, but rather only beneath the surface of our defunct mythological memory?

Romantics, however, have always favoured somewhere off the Cornish coast as being where Lyonesse once was, assuming that the Isles of Scilly are all that's left. But look northwestwards on a clear day from a north

Cornish beach and you may glimpse out there, in the blueness, this Welsh lioness, her chin less than 50 miles away as the gull flies. So close enough for a Lyonesse do you think? Perhaps not.

However, this Welsh lioness/Lyonesse theory gains curious ground when we hear how the lion was, in ancient times, associated with flooding. To hear more we must take a stroll along the banks of a rising river Nile.

It was at the enlightened time when the ancient Egyptians saw the Nile as an earthly reflection of the Milky Way that they noticed that the lions of the desert places would quietly slink into the valley of the Nile to escape the dry season. This was always a prelude to the river joyfully bursting its banks to bring new life to the valley. Interestingly, this flooding happened each year when the sun was in the astrological house of Leo!

The Egyptians, never slow in honouring the events of the natural world about them, especially when seen to be allied to events in the heavens, thereafter always had the head of a Lion carved upon the irrigation sluice gates of their holy Nile. The same delightful imagery found itself transported and perpetuated far from Egypt in the form of many a lion-headed fountain; even Glastonbury's own Chalice Well, where Jesus may once have cupped his hands, still gushes its cool, and some say healing, waters from out of a lion's mouth.

Back in Britain at the same time, when the tales flowed as plentifully as the mead on winter evenings, floods of greater proportions than those of the Nile fired imaginations. They even saw Hu or Menu, the Celt's own Noah, as actually making his first steps back on dry land upon British soil. And with that are our own imaginations fired up when we compare it to what we know now? Knowing that Britain has taken upon herself the shape of an enormous ark, is it not tempting to wonder if old Hu's first steps were upon its own dry deck?

We shall hear more of Hu when later on we

walk into the constellation of Taurus, but staying with Druid beliefs I would like to quote a most interesting snippet from the research of Dudley Wright into the cause of the flood that engulfed these islands and all the world. The following comes from his book *Druidism, The Ancient Faith of Britain*: "*In common with most nations the Druids had their own Deluge traditions, but represented the event as occurring in a lake called Llyn **Llion**, the waters of which burst forth and overwhelmed the face of the whole world.*" *Llyn* is most definitely Welsh for lake and, because an almighty lion of over 100 miles in length devours the land of southwest Wales, can you blame me for again feeling that we are here treading the land of fabled, and flood prophetic, Lyonesse? Indeed, was this the land where the giant mythological lion-headed floodgates of the world were first thrown open, and where the ark first took to water? Or then again, is all this not, in fact, a memory of the past but a prophesy of imminent events?

Either way, the lion/Lyon has become, and perhaps not so curiously now, synonymous with floods and fountains. Though because Leo is a zodiacal sun sign, a sign of fire, we must take note that in this coming together of opposites, fire being quenched by water, is (as all alchemists once knew) the poetic chemistry which has been behind every convulsive new beginning and ending that this old earth has ever been through. Simply, it is a duo that spells *change*. Remember this when on our clockwise journey we enter the sign of our presently dawning Age of Aquarius, for we'll see then these same two elements explode off the map in a most telling picture of what must be imminent global *Change/Rebirth*, upon the back of what can only be an equally imminent period of chaos.

A lion on a lead?

Now look at the cover and see how this big

cat has taken up what seems a protective stance almost between the legs of the Earth Mother. Indeed, put a lead in Virgo's inviting hand and connect it to the lion's neck and you will see the fiercest guard lion or dog ever! Or, looking at this ever-so-close twosome in another way - could the Mother be actually cocking a leg over the lion's back with a view to riding it! But do not think my suggestion flippant, for that's exactly how the Greeks sometimes portrayed the Mother of the Gods, their goddess Rhea, yes, riding on the back of a lion!

The Great Goddess has been known by many names in many different cultures where the portrayal of her in close proximity to a lion, more often than not with a foot, or feet, upon its back, also seems to have been an obligatory requirement. Ishtar, Hera, Cybele, Astarte, and Artemis, all seemingly befriended lions. And do not forget Britannia who is the personification of these British Isles, whose first incarnation may have been as the Celt's Brigantia was many times depicted with a lion at her feet. Quite rightly then even the zodiac places Leo next to Virgo - not only in the night sky but also on this otherwise purposefully out-of-sequence zodiac on the ground. Seems they must never be parted!

Note: the traditional zodiacal pairing of Taurus with Gemini, and Sagittarius with Capricorn, is also correctly copied by Albion's landcraft.

Found - a 4300 year old Sumerian replica of this Welsh twosome!

However, it must be the ancient Sumerian's Earth Mother who points most forcefully of all to the fact that Albion's portrayal of the mother with one foot on her lion's back is no coincidental freak of nature, but a depiction in shocking sympathy with the wisdom of the ancients.

Cast your eyes back some 4,300 years and

become, as I was, astounded at the sight of a cylinder seal design from the Akkad period, which portrays the goddess Inanna, Sumerian Queen of Heaven and Earth, and her fierce pet, in a virtual carbon copy pose to the one chosen by the Mother herself to sing out of Albion's miracle. Look again at the cover and see how she, as the Welsh Virgo, seemingly places her right foot upon the back of Leo; now look at my illustration of that incredible seal. Surely this is archaic proof that the strange self-portrait of the Mother in her masterpiece of Albion is not so strange after all. Indeed, we find now that it is a side of her that she has

Inanna - as Queen of Heaven and Earth.
Akkad period, c. 2334-2154BC.

been pleased to instill into the mind of that Sumerian artist to herald her high-stepping arrival into our startled gaze today. No wonder she laughs and dances in our faces!

Anne Baring and Jules Cashford, in their wonderfully informative book *The Myth of the Goddess*, where I found the above bombshell of a photo, shine a light into the many faces of the Mother. In their text relating to Inanna there is a very lovely description of how the Sumerians saw her. Their *'Green One'*, we learn, was clothed in heaven and crowned with the stars. Around her neck was a rainbow and her girdle was the zodiac. Is this not pure unadulterated Albion!

Now, venture with me northwards so that you may meet this very lady, the ultimate *Green One*, who has in her bridal gown of all

Albion literally clothed and girdled herself in heaven and its zodiac. Truly she is the Queen of this Heaven now brought down to earth.

Prepare now to dance the jig of life!

LEO

How marvellously have Silurian Llandovery, Ordovician Ashgill and Caradoc layers conspired to perfectly endorse fathoms below our feet the thrust and surge of Leo's aggressive movement, almost to the point of animation. Even a tail and flowing mane seems evident. And I just love that granite eye, shown in red on my coloured version.

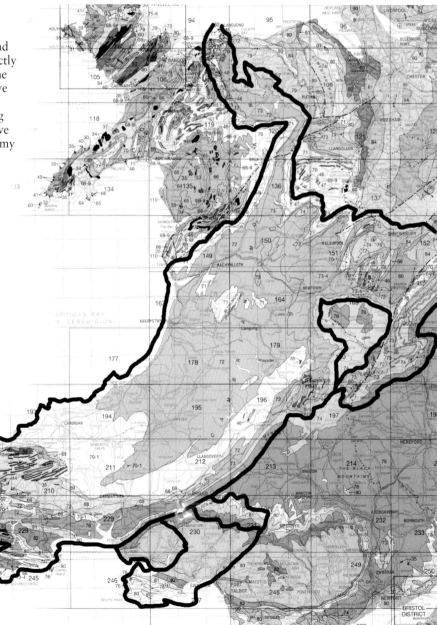

Based upon Geological Map of the United Kingdom by permission of the British Geological Survey, IPR/26-11C

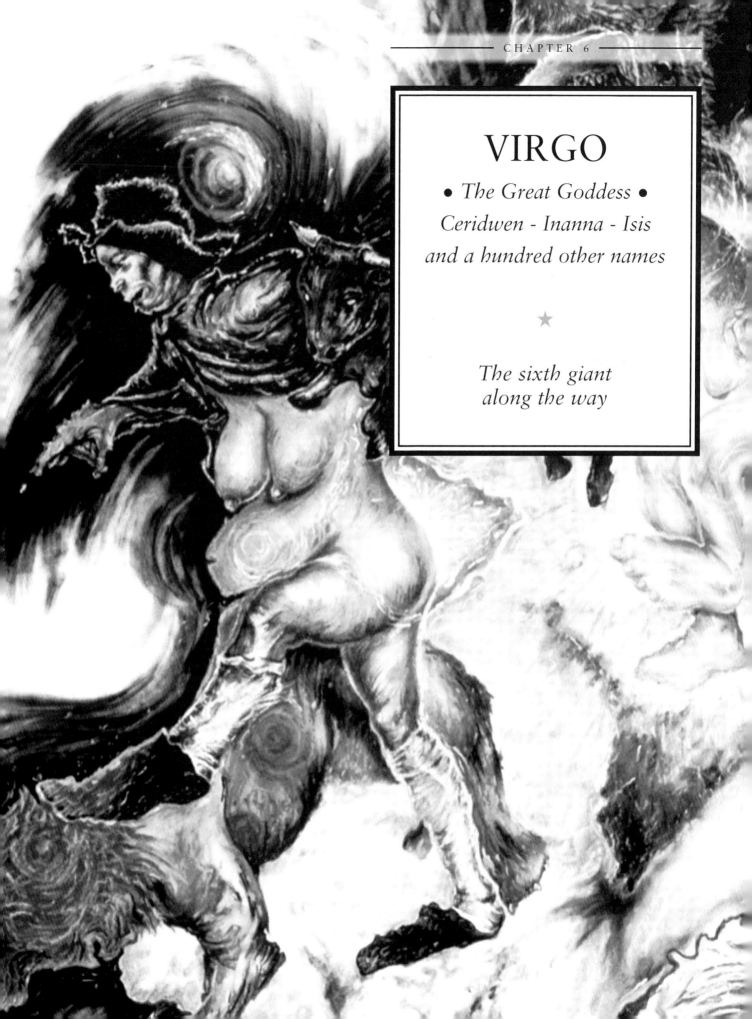

CHAPTER 6

VIRGO

• *The Great Goddess* •
Ceridwen - Inanna - Isis
and a hundred other names

★

The sixth giant
along the way

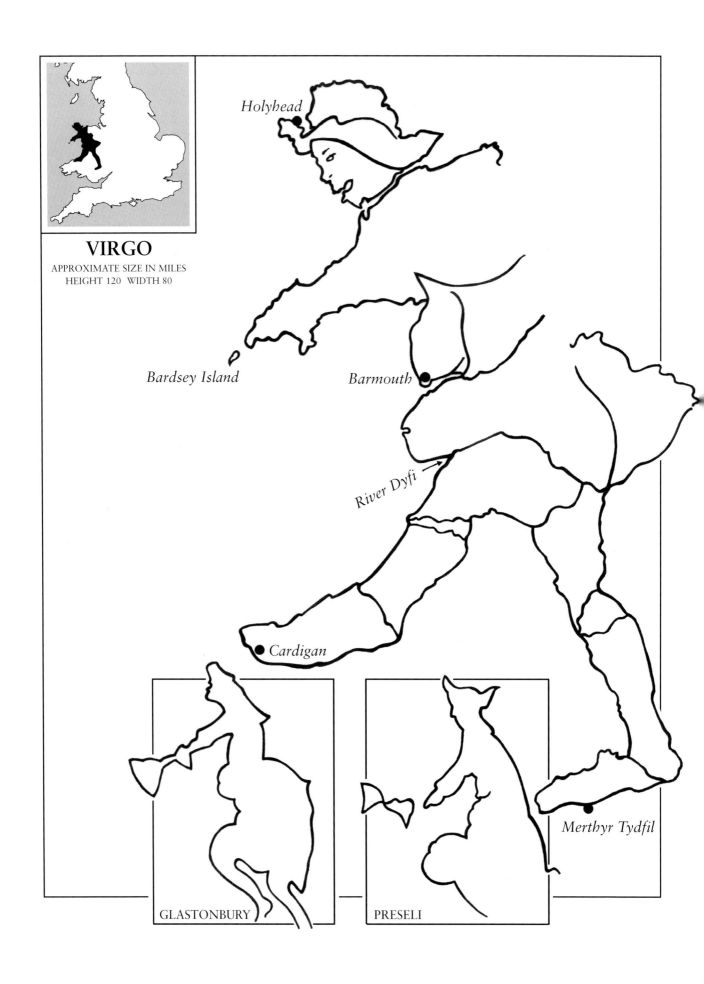

VIRGO

APPROXIMATE SIZE IN MILES
HEIGHT 120 WIDTH 80

Holyhead

Bardsey Island

Barmouth

River Dyfi

Cardigan

Merthyr Tydfil

GLASTONBURY

PRESELI

Oh, to be swallowed by the Goddess!

"I am the first and the last. I am the honoured one and the scorned one. I am the whore, and the holy one. I am the wife and the virgin. I am the mother and the daughter... I am she whose wedding is great, and I have not taken a husband... I am knowledge and ignorance... I am shameless; I am ashamed. I am strength and I am fear... I am foolish, and I am wise... I am godless, and I am one whose God is great."

Gnostic text discovered at Nag Hammadi entitled
THUNDER, PERFECT MIND
The poem is intended as being spoken by the voice of the Divine Feminine Force

GENERAL AREA:
THE BULK OF NORTH AND MID-WALES. HER HEAD IS THE ISLE OF ANGLESEY, WHILE HER FEET ARE AS FAR SOUTH AS CARDIGAN AND MERTHYR TYDFIL.

I would hazard a guess that anyone who has bothered to come this far upon this strange journey has, for some time, felt ill at ease with the state of our poor palpitating planet and the destructive course upon which mankind seems hell bent on keeping it. That ghastly hole in the ozone layer, and the rate at which the ice shelf is turning to slush, are providing ample grounds for such concerns. You might also be troubled by our tampering with genetics and feel we are playing fast and loose with what Prince Charles has rightly termed 'the building bricks of life'. You may feel that we have already unbalanced nature to a point where some kind of backlash seems inevitable.

Harbouring similar feelings, and after studying for years what the land has done, I have come to read Albion's arrival, this beautiful affront to all the beliefs and values which have led to the demise of our planet and its life forms, as a mother's scream of *"Stop!"*

to us her children. We are like hordes of delinquent gods gone mad, who arrogantly strut our greedy 'couldn't give a shit' stuff upon a terrible brink, to which most are utterly oblivious.

And yet, behind this visual wail of nature, just see how much love there must still be in the heart of her whom we have by the throat; a love powerful enough to cause the very stones to speak to us in images that we thought were our own!

For me, this wonder under foot could only have come about via the Earth Mother and Sky Father met as one in everything - from Devon's cliffs to Cumbria's worms! This marriage, this holy fusion, has then caused a body of earth, the size of Britain, to animate itself as a picture of heaven - so think what such a union would do if celebrated within a man! This same wondrously creative and transforming potential resides latent, I believe, within us all. We have, however, become so spiritually sundered from the rest of creation that to even broach such a subject usually guarantees yawns or embarrassed looks toward the ceiling. Indeed, as I type this I immediately squirm at what I've just written. It is hard to break out of the straitjackets of perception that our present culture shoehorned us into at birth. Sometimes, you know, even I look at what I've found and turn absolutely chicken!

Anyway, let's forget about us for a moment and return to what the land has done, and know that whatever upheavals this old planet is about to shiver through, Mother Nature will never cease her shindig of life, whether coiling through the laughter of children, or swirling within the nucleus of the furthest star of all. Look, even in the very face of continued abuse and pending catastrophe, the image that the old girl has chosen to emblazon 123 miles tall upon the face of the world is of herself *dancing* - indeed, *pregnant* and dancing! And oh, how that word 'dance' shall explode off Albion's cross at the end of our journey, for we shall see there even her Son dance off its planks, heralding all of us doing likewise!

Without doubt a great change must be coming, but because of the sheer beauty of this visual imagery, that change can only be ultimately for the best. This change is in itself a chance, and perhaps the greatest chance ever put to mankind en masse, to finally take up our rightful place in the Dance of the Universe. I can think of no other reason why the earth has done this to Britain.

Smile then, at her exuberant can-can of life. Smile even wider when you shift your eyes to the legs of her little sister at Glastonbury whom Mary Caine found also to be dancing beneath the green pastures there - and just check out their identical bellies! But it gets better. Take a look at her absolutely staggering look-a-like at Preseli. And why shouldn't they be twins, for both these Earth Mothers are proud to be Welsh and therefore each a Ceridwen, the name given to the Great Goddess by the Celts

of these parts. And as though to underline their Welshness notice how both wear the same distinctively brimmed bonnet, so similar in style to the traditional black top hat worn to this day by the women of Wales - and while you're at it just check out that identical breast too!

"Pure coincidence!" some will sneer when faced with this treble-take of ladies in the landscape - but for me it's just another day in the discovery of Albion. Once more we see all three zodiacs proving each other beyond coincidence via almost copy-cat imagery; even more so in this instance, for this is not the modern day image of a lath-like Virgo, but one who is rotund and in total accord with the Celt's own idea of the Mother.

Three in One

Virgo, the 'knees- up' fat mamma of this whole miracle has, however, many faces and these anciently linked to those of the moon. For instance, our ancestors saw her in the new crescent moon as the demure virgin, associated perhaps with the fragile spring, raw and yet with a subtle promise on the air, laced with the seductive scent of elder blossom, married to the yearning throat of the blackbird.

The summer Mother was then twinned to the full moon, under whose light she was seen full pregnant and frolicking amid her multifarious births. Her swollen breasts were feeding not only all who drew breath but also the inanimate, for, because of Albion, we know that the very rocks must be, in a sense, alive and pulsating with her rhythms. So, from sandstone to sandpipers, everything was seen to be joined in a spiritual conga (if I can put it that way!) behind her happily rolling rump, in a summer dance of riotous regeneration.

Her third face came with the darkening moon, which cast her in the rags of the crone or wise woman. In this guise she was seen to be withdrawn into herself, and yet perhaps her works were more vibrant in this inner state than at any other seasonal time. She was now working deeply through the dark months, rousing her dance within the nucleus of the snow drop, the lamb, and a myriad other life forms that do not slumber in winter, but are ever rising and spiralling back towards new birth. If only we had eyes to see the dazzling ethereal energies dancing through the bone hard frosty soil, or in the outwardly dead oak - then winter would seem as colourful as summer!

Such is the triple-faced goddess. As we witness her dancing out of Wales see now a spectacular composite of those three made one. From the head surely cackles the crone, though in the size of those swinging breasts and belly we can also detect her bounteous summer side. But notice the legs; it can only be the motivation of the maid that is behind such dainty high stepping jinks! In Wales we are thus privileged to look upon all her cycles dancing in one amalgam of joy, fertility, and wisdom.

But what the hell am I talking about?

I have just given three seasonal cameos with a bent towards the pagan, and thus for most readers, three more examples of pathetic silliness - and I would agree! Having just reread my three-paragraph indulgence I utterly retract my every word, for the truer vision of her today, regardless of moon phase and season, would be that of her globally decapitated head stuck upon a pole and stabbed into the toxic ground, alongside both the stinking tuskless elephant carcass, and the suicide child who could not bear to fail her exams for the System had never told her that she was beautiful beyond learning. And I feel sick with anger.

Her wounds are our wounds

On Albion you should know, even after this short distance, that this land doesn't forget a damn thing. It is then time to see right through this Mother's facade of jollifications. Observe how, for all her dancing, her throat has been slashed, indeed, she has been decapitated via the Menai Strait! Thus the crime of the male against the female, against all nature, is held up for all the universe to see!

"The land remembers everything and is a witness to history in a way we cannot fully appreciate"
ENCYCLOPAEDIA OF CELTIC WISDOM
Caitlin and John Matthews

I shall speak more of this glaring and most damning wound shortly, but for now let every man, or woman, believing too much in men, admit to the crime.

Since the demise of the goddess in favour of a more masculine god (or indeed, of no god at all), and greed and power became our truer religion, men have set themselves triumphantly above the rest of nature. This a crime perpetrated on two levels.

First, in denying the mineral make-up of the planet any semblance of intelligence, and only offering a grudging nod to the intelligence or self-awareness of its myriad animal, bird, insect, fish and vegetal life forms, it has been easy for generations of us to view the planet as not much more than a vast storehouse of help-yourself commodities, and these pretty well free to anyone with enough 'get up and go' to plunder, without searching their conscience at all. Indeed, until relatively recently, the Church itself helped matters along nicely by looking upon nature in the raw as almost evil, and therefore a thing to be cleared, cleansed and beaten into submission along with any native cultures that still upheld the view that a god could be in a landscape, a tree, or even a stone.

But most cunning of all, because we in the western world worked so hard at all but wiping out the usage of the word 'Mother' as relating to the earth, we, at the same time, eliminated any worry of the planet 'itself' ever achieving recognition as a Being in its own right. In this one psychological masterstroke we gave ourselves licence to bugger her and hers by the hour without the slightest pang of remorse - for 'She' was officially non-existent. She was a thing less than a whore, and thus we could take our pleasure of her body without the fear of having to pay a fee afterwards! You do not need me to tell you that this western way of doing things is now pretty well prevalent across the globe.

So ingrained and time-hardened has this denial and devaluation of the whole range of the feminine / mother / negative / left / black become, and so shored up the valued hierarchy of the male / father / positive / right / white principles, that one almost suspects that 'the great lie of it all' must have become so effortlessly passed on through the genes as to warrant seeing it as a veritable natural Law of the Universe! Why, even today in some families, whether in the west or east, the birth of a daughter can prompt in both mother and father an unconcealed disappointment, while in some other parts of the world her arrival is almost a curse.

And don't talk to me of today's leaps and bounds in women's rights, allowing them to rise to professional positions of power, to climb into pulpits, to fight alongside men in so-called theatres of war, and to go out to work while dads stay at home to look after the children - because the real problem of feminine recognition goes down a whole lot deeper than equal job opportunities!

Female liberation is for us all. On the plus side, we now find some men who value a feminine sensitivity in their character after generations of classing it a weakness. But for me, the greatest sign of the return of the feminine is in the stirring in the hearts of people of both sexes that prompts them to put their own life in danger for that of a tree in the face of a developer's bulldozer. These and many other signs, including this shocking slap in the face from Albion, are but the birth pangs of a coming new age - a new way of perceiving this whole miracle of life on earth.

Though it is not only on the outside that we've decapitated the essence of the Mother.

It seems that through our physical devaluing of the Mother and thus the planet there has accrued an injury to the entire feminine psyche, and because, in a wiser time than this, the soul was seen as essentially feminine (the spirit being masculine) I fear that in addition to the all-too-visible physical crimes, both the soul of the planet and that of every individual man, woman, and child may have become wounded to the same degree. The symptoms of this are many tiered, the implications vast, but often all summed up in that now widely used phrase, 'The Soulless Society'. Unbalance is not only visibly ransacking nature but it is gnawing away at every facet of human existence, and with every rise in the figures of drug users there may be hidden a far larger increase in those suffering physiological problems due to having to exist in such an atmosphere.

To stop this self-perpetuating rot, and only because of what I have read into Albion, I think we shall need a totally new way of perceiving just about everything under the sun. It will not be easy to admit that we've been so wrong on so many things. Indeed, I know it will be downright painful!

Mirror, mirror on the ground...

So try perceiving this: in the most simplistic terms possible Albion, before anything else, must be showing itself to us as some kind of mirror, for aren't the heavens reflected there? With such a premise in mind, could this same vast mirror, and I include the entire surface of the earth, also be a super sensitive reflection of *us*? And what if, in that same topographical mirror, our every deed and thought was somehow caught within it and thereafter reflected back a trillion, trillion times, not only back onto us, but onto the trees, upon clouds, upon our next door neighbour, even upon our own babies. *"Ludicrous!"* you say - but if you think that, what are you doing on this journey, so far from home?

I am not saying that this is a fact (because I'm no guru) but pondering on this while looking upon this growing body of evidence on the ground, forces me to concede that anything is now possible.

So let's kick the 'impossible' around a bit longer. If this crazy mirror theory is true, think of those daily and global acts of sickening aggression; think about the still starving millions; of the depressed and homeless; of the rapists' victims crying in the alleyways; think even about your own domestic angers, fears and concerns. Then think of the loneliness of the last whales - their calls not answered; of the reflected pain of the millions of trees felled in the decimated rain forests, through to the sickening moment, and one which must have sent a shiver through the entire universe, when man even thought about putting his own genes into a pig so as to make the meat more tender and lean. Think about it all, and worry as to whether it is all being perpetually thrown back into our faces in a myriad ways - image upon frightful image - a multiplicity of amplified sorrows and discontent which are imperceptibly leaching back into your own system, your own psyche, where even now such feed-back lies decaying, subliminally dulling the true shine of your life in this never ending two-way traffic of unbalance piled upon unbalance. Result - a global dis-ease.

New medical belief, (even without going onto the dodgy ground of my planetary mirror theory), is, however, suggesting that thought and feelings really can directly effect the physical, to the extent where stressful thought can of itself cause actual harm to the body in which the condition exists, even possibly causing cancer. I put it to you that the body of the earth may be liable to the same.

But all is not doom and gloom

Of course, as well as pain and unrest, a whole lot of love and laughter must also be reflected in and out of this same mirror; but I would wager that, on the world stage, the pendulum has been for a long time weighted on the side of suffering and sadness.

Having said that, just imagine what wonders could jump out of this same hypothetical looking glass if we, at last, sent into it a genuine, heartfelt acknowledgement of the fact that even bedrock is alive and has a creative mind. If such credence were transmitted en masse would we find ourselves suddenly communing with mountains and working hand-in-hand with nature as joint creators of a heaven on earth? If so, we would become true lords of the earth, not as domineering plunderers, but as protective shepherds and loving gardeners. Our pulse would no more be quickened by selfish greed, but by the seasons and the revolutions of the silver above our heads. And how nature might bloom in response - knowing that its God walked again, all seeing and knowing amongst its riches - he half man/Father, half animal/Mother, at last the ever intended God-Man!

"If ye have faith as a grain of mustard seed, ye shall say unto this mountain, remove hence to yonder place; and it shall remove; and nothing shall be impossible unto you."
MATTHEW, Chapter 17, Verse 20

Seeing what the mountains of Wales have done - do not dare water down the meaning of the above!

But all this is not a new theory, indeed, isn't the simple gist of its 'pay-back' theory no more than the message that often ran through the advice of Jesus:

"Therefore all things whatsoever ye would that men should do to you, do ye even so to them: for this is the law and the prophets"
MATTHEW, Chapter 7 Verse 12

Simply he is telling us to do good and that good shall be returned or reflected. Likewise that phrase of 'What you put in is what you get out' may be truer than we ever realised.

These words may become more meaningful than ever before when now we find ourselves walking over a magic mirror; as transparent as Glastonbury itself, now seen to be the glassy eye of Pisces, a place which may, in a mirror, translate as the location of the 'buried looking glass'. When on our journey we linger on the centre of the forehead of Albion's Christ, we will also take a mirror to the place that marks this prime spot, symbolic as it is of enlightened perception, and find there Glasonby reversed into something like 'by the glass son' - the Son revealed in the looking glass.

Tantalising stuff, but if this is exactly the imagery we are supposed to see then think whose face will shine out if you are brave enough to look into that face of the dazzling Son - *yours* is going to be the answer!

But, when I saw her boobs, I panicked!

Out of all these zodiacal giants, Virgo is the most animated. She is certainly the one to put a smile on our faces, and why not? Creation is a joyful thing, a physical manifestation of love. Her laughing head is so clear that once it is pointed out we could be forgiven for laughing at our own stupidity for not seeing her sooner.

I had first seen her when I was 11, though only her head and outstretched arm. Another 30 years were to pass before I was permitted to see that she also had a full body, a 123-mile high figure of dancing nudity - and that's when I panicked! You see, my upbringing branded her as outrageous and irreverent, for what was holy surely should never be seen naked, let alone pregnant and exhibiting it so unashamedly! I'm certainly no prude, and only ever attended church for the obligatory weddings, christenings, and funerals, but my reaction was, I guess, based upon the sanitised Christian dogma which had been implanted in me some time some where, and although never impeding my life previously, it was certainly rearing its ugly head now. Judged on this criteria, what I had found must be either a misjudgment or something downright pagan, and thereby more than likely degenerate.

Under such an attack, my unencumbered inner child must have had to hang on for all it was worth to urge me to draw her out as the land seemed to demand.

Sheepishly, after I *had* been true to the map, I waited for my two daughters to return home from school. Fictitiously casual, and expecting frowns, I said to them "Look who I've found, it's the Earth Mother, what do you think?" The girls' faces lit up and they giggled. But what they saw, although funny and a touch naughty, was no big deal to them, moreover, she seemed exactly as they expected: fat, pregnant, and proud of it! It was only the narrow-minded old ghost within me, 'the marketing man' with an eye on product acceptance, and the 'preacher of old time religion', who was threatening me with that big word 'blasphemy'.

The laughter of the girls soon made everything all right, however, and I joined in with them; thus the marketing man fled, ashamed at having labelled 'innocence' as possibly 'pornographic' in the eyes of the punters; and the preacher followed him, for although he sang *All Things Bright and Beautiful* he never wanted them to be stark naked and beautiful.

And tell me - if the Motherland wished to portray herself dancing a naked jig of life and love, then how dare I even think about censoring it! *Life* is the rhythm of her conga and its continuance via *love* is what Albion must be all about. It is obvious that even in her pain, the Mother wishes only to send us, her children, this dance of fecundity as a visual token to hold on to and to remember her by when on a chaotic day of our own making, our intellect takes flight screaming *"There is no God!"* At that time, and even above the howling of the elements, she wishes us no ill - what true mother would?

Words not permitted in the Bible

Jesus knew of her love and spoke of it in words not permitted in the Bible. Translated by Edmond Szekely from ancient Aramaic manuscripts dating from the first century AD, come teachings, allegedly from Jesus himself, and relating specifically to the *Earth* Mother. These manuscripts are reportedly in the possession of both the Vatican and the Austrian Government.

Now whether Szekely's translations are unerringly accurate or not, I cannot resist quoting some of these beautiful words of Jesus, for they could well come from a boy who had once come to Albion and found a Mother waiting here, and in whose herb-scented arms lay awhile in wonder. From Szekely's book *The Gospel of Peace of Jesus*, allegedly penned by the disciple John, I offer these warming words:

"And he who clings to the laws of his Mother, to him shall his Mother cling also. She shall heal all his plagues, and he shall never become sick. She gives him long life, and protects him from all afflictions; from fire, from water, from the bite of venomous snakes. For your Mother bore you, keeps life within you. She has given you her body, and none but she heals you. Happy is he who loves his Mother and lies quietly in her bosom. For your Mother loves you, even when you turn away from her. And how much more shall she love you, if you turn to her again? I tell you truly,

very great is her love, greater than the greatest mountains, deeper than the deepest seas. And those who love her, their Mother never deserts them. As the hen protects her chickens, as the lioness her cubs, as the mother her new born babe, so does the Earthly Mother protect the Son of Man from all danger and all evils."

And these too:

"And pray every day to your Heavenly Father and Earthly Mother, that your soul become as perfect as your Heavenly Father's holy spirit is perfect, and that your body become as perfect as the body of your Earthly Mother is perfect. For truly, no one can reach the Heavenly Father unless through his Earthly Mother. Even as no newborn babe can understand the teachings of his father till his mother has suckled him, bathed him, nursed him, put him to sleep and nurtured him."

With that let us approach her.

Her severed head

We shall certainly have fun in map reading our way around the ample curves of old Ceridwen, although I can start at no other place than that great head of the Isle of Anglesey, which although so obviously laughing, is nonetheless, horribly severed at the neck by the watery Menai Strait.

At first I did not feel there was any relevance in that watery slash of a neck, because the old girl's jollity was so overwhelming. But that was in the early days before I had discovered that such glaring strokes upon Albion's canvas are rarely made without significance.

Delving for a reason I found myself amongst the myths of ancient Egypt where we shall find so many hints to Albion's mythological lineage, as we progress on our journey. Anyway, a fragment from the affairs of the great goddess Isis and her son Horus caught my eye. Briefly, it transpires that in the midst of a mother and son tiff, Horus, in a fit of temper, cut off his mother's head. Fortunately, the two were soon reconciled, and by magic, so too was that precious head to its neck!

On the face of it, there is no big revelation here, but I can't help wondering if this decapitation of the Mother by the son should be read as a reflection of the sin all we sons of the Mother commit daily against, not only her body, the earth, but also against that feminine or soul part of each of us. If so, does that lopped-off head of Isis poetically hint at what the land has made so exceedingly plain here? And when we too are hopefully reconciled with her, will the Menai Strait one day become dry land?

Staying with that gash, another hunch has me tonguing my cheek while dwelling upon the name Menai. Now I don't know whether it translates into English, but what I do know is that as it stands the word *men* is most prominent within it - so could it be a tongue-in-cheek label to the effect that *"Men did it to me"*? Is that nonsense? More than likely. Let's just forget I mentioned it.

Enough speculation then; time now to focus on the details of this head that are beyond doubt, and are hammered into the map. For a start, just look at her chin hair at Abermenai Point and Llanddwyn Island; not even Arthur Rackham, the Edwardian children's book illustrator famous for witches and the like, could have drawn a finer set of old dame's whiskers! Look, too, and smile, at that cackling mouth that is formed by Malltraeth Bay. The mouth is full of golden sand, with Malltraeth itself acting as her tonsils. And oh how I'd just love to play with that name Malltraeth by firstly separating *mall* with its English meaning *to grind*, and then cheekily swapping the *'ra'* in *traeth* for an *'e'* and thereby filling her mouth with the sound of *grinding teeth* - but I'll chicken out of that one too.

Now come out of that toothless grin, and sail up past her hairy top lip to that lovely stub of a nose where Aberffraw is the plug in her nostril. I hope she will forgive this intrusive tour of her anatomy, but I feel sure that she is chuckling at my rudeness for she must have the earthiest sense of humour. So laugh again with her at the sight of that perfect wart which sprouts out of the bridge of her nose. Its name is Barclodiad y Gawres, where a burial mound holds the decaying body and trappings of a Welsh chieftain. Perhaps his entombment in her wart was for once upsetting her in some way!

Her forehead has Rhosneigr as her all-seeing third eye. Then it's onto the brim of her delightful hat, peaked at the front by Holyhead mountain where, as a youth, I found a strange ring that I still wear today on my wedding finger - it refuses to fit on any other! A lovely place to hide a ring. However, she has even more surprises in this, the most voluminous hat of all time, for at the very top of it squeak the islands of West and Middle Mouse! Why, even old Walt Disney couldn't have conjured up better tenants to take up residence in the hat of one who is the Mother of all witches!

But that's not the only play on words she has under her hat.

Just around the inside of that bent-up front rim tip is Holyhead, the main port and town of Anglesey. How odd then that we should all persist in pronouncing Holyhead as Hollyhead. Perhaps we do it out of guilt for our refusal in acknowledging the existence of this, her head? Let us then pronounce it properly as HOLY-HEAD for indeed it is!

And there's more.

The great centre cone of her hat is tipped at the front by Carmel Head… and another name to conjure with. In my own head I hear the verses of the Bible's *Song of Solomon/Song of Songs*, though in my opinion here is no love duet between the black Shulamite (who the Bible claims represents the Church as a bride) and her beloved (who is equated with

Christ/the bridegroom) but rather a dialogue of love between the goddess and her beloved consort, and, if true, it must also be the Song of Albion. Indeed, I'm not alone in thinking that something erotically pagan has crept past the Bible's editors. Hear what Robert Graves says of its verses: *"The fact is that originally they celebrated the mysteries of an annual sacred marriage between Salmaah the King of the Year and the Flower Queen."* And if that's true, too, then surely Albion must be their bridal bed, indeed, just look what their love-making beneath those pastured sheets has created!

But it gets better - the *Song* takes the form of shared compliments between the two lovers, though excitingly many of these seem to extol topographical rather than human features. As a traveller of Albion, I'd strongly recommend reading it along the way, because it so often seems to be in curious harmony with the visual poetry we're walking on. For example, and especially for us now standing upon the Mother's head, hear the beloved praise the beauteous head of his lover (the so-called Shulamite) in terms that can only be viewed as gigantic. Listen:

"Thine head upon thee is like Carmel"

Mount Carmel, much mentioned in the Bible, is a prominent mountain in Israel, which stares out to sea near the port of Haifa - just as Carmel Head stares out to sea on this head of the Mother - you get my drift?

A head like Carmel - Carmel Head - what more can I say? Is this coincidence or another case of hitting the nail bang on the head? The choice will always be yours, but for me even this stacking-up of coincidences seems miraculous in itself. I mean to say, put that Carmel Head on Virgo's knee, upon her breast, or smack in the middle of Sagittarius's forehead, and it would count for nothing - but placed here on the head of Albion's Flower Queen it is disarmingly relevant.

"Well whoever named that Welsh headland "Carmel" must have been an avid Bible reader and wished only to bring a Biblical place name to Wales."

This explanation may well be the less-than-fantastic truth of the matter. Though why that Bible fanatic chose to bring Carmel to the *actual head* of Albion's own Black/Yin/Shulamite, and not, say, to her thumb or right nipple, is for me another case of man aiding the miracle underfoot. And whether or not he, like the many other provocative name-droppers on Albion, knew what he was doing, this same lady now doffs her great bonnet to him!

Let us now finish the drawing of this bonnet. From Point Lynas upon the rear corner of her hat's centre cone just sail on down into Red Wharf Bay and round past Penmon Priory which tips the brim. Then just catch the poetically bloody tide past Beaumaris and back out through her throat to those hairs on her chinny chin chin. There I go again - forgive me, Mother.

To complete this awesome head, hear again her beloved sing out of the *Song of Songs* in topographical praise of her eyes:

"...thine eyes like the fish pools in Heshbon..."

Well I dare say that there are fish, too, in the lake of Lyn Maelog that give Albion's Shulamite one sparkling green eye. Such is the delectable detail upon this bridal bed's coverlet of the heavens.

Now for the prize at the end of her outstretched arm and hand - the prize which must be Bardsey Island

Caernarfon marks the front of her neck, so just head west and let the coastline of Caenarfon Bay do the work of drawing her arm down to that lovely wrist at Nefyn. From here the same coastline draws the back of her knuckled hand and that menacing finger, tipped as it is by Braich y Pwll. Now we're in the palm of her hand, but there's a warning not to tarry long, for Hell's Mouth is written on the map - get caught here and that's where you'll end up! Her wonderfully hooked thumb has its nail at Trwyn Cilan; then the handiwork of Tremadog Bay completes the underside of this arm to Porthmadog in her armpit - sorry Porthmadog!

But look, her open hand has seemingly let go of her wheatsheaf - a sheaf that is now nowhere to be seen! Certainly her reflections at Glastonbury and Preseli each hold splendid examples of that ancient symbol of fertility. Thus the pathetic apology for such a symbol on Albion must be the minuscule Bardsey Island or Ynys Enlli, as the Welsh call it, which lies just off the tip of her finger and to which she most obviously points. Sad or what! Albion seemed for the first time to have short-changed me!

Maybe as an excuse, I could say that her sheaf has been threshed too many times by westerly gales and here's what's left. No, I wouldn't buy that either. So, grasping at straws, I phoned the Bardsey Island Trust and was told that there is evidence that the island was once larger than it is today, for the sea is in parts quite shallow around its coast, suggesting that there was once more dry land to be seen. Still pretty unconvincing? Tell me about it! There really was no concealing the fact that it seemed that instead of a whole sheaf, Albion had fobbed me off with no more than one measly single seed of Glastonbury and Preseli's glory.

Somewhat 'peed off' I went back to the book shelf to find what, if anything, Bardsey had going for it to make up for this disappointment, indeed, the first serious disappointment I had had since embarking upon this madcap adventure. Anyway, things bucked up considerably (with a rush of adrenaline thrown in) when I found out that this tiny island was, supposedly, where Merlin

now sleeps surrounded by the so-called *"Thirteen Treasures of Britain"*. Not a bad resting place for this most famous of all wizards, I thought, for he was, indeed, surrounded here by these 13 zodiacal treasures of Albion!

With this, I reminded myself that, as with her neck, nothing is for nothing on Albion, and because this whole miracle is obviously meant for our 21st century eyes, any shapes that once were visible, but aren't any longer, should really be of no consequence to us. Simply, and my line of thought seemed logical enough, because Albion had, up until now, never put a graphic foot wrong, perhaps as far as this great zodiac is concerned a wheatsheaf *never had been intended* as part of its overall message for this, its day of unveiling.

I decided then to really scrutinise the actual shape of Bardsey, and things were primed to go from 'miserable' to 'quite bloody marvellous'! My earlier jibe of 'one measly seed' was about to tie up in quite a remarkable way with something that was waiting to smack me right in the face. In short, I was about to see that we had in Bardsey something of far greater worth and relevance, for us living now, than a mouse-nibbled wheatsheaf.

Magnifying glass in hand I zeroed in on that tiny shape to which our pregnant Ceridwen is so vigorously pointing, and I emphasize that word *pointing*, for just look at that hand position; take an artist's word for it that its shape is not, and never was, intended for the actual 'holding' of a flapping bundle of straw! In fact, when one looks very closely at the whole hand we can further see that, not only is she pointing, but in the next movement is about to 'pluck' or 'pinch' up the particle that is Bardsey Island between her forefinger and that dauntingly hooked thumb.

Check out that face too. Full of cackling glee, isn't it? She must then, in that speck of Bardsey, have laid her piercing eye upon something far more wonderful and symbolic of fertility than a wheatsheaf could ever be. Indeed, I fancy she's trying to get us to look really closely at it, demanding we work out the riddle to which she so fervently points, a riddle she could only ever share at a time when men could see as minutely as she, via the eye of the microscope. What is more, if Merlin chose this tiny place, above all others in Albion's zodiac, in which to be enshrined, then the significant shape of Bardsey must be massively underlined as Merlin's personal gift to us who now peer at it with a new eye. Indeed, put that eye to a microscope and it will verify what our naked eye can now see for itself - Bardsey Island is one waggle-tailed *sperm*, the ultimate symbol of life and potent herald of new birth - that's what!

Look at it yourself - turn that shape this way and that but it can spell nothing else - a single precious seed is exactly what was intended all along!

Thus *Life! Life! Life!* is again proclaimed as the force behind our old Mother's kicking up of her legs in a mighty jig of delight, for as old as she is and as many babes as she has given birth to, the sight of that glittering seed is the perpetual symbol of her union with her beloved, for while sperms still vibrantly swim, there will always be life and hope upon this blue orb. Indeed, that tiny seed is the most wonderful and holy thing in the universe.

And if I have cracked the code of that shape, then how poetically breathtaking has the ancient sign of fertility been upgraded for us to see now, in a time when that most divine spark of all might be in its greatest peril. Indeed, is this the sobering reason behind the Earth Mother's pointing finger?

However, I can see you want more proof

Because we're looking in mirrors I now want to take you back to that archaic Welsh book the *Mabinogion*, and in particular to the story of Ceridwen, the Welsh Earth Mother, and of

her giving birth to the wizard Taliesin. In this we will find what is for me and my child *within* sparkling proof that we have, in Bardsey, found the seed of man rather than of wheat - and yet even these two shall become poetically one in the final analysis.

Before we hear the tale, though, something more on the mysterious Taliesin, whose silver tongue we've already heard in Leo, singing of his knowledge of a lion in the landscape.

On the face of it, Taliesin was a sixth-century Welsh bard or wise man, but reckoned by some historians to spring from a much earlier time, some even equating him as possibly the physical truth behind the mythical Merlin himself. So is it Taliesin and not Merlin who is buried on Bardsey Island? Certainly, some of our earliest written poetry is attributed to this bard; poetry that to this day continues to smoulder within the pages of the *Mabinogion*. And why smoulder? Well, we've already had the description of a very topographical lion, and Taliesin seems to delight in taking other opportunities to hint at what can only be more of his knowledge of *this* great zodiac of Albion throughout his strange bardic verse. In one poem, *The Hanes Taliesin*, for instance, he teases thus:

"I was with my King in the manger of the ass, I have been instructed in the whole system of the universe; I shall be 'til the Day of Judgment on the face of the earth."

And I for one believe every word he said! Why? Because I have been myself in that same manger, indeed, millions this very night will sleep snuggled up to that same King! I'd better explain.

We will learn later under Cancer, which is Albion's great all-enveloping ark, that hidden, and now almost forgotten, at the very heart of its heavenly constellation, is a cluster of faintly glowing stars which the ancients called *The Manger*. To strengthen this hint of Bethlehem, this same cluster is also partnered on either side by two stars known affectionately as *The Donkeys*. Thus Taliesin's riddle is perhaps not so outrageous after all, for his poetic meeting with the boy Messiah was not under Bethlehem's star, but must have been *upon* the land-stars that stud Albion's constellation of Cancer, which, and as though to emphasise the bard's teasing words, has Gemini's holy Christ child sleeping as though in a manger, arguably at its very centre!

So do you get the picture? That Welsh wizard may well have been alluding to the fact that he had visited Albion's babe of hills and flowers, there lying in its manger of the Cancerian ark. But wait, could even his bardic cunning be double-sided? Could he also be, at the same time, hinting to an actual *physical* meeting with Jesus when that boy passed through these same green constellations?

Anyway, time to hear now just how Taliesin acquired his wisdom in the first place, and as the *Mabinogion,* and indeed Bardsey Island give up their secrets, keep the pose of Albion's portrayal of Ceridwen in mind. Get ready to be delighted!

Ceridwen once brewed a *Cauldron (Grail) of Inspiration,* and from just a taste of its fabulous liquor one would know the mysteries of all things by *becoming* all things. "*And she herself, according to the books of astronomers, and in planetary hours, gathered every day the charm-bearing herbs*" for this elixir.

Anyway, she entrusted the job of stirring the Cauldron to a little boy called Gwion, warning him never to taste the contents. However, and as you might expect, he did manage to taste three drops by accident, whilst Ceridwen was out gathering herbs.

Seconds after Gwion had tasted the liquor the kitchen door flew open, Ceridwen had returned and saw instantly that mischief was about. In a flash the wrathful hag flew at poor little Gwion, and a fearful chase was on!

Over hills and streams they fled, but because

Gwion was himself now gifted in great wisdom, a grand game of wizardry versus witchery was to be played out. First, Gwion changed into a hare, but Ceridwen chased it as a greyhound. Next the boy, on reaching a river, became a fish, but she became an otter bitch, then he a bird and she a hawk, and just as she swooped down upon him for the kill, he saw below a heap of winnowed wheat in a barn and he dropped amongst it and became one of the grains. Not to be outdone, the wise woman became a black hen that immediately began to scratch at the grains, the way that only hens can, until she found the one with him in it - and promptly swallowed him!

After nine months Ceridwen gave birth to a handsome boy child and being the Mother of all Mothers she could not find it in her heart to kill him - as I fear she originally had in mind to do. So she popped him in a leather bag and cast him into the sea. On May eve the bag got caught in the fishing nets spanning the weir of Gwyddno Garanhir, a Welsh nobleman. The weir chronicled as being near the mouth of the River Dyfi.

Elphin, Gwyddno's son, was apparently not pleased to find there wasn't a single fish caught in the net, but, on untying the strange bag, was more than delighted for out jumped a child, not a bawling babe, but a small boy "*full of fair speech and prophesy*" and most beautiful to behold. Taliesin was the name they gave him, which meant Radiant Brow or Shining Forehead - obviously suggestive of his enlightened foresight.

So, look at the cover, and because the look of any plant seed that has sent forth its initial taproot is not too dissimilar in shape to the shape of Bardsey Island (indeed to a human sperm - *see following diagram*) I ask you if this colossal picture of Wales is not a graphic reanimation of the above tale. There's Ceridwen changed back from a black hen into her true shape, and just about to gobble up that grain containing Gwion - the future wizard

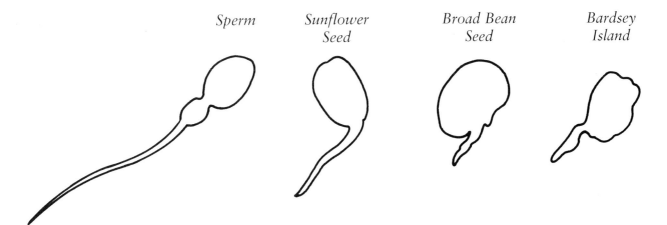

Sperm *Sunflower Seed* *Broad Bean Seed* *Bardsey Island*

Taliesin? But hear something more before you make your mind up.

No need for blushes, only another Wow!

First of all, and don't be shy, join me in putting a finger on Ceridwen's vagina - the portal place of love and birth of this Welsh giantess, the place where poetically so many babies' heads have popped out, along with roach and rowan trees, deer and dandelions, mountains and moths, and the rest of that paraphernalia of creation - her topographical yoni. Go to the line drawing and you can spot its inlet just above that raised up knee, and just a few miles south of her distinctive belly button. Found it? It is the mouth of the river Dyfi, its birthing waters flowing directly from out of this Earth Mother's almighty womb.

Remember that, after being thrown into the sea in a leather bag, the child floated into a netted weir; the exact location of that weir is not recorded in the tale but was said to have been somewhere between the mouth of the river Dyfi and Aberystwyth. Now if you look at any map of this area, irrespective of this land lady's bodily parts, you too may conclude that the most obvious place for that weir would be upon the river Dyfi itself, as between it and Aberystwyth there really isn't much river action at all, certainly none to match the splendour of the Dyfi. Thus, if I can persuade

you to agree, watch again the land poetry confirm the legend, for if found on the Dyfi this divine child was indeed reborn in the salmon net which hung across Ceridwen's yoni - thus he was, in full topographical truth, reborn from out of the knowledge of THIS dancing goddess of valleys and mountains!

Some, however, may say that my locating of Taliesin's rebirth at the mouth of the river Dyfi is taking a liberty, arguing that if that weir of Gwyddno Garanhir *had* been on the river Dyfi it would have been jolly well stated as so in the *Mabinogion.*

Fair comment. But time and myriad retellings of a myth can sometimes render actual locations a touch fog-bound. That said, I also knew that if this weir were nowhere near Ceridwen's vagina, my tying up of this part of the tale to the landscape perhaps wouldn't have quite such a strong case. Of course, I could have left the matter shrouded in mist and therefore hedged the bets in favour of the Dyfi; that said, you must by now know that you're talking to Mr Doubting Thomas himself, and, by Christ, he himself wanted convincing! So I went back to the *Mabinogion* and began trawling through the notes of Lady Charlotte Guest, the original translator of the texts. In her appendix to that tale of Taliesin's birth I found exactly what I needed to legitimately include this Dyfi/yoni theory in my book.

This subsidiary tale has Taliesin, some time

after his rebirth in Gwyddno's weir, enjoying a spot of fishing from a coracle. However, an Irish pirate ship sails up alongside and abducts him. But Taliesin, while the pirates *were at the height of their drunken mirth*" manages to sneak back to his coracle. I will let Lady Guest tell you what happened next: "*...he had no alternative but to be driven at the mercy of the sea, in which state he continued for a short time, when the coracle stuck to the point of a pole in the weir of Gwyddno, Lord of Ceredigion, in Aberdyvi; and in that position he was found, at the ebb, by Gwyddno's fishermen.*"

Know that Aberdyvi is today's Aberdyfi, and Aberdyfi is the place that sits directly on the river Dyfi's yoni/mouth - and with it I think the land's explicit picture has made its incredible point!

Ceridwen's Grain of Truth

Taliesin's marvellous mythological conception and birth, and its message for us today, can now be seen to be unquestionably cast into the very fabric of his Mother, the land; no more a tall tale but a gigantic physical and dancing truth. Again, see how Ceridwen's chase still goes gloriously on, watch her constantly reaching for that vital spark of life - yes, in the story a grain of wheat, but now metamorphosed for new eyes into a sperm. Both images hover within the Mother's grasp as the one supreme logo of the wonder of life, yet which, at this very moment, hangs in the balance. For are we not altering the genetics of the wheat while tweaking the last drop of divinity out of the sperm? Thus, it seems there is no time left for riddles; everyone must become an initiate of the truth of this earth and the gift of a life upon it before it is too late.

Later, and far to the north on this vast zodiacal clock, upon a lonely moonlit bridge, we shall watch the joint symbolism of both sperm and grain flood as one in yet another glittering masterpiece of living land poetry. On this bridge we shall again remember the knowledge won by the boy Gwion and his lesson to us on how we, too, if we allow ourselves to be swallowed into the great mystery, may learn to glide with the fish, soar as birds, and with glowing brows, speak with fair speech and prophesy.

After sacrificing ourselves by plunging into the deep guts or mystery of the Mother Earth, it is intended that we shall at the end of it rise to the dizzy heights of what shall be the full wonder of our own physical nature. This is charmingly sign-posted by taking a peep at the place-name within her grasping claw-like hand, for in it is betrayed exactly where little Gwion was also heading once given up to her clutches; it is Hell's Mouth, obvious portal to the underworld and thus the beginning of that journey which can only be towards enlightenment and rebirth! And there should be no surprise that deep dark hell should be the initial starting place for one seeking to fly so high, for mythology is littered with heroes who also freely ventured through the jaws of the underworld to seek the crown of self-knowledge. They knew that before they could attain the spiritual heights they must first experience their equally beautiful physical depths. And this plunge to the underworld was, I imagine, symbolic of the unrealised depths of one's inner self.

It seems then for us accursed, but perhaps ultimately lucky ones, who are upon the brink, that this underworld, frightening to some, awe-inspiring to others, that forgotten plane of buried wisdom, is now brought to the surface in the shape of Albion. Its gates are thrown open to all - should we have the guts to walk through the wisdom of the past and into the future before the clock strikes twelve.

And if you still don't understand, hear your Mother shout at you from out of that same hellishly beautiful mouth: *"Listen! Gwion/Taliesin/Merlin is still buried at the heart of that solitary grain of truth just as the Bardsey legend says he is - so follow his lead, taste of my Cauldron, this starry broth of Albion, and I'll chase you back through the memory of all you have lost - I'll run you as a hare, as a fish, and as a bird; I will chase you until you realise that you are all these things. Then, too, will your brow glow with the expanded perception that you are God. Never again will you injure this good earth, or indeed your fellow men."*

Simply. In Bard-sey we are being permitted to see as the Bard-*saw*!

Hellish - and yet the presence of the dove will mark the journey as holy

Before we journey around the rest of her lusciously swaying lumps and bumps, one last look at that river Dyfi, for I'd like to clinch its sacred place in the scheme of things.

If I have rightly read its purpose in both Ceridwen's anatomy and the story of Taliesin's winning of wisdom, then we may not be pushing our luck in looking for its own personal mark of sacredness, for such a birthing water worthy of carrying Gwion from dark womb to radiant rebirth, both in story and topographical fact, must be blessed in its own right with a resplendent signpost. We shall not have to look far, as the English name for this river is the Dovey - of course meaning *dove*; then add to this the fact that *Aber*, as in Aberdyfi and Aberdovey, means *mouth*, we suddenly get the message that Taliesin was born out of the *mouth of the dove* - that very bird which was the key (remember the Libran dove) to our, and perhaps *his* too, stepping through the door of Albion's underworld miracle! And as we add all this up, surely too our earlier musing upon that dove-encoded Awen or Word of God (*see Libra*) begins to gel into even more significance.

It seems then that our guiding dove has found yet another initiatory gate of rebirth through which to coo its glad tidings, to the effect that from out of some act of perfect harmony or balance (just perfect for Libra) has been born another wonder. Listening to it I cannot help but think, too, of the dove of the Annunciation - the one that signalled the birth of another divine child to another mother. But again, place this river of the dove but a few miles south and it would be pouring from her knee and as a consequence totally invalidated for the purpose I have identified it for. Seeing it flow from her yoni, however, is another miracle amongst the many - too many even at this still relatively early stage of our journey, I think, to argue away as a string of 'flukes'.

Defining the body

Let's now conga around the rest of her - starting with those pendulous breasts!

From Portmadog in her arm pit, cross the estuary and sail down the descriptive coast to Barmouth, upon her stout and squared off nipple! After Barmouth take either the A496, or a boat up the Afon Mawddach to Llanelltyd and there complete the right breast.

For the left one, start at Trawsfynydd and head south on the A470 until it curls wonderfully with the waters of the Afon Wnion around the hamlets of Dolrhyd and Pens-y-coed, upon the nipple itself, then continue with the A94 to Bala and completion. However, this left breast is not only drawn by roads as it can just as easily be more fluidly prescribed by earth's own milk. From Trawsfynydd then, take the river Eden (intriguingly, a river of this same name draws virtually the entire right side of Albion's Christ) which outlines it down to Ganllwyd - and what a lovely river name by which to draw the milk and honeyed breast of the goddess! The rivers Mawddach and Wnion then combine to draw the brilliantly pouting nipple. Cymmer Abbey, like a child itself, suckles at this place. Lake Bala and several streams all then lend a hand in completing it. Thus the pair can be traced almost entirely by life-giving water.

Note: find upon the right breast Harlech, where the severed head of Bran (see Sagittarius) gave verbal succour to his people for a while.

Belly laughs!

From near that left nipple of Dolrhyd, cross the river and follow it out into Cardigan Bay which draws her bulging belly down to Aberdyfi and its river Dyfi. Near Tywyn, though, do notice her water-filled navel, and hear another verse from the *Song of Songs*:

"Thy navel is like a goblet which wanteth not liquor:
thy belly is like an heap of wheat set about with lilies."
SONG OF SONGS, Chapter7 Verse2

That description of *this* Shulamite of the land is gorgeous, and so spot on. Wheat really does poetically fill her belly in that overlaid inference of little Gwion, himself encapsulated in a single grain, and who bulged her belly for nine months. And look at her navel, just a little north of Tywyn, and it too *"wanteth not liquor"* for being the largest body of water of any note in this area Broadwater has been scooped out like a dish, exactly where it should be, right in her navel, and is, I imagine, replenished regularly by the river Dysynni.

Continuing from Tywyn, stay either on the A493, or opt for a coracle on the river Dyfi, and, heading upstream, imagine another journey in honour of Gwion's. Imagine taking a boat from Bardsey Island to Ceridwen's

grasping fingers, then, as the name in the palm of her hand suggests, on into her mouth. Thereafter on land, sliding down her gizzard and into her vast domed belly and then out again with the flow of the Dyfi/Dove. What a wonderful circular journey it would be - as is life itself. For now, though, just take note that by going up the Dyfi we have poetically been within the womb of the Mother.

Her heart, by the way, I would like to think is the magnificent Mount Snowdon, the highest peak in this entire land zodiac.

Ceridwen really does not end here though, as to my artist's eye there seems such a strong case to see two brilliantly proportioned legs daintily skipping to some dance of creation, revealing not only a pair of lovely knees but stockings too! While on her feet we'll find what appear to be clogs. The detail really is astounding.

Upon her knee sits Taliesin

Incidentally, I found that on her left knee is the legendary last resting place of her son Taliesin, fittingly called Bedd Taliesin. Though, mythologically speaking, perhaps he only sat here to lay his head against the Mother's breast while she sang to him of the mysteries of stars, snowdrops, sperm and of all else.

There is certainly a magnificent view of his birthing river Dyfi from here. Indeed, I saw it for myself on a sultry July evening, the Dyfi glowing with the colour of beaten copper. My family and I had found my old friend's bed - a domed pillow of earth set amid a sea of sweet-smelling new mown hay. Propped up, an unspectacular slab marks the spot, though a curious sense of smiles upon the air more than compensates.

At the edge of the mound grew just one clump of exquisite harebells; each bell was of that rarest blue, all except for one bell, for on the same stem as the blue there hung a bell of purest white. On the crown of the mound itself clung a solitary spray of English stonecrop, tiny white five-pointed stars; a constellation for him whose life I know turned, and still turns, with this zodiac underfoot.

Silently I thanked that old seer for the blazing comet trail that he has left behind him upon Albion's starry wheel; without him I would have been lost many times. As we left I laid upon his slab a farewell bunch of foxgloves in acknowledgement of his charming cunning!

Now for those jigging legs

First, though, the rippling hem of her dress, that flies high in the whirl of her jig.

Start at the mouth of the river Dyfi and head inland. At Glandyfi follow the county line between Dyfed and Powys south and you'll see what a beautiful rippled hem it makes as it lifts over her raised knee; continue following it until it passes over the river Yr Allt. Now it's the country road to Rhayader, here picking up the A44 to cross her right knee to Crossgates, in the bend of that knee. We're still following its ripple as we continue with the A44 to Walton. Here we pick up the border line between Powys and Shropshire plus old Offa's Dyke, which again we find lending a hand in defining a giant. Follow this route north to Llangedwyn and on to the south of Oswestry, where the county line and the many waterways that separate Powys from South Clwyd unite to carry the rush of it away towards Taurus.

Note: if you wanted to be naughty the road from Glandyfi right through Caersws, and then beyond through Newtown and Welshpool, thereafter joining the county boundary to Llanymynech, gives us an alternative hem line and an altogether more risqué garment!

And the high stepping left leg

Start at Caersws on the A470 just west of Newtown. Head west and join the flow of both the A489 and the river Dyfi. At Eglwysfach, on her knee, the road becomes the coastal A487 and this, with the sea on your right, takes you down to Aberaeron at the start of her clog. From here just follow the coast down to Gwybert on her toe. The river Teifi from Gwybert fluently shapes the sole through to Lampeter upon her heel.

Across country now to draw her calf muscle; so pass through Llangeitho, Ysbyty Ystwyth, Devil's Bridge, and Ponterwyd in the bend of her knee. If you go from here to Aberystwyth, you'll have drawn her stocking top.

Back at Ponterwyd, it's now the A44 to Llangurig from where the A470 will take us back to where we started at Caersws.

Her right thigh starts at Llangurig. Head south on the river Wye that, faultlessly, draws her bump of a knee around Gwasteddyn Hill, then tumbles down her shin to Llyswen.

Now the A478 takes over and takes us south to Tretower; and on up to Talybont-on-Usk at the start of her clog, so we can follow the shape of the Talybont reservoir. Cross now the Taf Fechan river before crossing over the A470 to join the A4059. Follow this road around the toe of her clog and look for the A465 through Merthyr Tydfil to Abergavenny on her heel, after which go a few more miles on the A465 to just past Pandy where you'll pick up Offa's Dyke (yet again!) to Newchurch on her calf.

From Newchurch (I'm sorry it's a touch of artist's licence here) take a short hike across country so as to make contact with the A44, then onto Crossgates in the bend of her knee. The A483 will now easily finish this leg off to Newtown. Oh, and I nearly forgot that the river Severn from Newtown to Welshpool washes the curve of her bottom. Sorry Mum!

Stand back and look at her, an explosion of the spice of life! Her animated proportions designed not to cause a hush but a rousing, "*Yeeeah!*"

One last look into her face - and there detect another flicker of pain

Having now danced ourselves around her lovely figure, we should, I guess, be left with a lingering smile - but for me it doesn't linger long. You see I can't help going back to that face where I fear there is as much pain as there is delight.

Her head, you see, although now known as the Isle of Anglesey was once called Mona - another enigmatic lady if ever there was one! However, in this Welsh lady's case Mona was, I believe, pronounced as *Mooni*, and rightly so for what could be more feminine than the moon to light that face - her very own celestial bauble which, for age upon age, has been seen as so intimate to the mother and womanhood the world over. Indeed, remember that it was its very phases that inspired our ancestors to visualise their triple-faced goddess - so how beautifully apt it was to have her face signed as Mooni. Again, another slice of sublime coincidence.

And the pain? Well, it was to her Mooni head that the last of the Druids fled, pursued by the Roman legions under Suetonius, in AD 61. His legions crossed the Menai Strait and put not only those old men to the sword, but I sense beheaded the Mother religion of this land at the same time. On that day upon the very head of the moon goddess was the holy feminine force historically put to the sword - a blow perpetuated, perhaps, with each tide that spills through the Menai Strait.

Smiles, however, are never far away on Albion, for even in the silence of the above discovery I couldn't help a smile, albeit an ironic one, at this disarming expertise of the land in recording events both mythological and historical. This last passionate flight of the Mother's sons could have been to anywhere - to the head of Taurus, to the fist of mighty Sagittarius, even to the heart of the unicorn; but as any frightened children would, they sought the soothing words of their Mother. True, their flight was in vain, yet what better death for them than at their Mother's lips. So uncanny this, that one cannot help but muse whether those Druids knew exactly where they ran to.

Whatever, on that fateful day, the Mother and her followers melted into Albion's every sod, into every acorn, into every grain of wheat, and into everyone who has ever since filled with untranslatable longing, or even tears, at the sight of any one of nature's myriad wonders. I hope, for you, Albion comes to break your heart with similar bliss.

Lastly a confession - Hugh Hughes spotted her before me!

Whilst working in his studio in Caernarfon, upon the throat of Ceridwen, Hugh Hughes returned from an artist's reverie upon a map of his own locale and produced, just for fun mind, a rendering of what his sudden insight must have shown him. When more than 100 years later I saw what he'd done, it had me thumping the air and under my breath shouting "Yes!" for my own artist's eye, let alone my sanity, had there and then been totally vindicated! So, I am now immensely glad to announce that I am *not* the first to see Anglesey as the bonneted head of an old lady, or the bulk of Wales as the rest of her body!

It came about like this: back in my writing up of Sagittarius, my research had taken me one Saturday morning into the cloistered and cavernous silence of London's map library, part of the British Museum, itself embedded in the great thumping heart of that particular giant.

There I was then, smiling from ear to ear at

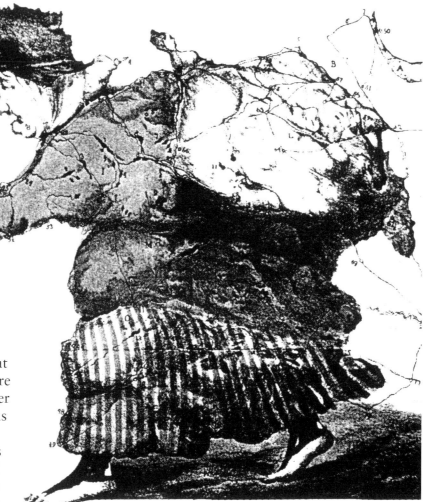

the antique artwork before me in the shape of the already reproduced illustration entitled *Geography Bewitched*. (*See Sagittarius*) Of course, I was amazed, but delighted too, for I had in Robert Dighton found another who had also seen the beginning of Albion, albeit whimsically misread. However, my smiles were soon to be sucked back in with a sharp intake of breath as out of the library's vaults, and delivered to my quiet corner by the helpful, though unexcitable staff member, who had no idea what he had unearthed, came an even more astonishing picture by yet another artist whose eyes had seen exactly as mine had.

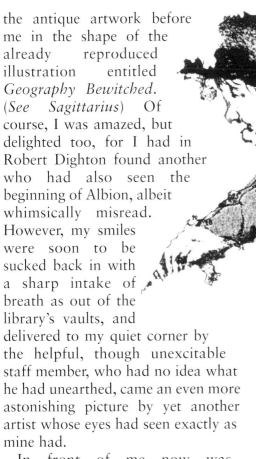

In front of me now was ceremoniously placed a virtual replica of my Virgo, the only difference being that Hugh, using perhaps the less-than-perfect maps of his time, had not seen her dancing nakedness, so had properly clothed her from head to toe. Oh, and another thing he did was to make her boobs become her belly, and her belly her knees; while Taurus he saw as no more than a sack upon her back! But my, her whole head and bonnet was a perfect mirror image of that which hung on my own studio wall; her outstretched arm was also exactly as I'd seen, although the artist had not made use of the coastal promptings to pronounce that hooked finger and thumb - again perhaps only owing to poor map reference. Interestingly, though, he had for some reason felt compelled to weave a strange and ghostly menagerie of all

Dame Venodotia - North Wales.
By Hugh Hughes. The British Library

manner of creatures into her clothes, including goats, dogs and rabbits, half-hidden amongst the shadowy folds. Witch-like he had certainly made her and in whose demeanour one cannot help but catch the scent of Ceridwen herself!

Needless to say, I was, and still am, thrilled by her company.

But John may have beaten the pair of us

For the last piece of overlapping imagery I'd like you to now try to see through the Revelation-filled eyes of John:

"And I, John, saw the holy city, new Jerusalem, coming down from God out of heaven, prepared as a bride adorned for her husband."
REVELATION, Chapter 22, Verse 2

Surely in heaven's name this island, this New Jerusalem, this entire earthly zodiac, *is* She - the Bride of God adorned in a gown of heaven's constellations, sewn together by Britain's spring flowering hedgerows. Is this John's Revelation made breathtakingly physical?

We now go east, towards the bellowing bull of Taurus.

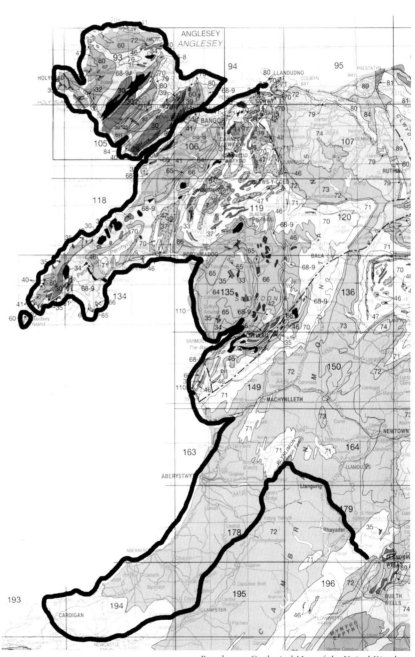

VIRGO

What a colourful geologically grinning mask our Mother wears, aptly swiped by so many sedimentary warpaint-like streaks, or is it more akin to those strangely terrifying masks seen flitting along the canals of Venice in the dusk of their somewhat eerie yet enchanting carnival, when for a few hours something gorgeously supernatural stalks the laughing throngs. How Ceridwen would love to shape change to her heart's content amongst them! However, also note how the riotousness of those sedimentary eddies suddenly slow and spiral more placidly around the area of her right breast - time for peace and contentment?

Based upon Geological Map of the United Kingdom by permission of the British Geological Survey, IPR/26-11C

CHAPTER 7

TAURUS

● *The Bull* ●

★

*The seventh giant
along the way*

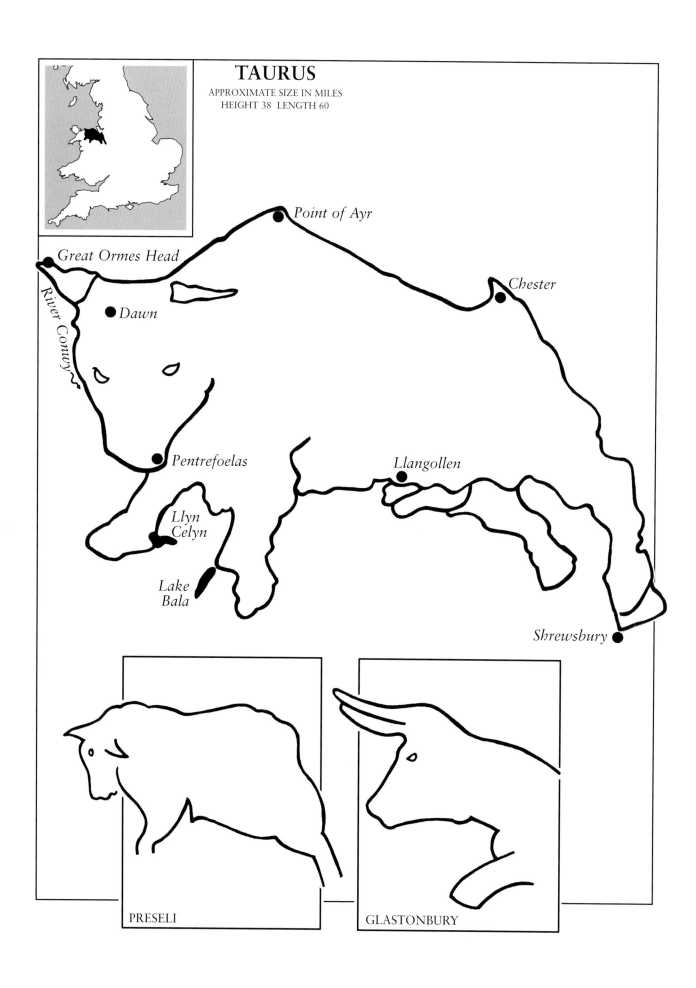

TAURUS

APPROXIMATE SIZE IN MILES
HEIGHT 38 LENGTH 60

Point of Ayr

Great Ormes Head

River Conwy

Chester

● Dawn

● Pentrefoelas

Llangollen

Llyn
Celyn

Lake
Bala

Shrewsbury

PRESELI

GLASTONBURY

Even the Bull bellows "Beware of rising waters"

"Demandest though O Britain, to what this can meetly be applied!
Before the lake of the son of Erbin, let thy Ox be stationed.
The sacred ox of the patriarch is stationed before the lake"

Taliesin

GENERAL AREA: THE NORTHEAST CORNER OF WALES. THE RIVER CONWY CLEANLY CUTS THE PROFILE OF THE HEAD, WHICH HAS THE GREAT ORME'S HEAD PENINSULA FOR ITS RIGHT HORN. HIS REAR HOOF GOES AS FAR SOUTH AS SHREWSBURY IN ENGLAND.

hat a magnificently masculine bull is revealed here, although up until my Geminian discovery, which lead me to find that all these giant figures had complete inland bodies (except for Sagittarius), I had for years been more than happy with just the sight of his menacing head, back, and right fore leg, all masterfully defined by river and sea.

Curiously enough, my initial view of a somewhat truncated bull was precisely as the original astrological artists saw Taurus in the heavens, and Glastonbury's version shows no more. Although, because this bull of Albion resides in Wales, and Preseli's own version is virtually complete in its form, I should have guessed he would not be outdone! Thus these Welsh bulls are proportionately almost mirror images of each other.

His actual positioning within this out-of-sequence zodiac is, I feel, quite significantly descriptive of the role our ancestors endowed upon him. He not only stands next to the Earth Mother/Virgo but seems provocatively to nudge her too. He is utterly justified in this stance, for he was traditionally seen as the consort of the Goddess, the epitome of the vital male principle in the great fertility merry-go-round.

The inseparable lovers

Those two inseparable lovers from ancient Egypt, Isis, *Queen of Earth and Heaven,* and her beloved husband Osiris, *Lord of All,* were at times represented by the cow and bull, a divine pairing that would guarantee the eternal regeneration of all life. The beautiful Isis is still

seen today in hundreds of depictions as being crowned by the horns of the cow, the crescent moon-like horns carrying the disc of the sun resplendent between them. Together now in this Welsh Virgo and Taurus we see these two eternal lovers coupled forever, and the promise, I hope, of earth's ongoing fertility, underwritten in the stars.

It was the god Zeus who, in Greek mythology, shape-shifted into a bull to win the love of the goddess Europa. The story goes that while Europa was out picking flowers a herd of cows passed close by, being led by a magnificent bull (Zeus) whose breath was saffron-scented. Europa, struck by the beauty and gentle manner of the beast, decorated him with flowers and climbed upon his mighty back. But once there, the bull charged headlong into the sea carrying the goddess with him to the island of Crete where she became his lover.

With the name Crete upon the page I cannot resist bringing back the weird and wonderful theories of Comyns Beaumont, for he believed that Crete was another place that received much of its mythos second-hand from Britain, some time after the deluge. Certainly, his theory comes to life if you now poetically overlay the 'island of Crete' upon this Isle of Albion and then rest your eyes on Taurus/Zeus and Virgo/Europa cavorting massively across Wales.

There is another myth we may visually overlay upon this corner of Wales: it seems that Ariadne, yet another goddess of the Greeks, whose name meant the *Very Fertile Mother of Barley*, chose not to consummate her marriage with Theseus but rather with Dionysus, the bull god, fertility god of the land.

Thus, whether you call her Isis, Europa, Ariadne or any other of the dozens of names the Great Goddess has worn, she is, all one and the same, the Mother/Lunar-Cow Goddess who ritually copulates with Osiris, Zeus, Dionysus and a phalanx of other male deities, all similarly personified as the solar bull. Because of this act, the Hellenic barley rolled like the sea, the Nile yearly burst its banks, and the wheel of life turned in splendour. In Albion's sympathetic and loving placement of Virgo and Taurus, these eternal incarnations of the Earth Mother and the Sky Father are perfectly bedded side by side. Out of sequence with their reflection in the heavens they may well be, but on earth, and at this vital time, their coming together must be a sign which nature wishes us to read out aloud. So see *Life* written in letters 38 miles high, for that is what this bull and his starry brethren have come to bellow for and to celebrate.

Defining the Body

In the mapping of Taurus I will start with the parts I have seen for many years, the head and foreleg. So let's begin upon that great jutting sea-sharpened horn they call Great Orme's Head.

The clue in the cave

What a strange name tips the perfect spike of this peninsula horn: Orme - deriving from the Norse for *dragon* or *sea monster*. It seems then they had the sniff of a beast when naming this point of land, and doesn't Orme itself sound like horn? Well it does to me, and perhaps someone else, too, when they gave the cave on the very tip of this horn of Taurus the name, Hornby Cave - in the mirror *Cave by Horn!* Funny isn't it - yet we should take it seriously, too!

One other word on this lovely horn: I understand that this whole headland is geologically composed of a creamy-coloured limestone; so what an apt colour from the Mother's landscaping palette by which to highlight her bull's horn.

From that horn westwards his great broad head now needs only water to delineate its unquestionable shape. Let the coast take our eye easily into the charmed river Conwy, for no other defining line is needed for the next 25 miles and more, because on its own, this river will deftly sculpt this masterpiece of a bull's profile from horn to hoof.

Join me now in sailing down his great head

With an incoming tide, and beneath a star-filled sky on a warm Taurean May evening, with the sound of cattle lowing somewhere amongst indigo fields which roll down to the river's bank, let us drift languidly along the inky Conwy in an imagined boat. The boat shall be shaped like an upturned crescent moon in honour of the Sacred Cow/Mother and her consort the Bull/Father, and we shall sit between those glittering horns.

From here we go south, letting the current use us like a pencil, which describes upon the landscape the same sinuous line as the stars above described to the eyes and psyche of those first astrological artists. Like Tennyson's Lady of Shallot *"Under tower and balcony, By garden wall and gallery"* we pass beneath the battlements of proud Conwy Castle on Virgo's western side of the bank. Easily, as in a dream, we glide down the vale of the Conwy, stroking the vast solar forehead of this celestial god on earth until, sailing through the spangled reflections of Llanrwst, and with an inspired will of its own, this knowing water manoeuvres our moon ark into a subtle indentation to the east, precisely where it should, to draw the dip where the forehead ends and the muzzle begins its taper, at about the level of the eyes. Llanrwst is the right eye, whilst the left I've targeted between Gwytherin and Pandy Tudur.

The proportioning of the head here is near perfect, even seeming to suggest a telephoto-like foreshortening as though to emphasise, from where we view, his overall 'head down and preparing to charge' pose.

Gliding down the straight muzzle, feel our boat now veer to edge to the east, opposite Betws-y-coed, and begin the big curve that will take us around the nose. But now hear the roar of tumbling water before us for we are in sight of the delightful waterfall at Conwy Falls - that's right, pouring directly from the tip of his nose like snorted mucus! What gorgeously graphic imagery we have here, and what a bullishly broad snout it is too. As we sail by, spare another smile with me over the name of another river which adds its own flow to that mucus-like outfall, it's called the afon Machno - a bullish attempt to snort *"Macho'* I wonder...? Perhaps not!

The current now hugs the A5, but just past Padog take note that from Pentrefoelas the A543 goes north to draw his lower jaw to Bylchau.

At Padog, notice how we're punted almost sharply to the southwest - sharply but right on proportionate cue, for we now leave the nose and begin our watery way down that straight right foreleg. The B4407 runs at our side for double confirmation. However, halfway down this leg we have unfortunately to tie-up our boat and go with that B4407 down to Pont yr Afon-Gam, at the tip of the hoof. Afterwards it'll be the A391 east, but do look out for the place where this road joins the A4212. Another river, this time the Prysor, will guide us into Llyn Celyn and with it, the completion of that hoof.

Once there feast your eyes at the way the lake indents the rear of this hoof perfectly to suggest the ankle joint, forcing men, too, to emphasise the same anatomically correct feature by introducing a sharp and sudden hairpin bend into their A4212, confirming the line that the lake had already insisted upon.

But again, applaud the river Conwy and the magic it has performed, almost single handedly, in bringing these stars of Taurus down to earth. Indeed, he is so clear that the rest of his body is but a bonus!

Now the rest of him

This right foreleg along with the head, single horn, and great humped back, which follows the coast from Colwyn Bay all along to Chester on the river Dee, was, as already mentioned, all that I (and those first artist-astrologers) saw of this sign originally. Only years later it again turned out to be the case that once the outer edge of the puzzle had been found, the inner clues would just fall into place as a natural matter of course.

His humped back, I think you will agree, needs no guidance from me for it is all coastal and therefore utterly pictorial, even down to that characteristic conical tuft of shoulder hair, so common a sight to Spain's matadors! On Albion someone marked this tuft as the Point of Ayr, or did they really have hair in mind?

Now that we are on his back, let us continue eastwards to trace the rest of his bulk and finish where we left off on the ankle bone of Llyn Celyn.

So plummet down the hump and into the river Dee, or, in Welsh, the Afon Dyfrdwy, and from Chester we'll draw his hind quarters and left hind leg. Leave Chester on the A41 down to Whitchurch and, as you do, look back on a lovely curved leg joint. Now take the A49 and old Roman road down to where it meets the B5063 going to Shawbury, High Ercall, and on to Shrewsbury via the B5062. This completes the rear delineation of the left hind leg and underhoof that dips magically into Shrewsbury's river Severn to cool off. From Shrewsbury, and to finish off this leg, we now head north on the A528, then the B5476 to Wem to pick up the B5063. At Northwood just follow the county boundary line between Shropshire and Clwyd westwards and that should finish it off nicely.

Where the county line passes near Erbistock we need to pick up the A539 to Llangollen and then the A5 to draw his underbelly. After Corwen we want to head south to draw the rear of his left foreleg, so follow the B4401 past Llandrillo to where we can continue with the county boundary between Clwyd and Gwynedd. Later, where this border touches

the border between Powys and Gwynedd, we'll go southwest a little to draw the underside of this left hoof. Skirt now the Aberhirnant Forest upon that graphically pawing hoof, whilst looking out for an unmarked road that will carry us north through Aber Hirnant to Bala.

Just beyond Bala look now for tiny Llanfor from where a track seems to be heading off northwest but then appears to fizzle out. Anyway, my artist's licence allows me to carry on its general course but leaning perhaps more to the north in the hope of meeting the Clwyd/Gwynedd border under the shadow of Foel Goch. Now follow this border west to draw his chest before heading off southwest to Carneddy Filiast, another mountain. From here follow your nose two miles across country, using the Nant Ty-nant stream as your guide, and back to that lovely ankle kink of Llyn Celyn on his right leg.

Note: by the way, and as you may have guessed, my use of that tongue-in-cheek 'artist's licence' is no more than me using a little imagination! Rarely, however, throughout the course of this Grand Tour have I had the need to indulge in its use, for the way around these giants is more often than not faultlessly prescribed, indeed, these moments of flashing the 'licence' have accounted for but a handful of miles out of the many hundreds we shall travel. That said, when I have had to make short hikes across unmarked ground it is only because the scale of my maps fail to show any feature there to guide me otherwise. This lack of apparent guidance, however, does not mean to say that when one is actually in situ on the ground there is not some subtle feature on the immediate terrain to guide the way, whether it be a dry stone wall, a line of trees, or any other thing that would take the eye and lead the seeker along the right path after all.

No blushes please as we now take a hike around his awesome genitalia!

From Llangollen take the unmarked country road to skirt around Plas Newydd, past the telecommunications aerial, and then via Froncysyllte to run into the A5 and a little beyond to Pont Cysyllte. For his testicles, start at Pont Cysyllte and run down into the A5 again, this time going east with it until you can take the B4500 to Glyn Ceiriog. A little way beyond will have us back upon the tip of his phallus - and at a stroke complete the ultimate intent of his fertile purpose in the mythological scheme of things.

From our previous travels upon Virgo we should know that nature does not blush, indeed, she seems to revel in such displays of fertility, and with a smile I must again mention those weighty testicles, for standing proudly upon them I discovered another wonderful signpost and bastion of masculine pride, this in the shape of Chirk Castle no less!

The last leg of this journey

The right hind leg starts behind the testicles. Start at Knolton on the A528, then south through Ellesmere to Burlton on the corner of the hoof. The under part of his hoof is shaped by the B4397, to where it crosses the river Perry. Now follow the Perry northwest until it meets the A495, but soon picking up the B5069 though Gobowen and on back to Chirk.

His tail by the way, seems to be out of view behind that hind leg, however, that conical shape in and around Chester seems to suggest its presence. Oh, and if you'd like a second horn, one can be suggested from Abergele on the north coast to St Asaph on the A55, then back to Abergele on the B5381 and A548.

More bellows of approval?

Lastly, two more bellows of what I would like to think is the land's own approval towards my sighting of a bull here.

The first bellow sounds like 'Baal'

The first of these bellows I heard booming out of the research of Dudley Wright, as documented in his book *Druidism*.

On the eve of Beltane, 30 April, when the sun has entered Taurus, the Druids held a festival in commemoration of the leaving of the ark by their Noah, one Hu the Mighty, and his return to *terra firma*. Next morning, being May Day, they would then perform a ceremony that would re-enact this event, and it went something like this: oxen were tethered near a lake, in the centre of which was an island (probably a raft of sorts), which was regarded as holy and upon which a shrine or ark was kept. This was then drawn across the shallow water to dry ground by the oxen by means of a chain, whilst the best singers in the district gathered on the bank and chanted the *Cainc yr Yehain Banawg*, which was said to resemble the lowing kine and the rattling of chains!

What a haunting choral spectacular that must have been echoing around the newly greening valleys. However, when reading this, it immediately struck me that Albion's giant bull has lake Bala directly in front of, and touching, his left foreleg (not to mention Llyn Celyn at his right foreleg) and thus, pictorially speaking, he too stands as written - tethered before his lake.

Now, I don't know if the muddy bed of Lake Bala still clings to a few golden trappings fallen from a long sunken ritual raft, neither do I know what, if anything, Bala means in Welsh, but what I do know is that another name for Beltane was Baal - close enough for my comfort, if no one else's! Add to this the knowledge that the last three principal locations in Wales where the Druids performed these ceremonies, according to Wright, were Pontypridd, Borth and, would you believe,

Bala - and I've got every right to get excited!

To pile on the pressure of Bala's place in Albion's scheme of things, let me add the poet Robert Graves' own weight of knowledge when he says that Baal was in fact the white bull-god Baal Zephon, worshipped by the Canaanites as king of the Northern Otherworld (Britain?) His name was eventually corrupted into Beelzebub!

For me then, the bull colossus of northern Wales is tethered precisely where he should be - by the lake that reflects both his bowed head and his own true name.

And the last bellow is to the dawn!

This second bellow of approval is for me the loudest of the lot - ear-splitting enough to be heard even in the Egypt of 6500 years ago!

Let us venture towards this resonant bellow while chewing over another riddle from him who will never be silent on matters of Albion; listen again to the Bard of Albion, Taliesin/Merlin, indeed, listen to the bard in bull's clothing!

> *"Then let the giver of the mead-feast cause to be proclaimed*
> *I am the cell; I am the opening chasm;*
> *I am the Bull Becr Lled.*
> *I am the repository of the Mystery;*
> *I am the place of reanimation...*
> *As for him who knows not the ox-pen*
> *of the bards*
> *May fifteen thousand overpower and afflict him at once."*

I discovered this magic-loaded verse in Mary Caine's book, along with the translation of his strange self-proclaimed title of the *Bull Becr Lled,* which for hikers of a topographical bull will become music to our ears. According to Mary it means *Bull of Dawn.* OK, nothing instantly wonderful in that, but please bear with me. Apparently, it seems that this bull of

Dawn was an image revered from about 4500 BC when for some 2000 years Taurus *'Opened the year with its horns'.* Caine's own source, a Mr Davis (she doesn't give me his first name, though his own book *Mythology and Rites of British Druids* was published way back in 1809) relates this to the new year/sun rising at that time in the astral ox-pen of Taurus at the spring equinox.

With such imagery in mind can we then visualise the disc of the sun poetically rising on that Taurean dawn, upon that magical New Year's Day, actually *between* the bull's horns? Certainly it would have been a potent image, and indeed one emphasised and cast in solid gold for the 'Sun between the Horns' crown of Isis, the Mother.

And so with this visual spectacle teasing my imagination, my childlike self became alert and prodded me to 'take a chance', and go and scrutinise the map between the horns of Albion's own bull. So I did!

Yet again, this was at a time when I thought that I had already listed everything there was to list to give this long-lost bull his reality back. So I dived again amongst those tongue-twisting Welsh place names but almost immediately dropped upon one that not only could I pronounce with ease, but could likewise translate too, thanks to Mr Davies. For there, at the absolute centre of the bull's forehead, indeed, smack bang between his horns, and it must be said in an area short of habitational blocks of grey, I spied a village all alone and yet gloriously glowing in the dark of today; its signpost said... DAWN!

Of all the names to find in that telling spot! Thus Albion's bull *IS*, for a mind-blowing fact, crowned by the dawn, in precise and staggering honour of the rising of the New Year's Taurean sun of some 6500 years ago!

Taliesin, teasing the unenlightened by speaking on behalf of this secret bull, knew it too - *"I am the Bull (Becr Lled) of Dawn!"* he cried, and laughed his own woolly Celtic socks off at their stupid bemused faces, for his baffled audience may have themselves been standing upon this very bull when he made his grand jest!

Now try to pooh-pooh all this away as coincidence! Incidentally, not only Isis wore a crown of the sun's disc enclosed by horns, but so did her beloved Osiris. You see, after his murder, the soul of Osiris was said to have entered an Apis bull, an animal that was to become highly revered as a consequence. So look with new eyes at the illustration below, their Apis bull with the dawn sun disc between his horns, and know that the land has in Albion poetically replicated that same revered creature, resplendent with horns, blessed at their centre by the unsuspecting village of the Dawn, and signpost surely to the promise of a newly-rising sun/perception. Therefore we can see in this landscaped Osiris the Bull God, nudging his Cow Goddess Isis, paired once more in the harmonic cycle of life and fertility here in Albion's constellations, another sign that it will be via a new perception that a New Golden Dawn will rise. What else can it mean?

Isis wore her crown in reverence of the sun in Taurus; on Albion, Taurus wears his crown in reverence of *You*. Truly if you see all this through the uninhibited eyes of a child you will know that the heavens have dropped at your feet, along with a legacy of thousands upon thousands of years-worth of mythological wisdom. As Taliesin said from the mouth of this fabulous Bull of Spring: *"I am the repository of the mystery, I am the place of reanimation"*. **I say that repository *is* now open before you, and look, the bull *is* reanimated!** And I was, and still am, like a child on Christmas morning at the sight of all this wonder.

In Welsh, by the way, I believe the word dawn translates as *talent,* a gift, whereas *dawns* means to *dance.* On the head of our solar bull, whether then in English or Welsh, I repeat that I see nothing but the gift of a new perception of this dazzling life on earth, and another invitation to rejoin in that dance of the universe.

Quietly now step through those golden horns and across the river Dee to where the precious unborn Christ Child of Albion sleeps; you will not have to travel far though, for the same child kicks within *you,* kicks even though you may have locked it away, out of sight and mind.

*Note: the signs up to and including Taurus I intuitively feel are (although part of the overall message and vital to the coming of the New Dawn) hours on this land-clock which have in a sense already ticked by. From our next chapter, Gemini, onwards, I believe, are the signs that denote what is still to come; these last few hours I believe will fly past.

CHAPTER 8

GEMINI
Part One

• *The Fetus* •

*- The Unborn
Christ Child Within*

★

*The eighth giant
along the way*

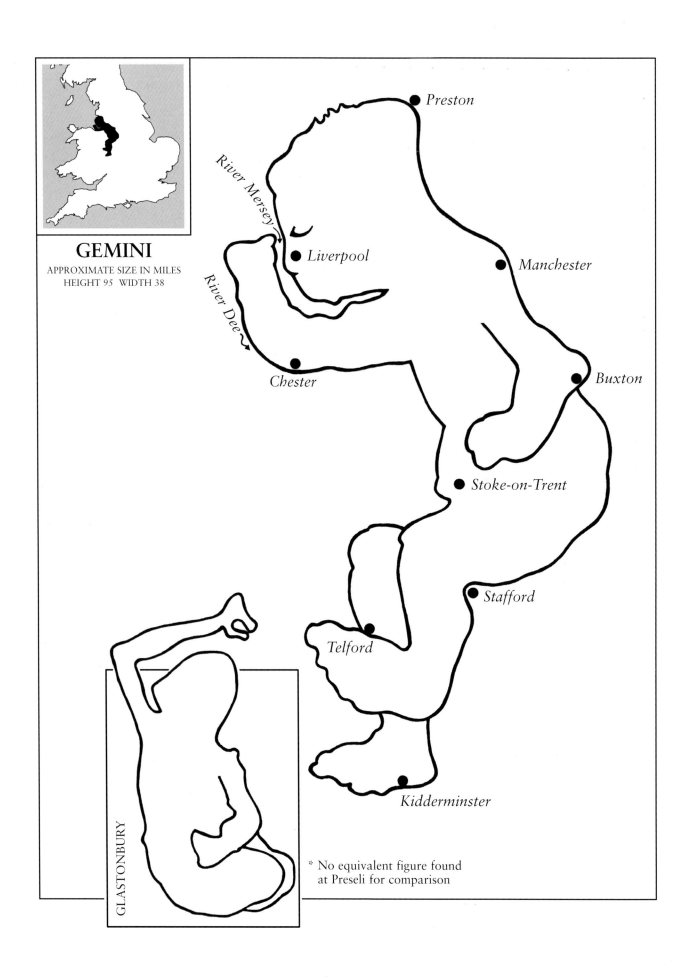

GEMINI

APPROXIMATE SIZE IN MILES
HEIGHT 95 WIDTH 38

Preston

River Mersey

River Dee

Liverpool

Manchester

Chester

Buxton

Stoke-on-Trent

Stafford

Telford

Kidderminster

GLASTONBURY

* No equivalent figure found
at Preseli for comparison

Beneath the streets of Liverpool...the face of the Christ Child

"The Chief of thirteen gold and silver idols, bowed its head westwards for its face was from the south, and twelve other images can be seen to this day half buried in the earth."

Saint Patrick, relating what he saw on approaching the shores of Britain

GENERAL AREA: ITS UPRAISED ARM HAS CHESTER FOR AN ELBOW. PRESTON MARKS THE BACK OF THE HEAD WHILST KIDDERMINSTER ON THE FOOT MARKS ITS MOST SOUTHERLY POINT. LIVERPOOL IS ITS FACE.

Deep and near untranslatable emotions, aligned to an immense sense of calm, always bubble up in me whenever I contemplate this child's astonishing and fragile beauty. It's the small tender heart of Albion's otherwise mighty array of power and purpose. And yet I have a feeling that, if this little one does not open its eyes at the core of each of us, then this entire spectacle will have been in vain.

In a nutshell, this child is the icon of the potential that I must call Christ Consciousness realised in a man, and yet the title is, in itself, joyfully free of any one religious dogma. It is rather an embracing of the essence of many: from the beliefs of the indigenous North American to those of the Egyptians 6500 years ago, a concentrated droplet of the universal truth which is God. Therefore, if you would prefer, just call it simply 'enlightenment' or even 'a heightened awareness of the god within', or whatever else you feel comfortable with. Either way, *it* already lies dormant in us all; from the beggar beseeching in Bombay to the baritone barrelling his chest in Budapest,

we are all primed with the consciousness of a Shiva, of a Buddha, of a Christ, of the highest state of *knowing* possible, and in this sleeping fetus of Albion that latent potential has been fragilely sculpted. But look, its eyes are tightly closed!

So what is it to be - do they remain shut? The whole universe hangs upon the answer. Give it birth it with eyes open and join a revolution in the perception of our existence - see heaven in the palm of your hand. But if we abort it down the back streets of ignorance and fear, such blindness will assuredly lead to a point where the earth can no longer healthily regenerate herself. We must already be very near to this point of no return otherwise why this screaming miracle beneath our feet?

Once again here is another figure whose shape and pose is so incredibly akin to its twin image at Glastonbury, where there is another baby with one distinctively bent and upraised arm. Looking at Albion's child it is as though it has fallen asleep after sucking its thumb, indeed the more you look, the more the whole pose seems to be that of an unborn babe still safe and floating within the womb. However, as with any baby, it cannot stay in there forever, as much as it would like to, and this one *must* be born for the very continuance of the human race may depend upon it - so suggests this writing on the walls of Albion if I have read it correctly.

And Liverpool shall bear either its smile or its grimace

Perceptive Mary Caine pointed out that near the knee of the Glastonbury babe there is a place called Liver Moor which, she suggests, is a sign of the bleeding Christ, the bleeding God-Man who is still yet to realise his own true potential. She also saw it standing for Christ the *liver* - the lover of life.

So with Mary's thoughts in mind see which city just happens to fill the entire face of this great zodiac's own babe - it is, and I think could only ever be, Liverpool - the pool of life - *the Christ lives!* Hence it is Liverpool that is the potentially life-illuminating wide-eyed smile of this Christ child in waiting.

By now you should know that I read only pictures and whether I read correctly is up to you. Even I have doubts as to my interpretations. But what I *do* know is that when I see that no other city in Albion dominates the face of any of the other giants as Liverpool dominates the face of this child, I cannot but feel obliged to put my ear to what this city may be crying out in its sleep. In its character and psyche, in its streets and happy Friday-night faces, there might just be a subtle whispered word coming from the lips of this awakening child in the unplumbed scary depths of us all. So let us put our ear to the ground of this most individualistic of cities.

A word of advice though - only intuitively can we ever expect to hear anything here. Only by trying to tap into the unique psyche of this city may we have any hope of gleaning the inner nature of the sleeping Christ child that it

hides just behind the mask of its noisy and bustling face.

Cursory though my knowledge of Liverpool, and indeed of astrology, is, I nevertheless really do sense this city's nature to be most perfectly Geminian. Possibly more than any other city in England it is a place of split personalities, for me a city of two very definite faces: one lined with laughter and friendliness while the other touched with pain and suffering. These seem to me to be the traditional astrological traits of true Geminians. And while we talk agony and ecstasy, have you ever known a birth that does not attract to itself these very same emotions? The birth of enlightenment may be no different.

But let us see if my gut feeling pans out - is the zodiacal poetry of this place reflected in its communal face? Let us observe the Liverpudlian face of this child and see what news we can read on it.

First and foremost I see a lovable and unconquerable community spirit full of enormously youthful energies, and I wonder if it was in the 1960s that the child beneath their homes first began to stir? I say this as it was from this same face that the Beatles first stepped out and thrilled the young of the world, and with them came a tidal wave of new and creative thinking. The whole atmosphere was colourful, youthful, and fresh; never had there been a time before when the young could express themselves so creatively. It was as though after the long winter of the war years the psyche of the planet had vibrantly re-emerged and came singing back like the spring. For millions it was an enormously exciting time to be around and to drink in its freedom, and for many at that time Liverpool was its fountainhead.

Without doubt, the young in the '60s were at the vanguard of a mini-leap in the perception of life, the suffocating values of the Victorians were finally washed away, and to be living at that moment upon the face of this child was the perfect location in which to reap the full benefit of what must have been in the air.

I also detect an impish curl at the corner of Liverpool's mouth due to its own unique and warm brand of self-mocking humour, a humour with a happy knack of making light of that city's many social traumas. Yet when it needs to cry it does it openly, unashamedly, and from a massive heart. Here is a city whose collective psyche, I sense, has always sung of hope - smiles are never too far behind the tears in this place.

Sadly some of these tears, in true Geminian fashion, are sometimes the result of self-inflicted wounds: its own council very nearly financially crucified the city it supposedly loved and looked after - and remember the self-destructive riots in Toxteth.

More pain flitted across this face of Gemini at the time of those horrendously twinned football crowd accidents, both causing world-wide shock: Hillsborough seemingly the reversed mirror of the earlier Juventus tragedy. At Belgium's Heysel Stadium it was alleged that it was Liverpool supporters who caused the crush which claimed the lives of so many supporters of Juventus, while at Hillsborough it was 96 Liverpool supporters who died - this time accidentally crushed by fellow fans. How strange then that it was Liverpool supporters, the bulk of them again youngsters, who lived or died at both venues and these two disasters within but a few years of each other. And as much as I hate using the word 'unique', for one football club to be involved in two disasters like this in quick succession is a horror undoubtedly unique to Liverpool.

Certainly this child of Albion has, in recent years, lost too many of its own children, and there are more examples than the ones I have just given. To my mind Liverpool has had too large a share of anguish, for each incident detailed above I'm sure caused a flicker of pain across this babe's sensitive face, pain that will likewise forever haunt the faces of the folk who live upon it, for this is still a tight-knit city. After each trauma, however, they seem to rise from the ashes, each time with an even stronger community spirit perhaps for the sharing of their pain - taking every blow to its collective heart, but never letting it fester therein.

"Walk on, Walk on, with hope in your heart" not only the anthem of one of its two football teams but I think for the whole city.

Of course, other cities, towns and villages hurt for many and varying reasons throughout all Britain and certainly many more times so in other parts of the world. However, I feel that Liverpool, because of the ultra-sensitive location of where it sits in this zodiac, may act at times as the microcosm conscience of all who live upon this mirror of Albion - and for all I know perhaps of the rest of the world, too. If so, in the psyche of Liverpool maybe the conscience of us all, at times, is laid bare and bleeding. At other times, though, it is an example of mankind's aptitude for forgiveness and community spirit, or of seeing the funny side of life even in the face of adversity, that shines through as a lesson to all who observe this city's trials and tribulations. Maybe, then, we should look towards this city, for its people may be amongst the first to open their eyes upon this bright New Age - so come on Liverpool show us the way, open your eyes and sing *She Loves You Yeah! Yeah! Yeah* - because if the Mother has chosen to sculpt her baby's face beneath your streets, *she* really must do!

Hard to comprehend, I know, this whole cause and effect land mirror stuff; it certainly is for me. If, however, Albion is not the biggest freak that nature has ever thrown up, but is instead both the awesome product and proof of a knowing and purposeful creation, that has from the beginning made itself a receptacle in which our dreams may become landscaped realities, then surely too the same sensitivities must be open to the nightmares we have created for ourselves. And if like really does attract like, do those glittering dreams and acts of love attract a sympathetic resonance, and, by the same token, do those who carry no hope attract exactly that?

And it may not only be individuals who are open to such subliminal traffic, but the collective psyche of an entire nation may also be affected by what it has, over generations, laid down upon the soul of its own landscape. But again, try convincing a guy in London's cardboard city to think lucky and he'll be lucky!

I would agree, we are talking of one hell of a crazy theory here and I am but sticking a naïve toe into it, but when we get to Scorpio we will be faced with more devastating evidence to the effect that the theory may not be so bizarre.

Dissecting a little more of the word 'liver'

We have already heard how Mary Caine found a place called Liver Moor upon the Glastonbury child and her reading into it as a sign for Christ, the liver of life, with which I vigorously concur. However, before we leave Liverpool in search of the rest of Albion's baby let us just toy some more with that word "liver".

Apart from its bodily functions my dictionary tells me, *"the liver is the seat of emotion"*. I ask you, after all that I have just put to you, does not Liverpool admirably fit the bill? So what a perfect sub-title for this child's role in the land's scheme of things - without doubt here could well be the emotional seat of all Albion.

Here's another dictionary definition of *liver*: *"One who lives in a specified way"* Surely Christ, and indeed all other masters, have come to show us how to live in a specified way and thus to *live* like never before. Why, even in death, Jesus was really showing us how to *live* - and soon upon Cumbria's heights I'll also show you how he dances off the cross so as to ram home his own ultimate message: that in a life on earth we have a greater gift than even

the Angel Gabriel's wings! Albion sings no different message from its every stream and hillock; a song whose first and last verse is that Jesus did not come to die for our sins (because we'll die for those ourselves!) but to show us how to be reborn instantaneously to the realization that it is in the living flesh, yes, right here in the present, that heaven is to be won. *Find heaven on earth* was for me his first and last verse.

In Liverpool's child we are shown by the Mother herself just how we can push out of the dark and find ourselves in a paradise on earth. So see your own face smile back out of the sweet dirty tracks of Liverpool's bittersweet tears and hope that your eyes begin to open and you perceive truths we've never dared contemplate - truths of the aware god residing in every grain of sand, of the god residing in every man and woman, even though in us he is gagged and blindfolded.

It all stemmed from a baby's cry!

Before we trace out the lovely form that this baby presents as it lays in its lambswool fleece (see how the land has lovingly lain its child on the back of Aries' lamb), I would like to relate how my own eyes were opened one afternoon when I had foolishly accepted that I had documented all the flowers in this vast zodiacal garden.

From the beginning I had never given a thought as to whether any of these giants had inland limbs, having always been totally convinced by the coastal template alone. However, it was late one spring afternoon that this babe cried out and, in an instant, showed itself, not only as a coastal head and arm, but also as an entire and beautifully-crafted full figure. I would briefly like to relate that special moment of his finding, for it again illustrates much of the off-the-wall way in which this whole wonderful thing has dropped into my lap.

I had, by the time of writing up Gemini, already finished the writing of the preceding seven signs via my findings in the coastline - only in Pisces did I suspect a head lying deep inland, though I had not bothered to pursue it on a map - I was again content with what the coast alone brilliantly indicated. That said, that full figure depiction of Libra's dove should have tipped me off far sooner!

Anyway, there I was looking at my map, and jotting down a few prominent place names upon the child's head, when I heard a baby crying somewhere in the busy street outside. Instinctively I looked out of my window and then back to the map where I saw, in a flash, a fluid set of unbroken lines which drew the entire inland body of Gemini's baby, looking so incredibly fetus-like. It was as though that baby's cry outside had, in a moment, uncannily cleared my vision, and out of that almighty tangle of roads, rivers and cities the full and breathtaking babe of Albion also cried out to be found. I was astounded.

Needless to say, within moments my pencil was charging excitedly around the map to catch what I'd seen, before it melted back into the maze.

I must admit, though, to doubting whether that vision would unravel a second time to the demands of the pencil, or whether it would have to be remembered only as a lovely mirage on an otherwise uneventful afternoon. Nevertheless, five minutes later, reality or mirage, it was there for all to see. I also knew I had now no alternative but to record the entire co-ordinates of this vast giant, a giant task in itself, but my what an exciting one! But then, as usual, one thought led to another, and apprehension arose out of the clear spring blue inside my head like a great bank of cloud, and with it the daunting prospect that, if this figure was meant to be shown in its entirety, then so must all the others, and an estimated one year's work in completing the manuscript would be blown away into God only knew how many

more to come! Tentatively I looked again at the other giants - and you know the rest!

Defining the body

Time now to retrace what that afternoon brought to bear.

Chester marks his right elbow and from there the river Dee flows seawards drawing his raised forearm in its wake; Hoylake, Wallasey, and Birkenhead sit upon the closed fist and from here protrudes a sucked thumb, tipped by New Brighton. Please note that the angle of this forearm is a virtual carbon copy of the Glastonbury child and I can only imagine that there must be an important reason for this unique feature. Mary Caine herself saw the same sharp right angle as being suggestive of a mason's square and deduced from it that it graphically illustrated the child as the son of the architect of the world. Whatever the reason, the sea obviously demanded it thus.

Come back now to Chester and take the A54 to Northwich, giving us a lovely underarm. The river Mersey (or Mercy as I'd like to call it) washes the profile of the delicate face into shape along with the inside of the arm, before flowing into the throat. Hale marks the chin and Warrington his Adam's apple.

Follow the coast round past Speke (in hope of a spoken word?) also upon his chin, past Grassendale which is in the area of the mouth, and then on along the long noble nose (it seems to sniff the flowers in the Festival Gardens!), which marks at the same time the profile of bustling Liverpool. Bootle marks the bridge of the nose; Crosby (by the cross?) the forehead, perhaps in anticipation of the cross that this same head would one day lean against. After Crosby, the towns are left behind for a while as the coast flows north to draw the top of his head past Formby Hills and

Southport. The back of his head is drawn by the river Ribble all the way down to Preston.

Using the M6 from Preston, one can draw the rest of the back of his head and neck down to Manchester, which sprawls over his left shoulder.

Heading south to a baby's bottom and beyond

Leaving Manchester head now to Hazel Grove, then the A6 to Buxton. From Buxton let's forget about roads completely and let the river Dove do us proud. So after Buxton just go a short way along the A53 as though making for Flash, but just before, pick up the Dove and the county border line between Staffordshire and Derbyshire and follow the pair right down to Uttoxeter, and with that the smooth curve of the baby's bottom is complete. Look over your shoulder, too, and note the fabulous bump of his left elbow between Whaley Bridge and Buxton.

Now take the A518 to Stafford, in the bend of the knee, and follow that inner curve around the town on the M6 which goes on to draw the calf muscle until Junction 13. Here we need the A449 to Wolverhampton and where crossing the M54 at Junction 2 should hopefully bring us to a major roundabout right on the baby's heel. Head then to Sedgley, Wombourn, and thereafter to Bridgenorth upon his little toe.

From Bridgenorth the A458 draws the outer silhouette of the other toes as far as Cressage. Cross the fields now and walk along the river Severn to the A5 near Attingham Park to draw the tip of his big toe. As I was writing this I suddenly realised that the child was actually dipping his toe into the river Severn - as does Taurus. This same river also separates the big toe from the next toe along on this foot.

Where the Severn goes beneath the A5, turn towards Telford, here get the M54 to Tong at Junction 3, then it's the A41 to Newport.

Once at Newport follow the line of the county boundary between Shropshire and Staffordshire northwest to Loggerheads on the A53. We have then outlined the shin of his left leg. Now it's on to Stoke, joining the M6 on the outskirts and following it to Sandbach. This motorway, from Loggerheads on the top of his knee to Stoke, marks out the top of his left leg and from Stoke to Sandbach, his tummy. His chest from Sandbach to Northwich in the armpit is traced on the A533 and A530. We have not finished yet, though, for he really is colossal!

Next we trace his right leg. Start at Loggerheads on his left knee. Head for Hodnet on the A53, which marks his right knee. Carry on to Telford on the A442 where visually this right leg goes behind the raised left foot, and continue on that same road until the ankle appears. Go then on to Quatt. From here it's all country lanes first to Hampton, then Sutton, Billingsley, Stottesdon, Farlow, and Hopton Wafers on the tip of his right foot's big toe. Like the other big toe, it is delightfully tickled by a river, this time the Rea; though, again, the Severn, that veritable foot bath, washes across the bridge of this foot.

Onwards we go. From Hopton Wafers we will trace the rest of the toes by following the A4117 to Bewdley, then via Kidderminster to Hagley. Again I note another major roundabout on this heel, just as there is on the left heel. From Hagley take the A491 to Sedgeley where once more the ankle disappears behind the raised left heel.

Lastly, the left arm

Now to trace the left arm go back to Buxton where that lovely cartoon bump of an elbow is. Take the A53 to Leek, which will draw the elbow down to the left wrist. His slightly folded hand is drawn from Leek to Stoke, but once there, head north west to Kidsgrove where his navel is.

Proceed to Congleton on top of the hand, though be sure to take the A536 to Macclesfield to trace the bend in his arm. From here we draw the last part of this upper arm by going on the A523 for a short way, then taking the A538 to Wilmslow. Carry on to Junction 6 on the M56 and this will take us into the armpit and completion of our journey through the earthly constellation of Gemini.

By the way, and I mention this for obvious reasons, there are three other places on this sign with *kid* starting the name, Kidsgrove, Kidmore Green and Kidderminster.

Note: in esoteric healing based upon chakras the kidneys are looked upon as the area of the body where are kept the emotional traumas of childhood. Bang on for this sign!

And his eye?

That left eye flickers beneath Liverpool's suburbia where thousands must sleep nightly, unknowingly, upon its covered brilliance. Well, I'd guess that the line that follows its closed lid would be the 506 from Kirkby into the city. Aintree could be the pupil beneath it.

Did a Saint see or sense it too?

St Patrick in the 7th Century must surely have sensed Albion's slumbering babe when sailing to these shores from Ireland. Hear him again tell it as it was: *"Chief of thirteen gold and silver idols, it bowed its head westwards for its face was from the south"*. Who can say this is not Gemini described exactly, along with the rest of Albion giants?

Now I know Mary Caine has equated the above reference to the saint's first sighting of the Glastonbury child, but I now feel safe in claiming it as pertaining to this greater child of

Albion.

What is more, I would call into question Mary's assessment that the Glastonbury child bows its head westwards. According to her own compass setting, next to her illustration of the child, it is to the south that its head lolls, whereas Albion's own towering child, near 100 miles tall, does indeed bow its head directly westwards, lolling it sleepily into the hushabye waves of the Irish Sea over which St Patrick sailed, and thus, more than likely, looking up to the colossus babe from the south - just as written.

But shouldn't Gemini be the sign of twins...?

Yes, but I feel this extraordinary picture in a landscape asks us to consider rather 'twinning' as the vital key word in the deciphering of this solitary star child's contribution to the overall topographical message.

Under Capricorn we touched upon the possibility that this miracle was, in part, perhaps urging mankind to rejoin all broken opposites - to reclaim the sight that without the goddess/the feminine force, the god/the masculine force is weakened; that without the black/negative, the white/positive may drift out of control; that if the spiritual is lost, the material becomes hollow, and if mankind does not embrace nature as a part of his own intimate makeup, then the writing on these headlands of Albion seems to spell out that he could be doomed. Thus, the land might be telling us that to remarry the Yin to the Yang, in the understanding of all men, will be to cause the rebirth of a new and wiser mankind - perhaps even overnight. And then what wonders we'd work, and what healing we could carry out to both the planet and ourselves by working in tandem with this now proved to be God-infused nature, rather than against it.

I then consider this Geminian child, this icon

of the embyonic Christ Consciousness asleep in us all, to represent the chance of a mystic re-twinning (if you like, a sacred marriage) of the many sundered opposites stored in the intellectual core of man. But then again, never forget that the land has willed it that as a fetus its eyes are shown tightly closed. For them to open, the child must be born. "*Open your eyes!*" must be the message.

However, Geminians may still argue that their sign *is* of the twins, so where's the other one? Well, the land has obliged. So walk this way to the griffin, although I repeat that it will be *twinning*, or the issue of sacred duality, that will still be the key that unlocks the message that this northwest corner of Britain has writ large upon it.

GEMINI

Unfortunately the underground swells seem not interested in giving our child a lower half, unlike the surface currents. But how those Triassic mudstones and sandstones bring a pool of hushed stillness amongst the swirling mayhem so as not to disturb that still sleeping child shape that swims there.

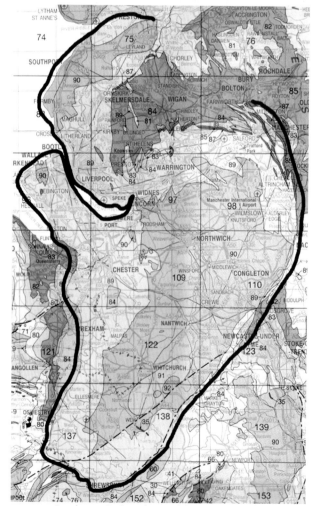

Based upon Geological Map of the United Kingdom by permission of the British Geological Survey, IPR/26-11C

CHAPTER 9

GEMINI
Part Two
• *The Griffin* •

★

*The ninth giant
along the way*

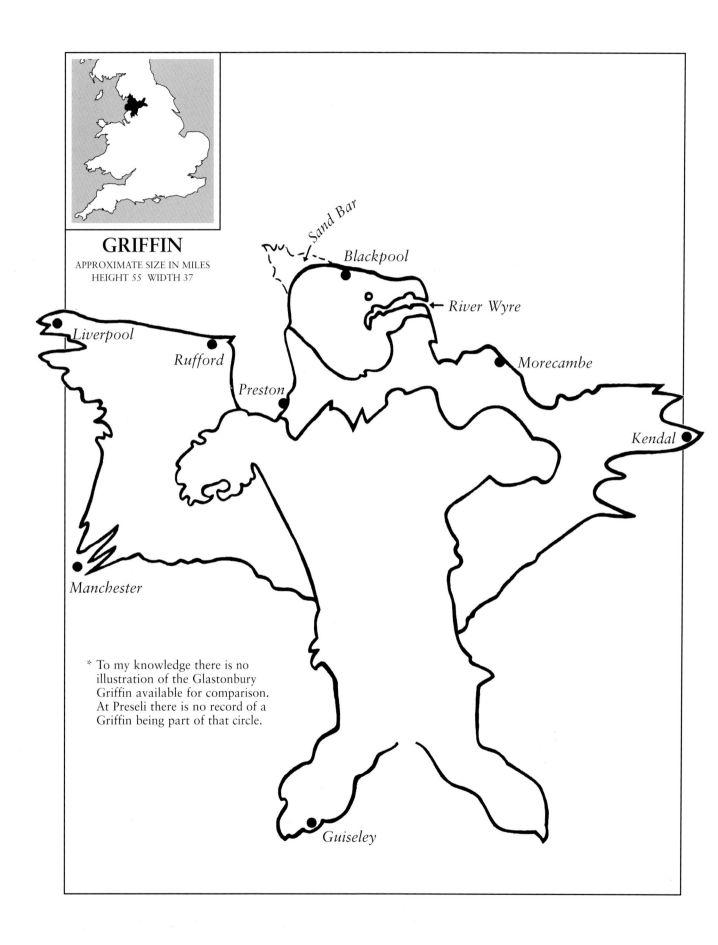

GRIFFIN
APPROXIMATE SIZE IN MILES
HEIGHT 55 WIDTH 37

Sand Bar

Blackpool

River Wyre

Liverpool

Rufford

Morecambe

Preston

Kendal

Manchester

* To my knowledge there is no
illustration of the Glastonbury
Griffin available for comparison.
At Preseli there is no record of a
Griffin being part of that circle.

Guiseley

A sign that we must be near the Grail, and thus great danger too

"This creature is found widely distributed in the world. He is said to have the beak, head and wings of a bird, the ears of an ass and the body of a lion. When his position in the design is known, it may be possible to guess at the treasure that he guards so carefully."

GLASTONBURY & BRITAIN, A STUDY IN PATTERNS
The Somerset Zodiac, Elizabeth Leader

GENERAL AREA: THE MYSTIC CREATURE LIES UPON ITS SIDE, ITS HEAD TURNED TO FACE THE NORTH. BLACKPOOL SITS UPON THE TOP OF THE HEAD WHILE THE OUTSTRETCHED WINGS REACH AS FAR AS LIVERPOOL TO THE SOUTH AND KENDAL IN THE NORTH. HEALEY AND SHIPLEY IN YORKSHIRE MARK ITS FEET.

I have to say right now that this griffin was totally unlooked for. I had no reason to look for him, as I had already been gifted with the standard 12 signs, and felt that the 'seeking' part of this whole project was complete. Having said that, I do remember at least once having just a wee grumble to myself as to why, if every inch of the English and Welsh coastlines had been so fabulously figured, that glaring gap of nothingness between Gemini and Aquarius had been so overlooked. But I guess I soon let the little nagging thought fly away and fell back to patting myself on the back for an otherwise job well done. And that's the way things stayed until some months later when the head of an Imperial Eagle suddenly screamed out at me - not from my trusty Reader's Digest Atlas from where all the other giants had initially leapt, but from that *Geological Map of the United Kingdom* - no real map at all!

This map isn't the sort to get you, say, from Doddiscombleigh to Hope-under-Dinmore, but it is a very pretty map to look at and one that shows the flowing waves of strata that form the foundations of Britain. And sure, we've already seen how these geological swathes seem at times to lend an uncanny hand in enhancing the presence of these land giants, but I never expected it to show me a giant that my trusty atlas had failed to expose!

It did just this while I was writing up the chapter on Gemini and admiring the baby in its purely geological make-up; I noticed that the child's pink-coloured head of permian and triassic sediment was seemingly overlapped by a very graphic grey wing of carboniferous material. Naturally enough my eye then followed this wing shape to where one would expect it to be attached to a body - and wham! What it did was to attach itself to that hitherto blank coastal area around Blackpool, however, it was now no longer void of magic, for that wing was connected to an eagle's *head* and the head to a *rampant and furry body* - Hell, it was a griffin! Its head was coastal cut as the rest of

Albion's giants had been, except Pisces, but its body was totally formed from the primordial sedimentary slips and slides of Britain's underground foundations and, of course, not noticeable on a normal map - no wonder I'd missed it. Yet so good was this subterranean outline that for the first time I didn't even need to follow roads or rivers for back-up, so accurately did the coloured sedimentary tide-marks present him.

Moreover, because these deposits were laid in the infancy of our planet's formation, one can only assume that this griffin was waiting here long before Ceridwen had her thumb crooked and Pisces its fins fanned.

However, I really should have expected his company some time or another, because Katharine Maltwood had also found a griffin in the Somerset circle. This griffin was also stationed back-to-back with Gemini's child at the stern of the ark - just as Albion's pairing of these two is also uncannily at the stern of its own ark!

Guardian of the Grail

Admittedly a griffin is, at first sight, a perplexing addition to the zodiac - certainly as a twin for Gemini's baby! That said, if the bedrock of Albion has given birth to such a one, he must come with an almighty purpose. Indeed, as unprecedented as he is, spread-eagled upon the horoscope, we shall find that there could be no finer twin or 'minder' for Gemini.

The clues to its empathy with Gemini start becoming apparent even in its own mythical make-up, for see how two creatures, the lion and eagle, have harmonised as one to give rise to this magnificent hybrid. Our stalking of him will further confirm his twinning traits and also the wisdom of the Earth Mother in letting this creature enter Albion's arena of stars.

Another reason to be excited at his inclusion is that, for seekers of the Grail, such a creature was more often than not found guarding the gate of the very last portal to that ultimate treasure. We must therefore assume that on Albion we have reached the same threshold.

Though he is more than just a doorman, for his credentials sign him as a protector second to none. See this long-standing belief verified, even at a prosaic level, when the griffin's image was carried as an emblem on a battered shield; he was a favourite to repel blows, both on the battlefield and on tournament grounds across medieval Europe. It stands to reason, then, that in such a guise this stranger in Albion's firmament might be taking up his traditional position as a repeller of blows; certainly his stationing directly at the rear of Gemini's child seems to be a hint of a strategic manoeuvre; and in that gentle placing of one wing over the babe's face I think his protective intentions are fully illustrated.

If this is so, we must also assume that out of all the giants on Albion, it is this 'little one' who must be in most danger. Why? Because that child must be representative of the Grail itself! *Read again Elizabeth Leader's findings at the head of this chapter.*

And if my reasoning is correct, I would even go so far as to say that the griffin's pose and placement must be highly prophetic of a precarious moment when that Grail could be either won or lost - or in poetic language, when those eyes will either be opened or disastrously sealed for ever. Look at the forceful gesture of those wings looking like arms on a signpost; see one pointing to that child, but notice where the other one points - directly at the sign for this age: Aquarius, and if I could put words into his mouth I would say *"Under my right wing is the Christ child/Grail - it will be born or aborted at the time that is under my left."* Look right, look left, and *know*.

So, this mysterious creature has seemingly bided his time, out of sight and mind, deep underground in readiness for these days of reckoning. I say 'reckoning' for take it from the ancient Minoans that the sighting of a griffin presented a most awesome line in the sand. To them it was a griffin that sat upon the actual throne of judgment and only by his approval could one pass on into the last and ultimate mysteries of the Goddess, and, if heeded, thence to the Tree of Life and the fruits thereof - the Grail in any other words.

It seems then that the Way of Albion may be no different; its last stages, its most intimate secrets, are now seen to be guarded by a stony-faced glare. Who will dare approach for approval to pass? I'm afraid only the childlike can.

Returning to his provocative posting at the rear of Gemini, any dictionary will confirm what we questors already now suspect, that his credentials are: *vigilant, a chaperon,* and a *guardian.* Surely he represents all these as he takes up his station of strength and defence by standing back-to-back with that baby, obviously guarding the little one from the rear. But what *is* to the rear? The answer: the pincers of Scorpio, that's what! And Scorpio is our next starry port of call. Now do you get the picture? That child and its potential of Christ Consciousness in us all *is*, for sure, the Grail - so the danger must be in us never achieving that, and, if so, Scorpio must be the reason why. More of this later.

Adding two and two together

Because we're still in the House of the Twins, let's start adding a few more two and twos together to determine why a griffin has been allowed to gatecrash what has been, up until now, a strictly zodiacal party.

Here, visually joined back-to-back, like all twins who would rather be one, is the unlooked-for other half of Gemini. Although he hasn't arrived as another child, he is again as perfectly Geminian as could be: a succinct example of the two become one, the repetitive underpinning of all Albion.

First and foremost, see in him the symbolic union of the two most potent creatures of earth and sky - lion/Earth Mother, eagle/Sky Father, met in one mythical creature from the Dreamtime. In this he represents a spectacular graphic twinning of holy polarities, and speaks a thousand words without making a sound, like any good picture should. Therefore within the griffin's shape one may simply see, in pictorial language, the divine embrace of the parents, which, if performed within a man, would give birth to a Christ, and in a beast a griffin. We are talking here of the poetical optimum outcome from whenever the lovers are met as one, and totally aware, in anything. In the case of the griffin we are presented with a perfected beast, a hermaphroditic creature that is both queen of the land and king of the sky, symbolically free to move in both physical and spiritual dimensions. And this is the promise to us all, should this same sacred marriage take place within our bodily temples, which are as yet rarely visited centres represented by that icon of a still sleeping Christ child.

You may, however, think the twinning of an infant Christ and a griffin too odd a couple - I did too, until I looked a little deeper than the first impression.

For instance, after the Resurrection, those who saw the risen Christ have, with purpose, recorded that he too displayed double attributes which allowed him to operate on two different planes at the same time: they marvelled at him as a spirit passing through closed doors, and yet as a very physical man he let Thomas feel his warm wound. So to my eyes, at least, the risen Christ, that fully enlightened Jesus, had become, in a poetic sense, a griffin in the shape of a man; a master of all dimensions; the perfectly balanced Son who held the divine polarities of Mother/Father, Matter/Spirit, within himself and knew it! And if my theoretical reading of the mythology behind the Resurrection is correct, is it any wonder that it is a griffin that has been chosen to partner the sleeping holy child which, should its eyes ever open, is the token of that same metamorphosis of man into God-Man. Indeed, with its Liverpool eyes still closed, is there not a further poetic token of Jesus himself lying in his womb-like earth tomb waiting to walk out three days later as a man reborn as a Christ, the ultimate *Liver* of life?

Thus this amalgam creature not only protects that soft and fragile expectation of new perception in us all, but underwrites their joint message to the effect that they are the promise of each other; whoever gives birth to that child *within* will likewise soar as a Lord of All - a lord of all planes, and an evolutionary leap in man's concept of life on earth will have been gloriously undertaken.

Robert Graves' own research seems to validate a similar mythology revolving around the presence of a griffin.

In the *Song of Amergin* (Amergin being an almost Taliesin-like chief bard of the Irish), for instance, the wise old man proudly proclaims in otherwise mysterious tones: "*I am a griffon on a cliff...*" In trying to get to the bottom of this announcement, Graves gives the following wisdom-laced pedigree of both the griffon-vulture and the purely mystical/heraldic griffin: "*..the griffon-vulture sacred to Osiris, a bird also of great importance to the Etruscan augurs and with a wider wing-span than the golden eagle. In the Song of Moses (Deuteronomy) Jehovah is identified with this bird, which is proof that its 'uncleanness' in the Levitical list means sanctity, not foulness. The heraldic griffin is a lion with griffon-vulture's wings and claws and represents the* **Sun-god as**

King of earth and air.

The name Osiris will later flare up many times as Albion's own riddle untangles, but for now let me mention that, to some, this god of early Egypt was in a sense a prototype of the Christ himself, as were many other deities from around the globe; while the mere nearness of the name Jehovah to that of a griffin obviously speaks volumes in itself.

However, Graves had more. Further on, and whilst poking around in mystic calendars, he uncovers the griffin being allocated to an auspicious one-off day when enlightenment was there for the taking. This time it is a griffon-eagle which shows the way, for it seems that such a bird was mystically perched upon that all important 'extra' or 'odd day out' in the 12-month calendar, which was decreed as that day when a chosen one could become a God-Man **in the form of a griffin no less!**

So ask yourself now if Albion's griffin is not the odd giant out in Albion's 12-giant spread? Funnily enough, he was also the 13th giant that I found. Indeed, he and Cumbria's Christ combined are truly always going to be the 13th and 'odd ball' guests in any reading of the stars - but, God, how we shall watch them make sense out of it all.

To clinch this harmonious twinning, listen to what happened to Sir Galahad when he achieved the Grail, albeit only in a dream. It is his father Sir Lancelot who is doing the dreaming for us: "*And he who had come down from heaven went up to the youngest knight of all and changed him into the likeness of a* **lion, and gave him wings,** *and said: 'Beloved son, now canst thou range over all the world and soar above the ranks of chivalry.' And straight away he took wing, and his pinions waxed so huge and wondrous that they shadowed all the earth. And having left everyone breathless with his powers of flight, he soared up to the clouds; and at once the heavens opened to receive him and he entered in without further stay.*"

The dream is recorded in *The High History of the Grail*, and with it I think the griffin's place in Albion's scheme of things is cemented in the sediments.

Defining the body

So let's dig out another work of disarming cunning.

An ear or a sure sign of enlightenment?

He makes himself known from Preston at the base of his neck, from where the river Ribble flows seawards while washing the back of his head. Notice the sand bar at Lytham St Anne's which looks very much as though it would like to give our griffin a large flap of an ass-like ear - this is entirely in keeping with some depictions of griffins. However, another and more exciting way of seeing this same distinctly shaped sandbank is sparked by reading the following griffin lore as researched by Elizabeth Leader: *"The treasure he guards is Light in the sense of intelligence or enlightenment, and it is interesting to find that his conventional representations always give him an excrescence, either a knob or a flame, arising from the top from the top of his head"*

Look at my line drawing of that sandbank in conjunction with the words above; are we not looking at nature's own representation of a sand-gold flame? Though I have to laugh when noticing that of all places it just had to be Blackpool which actually crowns this creature – that town with its own famed brand of electrical illumination!

Carrying on, it is the Irish Sea, which takes over and draws the top of his head and beak. Fleetwood is at the beak's tip from where it curves wonderfully into the mouth of the river Wyre - why do I think of wyvern, another strange griffin-like beast? Knott-End-on-Sea is on the tip of the lower beak out of which sails

the ferry to the Isle of Man. The neck then continues down to bird-sounding Cockerham and with it completion of the sea-sculpted head. The eye, I'd say, was somewhere around the zoological gardens on the outskirts of Blackpool.

To do justice to the way this creature came to me via the underground magic, I feel it would be wrong of me to even think about proving the rest of the body by roads and rivers, so I will only drop a few place pointers onto that figure secreted away in a subterranean sandwich. The only liberty I will take is to reverse and transfer the cat-like right fore and hind legs so as to provide legs for the left side, as on the geological map the limbs on the left are not defined.

Starting with the southern wing

Its perfect feather tips flick Liverpool, whilst the tip of the northern wing touches Kendal in the Lake District; interestingly this particular wing's geological outline seems to echo both the path of the M6 and the county boundary - although perhaps I ought to say *they* echo *it!* Is this another case of subliminally prompted embellishment perhaps?

The right hind leg seems to take in the curve of Rombalds Moor from Skipton down to the area of Shipley, while the paw of the right foreleg surrounds the Chorley and Adlington areas.

Appreciate for yourself this underground poetry in motion - this magnificent adagio of eternal patience. See that wing and that gorgeous paw. Look with the eyes of a child and you will see the griffin and therein gain entry into the last mysteries of Albion.

The beginning of the end

But, you hikers of Albion, let's linger on this sign of protection, and assess what is revealed

Based upon Geological Map of the United Kingdom by permission of the British Geological Survey, IPR/26-11C

here along with what is still to come, for here is a good place from which to turn back.

Why do I suggest turning back? Well, from here on in I must warn you that our journey is to be strewn with sights and sounds which, more than anything you have encountered to date, may cause great insult to your adult sensibilities, and to such an extent that you might even be tempted to laugh away the child within you so as to save your ego-fuelled self which, you think, already *sees* the reality of your existence, the solidly educated, rational and sensible *you*. To those who would risk going on, however, I offer only increasing evidence of the 'extraordinary'. We shall enter territory that will test any sane person's staying power; though for those of us who can still hang on and see with child-like eyes, it will be territory filled with the most terrifyingly beautiful things ever to confront us, things more disarmingly absorbing and testing than anything we have yet seen.

Understand, then, that this griffin is the turning point of our entire journey. From here on the terrifying and the marvellously beautiful will vie equally for your attention. To take the step beyond the griffin is to toss a

lifetime's worth of beliefs into the air like chaff into a tornado, and even Albion may seem at times more a picture of hell than of heaven.

This griffin is the terrible, though unavoidable, doorway to the culmination of all Albion. And sure, that Cumbrian cluster of Christs *is* it; indeed, this griffin's northern wing points beyond Aquarius to the same conclusion - one wing guarding the unborn Christ child (our sleeping perception) the other showing that same child full grown and fully aware upon the cross. But don't rush on to Cumbria, as we must first travel the miles in between, where other giants already queue up either to prepare you for that final mind-blowing mile or two, or else to have you running scared all the way back to the technologically-tamed world you knew yesterday. So be warned that almighty stumbling blocks bar our path, and the only way to get over them is to remain a happy-go-lucky griffin-spotting child - even when the sting of Scorpio hovers within an inch of your face, don't scream, but just be amazed at its beauty - touch it even!

I know it sounds foolish advice by today's

standards, but by the standards of those who have already sought and found the holy Grail such advice would be looked upon as 'gloriously foolish' ...just ask Perceval.

It seems it was exactly this 'fool's trail' which this Grail-seeking knight adhered to; a path which, incidentally, and whether you know it or not, you have been following ever since the day you so marvellously decided to read *this* apparently foolish book!

Perceval, you see, was a simple backwoodsman who became a knight beloved of Arthur, and who, through his childlike innocence, achieved the Grail where other knights of greater renown and intellect failed utterly. With this in mind, and to those of you brave enough now prepared to head northwest with me, I'd like to draw your attention to a piece written by John Matthews in his book *The Grail Tradition*, as it is a timely reminder how best to continue the rest of this journey towards its crescendo. Here Matthews writes of Perceval and the state of mind that allowed him to seek out and lift the Grail. *"And this is indeed a most important function of the would-be Grail seeker. To be able to relate the realms of the everyday and the otherworldly into some kind of unity is to move close to the central mystery of the Grail, the ability of which to do the same thing in non-finite terms is one of its greatest gifts. To have one foot in both worlds, the infinite and the mundane, is a blessed state and one which only the truly innocent generally attain.*

One could even say that it is necessary to *learn how to become **truly 'foolish' before one can begin the quest, for as long as we are enamoured of the 'serious reality' offered by the outside world, we can hardly begin to step outside ourselves in the manner necessary to perceive the Grail."**

Well said, John, you have taken the words out of Albion's mouth!

*Note: Perceval's quest for the Grail has been read as being closely linked to that of Sir Galahad's own, indeed, it has been suggested that these two were themselves mystical Geminian twins - Perceval being the earthly knight who had to struggle for what he got, whilst the almost Christ-like Galahad was the heavenly and thus guaranteed of his own achieving of the greatest prize.

Gloriously foolish, let's head now to the first of those stumbling blocks.

To get there we must now, for the only time on this journey, leave the safety of this ark of Albion for a while (which, in itself, should tell us that danger is about) and cross the dividing ocean to the place where this zodiac's Scorpio dwells; a coiled and malignant force, yet a sign whose role is a vital component to this overall prophesy, indeed, as vital as the addition of the Christ, for without Scorpio's sting there is no stab of pain to shock us back into our true senses.

Away now across a tempestuous, bilious sea to Northern Ireland, for a storm is brewing.

CHAPTER 10

SCORPIO

• *The Scorpion - Mordred* •

★

*The tenth giant
along the way*

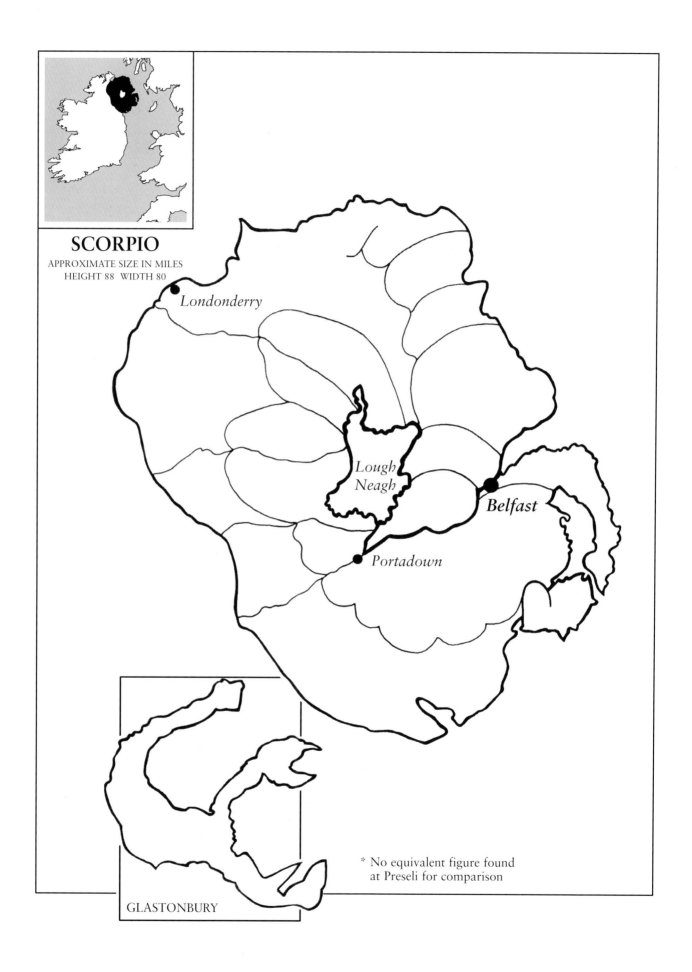

SCORPIO

APPROXIMATE SIZE IN MILES
HEIGHT 88 WIDTH 80

Londonderry

Lough
Neagh

Belfast

Portadown

GLASTONBURY

* No equivalent figure found
at Preseli for comparison

And does Northern Ireland mirror the crimes of all mankind?

"...And when he had dipped the sop, he gave it to Judas Iscariot, the son of Simon. And after the sop Satan entered into him. Then said Jesus unto him, "That thou doest, do thou quickly."

JOHN, Chapter 13 Verses 26-27

GENERAL AREA: NORTHERN IRELAND. THE SCORPION FACES EAST TOWARDS ENGLAND AND THE SIGN OF AQUARIUS. BELFAST SITS PARTLY UPON ITS STING.

e have left the safety of the ark and now find ourselves hung high above its stern as though caught up within an approaching tornado.

As we hang in this buffeting station you ought to know that when I first saw those sinister arms protruding out of this corner of Ireland I immediately looked away, consoling myself he wasn't there and that I'd find him elsewhere on Albion's mainland. Why? Because I'd rather have found him anywhere upon the globe than sitting on the streets of Northern Ireland, for would it not seem too cheap a shot to have him, of all signs, occupying that tortured plot. But as the ark slowly filled up with all the other giants I became sadly aware that there were no telltale pincers protruding from anywhere else. Simply there was never, ever going to be room aboard the ark for Scorpio, only Northern Ireland could house him - the land would have it no other way.

My hands were tied, and my mind, I confess, has been troubled ever since finding it by the all-too-obvious ramifications of this provocative placement. Yet, I also know that in its deliberateness must be heard what can only be the most heart-felt cry of the Mother Earth. As you read on, you may, like me, also have to concede that no place upon the whole planet could better harbour the mythological threat to Albion's ark, and thus perhaps, to the very continuance of life on earth.

Building up to this worrying scenario, take William Blake's *Jerusalem*, for me a veritable prophesy of this miracle of Albion. Among the visionary verses the poet allocated to Ireland, would you believe, was one suggesting that that country would be both the *"redemptive and regenerative force that will via its ferocity* (sting?) *reawaken the half-dead giant Albion"* - and with his rising the return of a New Golden Age. (*My bracket.)

Sobering or what, when placed alongside what the Earth has sculpted in Northern Ireland's foundations?

Blake, however, goes further. To underline the threat to his New Jerusalem he marked its attacker's place with a compass reading of: *"But Westward a black horror"*. Though even if this wasn't enough; to ram the mystic message home he also allots a number to the whereabouts of this same terror, a number which for us looking at a clockwise round of giants is itself a virtual map reference, and one leaving no seeker of Jerusalem in any doubt where to look for the initial whipping up of that anti-Jerusalem storm of storms.

I shall tell you that number later, but in the meantime you must understand that, although this sign of the Scorpion does indeed have dark work to carry out, it nevertheless has in the end, as even Blake intimates, a God-given regenerative role in this grand stage play, geared towards the winning back of a global harmony and balance.

A return to balance is what every earthy inch of Albion craves, an equilibrium of the Yin and Yang that the ancients knew to be poetically imperative to the fruitful workings of all creation, the black Yin and white Yang being symbolic of the crucial feminine/negative and masculine/positive polarities. To them neither colour was good or bad, except when man chose to divide them to the extreme, when even the so-called good or white light could itself become an inbred and harmfully unbalanced force. Their goal was always to hover at the neutral quintessential heart of the Yin and Yang's complementary opposites.

So look at the artwork on the cover and see the absolute screaming epitome of division, or anti-harmony. Not only is Scorpio physically sundered from the rest of Albion's giants, his own starry family, but so too diplomatically from the rest of Ireland. **And this in turn forces me to wonder if the painful segregational struggles of those who live upon his back are in themselves some sinister reflection of the bigger picture that broods unseen beneath their floorboards.**

Do I go too far? Please hear me - or rather the land - out.

This Scorpion, however, is not purely Ireland's grief, for I think we'll find him representative of the disharmony shot through the whole of mankind, especially so in our relationship to the rest of creation. Thus, in this one damning portrayal of multi-layered severances, we are being urged to look urgently and deeply for both the cause and pending effect of our and Scorpio's alienation from a state of universal harmony, a split which may now be already threatening the whole structure of life on this planet. This must be the reason why an ark and all it stands for has docked on the face of the planet. And it has happened at a time when man has even split the atom for malevolent purposes, and with it perhaps finalised his own divorce from everything else. If so, he may now have dire need of a lifeboat for that day when all the disharmonies he has wrought might blow up in his own face, and it might be that in this ark there is stored for him a life-line back to the divine laws of the creation, and with it, perhaps, a way of living beyond our wildest dreams.

Focusing in

So let us try to make sense of this the land's blatant show of disharmony, for if we can see something of ourselves in it we may then have sight of not only how our protracted ignorance might have caused such a global dis-ease in the first place, but how we may bring about a return to a saving harmony.

Start by looking at the whole artwork and see again how all the other signs are gathered in the ark (*see also line drawing for Cancer*), while Scorpio, although as starry as all the others, has been visually pushed away, as though disowned, set adrift in an open boat, to become a breeding ground for further imbalance and discontent. Thus, *separation/division/anti-oneness* must be the pictorial key upon which the earth now wants us to sharply focus. Simply, I feel she wants us to see in that picture of alienation our own present position in relation to the rest of creation and from it attempt to gauge just what we're doing to present a threat to the ark, and thus to the continuance of all life on earth. For surely an ark lacking even one God ordained passenger is no ark at all, her cargo of the Word of Life rendered incomplete and thus fatally flawed. Clearly then, and if I'm reading this picture correctly, it is the inharmonious doings of man which constitute the coming storm that is set to rock the boat - coiled Scorpio is but our symbolic stooge.

But now I catch myself chewing my pen and feeling a fool, for when one starts bandying about suggestions of trying to harmonise with the forces of nature, most folk turn off with an: *"Oh, Christ, listen to this cheesy rainbow-jumpered New Ageist crap."* And why should we want to listen to a god buried in the landscape and seemingly trying to converse in mythical mumbo-jumbo, when we are ourselves on the verge of cloning a man in our own selfish image! In answer, and not feeling foolish at all, I believe we are indeed gods - though alas gods gone absolutely insane, and Scorpio seen stinging himself to death on Albion's prophetic clock face is the cutting caricature of the same; if it wasn't so deadly serious you'd have to laugh at this near ninety mile high piece of perfect satire!

Behind the satire, though, I sense that a terrifying race is on to make us understand something of paramount importance before it is too late. To grasp it, let us begin to ask some very disturbing questions, and then try to read their answers in the landscape.

First of all, I put it to you that if the land really could be some sort of living mirror, then Scorpio might be where it is poetically cracked - cracked by our every greedy and destructive act, whether committed against brother or brook. Recall some of the destructive acts perpetrated by man: the Somme, Belsen, Hiroshima, Lockerbie, through to one of those last few tigers left in India, as I write its pelt drying in the sun, while its supposedly medicinal bits are

already in a box posted to China. I could go on and on but imagine all of it reflected daily in Scorpio's remembering mirror, to fester there and then be reflected back as an invisible pollutant, a super-charged negative vibe - in a word *evil*, the very reverse of that wonderful word *live* (which in *Liverpool* covers the face of the Christ Child,) and so to infect another and another, even the very air and grass, to such a point where everything is spiritually dulled, everything robbed of a telling degree of vitality, until the concept of a New Dawn, a heaven on earth, is entirely laughable. Whereas the prospect of a hell on earth is far easier to contemplate.

I'm asking, then, if our myriad acts of imbalance have created a living force which can itself exhale, or reflect back, upon all and everything, an infectious anti-love and life vibe - a force which, for the sake of Albion's street theatre, I must now begin to personify as an unbalanced and incestuously conceived child of our own selfish making, and who now wishes to unencumber himself of the piteous weight of the wrongs we have put upon him. So don't blame him as he steps out of that ghastly Scorpionic mirror, wishing to hurl it all back in our ignorant faces. And we can feel him coming, too, by the blurring of the seasons which clatter around his head, by the rising seas at his heels, and the fumes of hell upon the radioactive breeze of his breath. We shall come back to him shortly.

But speaking of hell...

...is Northern Ireland the actual mythological location of the underworld?

Now wouldn't it do my case a power of good if I could bolster the brooding negativity I've already thrown onto this troubled corner of Ireland, by also trying to dump upon it the fabled location of hell itself! Below the belt or not, it wouldn't be hard to make a case based upon ancient belief.

It goes like this: more often than not the ancient peoples of the northern hemisphere believed that the land which lay upon their furthest western horizon to be the land of the dead, the otherworld or Hades. Always when someone died it would be said that they had *"gone west"*. Indeed, until fairly recent times, and perhaps even still continuing in parts, I believe that in the funeral processions of Egypt the female mourners would cry out *"To the west! To the west!"* in a tradition, according to Dmitri Merezhkovsky in his *The Secret of the West*, that had gone on without ceasing for six thousand years. The West being to them the location of the eternal birthplace of human souls, the kingdom of the dead - the *Duat*. Westwards would their shades drift on boats across the *waters of death* to where the sun disappeared beneath the horizon, and where would be found the *Fields of the Blest*, a place envisioned as a second or mirrored Egypt. Bliss beyond the horizon, however, was not guaranteed. Those Elysian fields being but part of a region beset by monsters and an eternal gloom, and through which the soul of the deceased would first have to find a path.

Anyway, because to the Egyptians the scorpion was sometimes considered to represent evil, even allied to the terrors anticipated in the passage of death, can you blame me for now suggesting that Northern Ireland's gloomy secret could be the flip side of those blessed fields - in a word, Hell! Certainly, these terrifyingly beautiful monster-filled fields of Albion still mark the spot where each night the sun of Egypt dips into the west; fields wherein, I propose, a soul, whether of one deceased or not, might well find something which could afford it a rebirth to the full splendour of just what a gift a life on this holy and conscious planet really is.

Could then, a forlorn 'vibe' of that scorpion coiled in Northern Ireland's foundations have been picked up by the seers of ancient Egypt, and who then interpreted it as the abode of lost souls? Whereas any vibe sensed rising up from English and Welsh fields, where the Mother Isis danced and a great bull of fertility bellowed, would logically be accounted by them as emitting from what could only be the Fields of the Blest. Oh, and while you muse on that, did I tell you that their Duat had twelve regions for a soul to pass through!

__Note:__ maybe Northern Ireland, Wales, and England are indiscriminately overlaid with both heaven and hell, and only via one's own particular stage of spiritual development does one or the other show itself as the vista before you? Certainly, such a two-way mirror existed in the beliefs of the Celts regarding the appearance of the otherworld.

Should you feel, however, that this my attempted grafting of Egyptian mythology onto Celt trod fields too far-fetched, well, towards the the end of our journey, and high on Cumbria's cross (see The Dark Twin), you will see in stunning pictorial detail just how much of the Egyptian rites of death and rebirth has seemingly been stamped onto this remote part of England. Though if you're more into the zodiac and can't quite accept my associating Scorpio with any land of the dead, then accept the following from astrologers Ariel Guttman and Kenneth Johnson and taken from their book *Mythic Astrology - Archetypal Powers in the Horoscope*:

"The connection between Scorpio and the underworld goes back to the very beginnings of astrology."

Time and again a hunch inspired by a myth seems effortlessly to find collaboration upon this landscape, and all you can do is shake your head and feel dumbstruck. Yet in the very simplicity of this revelation I am not unaware that there is the danger that many will judge it all as being 'just a little too simple', and therefore easy to brush aside as not worth serious consideration. And in this we have the one weakness of Albion, for its absurd simplicity will be an insult to the intelligence of many. What a pity.

Let us hope, though, some will actually warm to this same disarmingly simple rhythm of revelation and through this alone will stick with the uncanny tale longer than most. Indeed, its ability to disarm with humour and a child's amazement is, on the other hand, Albion's chief strength. For its hikers, happiness therapy on the hoof!

And so with cracked mirrors possibly reflecting back, even *paying* back, our every crime against the harmony of life, and this in turn fuelling more of the same; together with the evidence I've shown for the ancient world's thinking that the underworld, both terrifying and blissful, was situated pretty well where Britain and Ireland sit today, it's once more over to you to make of it what you will.

As for me, I think it means it is time for an updating of mythology

In order to see if a pictorial, mythologically-loaded message *is* rising out of Britain and Northern Ireland, and relevant for today, I feel we must attempt to read the seemingly purposeful rearrangement of the heavens, as shown upon Albion's fields, in conjunction with the myths in which our ancestors may have secreted away the very purpose of life on earth and its link to the harmonious workings of the cosmos - these tales more often than not revolving around the search for the knowledge of the Absolute/ Self Enlightenment/Immortality. And perhaps via such overlapping of myth onto these reshuffled constellations a pictogram will appear and be somehow strikingly applicable to today's global circumstances. For surely if message there is to be found, it *must* be screaming in the face of today, or else why this sudden unveiling of itself after ages in hiding and preparation?

With the above in mind, and because this shocking phenomenon has chosen these British Isles for its stage, a most useful myth to apply to the pictures before us must be that of King Arthur and his Round Table. Indeed, could not this circular tour around the houses of Albion's horoscope already be the fantastic, yet so simple, truth behind that very table? Each sign a seat of learning around it, and each seat leading ever closer to the Grail?

Whatever, in this proposed reapplication of an archetypal myth onto the present day map of Britain and Northern Ireland, we may even begin to read what could be the 21st Century's own chapter in the eternal cosmic myth; this again ever centred on the long awaited rise of man into God-Man. And should we (or else why this almighty depiction of an ark?) be the generation who are nearer than any other to obliterating once and for all the prospect of that ultimate goal, then this updating of the Arthurian Quest for the Grail might, even at the eleventh hour, educate us on how to avert the disaster and fuel instead that longed-for evolutionary leap - to conjure from a landscaped table, inlaid with stars, a new Golden Age.

Let's then begin this new take on Arthur's eternal quest by allowing me to further personify Scorpio, again for the sake of Albion's street theatre production, by now actually naming him. Let's give him the name he had when he last murdered the promise of a Golden Age on these shores - that name being Mordred. Though, as Mary Caine suggested when she found this same one hiding in Glastonbury's Scorpio, you may know him better as Judas, even Lucifer. His names are legion, his role has ever been the same - to sting us to new heights of enlightenment.

Note: and just as Mordred/Scorpio breaks the balance of these 12 terrestrial signs of the zodiac, didn't Judas before him break up the band of the 12 disciples?

Take centre stage then, you incestuously-created son of Arthur, conceived after the king had been tricked into sleeping with his sister Morgan Le Fay (who had for the occasion deviously changed her appearance), an act which ensured that even Mordred's conception would be stamped as another symbolic act of imbalance. Yet Arthur tried to make matters right again, albeit in a way that was to pile wrong upon wrong, and we can learn how from Malory's medieval epic of *Morte d'Arthur.*

Malory, you see, also saw evil unleashed in the shape of Mordred, and although never linking him to Scorpio or Ireland, nevertheless, under the guidance of his muse, had him expelled from the Round Table. Hear him give witness to what Arthur did when he had discovered that he (or *you* in the mirror) was the father and creator of Mordred, born to be the murderer of Balance. Why, even my computer's spellcheck constantly insists that Mordred should be spelt *Murdered*!

Arthur, wishing to put out of sight and mind the fruit of his illicit act, and very Herod-like, had all the boys born on that day put aboard a crewless ship and set adrift. And tell me again if this separation and banishment is not exactly remembered in Scorpio's situation, pointedly cut off from the rest of Albion? Bet your life it is!

Anyway, according to plan, the ship did get wrecked, but much to the future woe of the Round Table (this zodiac?), the boy Mordred was the only survivor, and was afterwards fostered by one called Nabur. Thus the mystic mechanics of payback were set into mythological motion for the tutelage of mankind.

Mordred sought payback, and boy did he get it! One vengeful blow to his father's skull sank Arthur's own ship - *this* ark of Albion - deep beneath memory, and with her his starry Round Table upon which was laid out the foundations for a livable heaven on earth - all sunk into the realms of tacky Hollywood adaptations.

Behind the scenes, however, Mordred was cemented into his role as the eternal personification of every act that disrupts the flow of love and harmony. While Arthur, albeit still synonymous with the quest to found a Golden Age, would nevertheless carry the scar of one who had allowed an ego fuelled by both pride and fear to gag the cry of a conscience and hence wreck all he had striven for.

However, it's rumoured that just prior to the fatal battle with Mordred, Arthur's conscience finally broke through, and the old king offered his hand to his son; sadly the hand was slapped away - it was all too late. But perhaps via Arthur's belated admission of the wrongs he had tried to bury, he won the prophetised promise of a return to his ancient realm in effort to right his symbolic wrong at a time when it has itself been so replicated and magnified that a Golden Age may now never dawn.

Has that time chimed in with this 21st Century? For look what has resurfaced off the coast of mainland Europe - his mystic ship (*again see Cancer*), and its cargo of the Round Table, risen once more out of the depths of our forgetfulness. Inviting the open-minded knights of this time to unplug their laptops and to instead log their intuitions onto this pictorial sign language in a last minute attempt to unravel the antidote to a Scorpion's sting - perhaps to be found in a sip from the Grail Cup? A Cup, incidentally, which Arthur's own lips never touched.

Who am I kidding though? How many of us today have the new mindset needed to read what the land is saying and to shout back at it

"*Stay your hand Mordred - I recognise my hand in yours!*" and mean it? Can we really overlay the essence of this recurring universal myth upon our present lives and times and finally get the bloody picture? Or do we just shout "*Bullshit!*" to the whole nonsensical notion? For what it's worth, I myself constantly battle with this same dilemma.

To help make our minds up, however, and what with that suggestion of Northern Ireland itself being overlaid with the underworld, and Mordred being its doorman, get this: Mary Caine found that the Persians named Scorpio's month of November (to them the month of Death) as **Mordad!** Again, get the poisonous picture?

***Note:** *only a passing thought here, but in that 'Nabur' did Malory mishear his muse whisper 'neighbour', making reference to a neighbouring land to Albion - Northern Ireland?*

Blake and the Celts had his number - and probably ours too

A good time here I think to further back up Malory's chronicle and my Irish hunch in seeing Mordred's banishment from the Round Table, or this ark, as something, mythologically speaking, highly significant for us today. So let's hear that mystic number, previously referred to, which Blake, in a sense, stuck on Mordred's back so that we seekers of his New Jerusalem would know to where and why he was banished.

We have already heard him mark Ireland as Albion's probable bitter medicine, but hear him now locate its numerical threat as "*The Ninth who remained on the outside of the Eight*". Exactly! Scorpio is indeed allotted the ninth station (if you count the griffin as part and parcel of Gemini) upon the face of this purposefully out-of-sequence star clock, and likewise *on the outside* of the first eight giants!

Certainly, the Celts would have had no quibble with the latter-day bard for citing that ninth station as one of intimated banishment as they too, according to Caitlin and John Matthews in their *Encyclopaedia of Celtic Wisdom*, saw '*retirement beyond the ninth wave*' as the traditional point of **exile from the land.** Exile = expulsion = our chosen separation from the natural laws of harmony?

It is interesting, too, that, in the Mystery Teachings, it was the number nine which represented the number of man and of initiation, for the one who could pass through the Nine Mysteries received the mark of the cross, the sign of his regeneration and freedom from the shackles of his own ignorance.

On face value then, it seems that the ninth square on the gaming board is one stacked with expulsion and negativity, although judging from the above, there's still a lingering chance of being stung into self enlightenment, however painful, and of thus finding one's way back home. That said, gathered here in this ninth house of Albion we must assume that that same number is painted on all our backs, because aren't we all in a sense so many self styled Mordreds? In environmental terms alone (God only knows the ramifications of how we treat one another) aren't we again all guilty to some extent of turning blind eyes to the imbalances we're aiding and abetting, from our daily adding to the pollution problem, to buying hardwood products without giving a toss as to whether they're made of trees from a sustainable forest or not? If so, even these socially permissible crimes, may amount to us bringing a blade, Mordred-like, down upon the head of our creator, and in our reluctance to fully engage in the bigger picture we underwrite our self imposed exile from the ark of planet earth and thus too the laws which make all her life forms possible. And in this I'm as guilty as anyone.

In mythic imagery see the above wind-chiselled out of Albion. See us number nines abandoned from the ark of cosmic harmony, hung in our couldn't-give-a-shit severance and placement high above the rest of nature, and preparing to snip the last rope that links life to God. Then the ark will sail back to the stars without us, except that is for the one returning Son, see him on the cover, nailed to its mast for absolutely nothing.

But pity Mordred, for he too is tied to this our wheel of fate, and there are moments when he would, I'm sure, put down the ghastly weight of wrongs and ignorance which he carries on our behalf, and return from the banishment we have imposed upon him (and ourselves) to take up his rightful place in the starry cargo of the ark. Until he does, we will not have heaven on earth, for again note that even the ark herself must be unbalanced without him, and her list alarming. So from across the chasm of time and sundering grey waves he cries into the wind towards Albion's ark and all of us: *"Forgive me, forgive yourself - release me, release yourself - accept your ignorance and unburden us both - accept me as your creation and allow me to become the last piece of the puzzle which will perfectly picture a livable heaven on earth."*

The audience, however, do not reply, we all turn our heads away just like every giant (but one) in that ark, for look at the cover - just like us, none of them can bear to look upon the terrible scenario we have seemingly laid the groundwork for. Tellingly, only the Aquarian phoenix - sign for our time now - dares a look westwards.

The stage is very definitely set!

Rise now above the whole stage, let's take the highest vantage point possible, and look down upon how the end game of this new myth for today is already written. Kill the lights - except the one on Mordred. Quiet please.

His piteous plea for mercy is then refused, and so he groans and sinks that sting into his own back in a perfect portrayal of the consequences of our own severance from nature. In this macabre side-show of Albion, Portadown takes that sting, while Belfast sits partially upon the bulbous poison sack from where the actual sting protrudes. My intuition suggests to me that each time that sting pierces his own back, somewhere in the ether is heard another baleful moan that is physically replicated by a crime somewhere in the world: from the cry of another mother for a son taken before his time, whether on the streets of Belfast or Birmingham, Alabama, to the whine of chainsaws taking out another slice of forest. It is all the same to Mordred, he is symbolic of all the world's ills, not just Ireland's.

To the chime of our new astrological Age of Aquarius, however, Mordred's self-pity begins to ebb. He reverts to type. His eyes become focused slits as he shifts his attention across the sea to Britain for the first stirrings of life from where that chime has sounded; the very same phoenix ground where he last left Arthur and another Golden Age for dead. Indeed, I think it no accident that, on Albion, Scorpio and Aquarius have been set provocatively side-by-side, five minutes between them. And five more minutes past these, the Christ is hung at midnight.

And tell me, as Mordred prepares to strike, has not Northern Ireland already been, for years, a political thorn and sting in Britain's side?

I do not, however, intend to promote a feeling that Scorpio dressed as Ireland will deal a blow directly upon Britain. I reiterate that whatever does come to wake us up will I believe be felt globally, and will be an entirely natural upheaval, albeit one instigated by one, or a culmination of the many imbalances we have committed against the natural workings of creation. Neither take this possible backlash as retribution from either the earth or God, for I believe retribution is a word inconceivable to both. No, what comes will be but the earth having to reinstate the balance of the natural order, and in doing so the seas may have to rise, the elements might well go berserk and perhaps new viruses will break out and run riot. Although what the hell do I know - only that when I see an ark I'd guess that major flooding is going to be part and parcel of whatever chaos may be coming our way.

Plainly, if I'm still on the right track, it is mankind, probably generations upon generations of us, who have primed Scorpio's sting to bursting point, hence our final disruption of the fundamental harmony out of which springs all life, whether it be a gnat or a man, must be a gnat's whisker away. Otherwise why this morning all this landscaped fuss?

Spot-lighted, watch Mordred now pace his banished corner of the stage, that Scorpion claw of a coastline opposite Cumbria, perpetually scanning eastwards to where the sun will rise, to where he knows Arthur is, still lying in his mystic barge - that gigantic resurfaced ark of Albion. How he hisses and spits his venom towards it. Not only this, but he also grows stronger with every new atom bomb test; with every song bird shot for a delicacy, and with every mugging; for with each shock wave, each tumble from the sky, and each grandmother left bleeding in a gutter, Arthur's Golden Age retreats even further out of mind.

Therefore he senses that the time has come when the balance has so tipped his way, that events call for his horrendous reappearance upon the starry stage, where he will again perform to the world by kicking it up the backside! So, as *Chaos*, he waits in the wings, ready to light the blue touch paper that will ignite the new astrological age which the land has seen fit to sculpt as a mighty pyre overhung by a phoenix. Snag is, the whole thing is inverted. The picture doesn't look good.

OK, let's now stand on our seats so as to broaden our view of the stage - we need to check out what's going on around him.

The previous sign to his was that guardian griffin, placing a protective wing over the face of the unborn Christ Child, seemingly to hide its sleeping vulnerability; here surely must be what's at stake - what's to be fought for - the birthing of a new perception of life, the Grail no less. Then directly in line with Scorpio's pincers is that worryingly upside down phoenix. This bird not only the sign for these present days, but it is also the next stop for us and Scorpio. Thus, if Mordred is also Lucifer, the lamp-lighter, you should not need a degree in commonsense to know whose mythological lot it is to provide the spark, in whatever shape or form, that shall ignite that pyre and the immense consequences thereof. Indeed does it already crackle?

Five minutes beyond that inferno, see the last scene, that of Christ crucified, and that part of the sign of Aries that is the lamb of spring - obvious promise of a new dawn.

In your mind's eye, watch now a cinema trailer to these last four scenes - indeed, see yourself as the hero or heroine. Simply, you need to give birth to Gemini's Christ Child within yourself so that you may have perception enough to rise from this dire position upon the funeral pyre of the present. If you can give birth to that child of newer vision and allow it, in the shape of a death-defying phoenix, to carry you into the next scene, you will become one with the dancing God-Man (*see You! the Lord of the Dance*) and all he stands for. Then you can pass beyond midnight on this land-clock and into a land signposted by the lamb of Aries and, I dare say, wonders beyond belief.

However, don't take your bow yet. Note that, in between that child and the spring, a Scorpion waits, even surer sign of a danger, and where we may blow our chance! Thus he appears to be the terrible fulcrum between success and failure - will his sting abort that spring child's birth or spur it on like a smack does to a newborn? Pondering this, shudder with me when I tell you that the brightest star in the constellation of Scorpio is upon its heart; it's called Antares, which Sesti translates as Anti Ares (Aries) or Rival of Mars - Mars being the ruler of Aries. Read his barefaced intentions!

Your own final scene, then, is left as a massive question mark, shaped by Scorpio's arched and twitching sting. God help us all on the day it jerks downwards.

Do not despair, however. In that phoenix, which is struggling to rise, we are to find overwhelming signs of Arthur's presence, he who was and still is the epitome of hope against all the odds, a name that lives on as a champion of every stumbling man who yet still clings to a dream of better days. Believe me, we shall find Arthur's force just as potent and alive as Mordred's when we enter that station of the firebird. Admittedly, in his life Arthur was no saint, but one who had a vision mirrored in his Round Table of bringing down heaven to earth for both beggar and king to enjoy - a Grail attainable by all.

In the grand animated mythology of Albion, this Once and Future King will be found to be rousing, as promised, in this hour of need. He too feels the shadow of the sundial touch his Cumbrian barrow and even now girds the truth-seeking Excalibur to his side.

Remember though, that the main player in all this will always be *you*!

Sorry, but I must ask it again

Time now to leave this stage for a moment, and prod a little deeper the possibility that Mordred's abandonment from the universal truth and, as a consequence his self-destruct nature is but a mirror held up to the faces of us all.

It's time therefore - and just as we did when looking into Gemini's Liverpudlian face - to dare ask again the admittedly outrageous question, albeit one that will not now go away, as to whether the land (assuming firstly that man can influence via his thoughts and deeds the spirit of place) as a self-aware and sensitive mirror can somehow reflect back on us that which we've given out, thus subtly influencing more of the same, whether born of agony or ecstasy. The answer to this question could be as damning as it is filled with the potential of our finally getting off the treadmill of what could be the most prolonged of self-perpetuating vicious circles.

Thus, whether ridiculous or not, I'm asking for a second time if Northern Ireland's troubles, when overlaid by either a zodiacal or Arthurian template, have a shared pain (no matter how poetic) too obvious to ignore. **Bluntly, has Scorpio's/Mordred's own wretched, yet natural enough, yearning to rejoin the rest of Albion's family of earthly constellations aboard the ark, to be a seat again at the Round Table, somehow seeped into the hearts of those folk who live upon his back, thus making its own need seem like their very own - or, indeed, vice versa?**

Again I balk at the suggestion and very nearly chicken out of voicing it for I do not intend in any way to trivialize the very real suffering of the people who live there. But that said, even if there is not one jot of direct interplay between the spirit of the place and those who live within it, you must, like me, still stand aghast at this all-too-obvious pairing of basic plights - Scorpio physically separated from the rest of the zodiac. While, at the same time, the people who live upon it are themselves segregated into opposing factions, some of them as desperate as Scorpio to be part of what lies across the waves, while others are just as desperate not to be. These the two defining faces of Mordred!

As barmy as all this must sound to a modern mind, it is not, however, an original theory. No matter how today's soapy astrological forecasts have cheapened that art, remind yourself that astrology has always claimed that men dance their lives, in part, to the rhythm of the stars, joyfully pirouetting or painfully tumbling as a direct consequence of those celestial influences. So what now, with the added weight of Albion's terrestrial constellations rising up beneath our feet and radiating these same undreamt of forces *upwards* through the entire crust of the world? The influence of the stars, or perhaps more to the point, our influence on them, is suddenly found to be of double strength and a lot nearer home to boot!

You gotta be joking?

"*So what are you telling us - that we're all just the damned puppets of these constellations, being pushed and pulled this way and that at the whim of one zodiacal puppeteer or another? And so great is their influence that the majority of those folk of Northern Ireland will never find rest because of what lurks under their beds; while everyone born upon the Isle of Wight is a born peace broker? Are they all fishmongers on Pisces or aquarium enthusiasts? And that poor lot who have the misfortune to inhabit Virgo, do they have to battle daily with an inner urge of wanting to dance in the nude at the drop of a hat? Some life!*"

Of course I'm not saying that - although who couldn't wonder at the entertainment value of living in some of those Welsh valleys if it were true!

No, what I am saying is that neither I, nor anyone else for that matter, really knows 'diddly squat' about the hidden forces of the universe. For my own part, I am but craning my head out into a vast lacuna of uncharted thought and asking questions that may, or may not, echo back with accurate replies from off this incredible landscape. What I can confidently echo, however, is a centuries old

warning of the wise of many cultures: namely if we do not live in harmony with these awesome forces, the self-perpetuating ills of imbalance might always dog our lives. Misuse, or be ignorant of that force, and we may well become its puppets, but if we acknowledge it as an awareness permeating everything and attempt to use it harmoniously, the most creative tool ever may be put into our hands. I believe this force aches to be just this, and Albion is its spectacular calling card.

A theory laughably childish? Too naïve a remedy for the world's ills? Maybe, but humour me for a moment more - once more muse as to what would happen if, say, we could suddenly all become gloriously innocent, so innocent that we could sincerely acknowledge that this scorpionic influence *is* capable of percolating up through our lives, and paying back all we have inadvertently sent to it. Then, in the next breath, we offered it compassion, for Scorpio is not evil, but only a product of our own imbalance. Could we by giving such simple credence to the impossible begin to retune its imbalance, no longer fuelling it with fear, separation, and destruction, but with harmony and peace? And would we allow that same force then to become a potent instrument for the creation of a heaven on earth?

Indeed, perhaps just to give credence to its presence alone, as mapped out on the land, would go halfway towards healing our joint wounds and stop the 'backlash influences' we may have set into motion. Again, I just don't know; I'm way out of my depth, and have to confess I have been ever since I began this journey.

What I do know is that for most of us to even begin to acknowledge the shape that is squatting upon Northern Ireland will be intellectually painful - though such pain may well be part and parcel of Scorpio's transformational sting. Sometimes the truth can hurt like hell! However, if we can swallow our pride and meet head-on these strange challenges of Albion, perhaps we could eventually draw out that sting on both the physical and spiritual planes and allow the 'unknown' to become the familiar and thereafter marvellously user-friendly!

Again, to try would cost nothing but a dent or two to our intellectual pride.

Science on the other hand will tell you that Albion is a nonsense, and to read God into it, is a one-way ticket back to becoming painted pagans worshipping tree and stone. In other words savages. However, this pronouncement coming from a school that has created the most savage and disfiguring weapons of all time, and who now turns a greedy big business eye towards that building block of life, the gene, has me, without a second thought, gladly taking my chances with whatever has caused such beauty to rise out of the face of this landscape.

Defining the body

The front of the head stretches from Downpatrick in the south to Comber in the north and is shaped solely by Strangford Lough. The same lough also draws the inner line of his longest arm, his left, which folds in front of the head from Newtownards in the north, down to Ballyquintin Point on the pincer's tip. The outside of this arm is then completed by the Irish Sea all the way round and down into Belfast Lough. Belfast itself sits partly upon the bulbous sting.

From Belfast take the M2 and M1 to Junction 9, joining the A3 to **Portadown, the point at which the sting punctures its own back**. Although to be absolutely accurate the sting tip is marked precisely by Junction 2 of the M12! After Portadown go back northeast to pick up the M12 and M1 to Junction 10 on the side of Lough Neagh. This then completes the whole sting.

The circular shoreline of Lough Neagh describes perfectly the inner curl and axis of

its coiled tail. I feel the very eye of the tornado must be here. The coastline again draws the outward contour of the tail by the curve of the North Channel, Antrim Coast, and Lough Foyle all the way to Londonderry. From Londonderry just follow the A5, N2 and A37 to get us to Dundalk, this giving us the western and southern outlines of the body.

At Dundalk we go out into the Irish Sea following the coast all the way round into Strangford Lough and round again to Downpatrick, thereby completing the right arm. Audley's Castle and Strangford tips its pincers.

Its eyes, may, I think, be Killyleagh for the right and Castle Espie, which I cannot help thinking should be renamed Castle I Spy, for the left.

Now stand back and take a look at that arched and poison-bloated tail and marvel how all the major roads rotate around it like spokes in a wheel, though perhaps more accurately the joints in his armour-plated tail! I also wonder whether those famous Mountains of Mourne echo mournfully to the sound of the underworld's lost souls.

I have suggested the legs in the areas to both sides of Carlingford Lough, although I do not think they're vital to plot - we've seen enough already to know what's here! Glastonbury's Scorpion, you will note, has no visible legs.

But what if you're a Scorpio, reading all this? And, worse still, what if you actually live upon this sign?

Whether a Scorpio, Ulsterman, or both, please do not fret! This is what the book *Mythic Astrology* says regarding the nature of those born of this starry house: "*Scorpio's process concerns life, death, and rebirth. This is a constant theme in the lives of Scorpio individuals - they typically experience a death or near-death experience, only to be reborn,* *and, like the phoenix, rise from the ashes of their former selves and soar to the heights. This process is seldom undertaken willingly. Scorpio is fixed water (Lough Neagh?); therefore it does not usually welcome change. The snake has to bite these reluctant Scorpios first, then their **atomic reactors are ready to fire back with a vengeance**".* (*Bracket mine.)

So, people of Northern Ireland, the eyes of the universe may be upon your homeland, but, be assured, you are not accursed! Hold up your visions of peace, of tolerance, of a de-segregated society, and, like so many lanterns, lead us out of ignorance and into a newer age of greater understanding, both of ourselves and our surroundings, to a time when we will never again cause division of those things that should be one. You peoples of the Scorpion may harbour our last chance of rising above ignorance.

And let's face it, sometimes we all need a push: Arthur needed his Mordred so that his name could live on as a byword for the return of a Golden Age; Jesus, too, needed his betrayal by Judas to accelerate his own magnificent metamorphosis, and underwrite the promise of our own. The mythological wisdom embedded in Northern Ireland may prove another keynote in man's evolutionary climb, no matter how dark its initial appearance.

Mary Caine, though, beats me to all these Mordred/Judas/Scorpio tie-ups and of Lucifer writes: *"And Lucifer, though he be the very devil himself, is nonetheless the Light Bringer, as his name implies"*.

In the final analysis, Scorpio's function in Albion's present scheme of things is as a cleansing castigation to all our imbalances. The Bible backs this by calling the Scorpion the *'Divine Scourge'*, although still acknowledging it as an initial symbol of *'desolation'*. This, along with Blake's *'redemptive and regenerative'* view of Ireland, secures the role of Albion's own divine scourge in waiting, and the antidote and balm for many wounds may come through our understanding of the cause and effect of its mystic poison.

Coincidentally spot on!

Lastly, let's return again to the above quote from *Mythic Astrology* regarding the nature of Scorpios, and to pick out just three (and I'm sure quite coincidental) words: **phoenix**, and **atomic reactor**. Take these with us as we head eastwards back across the Irish Sea to reboard the ark where the phoenix flares.

We'll make landfall on the wing of that firebird and on a spot where already the pyre is uncannily ablaze. Indeed, one of the hottest spots on the planet is here, as the land must have ordained, to reinforce this ancient myth so that we, living now, can understand it the better. This place is called Windscale, Sellafield if you will, the Thorp nuclear reprocessing plant, magnet for a planet's ills and perhaps ultimate symbol of an age out of balance with itself.

As always, make of it what the hell you like. As you do, don't take your eyes off the stage, watch again Mordred sensing the bleed-off from the plutonium-rich wound of Albion's Aquarian phoenix, tasting its salt-water discharge along his Irish coast and knowing that mankind must be near the edge - one final push that's all he needs. But he laughs, because he knows we're pushing ourselves - we're melting the North and South Poles, and we're on the verge of designing our own babies!

He puts on his blackened armour and draws a cloak about him, as the narrow sea which separates him from his target, his estranged father, indeed his entire family, whips to a frothy scum. The sun is rising.

Arise, Arthur! Put on your phoenix helm, as of old! The time has come for you to walk your Table of Stars again. The stage is set, the players are gathered, the parts allocated, and the old myth rewritten for a new audience. But will they want to read it?

★ STOP PRESS! ★

Just two weeks before going to press, and with Scorpio very much in mind, I strongly felt that the following should be added to Mordred's last page.

'Reaping the whirlwind' was the front page headline of *The Independent* newspaper on 3 July 2003, and from under its subheading of **'*Extreme weather prompts unprecedented global warming alert*'** I have culled the following extract:

"In an astonishing announcement on global warming and extreme weather, the World Meteorological Organisation signalled last night that the world's weather is going haywire.

In a startling report, the WMO, which normally produces detailed scientific reports and staid statistics at the year's end, highlighted record extremes in weather and climate occurring all over the world in recent weeks, from Switzerland's hottest-ever June to a record month for tornadoes in the United States - and linked them to climate change.

The unprecedented warning takes its force from the fact that it is not coming from Greenpeace or Friends of the Earth, but from an impeccably respected UN organisation that is not given to hyperbole (though environmentalists will seize on it to claim that the direst warnings of climate change are being borne out)."

The report goes on to list that in southern France, June temperatures were 5°C to 7°C above average, and Switzerland had the hottest June for at least 250 years; for England and Wales it was the hottest June since 1976. Even India's pre-monsoon heatwave this year was 2°C to 5°C above the norm, and caused at least 1,400 deaths. Heavy rainfall in Sri Lanka, claimed 300 lives and virtually wrecked the infrastructure and economy in the south-west of the country. China too is experiencing devastating flooding.

In the United States tornadoes have been rewriting the record books. In May there were 562, compared to the previous record of 399 for any month - 41 people died as a result.

The WMO confirm that *"Recent scientific assessments indicate that, as the global temperatures continue to warm due to climate change, the number and intensity of extreme events might increase"*.

The article concludes with *"The unstable world of climate change has long been a prediction. Now, the WMO says, it is a reality."*

Mordred himself concludes with *"I'm on my way!"*

CHAPTER 11

AQUARIUS

• *The Phoenix* •

★

*The eleventh giant
along the way*

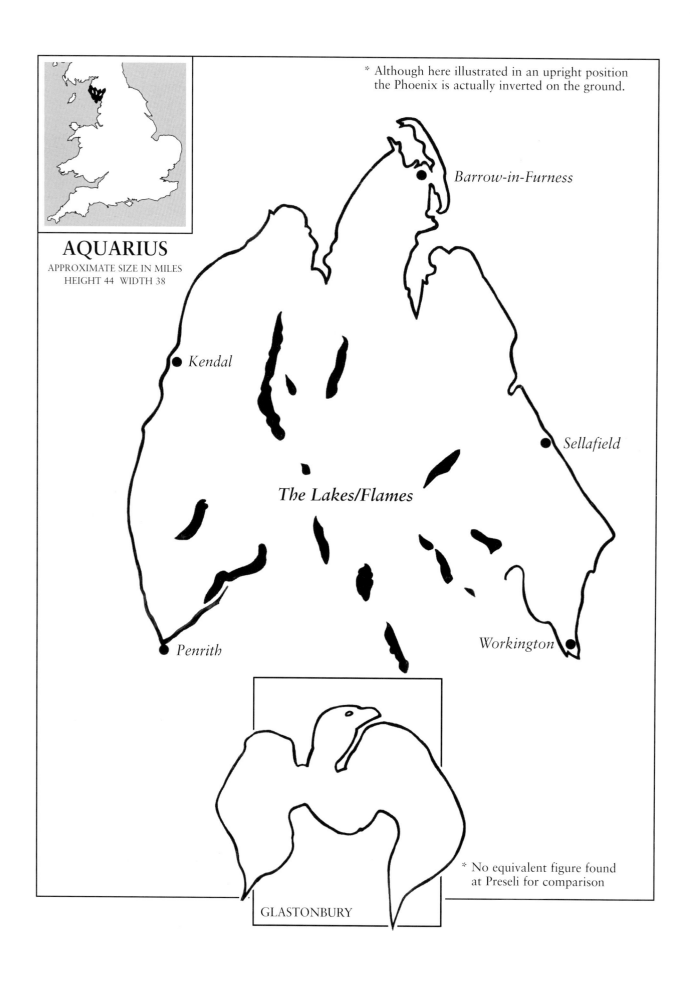

AQUARIUS

APPROXIMATE SIZE IN MILES
HEIGHT 44 WIDTH 38

* Although here illustrated in an upright position
the Phoenix is actually inverted on the ground.

Barrow-in-Furness

Kendal

Sellafield

The Lakes/Flames

Penrith

Workington

* No equivalent figure found
at Preseli for comparison

GLASTONBURY

Into the melting pot

"Are you willing to be sponged out, erased, cancelled, made nothing?
Are you willing to be made nothing?
Dipped into oblivion?
If not, you will never really change."

PHOENIX, D.H.Lawrence

GENERAL AREA: THIS INVERTED PHOENIX ENVELOPES THE ENGLISH LAKE DISTRICT, THE LAKES THEMSELVES BECOMING THE FLAMES OF ITS PYRE. BARROW-IN-FURNESS IS ITS EYE.

Enchanting! Out of all the areas of the British Isles in which to reveal the sign of the water carrier, Albion just so happened to choose the English Lake District! However, as with the Glastonbury zodiac, we are not given an image of pouring jugs but the disquieting, albeit spectacular, image of a phoenix, and a seemingly inharmonious clash of fire over water. Surely this is an error then? On first sight, some 15 years ago, that is what I thought until, that is, I was to learn from the land and a couple of old alchemists that, on the contrary, there was here a very beautiful coming together of two of the four elements - in short another sensationally choreographed example of the sacred marriage. Indeed, for ten of those 15 years I hadn't even noticed that the lakes themselves were the actual flames that leapt up to consume that mythic bird - harmony or what!

But why then do I say 'disquieting'? Well, if, as with the Glastonbury version, this phoenix is a sign of some imminent metamorphosis in the way all mankind views itself and the planet, then it must also warn that such a self-resurrection, rebirth of attitude or perception, call it what you will, will only happen if our present ignorant self is utterly shuck off as though it were a shell of ashes, from where one may, like this fabled bird, instantly rise anew. Though when I speak of shaking off ignorance, I fear that the opportunity to do just that might be forced upon us by some global crisis, only then will we be pushed towards the scorching crescendo of change that the presence of this bird must foretell.

The following is from the Nag Hammadi's rescued *Gospel of Philip*:

"It is through water and fire that the whole place is purified"

My feeling of disquiet is emphasised by the fact that we have here the only sign on Albion that is ominously inverted. Certainly, when a tarot card comes inverted out of the pack it takes on an entirely negative meaning, and its warning needs to be heeded. So, then, this upside down phoenix, the sign of our presently dawning Age of Aquarius, in Albion's own prophetic clock-spread of zodiac cards must itself be screaming a warning of something. For me, it can only add up to the predicament that envelops each of us. I sense it is the mythological writing on the wall telling us that either we immediately turn back from the damaging environmental and genetic paths down which we are at present racing headlong, and take on board a newer perception of the sacred balance and awareness which must sing throughout every atom of the creation, or else self-destruct through our own gross ignorance.

Either way, I think we can be assured that there is an obvious warning for us in this rare bird's provocative nose-dive. Although for thousands of years she has been the definitive logo of instantaneous self-resurrection, I feel the guarantee of us all rising with her must, at this moment, be very much in the melting pot. That said, in a more hopeful frame of mind, my own inner childlike self suggests another way of reading that same dive: it sees it perhaps as a pictorial directive to *where* exactly we must all head before we can rise. Perhaps it suggests that we too might have to first *plunge* deep down inside ourselves, to where the landscape has already indicated that an unborn child, symbolic of that newer perception, awaits to open its eyes upon a new world. And let's face it, a global cataclysm may be the only thing that *could* force millions to venture to think as they've never done before. At such a time our inner selves may be the only place any of us can flee to.

The marriage of fire and water

The things that are in the realms above
Are also in the realms beneath.
What Heaven shows is often found on earth.
Fire and flowing water are contraries,
Happy thou if thou canst unite them.
THE TWELVE KEYS
Basil Valentine 1599

Many years after finding this presumed inharmonious clash of fire and water, I discovered the above alchemist verse in A T Mann and Jane Lyle's *Sacred Sexuality.*

This, coupled with my finding that the earth's rendition of flames was conjured from lakes, made me realise that I had stumbled upon yet another pictorial masterstroke endorsing the union of holy opposites, and, according to those lines above, an alchemist's dream come true! Dr Irene Gad in her book *Tarot and Individuation* inadvertently agrees with me in that what the earth has done to Britain would most definitely have been a sight fit to blow many an alchemist's mind: *"The alchemists were pioneers, people open to the worlds within, who projected their inner perceptions onto outer symbols and thus found a universal language, transcending words, for communicating their experiences of the soul's architecture and dynamics".*

"The alchemists sensed the rhythms of the past and the presence of the goddess..." is how Mann and Lyle introduce the following quote from C G Jung's *Psychology and Alchemy: "...and they were aware that a vast unknown Nature, disregarded by the eternal verities of the church, was imperiously demanding recognition and acceptance"* In the shape of Albion this once *vast unknown Nature* is now recognised, and what is more, I don't think you have to be an alchemist to understand the gist of its universal song: out of perfect harmony shall come miracles that even we 21st century technological whiz kids cannot conceive of.

From another alchemist's verse of coded wisdom realise that only love could have created this firebird out of England's most watery corner:

There are two fountains springing with
great power,
The one water is hot and belongs to a boy;
The other water is cold and is called the
virgin's fountain.
Unite the one with the other, that the two
waters may become one.
THE CROWN OF NATURE
Johannes Fabricius, 17th century

Look now, the earth *has* united them and, for us of this time, has given birth to a water-born phoenix - transmutation of rock, peat, and water into poetic gold!

This language must have been universal, for what's burning the feet of Cumbrian shepherds was understood as holy by pharaoh and Hindu alike. Mann and Lyle explained the way the Egyptians saw things: *"In identifying with the myth of the Hindu creation, the masculine principle Atum, by the fire of its heart, projects itself into the feminine watery manifestation of its own self, Nun, in order to bring the world into being."*

England's Lake District revelation can only be a dazzlingly graphic projection of Atum upon Nun, the Sky Father coupled with the Earth Mother, and from such perfect union even the bedrock becomes alive! For me, this beautiful corner of Britain is pictorially yelling out that we, however, are at odds with this creative balancing act. We juggle like drunks with those building bricks of life and from the rain forests to Dolly the cloned sheep we are as though tearing those lovers apart, and in the process unpicking the divinely woven matrix of all creation. And sure, before the environmental and moral shit hits the fan, we can still make money from the wreckage: from hardwood window frames to babies made to order. Neat eh?

But let's return to our western traditions and in particular to the Grail.

In *The Castle of the Grail*, we are told that with eyes wide with wonder, Perceval once watched the procession of that cup pass silently by. He saw angelic figures carrying four holy objects: a sword, the actual spear used to pierce the side of Christ, a salver with a fish upon it, and last came the shimmering Grail itself. What the knight saw, according to Guttman and Johnson was a Kabbalistic magician's idea of a procession of the four elements: the sword being symbolic of air, the spear of fire, the salver of earth, and the Grail of water. Years

on, I see not only a loving embrace of fire and water animated in this phoenix, but also a wonderful amalgam of all four elements: water cloaking herself in flame, the earth forming the body of the bird itself, while air will be the vehicle of her ascension.

In this fusion of Albion's phoenix, a true sign of the *present*, all the elements, which in that visionary procession are shown to be the key ingredients of the Grail, have come together to now press that cup of all knowledge to everyone's lips, in the hope that we may rapidly realise both the fabulous and dreadful brink that time and the pay-back of our greed have brought us to. What the earth has done to Britain is a taste of what that knowledge can bring about, left as a gift upon the edge of the precipice in the hope that its terrifying beauty alone may cause a few to turn away and think again.

Astrologers Guttman and Johnson go on to satisfy my own intuitive soundings that the fullest blooming of the Grail will come about with the birth within each of us of that Grail-perceiving child. Listen to an astrologer's way of reading the demise of our present society, using the language of the Grail legend, and what may symbolically occur when fire and water mystically embrace at the core of an individual.

"Until the Grail is found, the world will be a wasteland. The inner meaning of the story is clear. It is the quality of feeling - symbolised by the watery element and the magic cup - which is most sadly lacking in Western Civilisation. The authors of the Grail Legend had already realised back in the Middle Ages, that our culture was leaning too strongly in the direction of science, of the rational intellect. A repression of the feminine principle (the symbolic Grail) has crippled the inner king, and now the world is a wasteland - curious anticipation of the current eco-crisis to which our scientific orientation has led us. According

to myth, healing for the culture can only come through the medium of feelings."

"The hot fiery emotions mix with the water and steam in a cauldron (Grail) several levels below consciousness (this place symbolised by the sleeping Grail child within) until a transit, eclipse, lunation, or progression sets them off and creates a highly volcanic eruption (sudden awareness or birth of the child). This is often true when Scorpio is involved, since Scorpio is the sign of fixed water (feelings), water that stays contained (suppressed) beneath the surface, sustaining the feelings before they can proceed. When positively integrated and expressed, the combination of water and fire creates people who are passionate, sensitive, fiery, and warm, encouraging their feelings to flow freely and spontaneously (alive, like never before)."

(*All brackets in this second quote are mine.)

Now I'm no astrologer, and neither do I understand entirely the alchemist's art, but is the earth through these fascinating fields of Britain attempting to condense and simplify their joint wisdom into a pictorially universal language for the common man to comprehend before it's too late? If so, and taking the bare bones from the snippets we have read, we might be being told that when the time comes, that mystic fire and water shall perfectly unite (the phoenix shows they already have) and some profound combustion of enlightenment shall be triggered throughout mankind if, that is, we first have the guts to be stripped of all we thought we knew. As D H Lawrence puts it: *"Are you willing to be made nothing? Dipped into oblivion? If not, you will never really change"* And certainly with Scorpio entering Guttman and Johnson's equation, Albion's arraying of Gemini, Scorpio and Aquarius in a triangle seems to vouch for the same chemistry containing something which, at the height of the storm, might have the power to

instantaneously catapult any survivor into a higher state of evolution. Is this not reason enough for a self-resurrecting phoenix to mark the spot for this time now?

A tongue of flame for each giant - and a pyramid of transformation?

As with the rest of Albion's giants, the closer you examine this one, the more the land will delight the eye and verify its presence.

But first, scrutinise the watery layout of this corner of Albion. Try imagining a blazing autumnal sunset over the western sea. Do it through the eyes of a hawk wheeling on a luxurious thermal high above this Lake District. Now count the most prominent of those lakes as each in turn catches fire in reflection of that sinking sun. I counted 14 tongues of flame - one for each of Albion's 14 giants? If the griffin is counted as one with Gemini's child, and the coming trinity of Christs upon the one cross is also viewed as one and the same, there are indeed 14 individual tongues to tell this tale of Albion!

Keep looking at these same lakes, but this time with a pencil, ruler, and map of the area to hand. Now, just as I once felt intuitively compelled to try out, put a ruler against the small town of Hawkshead (hint of the phoenix's own head?) which you will find in the centre of this bird's breast (it could even be its heart). Then shoot carefree connecting lines from there through eight of those 14 lakes: Ennerdale, Loweswater, Crummock, Buttermere, Bassenthwaite, Thirlmere, the northern straight of Ullswater, and Haweswater, noting as you go how the angle of each lake uncannily seems to follow the course of your pencil stroke. It's as if they are all endeavouring to lean and point inwards towards Hawkshead as though it were a vanishing point in a perspective drawing exercise. But more than this, notice how, as near as damn it, your ruler has indicated a classical bonfire shape with Hawkshead as its apex - though, like the bird it attempts to fry, this pyramidal pyre too is inverted.

Arthur - the mystic gold within the furnace?

It was while I was counting lakes, drawing bonfires, and musing upon mythical birds of resurrection, that my intuition brought up again the memory of King Arthur and suggested that this might well be a good place to find more news of that Once and Future King. Soon, not only the map and a few haunting lines of Tennyson, but also one or two historical 'maybes' were eagerly encouraging the feeling of Arthur's nearness.

Locations of Arthur's last resting place, along with the sites of his escapades, are I'm afraid as plentiful as Elvis impersonators. These locations are usually in beautiful and majestic settings, although I have never heard a certain industrial town in Cumbria lay claim to hosting that tomb in which they say the King only sleeps. However, let's allow the poetry in the map to lead us there, to what would certainly seem a sympathetic place on this phoenix where the King, who promised to return, might be mythologically biding his time, waiting to make his reappearance.

Hawkeshead, at the apex of the bonfire, would be an enticing spot to find him, but then again who cannot be intrigued by the wordplay of that intimated 'burial mound within a furnace' which is Barrow-in-Furness (locals actually pronounce Furness as *furnace*!). The town which was once the fiery birth place of nuclear submarines and the furnaces of an array of steel works is now the location for this firebird's own bright eye!

But wait, if we locate Arthur in this 'barrow within a phoenix's flaming eye' we would then be obligated to make a case for the Lake District over Cornwall and Salisbury Plain as the place where he bade us farewell and sailed into our deepest dreams, after his fatal wounding at the battle of Camlann. Let me tell you that to make such a case will not be difficult.

First of all, remember how Arthur's last wish was that Excalibur should be thrown into a lake. Well imagine that sword now cartwheeling into one of this Lake District's 14 tongues of poetic flame. As you do, tell me if Arthur's reason for casting it away here, above all other places, does not itself suddenly flare up with new import. What better place in all Britain than into the phoenix's own transformational flames for that blade of truth to return and thus be reforged in readiness for his own poetic return? Moreover, if Arthur did have that sword returned to the waters of one of these flames, we could rightly assume that he would have known exactly the pictorial layout of the vast stage he was dying upon. Indeed, I put the question again as to whether this zodiacal stage could have been one and the very same as his own Round Table, fashioned as it was in the orbits of the constellations, and groundplan for a New Jerusalem. Would not such fall wonderfully into place?

Remember, too, that it was the so-called Lady of the Lake who gave Excalibur to Arthur in the first place. Logically then, there is no finer place to return that blade to than the Lake District itself, surely no finer watery realm for her in all Albion than this.

But which lake would have taken back Excalibur? And what back-up do I have for claiming this?

Personally I'd like to believe that a gifted poet may glean as much truth of the past from his or her inspired heart, albeit condensed into a few verses of scintillating strangeness, as the archaeologist stooped for years with trowel and brush in hand. Alfred Lord Tennyson, Arthur's champion in Victoria's reign and the prime invigorator of the re-blooming of all things Arthurian throughout the English arts at that time, may have been one such poet.

I wonder then if, while he stayed near

Bassenthwaite Lake (one of those flames), whether he was inspired to weave it, without naming it, into his *Idylls of the King* as the lake into which Excalibur was thrown? If so, was it Tennyson's muse who whispered as *an actual truth*, deep within his poet's heart, that this, or maybe one of those other 13 lakes of fire, is where Excalibur sank back into the dream? The answer really doesn't matter, only that he wrote something that again has suddenly come of age for us today to be newly fascinated by when overlaid upon what the land has done.

Listen to a little of its gorgeous lament, and mentally replay its scenes amongst these boiling waters of Aquarius:

> *So all day long the noise of battle roll'd*
> *Among the mountains by the winter sea;*
> *Until King Arthur's table, man by man,*
> *Had fallen in Lyonesse about their lord,*
> *King Arthur, then, because his wound was deep,*
> *The bold Sir Bedivere uplifted him,*
> *Sir Bedivere, the last of all his knights,*
> *And bore him to a chapel nigh the field,*
> *A broken chancel with a broken cross,*
> *That stood on a dark straight of barren land.*
> *On one side lay the Ocean, and on one*
> *Lay a great water, and the moon was full.*
> THE PASSING OF ARTHUR
> Tennyson

*Note: only a poem, but there are no mountains in either Cornwall or on Salisbury Plain; and as far as lakes are concerned, neither Cornwall nor the Plain has one that could be seriously termed 'great'. The Lake District, however, boasts mountains and lakes galore!

Putting aside poetic innuendo for a moment, let's now touch upon something that may be considered a wee bit more substantial. In his book *The Landscape of King Arthur*, Geoffrey Ashe, a modern voice on Arthurian and such like matters, states that the name Camlann is derived from the word Camboglanna, meaning crooked bank. He goes on to point out that there was a Roman fort on Hadrian's Wall of this name, and the winding river Irthing passes by it where Birdoswald stands today. Ashe concludes, however, by tossing his cap firmly back into Cornwall's corner with: *"Hadrian's Wall is a long way from Cornwall and cannot be associated with the battle"*.

Hadrian's Wall is certainly a very long way from Cornwall, but then again it is *very, very* close to this phoenix and its lakes of transformational fire!

The battle to save tomorrow

In our attempt to marry myth to map, hear that Birdoswald/Camboglanna just so happens to be crucially located all but a few minutes east of the top of Albion's midnight-pointing cross; where we stand now is effectively five minutes to the top of that hour. Yet I feel that, due to the ebb and flow of the battle, Arthur, knowing perhaps something of his end, may well have chosen to take his mortal blow upon that land cross, alongside the Christ, although with the last of his strength, struggled back into the flames of the phoenix with the help of Bedivere, knowing that this station of his Round Table was resplendent in the imagery of resurrection - hence the possible grounding for that long-held belief of his return. Bassenthwaite is approximately 16 miles from that colossal cross in the landscape, while Ullswater actually lies against its horizontal bar.

But let us put ourselves into the script. Imagine, like Arthur, you had fought to bring about a golden age but, due to your own mistakes, were in danger of destroying it all, especially by your creation of Mordred, that incestuously-created son who wished to smash the dream you had banished him from. Thus, in the final battle, the only thing you could do was to make sure that the dream, whose foundational plans were scribed into the Round Table's surface, would be concealed and preserved for another time to strive for. At all costs, then, Mordred must be stopped from seizing that Table's highest seat, kept for the lamb and his spring and all hope of that golden time.

And so raged one of the most dreadful of battles ever recorded by legend. A battle that was impossible to win so the objective was to fight until a stalemate was reached, and thus take your adversary down with you. Arthur's destiny was to sacrifice himself in the defending of his Round Table of truth, there at the very apex of its mysteries, and upon the very threshold to that lamb of the new dawn, for that's where Camboglanna is situated. In doing so, he may have given his life to keep the secret of this great zodiac alive for us today, for if Mordred and imbalance had crossed into this cosmic clock's station of the lamb, that last square on this vast gaming board, then on that dark day winter may well have blighted spring for evermore. Even so, it was the well-named Dark Ages, which were to follow, indeed, have they ever ended?

Then rose the King and moved his host
by night,
And ever push'd Sir Mordred, league
by league,
Back to the sunset of Lyonesse -
A land upheaven from the abyss
THE PASSING OF ARTHUR
Tennyson

Do I romance too much, or is all this gelling into an extraordinary new insight into that most famous of legends?

Scan the cover artwork of this battleground of a gaming board for yourself - see how graphically it lends itself to one hell of a clash. Point just to the right of the top of the cross and gauge for yourself the pictorial significance of such a battle raging around this of all places.

Observe the Christ hung on that cross of Aries leaning so graphically westwards towards those phoenix flames, while, just to the east, rests the glowing lamb of the gathering new dawn. What a nail-biting geographical position this collision with Mordred would have been. And all this but a minute or two past midnight and only seconds more from the border of Durham, the only county in England that has been left pictorially vacant and therefore, for me, poetically holding the 'stilled' metamorphic moments before the opening of one's eyes upon a new dawn. Here, then, is a womb-like neutral space between the cross and the lamb, a magical peace aligned perhaps to those metamorphic hours spent in Joseph's tomb before Jesus himself rose up as a Christ. If so, today's Birdoswald in Albion's scheme of things would mark the beginning of the symbolic moments when the Christ Child or Christ Consciousness strives to be born. Justifiably Mordred wished to take this chunk of the gaming board, and widely scatter the pieces so that no one would ever remember that it existed. Game, set and match to imbalance!

Thus at that time, when, like today, the balance of the Round Table and of the world swayed dangerously out of kilter, Scorpio, cloaked as Mordred, made his lunge towards this tremulous and tender zone of Albion in an attempt to deny us the memory of Arthur, of golden ages to be won, and of his starry table of cosmic harmony, but most of all of the chance of that child ever opening its eyes upon a heaven on earth. But Arthur cried, 'No', and with colossal might pushed the shadow of inbred darkness back westwards, backwards out of the dawn and into the melting pot of these flames of the phoenix, fit, as John has told, for *murderers* and *liars*.

"But the fearful, and unbelieving, and the
abominable, and murderers, and
whoremongers, and sorcerers, and idolaters,
*and all liars, shall have their part in the **lake***

which burneth with fire and brimstone: which is the second death."
REVELATION, Chapter 21 Verse 8

And I can't help wondering if his vision of lakes of fire was a preview to what we all may now perceive on the Lake District - if so that Day of Judgment is doubly spelt out. But I digress.

Mordred, having then given his father a fatal wound, was, in turn, struck by Excalibur's cutting truth, and had then to bide his time until men, via their own ignorance, could feed him back to health and hate. He could, then, under a different name, but still under the same cloak, return in the hope of smashing that Round Table which has wrongly refused him taking up his rightful place, thus blinding itself via its own ignorance to the fact that even 'bad' has a right to be welcomed to the table of harmony. As already suggested in Scorpio, today's lesson must be to finally accept Mordred back for what he is - our own imbalances personified. Until we do, the Round Table or cosmic harmony on earth will be set only for upheaval. Indeed, in Arthur's own denial of his son and its terrible consequences there is parable enough, retold now for us who may soon have to face our own global Camlann.

Arthur then, in defending all that Albion brings, was alas dealt a fatal blow via the hand of his son (just as we may receive a fatal blow from our own unbalanced creations.) But in pushing Mordred back, Arthur had life enough left, with Bedivere's help, to make his own final way to the lakes, those resurrectional tongues of fire, and there have Excalibur cast back as a promise that all would be reforged and brought back to light in this, our phoenix time - the future he gave his life for.

Beside one of these same liquid flames, perhaps Bassenthwaite, Arthur also let his soul go and so be held in the essence of this phoenix. His body was perhaps then interred under Bedivere's knowing instructions in its eye, which is Barrow-in-Furness, that splendidly coded fiery grave, as an eternal sign of his own eyes reopening when another battle for a new dawn draws near.

Finally, and before I rest my case for Camlann being close enough to this phoenix for legend to be rewritten, I would like to draw your attention to the book *A traveller's guide to the Kingdom of Arthur* by Neil Fairbairn, in which, while debating the location for Arthur's final battle, settles for Camboglanna/Birdoswald as being the more probable site of the battle. He writes, *"Mordred's frequent association with the North would make a conflict in this part of Britain a distinct possibility."*

Believe me, if Camlann was fought upon that cross of Aries, the whole story of King Arthur and his knights of the Round Table should become more important to us now than to any other previous age. A whole new insight, triggered by this map, makes his story explode in both new life and meaning; no more a medieval frolic, but a time-capsule of meaningful advice as this evolutionary clock moves again to midnight and the Grail comes up for grabs - maybe for the last time.

Tell-tale names?

Further to my suggestion that Arthur's poetical last resting place could be at Barrow-in-Furness - scholars will of course be quick to tell me that the name Barrow in this case has nothing whatsoever to do with burial mounds, and that Furness has not the slightest connection with a furnace. Their rebuke I'd take on the chin, though I'd still wear an impudent grin to the effect that it is in this precise way, albeit still intellectually humiliating to most, that the Earth Mother has for centuries concealed her Treasure Island of Albion from us all, yet all the time dangling it under our very noses - and thus all the better to shock us with today! And let's face it, because it defies all boundaries of rational thinking, scholars will never be ready to accept what has arrived, even if it had been delivered this morning with a bow of red ribbon tied about it from The Wash to Fishguard!

However, for any happy-go-lucky fool blinking through newly-opening eyes, some of the place names found upon these giants do seem to have been uncannily primed to become cheeky verifications of whatever giant they are now found to be sitting upon. One cannot help but think that their own 'wordy' evolutions may be as divinely wrought as the giants they mark. I must stress, though, that never once have I found a land giant by finding a tell-tale place name first; the coastal contours alone have guided me. I have found these seemingly confirmational place names only months, or even years, after I'd discovered whatever giant they sat upon. And if the actual shapes of these giants have made me gasp with disbelief, then these place name pimples and warts have always provided me with the disarming, though affirmative giggles, however, one place name was to prove the exception - one which had the power to squeeze an instantaneous tear out of the corner of my eye. You'll have to wait to read of a night in Easter week, when I first came face to face with the Cumbrian Christ, to learn of the superlative place name that backed-up the fact that he lies in all truth crucified beneath it. This was another name subliminally caught from the Earth Mother's

own lips and jotted down on a map so as, one day in the future, to sing out another explosive "Yes!" to her great design underfoot. Such do I claim for Barrow-in-Furness, and I propose that, whichever Roman dignitary stood up in Barrow one day and added *in-Furness* (or something like it), was, whether he knew it or not, aiding and abetting holy and comically wonderful work!

However, it wasn't only Barrow-in-Furness that caught my eye as being perhaps an indicator of Arthur's presence here, or indeed that we were traversing a bird of sorts. You see, the Celtic communities of Britain's western extremes believe to this day that, upon his death, Arthur's spirit took flight as a raven - a bird which when overlapped upon this shape of the phoenix incites another glut of exciting questions.

So hear now that buried in amongst this fiery plumage are such substantiating signposts as Ravensglass, Ravenstonedale, Caw Fell ('caw' in my dictionary is the cry of a raven!), Crosby Ravensworth, and Ravenstown - not to mention Hawkshead and Eaglesfield; all of them huddled upon this sign of the firebird and seemingly of Arthur too. Personally I doubt if anywhere else in Britain has so many raven or bird-like place names gathered in such quantity and in such a relatively small area. And is it not said that ravens were always drawn to battlefields? Even that site of Camlann, today's Birdoswald, seems to tempt the same thought.

So a cluster of five ravens haunts this sign,

and, I believe that, in remembrance of one they no more disguise but brazenly advertise! Even Hawcoat upon the phoenix's beak seems to strive to 'caw' out the call of this bird; likewise Haws Point, and the more thought-provoking Haws Bed, Haws Scar and Rape Haw, all found upon its head, clamour to be recognised and accredited as the awakening cries of the Raven King - all of them demanding that *we* also open our eyes.

Open them, for instance, to more of the folklore surrounding the raven, sometimes seen as the very eyes and messengers of both gods and heroes, while other legends told that the bird could actually bring eyesight to the blind! So how tempting, again, to suspect the essence of Arthur twinkling within this raven-crossed phoenix's own eye! Note too that a raven was also a sure sign of death and destruction, even of pending storm and flood. Apt, or what, such a warning on this of all signs - beset as it is with water and flame and with a scorpion on its tail!

With eyes still wide open and a map in front of you, check out the head of this firebird, for without doubt it is split asunder, and it prickles the hairs on my own head to hear Tennyson in his *Passing of Arthur* sigh in Arthur's own voice to his friend Bedivere: "*I am deeply smitten thro' the helm, That without help I cannot last 'til morn*". So could even this bird's own glaring head wound be a mirror of Arthur's own? Was Arthur's helm itself crowned by a phoenix?

Enticing food for thought, but gauge my shock when such suspicion led me to view on a larger scale map what seems damning evidence of the very same - soon counting off a staggering **26 place names around that phoenix's head wound ending in _Scar_**! Places such as Haws Scar, Hollowing Scar, Meeting Scar and Cross Dike Scar to name but a few - 26 *scars*, not upon this mythological bird's chest or wings, but spattered like so many blood stains directly **upon its geographically smitten head**; the most pertinent of all being the one that was placed deepest of all inside its golden sand-barred brain, spliced as it is by the Piel Channel; that spot screaming off the map as **Head Scar.** Yet again the land seems to do my talking for me!

Such news should be of comforting confirmation to many who feel that Arthur has always lived on in the spiritual fibre of Britain, his name a synonym for hope of better days even in the darkest of hours, an exultation to the faint-hearted. But if a poetic interplay with the physical day-to-day world isn't worth a damn to you, then that's a shame, for I agree with another poet, Matthew Arnold, who warned that in the years ahead all our faiths will be so defrocked by scientists and academics that only in poetry, that faith of the heart, will we stand any chance of again rejoicing in the wonders that are contained behind the everyday. And with that I cannot resist quoting for a second time John Cowper Powys' own views of the same:

> "*What's Poetry if it isn't something that has to fight for the unseen against the seen, for the dead against the living, for the mysterious against the obvious?*
> *It's the only Lost Cause we've got left!*
> *It fights for the... for the... for the Impossible!*"
> A GLASTONBURY ROMANCE,
> John Cowper Powys

And is this the secret behind Arthur's charisma?

Changing tack slightly, have you ever wondered just what is behind the evergreen magic and charm of Arthur? Certainly he has an aura, which, if anything over the last two decades, has grown ever brighter, even though historical opinion rates him as no more than a conglomerate figment of several storytellers' imaginations. I find it fascinating to see bookshop shelves heaving under the weight of the constant arrival of new Arthurian titles, and the sight of so many people who travel from all corners of the globe to Britain in search of just a scent of the atmosphere that still swirls about the places where his legend grew up. Indeed, watching them get off their coaches at Tintagel and Glastonbury, it's as though they come as pilgrims to a mini-Holy Land, and are open-minded about his promised return at some time in the future, as though he were a Christ. But why such passion when he is a somewhat flawed figure of myth, his childhood given to a Disney cartoon, his name to a National Lottery ball machine!

For what it is worth my small inner voice offers me a reason that gives me goose-pimples, a reason urged on purely by what we have read upon Albion's wonder map. My theory is, as you would imagine, a continuance of the bizarre, but I'll lay it on you anyway!

In the chapter on Pisces I recounted the old legend of the arrival to these shores of the boy Jesus and his uncle Joseph of Arimathea. However, I didn't quite finish it. Legend has it that, after the crucifixion, Joseph and a group of 12 disciples (not entirely the original 12, and including Mary the mother of Jesus) returned to Britain to escape persecution in their homeland. What is more, they brought with them the cup used by Jesus at the Last Supper and which, in Joseph's hand, had caught a few drops of Jesus' blood from the side wound he received whilst on the cross; that cup becoming the Holy Grail. Their final destination was Glastonbury.

On arrival there, so the legend continues, they were welcomed by a Prince Arviragus who at once, and most generously, gave the visitors 12 hides of land (each hide representing 160 acres) upon which to live in peace. This gesture gave rise to arguably the first Christian church ever to be built on earth, Arviragus being baptised by Joseph into that new faith.

Now you may already be one jump ahead of me when I ask this next simple, and I hope not too naïve question, namely: was Arviragus

Arthur? Too simple? In its defence I repeat that such simplicity is Albion's very benchmark; indeed, is not Albion already proving that 'we've never seen the wood for the trees'? Anyway, indulge me by considering if, with the passing of the centuries, the name Arviragus could have become affectionately bastardised and familiarised into a virtual pet name, one that could be spoken of with love, whether in vaulted palace or before rude cottage hearth, initially a clumsy mouthful of a name which in a thousand retellings of a King of a Golden Time could just possibly have evolved into simply *Arthur*.

Let us further speculate. Let's say if this Arviragus was at least some 30 years old when Joseph returned to Britain; could we then not presume, with relative ease, that upon Joseph's first visit here with Jesus, this same prince, a lad himself then, met and maybe even befriended the young Messiah? Certainly his gift of so much prime land, part of the holiest acreage in all Britain (seeing that it sat within the Glastonbury zodiac, itself the glistening eye of Albion's Piscean fish) would surely suggest that these travellers were by no means strangers to Arviragus. It might also infer that he was already a friend of their leader Joseph, who had now brought with him the Holy Grail which was to ignite Britain's, and perhaps the West's, most enduring legend of all time, not to mention the remaining years of Arthur's life.

Talk now with your younger self, the one more susceptible to fresh, strange ideas as you once did when you were a child and your own world was new and boundless. Ask if those two boys, a young messiah from the East and a young prince of the West, once sat atop some grassy earth giant when spring was all agog. Did they discuss not only the beauty of what was still forming deep beneath the heather cushions on which they sat, but did they also then look north, or even journey there, to see or sense what the land was pushing through its breast to mark their own harrowing destinies.

Strangely, the cross that would claim them both, albeit in different ways, was also being writ large upon the land-clock in whose dappled green wooded hours and minutes they sat, watching the troubled story of man and the earth unfold. It will do you no harm to let your child go and sit beside them in this exciting possibility, and if, while sitting there, your own heart skips a beat as you admit *"It just might be simple enough to be true"* then I ask you if such a friendship between Jesus and Arthur/Arviragus could offer up a reason for that undying and *almost, but not quite,* holy aura that has grown around Arthur - a luminescence picked up from being once in the physical presence of the Messiah? Maybe they were, for a season or two, as close as brothers leaving a shining *hopefulness* swirling about Arthur's name, retained from boys' arms, once linked amid peels of laughter and boisterous gallops headlong over the snowy slopes of Glastonbury Tor in some Albion winter of nearly 2000 years ago. It makes my own heart skip a beat as I write it.

Thus, although but a mortal, stricken with all the common faults and weaknesses which are part and parcel of being a man, Arthur, in having known Jesus, caught a flicker of his light. He learnt from him, too, that a man could rise out of ignorance and achieve paradise on earth. He learnt also that the earth herself was preparing for that New Jerusalem on these fields of Albion for a future time, and that under their green mantle would be placed all the wisdom that would be won by his friend Jesus. In a sense, in sending that cup to Arthur's realm, Jesus may well have been symbolically *passing his cup* of wisdom into the care of Arthur and his topographical Round Table, a foundational token for the coming of this New Jerusalem.

Could, then, a subliminal knowledge of this account be the reason that, for some, the mere mention of King Arthur stirs up a curiously spontaneous affection, a fleeting sense of better times just around the corner? I'd like to think so.

If the hunch is right, and because of that afterglow picked up from Jesus, I'd like to think that the spirit of Arthur had melted back into the fibre of his landscaped Round Table, to percolate up through every sod of it - he becoming almost a rustic and blackberry-crowned Christ-like retainer of hope, becoming one with the simple and innocently beautiful everyday things - one with hedgehogs and dandelions, with owls and old men, still with the child-like innocence in their eyes. I see this same essence of Arthur melting at last even into the very atmosphere of Albion where he can still be acutely felt by some, as though he has left behind a tingling silver akin to a comet's tail, a tail into which we may still dip as though it were an invisible stream and get carried along for a while above the daily cares towards the Grail.

We may not swim all the way there, but when we return we may find for a short while that a new glitter has settled over our uninspiring surroundings. Suddenly that row of chestnut trees alongside the parked cars is shimmering as though just ruffled by Arthur and Merlin's passing, the flickering shadows upon the kitchen wall suddenly a tapestry of tingling expectation of *something*.

So look for him yourself in the growing perception that a sight of Albion has set in motion; catch his presence glowing behind every cock-a-doodle-do and dawn chorus; behind every winter solstice day when the sun stays its outward journey and begins to return again; behind the badger sweeping out her set after winter's sleep, daffodils bent at her doorway; behind that orchard suddenly overnight hung in a frothy pink wedding dress; behind the comforting earthy incense of new baked bread, or a scent of wood-smoke caught on a late evening breeze when a feel of Christmas jangles in the air, even though it's still only October. Behind all these, and a myriad other expressions of the innocently

earthly and eternally hopeful, is Arthur, and behind him, I'm sure, must tower the Christ with the face of a laughing boy.

In his book *The Death of Merlin* the Arthur-sensitive Walter Johannes Stein, an Austrian by birth but whose life was ever drawn to "the Matter of Britain" and to the aura of Arthur, seems also to have plunged into this same Grail stream and to have returned with almost a half glimpse of Albion's landscaped secret. He certainly felt that *something* wonderful was rushing back into our consciousness from out of Britain's spiritual ether which would one day, like a returning comet, shatter the scholarly blockade which has been thrown up to repel the name Arthur and the whole nagging 'Matter of Britain' - for that was how medieval Europe termed the enigmatic magic that hung over Arthur's isles.

Hear Stein probe his own depths to what he felt was still hidden from his senses, but which he knew *was* here biding some God-given time of revelation: "..*but the important question we must ask is whether there is still something remaining over which has not crystallised into the frozen tradition. The problem of King Arthur is more alive today than ever before*"

Stein wrote the above in 1932, since when the ice has melted and the crystallisation of the Grail is indeed seen living within the suddenly transformed shape of Britain, the unveiled Round Table. With it, in these unfurling wings of the Aquarian phoenix, the essence of its Once and Future King may also be returned to us.

Stein, however, had even more to share with his readers about what he sensed in the Arthur-sensitised aura of this land.

Elsewhere in the same book he again seems to feel the very breath rising from Albion's sleeping giants although couldn't himself fully crystallise it, sensing only that *something*, as yet intangible but nevertheless profound, *was* oozing out of every rock and leaf of the place and nearing some astonishing visual revelation

of itself. For me, he writes as if his fingers were actually upon the very cliff-faced hem of the green, hedgerow-stitched, city-patched, curtain that has hid Albion's miracle for so long - but 70 years ago was not the right time for all to be unveiled, so his hand was stayed while his intuition probed on. Listen again as he tries valiantly to lay hold of its teasing: "*Something eternal-universal the very breath of freedom lives in this land. It stretches out, embracing the whole of humanity. It still speaks to us through the hills and valleys, the rocks and caves mentioned in the Arthurian legends. The winds and waves sing of it, the atmosphere is full of it. It is necessary to find contact with this invisible Power, which, in only one of its forms, appears as the Arthur of the Legend. This Power is the Eternal Spirit of this country which we shall meet again.*"

He goes on to tell us that this same *something* is: "*English in its innermost depths. It speaks to all human beings wherever they live and to whatever nation they belong. The Round Table is the whole world, says the saga (Malory xiv, 2). Its knights still live, their search for the Grail still goes on and the Grail, as we now know, is the secret spirit which must unite all mankind in love and brotherhood.*"

What a fanfare to what has now come to light! Unfortunately, Stein's life-long inner and outer quest for the truth of Arthur, so brilliantly intellectualised and shared in both lectures and essays, would not be worth the paper it's written on to the presiding 'know-alls' of presently acceptable historical fact, for the mere mention of Arthur in any degree of seriousness in such circles would provoke nothing but a few polite, though nevertheless condescending, grins. It must be said in their favour, however, that they have of late given an 'official' inch by agreeing that if Arthur really did exist, his time would have been spent more probably amongst the fur-clad Celts, as some war lord, rather than dressed in the mirror-finished armour of the medieval jousting circuits.

Some 2000 years ago, maybe Arviragus would have fitted their bill perfectly!

As an interesting footnote, legend has it that, in later years, Prince Arviragus was indeed crowned king and was the first Briton ever to fly the red cross on a white ground as his flag, for this was the design on the banner which Joseph gave to him as a gift. Was it given both in memory of that boyhood friend who did not return, and as a token that the quintessence of all that Jesus taught would, thereafter, be found in the symbolism hammered into that cross of stone, that is hoisted at the height of England? It thrills me to think that it was.

That first red cross, by the way, was to supply the present Union flag with its first four spokes; later the overlapping crosses of St Andrew and St Patrick were to give the final device its 12 radiating spokes. And tell me if, in it, we do not have the wheel of the zodiac itself - a perfect device to flutter over the secret!

But enough speculation of Arthur; as enjoyable as I hope it's been, rekindling his legend upon this map, at the end of the day it matters not one jot to this phoenix if Arviragus wasn't Arthur, or for that matter if Jesus never met him. In fact, this land would remain unmoved if the truth was that Jesus never set foot upon it, or if it turned out that Arthur really was born out of pure imagination, for, whether my wild speculations are wondrously true or laughably false, our earth is right now bulging the floor plan of the Lake District with the gigantic 44 x 38 mile fact that a firebird encompasses it all within her fabulous plumage! So let's get down to some hard fact!

Defining the body

Barrow-in-Furness is its red-hot eye. Hilpsford Point marks the top of that damaged head from where the A5087 and Morecambe Bay's coastline draw the back of the bird's head down to Greenodd sitting in the gap between the neck and the arched shoulder of the right, or eastern, wing. From Greenodd, that shoulder arches around to Grange-over-Sands and the river Gilpin, which, along with the A6, outlines this unfurling wing down in the direction of the watery flames.

Go back now to Hilpsford Point and follow the coast along the Isle of Walney, which draws its forehead down to that savagely barbed beak. The coast down to Broughton-in-Furness defines the hollow between the throat and the arched shoulder of the western wing. After Broughton we still follow the coastline to Haverigg on top of this wing's arched shoulder, then go northwards along the Irish Sea to Maryport, which marks approximately this western wing's singed feather tips.

Those lakes are truly incredible in their efforts to attain near vertical alignments in order to exercise their sacred roles as flames. See how, visually, they all leap upwards in an effort to consume the bird's intended flight, not one spoiling the overall effect by lying horizontally. Remember, though, that these flames do not destroy, but only cleanse, for are they not water after all? The child in you, if you'll let it, sees through the riddle at once and claps its hands at the simplistic joy of it all.

Lastly, at the back of the bird's head there is definite sign of an entirely characteristic crest, which, like the one on the griffin, seems to be suggested by sand banks.

Archaic shouts of approval

Albion's Zodiac is, as we know with good reason, out of sequence with today's accepted processional order of the heavenly signs. However, at times upon our journey it is reassuring to hear voices call out from a wiser past in confirmation that the direction we are following is perfectly *in step*. So first of all, listen to a voice from ancient Egypt, where once they perceived a mighty Tree of Life standing within the great hall of their holy city of Heliopolis, and from whose branches they saw, and never forgot, the phoenix rise in splendour. Albion's cross will itself be overlaid by the image of the Tree of Life (we'll hear more of this later). See then how our phoenix, too, is perfectly placed to graphically portray its own scorching flight-path from off the great right arm (branch) of Albion's cross (tree). Indeed, could it even be seen, blazing from the Christ's own right hand, as a double affirmation of him being risen? If so, a symbolic picture to all students of Albion's mother tongue that perhaps high on Golgotha, Jesus, too, had to first plunge *down* into himself to be able to rise thereafter as the Christ, or should we say *as a Christ*? Look, too, to where that bird is actually flying; its diving headlong towards Gemini's sleeping babe and its attendant griffin; confirmation that it is to your inner child that you must descend in the hope of perceiving new wings of freedom.

Now from old Sumer, that early font of zodiac wisdom, comes a voice that doesn't argue with Albion's allotting of Aquarius to its visual 'eleventh hour' station, for the Sumerians also gave to it that same 'on the brink' position in their own arrangement of the zodiacal clock. Moreover they named its month *Shabatu*, which, according to Sesti, meant *Malediction of The Rain*. Is this perhaps a warning that we, who find ourselves actually living in the astrological house of Shabatu, should keep a weather eye open?

Another warning voice, though this time from a lot nearer home

The next voice we hear is ominous indeed. It calls out in the form of a prophesy found among the anonymously written pages of *The High History of the Holy Grail* where, in its latter pages, and with Perceval well upon his way towards the Grail, it recalls that he *"seeth a hermitage upon the sea hard by"*.

First of all, let's put a ring around the *"sea hard by"* for such a locale can in no way allude to the Glastonbury area, as Mary Caine suggests, (she too has made mention of this same passage and set it upon Somerset's circle of inland giants). Although low-lying and once surrounded by a lagoon or swamp, Glastonbury's higher ledges could surely never have been happily described as being edged by *"the sea hard by"*. Therefore, I propose we try resetting the scene of that hermitage upon *this* Cumbrian coast of the phoenix, itself in Albion's own latter stages, and then see what happens.

Perceval, on arriving here, sees a vision of a castle that he perceived as *"burning fiercely with a great flame"* and asks the hermit about it. *"Sir, saith the hermit, 'I will tell you. Joseus, the son of King Pelles, slew his mother there. Never sithence hath the castle stinted of burning, and I tell you that of this castle and one other will be kindled the fire that shall burn up the world and put it to an end"*

Since treading Albion, whenever I hear tales of sons murdering (earth?) mothers my ears prick up; also, from a distance, don't those square-towered holders of atomic reactors look somewhat like the keeps of Norman castles - and these modern-day keeps also contain fires that never 'stint of burning'? No need to remind you, then, that here on Cumbria's burning wing of a coast, and with the sea hard by, is Sellafield!

Think about this as well - if we sons have been slowly killing the Earth Mother for generations, then by building nuclear reactors could we have committed the deed that will all but finish her off? I also wonder if that *'other'* burning castle was Chernobyl - already a catastrophe that I fear may have caused more long-term damage than we, who had to breathe its filth for weeks, and perhaps will have to digest through our food for years to come, have yet been told about.

You must, of course, read all this as you see fit. However, there must be something more in the atmosphere here than suspected radioactive leakage. Listen to someone else trying to express it to us would-be Percevals.

Trusting that they didn't know of this prophetic phoenix beneath their walking boots when rambling near this same Cumbrian sore spot, these two men, nevertheless, felt compelled to write in almost prophetic words of the vibe they picked up around Sellafield. While gathering material for their book *England's Last Wilderness*, the well-known environmentalist David Bellamy and his co-author Brendan Quale, stopped dead in their tracks when catching sight of that great 'plutonium keep'. They fell, for some reason, into recalling matters Arthurian and the prospect of this area having once had the dubious honour of hosting that grievous battle of Camlann: *"Ravenglass on the Cumbrian coast, ironically now the home of one of the world's oldest, biggest and potentially most dangerous nuclear installations, the Sellafield plant, has even been identified as one of the sites where Avalon was placed. According to legend, the mortally wounded Arthur was taken from there to the Isle of Avalon - probably Ireland (Scorpio's underworld!) by the witch-fairy Morgan le Fay."* (*My bracket.)

Intrigued? Let's hear the same pair begin to air even deeper feelings, perhaps triggered by the potent interactive spirit of both raven king and phoenix swirling about them. Now listen to words as prophetic as those once quietly spoken by a hermit long ago, but in this new mythology of truth, only said this morning: *"The ravens that accompanied Arthur on his mythological journey no longer roost on the estuary that bears their name, preferring instead to inhabit the safer heights of Cumbria and Pennine mountains. There they wait and watch for the passing of Sellafield, and the return of the King."*

I don't know about you, but I've just had another rash of goose-bumps!

For me, knowing where they sat when verbalising such thoughts, their words, as frighteningly sombre as they are, take on a strange beauty, words obviously spoken from the heart of another knowing inner child, who also awaits a full return. Meanwhile, today's children of Albion suck in every day the all-too-real venom of Sellafield, even though they have never laid eyes upon the place. The following comes from a shocking report in The Mirror newspaper of 31 July 1997: *"Every Brit has traces of radioactive nuclear waste in their bodies, alarmed scientists warned yesterday. Professor Nick Priest, said, "We discovered Sellafield affects the whole country. It really was unexpected... there are likely to be plutonium traces in everyone in the U.K".* Chris Rose, a spokesman for Greenpeace added *"We have built up a radio-active legacy that will be present for tens of thousands of years"*

Is then Ravenglass, Windscale, Sellafield, or THORP, name the sore as you like, the place where the raven king melted into the spiritual glass crystal of Albion's mirror. Or, because ravens were once the trusted messengers of the gods, is all this a warning of a day to come when this blighted stretch of beach, where Sellafield broods, will be blasted into liquid glass? With a phoenix underfoot I shudder at the mounting and seemingly inescapable evidence given birth by the land and sensed by those who love her.

And last of all - are we standing in that upper room?

If Perceval did meet that hermit on the Cumbrian coast he was just a short step away from finding the Grail he had sought for so long, for that culmination waited but 50 miles away. But just before we follow him there, along with Galahad and Sir Bors, let us briefly examine an intriguing text from the New

Testament concerning a mysterious water carrier who directed the disciples to the upper room, the place of the Last Supper before the next day's sweat and blood.

And he sendeth forth two of his disciples, and saith unto them, Go ye into the city, and there shall meet you a man bearing a pitcher of water: follow him. And wheresoever he shall go in, say ye to the goodman of the house, The Master saith, Where is the guest-chamber, where I shall eat the passover with my disciples? And he will show you a large upper room furnished and prepared: there make ready for us. And his disciples went forth, and came into the city, and found as he had said unto them: and they made ready the passover. And in the evening he cometh with the twelve.
MARK, Chapter 14, Verses 13 -17

Most Bible scholars find this water carrier something of an enigma for as soon as he enters the story he is gone again, leaving us with a strong sense that no matter how brief his 'bit part' was, such an odd casting must have had pertinent meaning.

Astrologers, on the other hand, have argued an Aquarian suggestiveness to this player's role; even some coded astrological message spirited between the lines and meant for translation by those in the know. Radical Christians, however, would wholeheartedly object to any biblical star gazing, even though it was a star that guided the Three Wise Men, who were themselves perhaps astrologers, to the birthplace of the Messiah. Indeed, one may even say that not only did the New Testament begin with the arrival of a star, but if that water carrier *is* a sign of Aquarius, then it pretty well ends with a whole constellation of them!

All that apart, in what context should this water carrier-cum-guide overlap onto this area of Britain that is awash with lakes?

Well, here we are in Albion's own house of Aquarius, indeed, we're upstairs in that house which is near the top of Albion's pile of wonders. Now just take a look where we're going directly after we set foot outside this upper room of Albion. Perfectly in step with the Bible's own record of events, we begin to climb Albion's own Golgotha, risen upon the highest peaks in England! Thus, if the land is poetically echoing Mark, we in this house and dawning Age of Aquarius must be being offered exactly the same that Jesus shared with his disciples in that Last Supper. In short, I believe that all the wisdom contained in the Grail must be here being offered to us. And if true, then like the events that followed that Last Supper, tomorrow we may face not only our own Camlanns but also as many Golgothas as there are individuals upon the face of the earth.

"And he took bread, and gave thanks, and brake it, and gave unto them, saying, This is my body which is given for you: this do in remembrance of me. Likewise also the cup after supper, saying, This cup is the new testament in my blood, which is shed for you."
LUKE, Chapter 22, Verses 19-20

*Note: in my dictionary the word 'cella', so close to 'Sella'-field, is uncannily described as being the 'principle room of a temple' - thus could Sellafield, albeit disquietingly so, be that upper room where mankind has not only killed his Mother but is now preparing his own Last Supper? Indeed, I was particularly concerned when (and this long after this chapter had been completed) in the aftermath of September 11, one of the first things the British Government did in response was to station a Harrier jump-jet at Sellarfield. Obviously they too recognised the potential hot-spot.

We must now begin our long climb up to Albion's Golgotha in the stars, but do cast a long look back over your shoulder at this struggling to rise phoenix, and as you do, put the following concerns of others into your backpack: in the Daily Express May 15, 2000, the Government's own advisors on environmental issues warned that "*...the world is still proceeding at a reckless pace towards disaster.*" From the same report, Julian Salt of the Loss Prevention Council, which advises the UK insurance industry, said, "*The oceans have warmed and they are going to get warmer. The world is already locked into a spiral of catastrophe.*"

What a weight it all is.

CHAPTER 12

ARIES
Part One

• The Cross and the Christ •

*The Tree of Life / The Mast of
the Ark / The Sword of Truth*

★

*The twelfth giant
along the way*

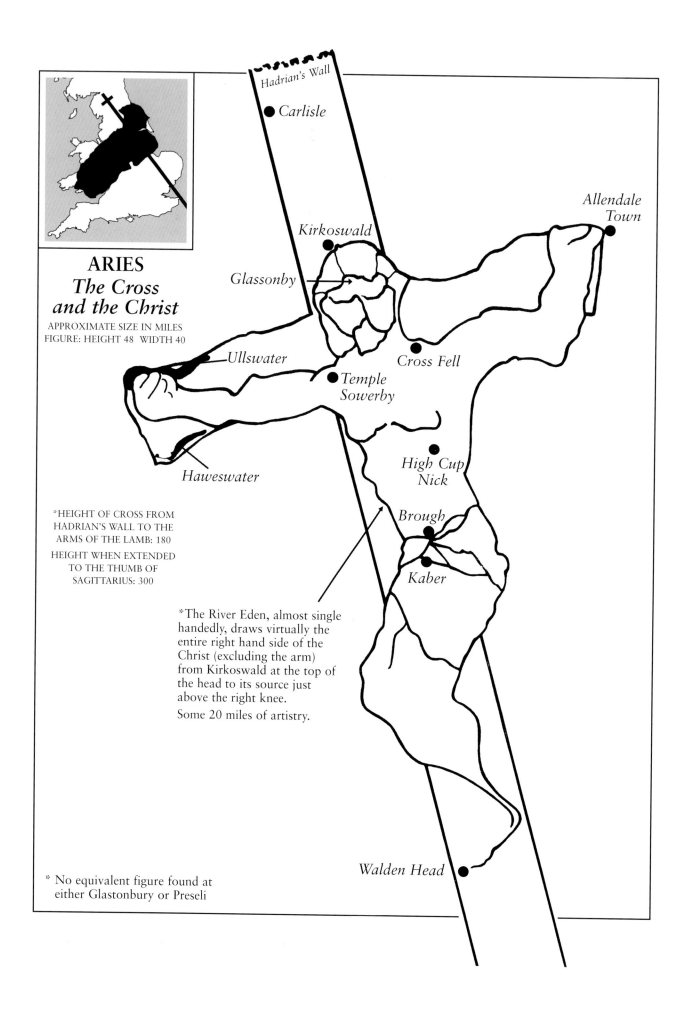

ARIES
The Cross and the Christ

APPROXIMATE SIZE IN MILES
FIGURE: HEIGHT 48 WIDTH 40

Hadrian's Wall

● Carlisle

Allendale Town

Kirkoswald

Glassonby

Ullswater

Cross Fell

Temple Sowerby

Haweswater

High Cup Nick

Brough

Kaber

*HEIGHT OF CROSS FROM
HADRIAN'S WALL TO THE
ARMS OF THE LAMB: 180

HEIGHT WHEN EXTENDED
TO THE THUMB OF
SAGITTARIUS: 300

*The River Eden, almost single
handedly, draws virtually the
entire right hand side of the
Christ (excluding the arm)
from Kirkoswald at the top of
the head to its source just
above the right knee.

Some 20 miles of artistry.

Walden Head

* No equivalent figure found at
either Glastonbury or Preseli

Unlooked for, unwanted, but devastatingly unmistakable!

And did the Countenance Divine
Shine forth upon these clouded hills

JERUSALEM, William Blake

Jesus replied: "Fear Not Albion: unless I die thou canst not live,
But if I die I shall arise again and thou with me,
This Friendship and Brotherhood: Without it Man is Not."

JERUSALEM, William Blake

**GENERAL AREA: THE TOP OF THE CROSS BUTTS AGAINST HADRIAN'S WALL.
ITS HORIZONTAL BEAM GOES AS FAR WEST AS THE TIP OF ULLSWATER AND
EASTWARDS TO ALLENSDALE TOWN, WHILE THE VERTICAL SHAFT TAKES A LINE
THAT CONNECTS THE HIGH PEAKS OF CROSS FELL AND ROGAN'S SEAT.
KIRKOSWOLD MARKS THE TOP OF CHRIST'S HEAD WHILE HIS FEET
TOUCH WALDEN HEAD.**

ries, on Albion's star clock, is seen as a colossal reclining lamb holding aloft a cross upon which the figure of the Christ is hung in astonishing detail.

This lamb and cross together form the largest of all Albion's flesh and blood giants by a long way, only Cancer's wooden ark dwarfs it. Its size is justified, I believe, on account of the magnificent message it bears, a message which tells that a spring of a new spirituality is just around the corner - a new dawn of global proportions that will see men bonding to the whole of creation like never before. This evolutionary leap, albeit on the back of some global upheaval, may even be sparked by the Second Coming, though the land doesn't say whether he is due to arrive in the flesh or purely within the consciousness of us all. Either way, for a sure fire fact he has returned today more than 40 miles tall upon the face of the planet!

But, first of all, allow me to separate this lamb and the cross it bears so that we may better appreciate each. Although I discovered the lamb a moment or two before seeing the cross, and many months prior to receiving the shock of finding the Christ nailed there, I feel that our next preordained step, after leaving the phoenix, should be to this midnight-pointing cross. Climb with me up to Albion's Golgotha, but fear not, the lamb and the new dawn it promises will follow the shepherd whom we shall find waiting on this cloud-tumbled height.

Before we begin our ascent, however, let us

rest in those foothills formed by the undulating fleece of the lamb, for I would like to relate just how the presence of this cross first dawned on me and my horrified reaction to it.

Smiles turned to frowns

They were, of course, happy and incredulous moments when I saw the return of the lost lamb into Albion's fabulous garden, his happy bleating being especially celebratory for me as his arrival meant, to me if no one else, that I was not mad after all. This discovery meant that, after more than 30 years of looking, I had found the full complement of the zodiac's starry family writhing beneath the whirling washing machines and sleeping dogs of the unsuspecting British. Moreover his arrival too, and I do not over-romanticise the occasion, began the springtime of my own life: from that day on, the world has become more magical than anybody had ever told me before. In short, the little boy's daydream was no longer just in his head, it could be seen from Hadrian's Wall to Land's End, and from Ramsgate to Londonderry!

Behind my smiles I also knew that, until the day of finding this lost lamb, I had in truth found nothing; Libra's dove, Gemini's child, Virgo's dancing Mother and all the others would have been but products of freaky erosion, allied to an over active imagination - but with this last piece of the puzzle my hitherto on-off dalliance with a map had been irrefutably confirmed: I had stumbled over a miracle. Unbeknown to me, however, other giants still waited in the wings for their own sacred time of return, their future arrivals providing the icing on the cake.

In the next chapter I will tell you just how the shape of this lamb finally dawned on me. In those moments when I first saw him, however, and which nearly had me dancing in the street, my eye was still working and was caught by that great rugged back bone of Britain, that north-south spinal column of high peaks called The Pennines. It seemed to lie across the lamb's body like a pole of some kind. As my eye followed the northward march of those peaks, which were beginning to look like an upright shaft, there suddenly swept into my view a very definite crossing of that shaft by a horizontal bar of further topographical promptings. In an instant I just knew that I was staring at a tall cross or crucifix, possibly being held aloft by the lamb itself - I *knew* within every fibre of my being - but I didn't like it one bit!

In those first few moments I also noticed that if there were a cross here, its top would be capped by Hadrian's Wall. There was, therefore, the prospect of Rome having had a hand in the making of it just as it did 2000 years ago in old Jerusalem - but again there were no smiles from me.

True, if there were a cross here, it would underline the existence of a lamb rather than the ram of today's accepted zodiacal iconography, for that image of a lamb holding a cross is undoubtedly a common one, gracing everything from altars to flapping pub signs from Jerusalem to Cornwall. That said, I would also have to take on board the fact that Christianity had just shanghaied the zodiac!

Though I was confused I couldn't get Blake's tantalising question out of my head:

And was the Holy Lamb of God
On England's pleasant pastures seen?

I should have answered him with a joyful, "Yes", but I again confess that I was anything but ecstatic; indeed, doubt ripped me apart. Simply, I didn't want any one religion to brand Albion's universal constellations as its own, a subtle behind-the-scenes blending of many, yes, but not this! Admittedly, we have on this journey suspected the parallel footsteps of Jesus, and, of course, everywhere there has been the glow of the Grail, so the finding of the cross would seem sensational confirmation of his nearness. However, I never looked for him to stamp this whole zodiac as his own, which that cross was now threatening to do in his name - to be sure it had, in 10 seconds, already christened the whole damn thing!

Inwardly I yelled in frustration: "But the stars belong to all, no one religion may claim them as their own!" So why had the very land itself, after giving to me one-by-one the shapes of 11 non-religiously dogmatised star giants, now branded this last of all with the irremovable sign of the Christ and his church, a church which, at best, would brand star-reading as 'just plain stupid', and, at worst, and more probably so, 'the degenerative work of the devil himself'. My confusion changed gear and slipped into downright anger.

My jubilation in finding the lamb was becoming smothered in a can of Christian worms and I was appalled. Luckily, I didn't know then that, several months later, the whole Christian thing would become amplified a hundred thousand times when I was to find the actual face and body of Christ hung so perfectly upon this same 'challenge' of a cross!

However, if this book finds itself in the hands of a Buddhist, a pagan, or any other faith, I appeal to you not to cast it away at such a late hour because of what apparently crowns this miracle. Instead wait, for you like me may soon find that, beneath this Christ of Albion are layered, one upon the other, many a sacrificial son and teacher of the many-named one God, who have, throughout the memories of mankind, graced this earth with their step, each in his own right a shepherd of man's climb back to his great self-knowledge. So, I hope that before our journey has ended you'll see, as I was myself to realise, that the land's portrayal of this great, green, cloud-strewn Son of God is but a reflection of them all - a final distillation of all the teachers, stretching from the beginning of the world to the end, now made one in his shape - arms spread out wide in the shape of a man, any man who has come to

know himself and all else to be filled with a loving God. And I ask, what could be more universal and inclusive than that?

Neither is the theory of a long succession of teachers, some even remembered as demigods, merging at the end into the figure of the Christ an original one. St Augustine must have heard some of their myths while upon his Christian travels to far off lands, and added two and two together:

"That which we call Christianity has been from the beginning of the world, until Christ came in the flesh, and until the true religion existing from the beginning received the name: Christianity."

I found the above quote in Merezhkovsky's *The Secret of the West* and I will let the author himself relate his own thoughts (and they will also do for me too) on exactly what he thinks the saint is telling us; *"This could not have been said with greater precision. This means, the shadows are leading to the Body; the gods of all perished worlds, the setting suns of all Atlantises, are leading to the non-setting Sun - Christ."*

As we head into the last stages of our incredible journey we shall be made conscious of a shining thread which connects Osiris and other God-Men of the deep pre-Christian past to Jesus Christ himself. Indeed, here at the height of England we shall watch the essence of them all converge into this figure upon the cross, even animating him into a dance - an act primed to be the most wondrous sight of our entire journey.

As our detective work goes deeper I hope any discomforts with this figure will ease and allow him to be seen in a new light. Indeed, my own discomforts eased, if only a touch, within a few hours of finding that cross, when I discovered that such a device should not be seen as the sole property of Christians. Thomas Macall Fallow in his article on the cross and crucifixion in the

Encyclopaedia Britannica underlines the fact that the cross had a religious lineage of far greater antiquity than that begun at Golgotha: *"The use of the cross as a religious symbol in pre-Christian times, and among non-Christian peoples, may probably be regarded as almost universal, and in very many cases it was connected with some form of nature worship."*

How beautiful, then, I thought, that with a cross built of mountains, lakes, and pastures, nature is reminding us of a symbol that men once used as a token to her own holiness. Yet, out of her breast of Britain, she has willed that a man should finally overlay that same symbol - as though she is now handing over her glory to him - handing him back up to us and all the universe, as a token to his potential of one day knowing himself to be the gentle lord of it all.

THE CROSS or TREE OF LIFE

The plotting of the cross

I shall always remember the incredible day several weeks after the initial mapping out of this lamb. I had planned to do nothing more than complete its floorplan by plotting out the exact alignments of that suspected cross. It was meant to be an easy task and that's how it started. I quickly found its horizontal bar to be magically aided in its construction by two lakes that endeavoured to turn right-angled corners! And because it had signposts like Cross Fell and Hartside Cross upon its span, I felt wonderfully guided, especially when I also saw that Cross Fell was the highest summit amongst the many bristling peaks here. It was 2930 feet above sea level and I had the gut feeling that the land was confirming what my eye, led by intuition, had told me existed.

However, I then turned my attention to the vertical down-shaft and, good heavens, was it going to be tall, especially if the lamb was going to play a part by actually holding the whole thing aloft. As I scanned the map,

misgivings suddenly bubbled up like swamp gas and for the first time on this journey I felt I was entering dodgy ground.

OK, those place names I have just mentioned were lovely confidence boosters, and that ridge of Pennine mountains did intimate the general drift of a down shaft, but what of the exact width of its plank, and of the true alignment of the thing? Even a quick glance at the map told me straight away that there were going to be no rivers or roads, neither straight nor long enough, to carry that central shaft's southward course into the arms of the lamb, nor even to give me any clue as to the weight of its construction. The truth was that, for the first time in 30 years of digging out Albion, I had come to an object where the coast had not cut a deep and foolproof template. Because of this all manner of nagging apprehensions crept through me, headed by the ugliest of the lot which reminded me that I never wanted this blasted cross to appear in the first place!

Wavering on the edge of happily conning myself that I'd never *really* seen its shape, and preparing to concentrate purely upon the lamb, I heard my inner voice. Calmly it reminded me that this cross was a man-made object, the first that I had encountered upon this journey (I had not as yet started to nail the ark together), and so I needed a totally different way of plotting its course than the trusty cliffs, rivers and roads I'd used on the other more sinuously shaped signs. I then suddenly received an insight into the line I should take - I would plot it through the highest peaks!

A novel idea, but would even those peaks give me the straight line that a cross needed, for surely their path, too, could be as meandering as a drunk's way home. Yet with the hunch came that same adrenalin 'buzz' of excitement which had, on many previous occasions along this crazy way, heralded an imminent and magical moment waiting just around the next bend; to get there I also knew from experience that the only requirement of me was to relax, have faith, and prepare to have fun.

And so with a grin I said to the child inside me, "OK - show me!" With red pen in hand I casually ringed a series of the highest peaks I could find in a roughly north to south direction, intuitively starting at that summit of Cross Fell. Anyway, let me tell you that in the space of a few minutes I could see as straight a line of red ringed peaks as Mother Nature could ever muster, stretching down to the peak of Rogan's Seat. This line was, though, still some way short of the lamb's forelegs where this cross would obviously have to be positioned if it wasn't going to come toppling down around my ears! My faith, however, was suddenly building up rather than being torn down. With pulse-pounding expectation I knew I had to zap a line through that string of peaks and continue it both north and south. To the north Hadrian's Wall was an easy target, while that southern line would have to go past the lamb's mighty head and down into its body to converge with those all-important tucked-up forelegs - if it missed there was no cross!

I knew for sure that these peaks were to be the star points that would either guide my path and build me a mighty cross or, more worryingly, turn my inner friend into a liar.

Calling my own bluff!

Half scared, half champing at the bit to get on with it, I allowed my wild inner child to take the driving seat. And what an exhilarating sense of puckish fun I felt, all I had to do was simply follow my intuition and, smiling, go with the flow over these peaks to where only the land knew, and return either with another wonderful tale to tell, or with egg dripping off my face!

I aligned the ruler's edge on those two high points of Cross Fell and Rogan's Seat at the top and bottom of my row of ringed peaks, and zapped through a pencil line to connect them, continuing it well beyond them both.

Tentatively I lifted the ruler. I was almost too scared to look where the line had run in relation to the lamb because, if this thing was going to work, that lamb was going to have to take firm hold of this towering symbol smack bang between those forelegs. If it didn't, the whole thing would look ridiculous, and that, in itself, would point a finger at my inner voice, intuition, call it what you will, as being hopelessly wrong, and, even more damning, so too might be all the other intuitive guidance I had followed up regarding this whole vast riddle. Simply, I had reached a critical moment in the entire discovery. Everything, but everything, now hung upon this cross - the tick of the clock, the beat of my heart, all seemed to hang on hold; would my trust be rewarded yet again or be now seriously undermined. I felt the child in me was on trial, no grin puckered my lips as I removed that ruler.

But, oh God, did that grin return like the rim of the sun from out of an eclipse? To my blessed relief I could see that, not only did the line fall magically balanced behind the lamb's head as though lying against his shoulder for extra support, but, more than this, I also saw that it had followed through southeasterly and fell like a charm between those crossed forelegs - bingo!

What could I say? For the perennial 'doubter' in me it was another case of, "You lucky beggar", but for the child in me it had the magical hallmark of Albion. To back up what was happening, the map then began to sprinkle along that line's route names that not only giggled out Cross Fell and Hartside Cross, but also so many 'by the cross' place names: Crosby-on-Eden, Crosby Ravensworth, Crosby Garret and Lower Crosby, - yes, there *was* a Cross here! As regards the horizontal beam, the lakes of Ullswater and Haweswater had already given the western arm upper and lower corner tips by bending themselves into almost liquid right angles! But was it just luck? Again you must answer that yourself, but for me I felt as from the beginning of all this seeming madness, either being guided by the hand of a far greater artist than me, or else the land was itself aiding and abetting a madman's dream - either way I was, and still am, enchanted.

I saw that the line I had just drawn between the two high peaks had uncannily also passed in and out of the other nine red ringed summits I'd earlier marked, without missing either of them by so much as a gnat's whisker - that line virtually touching four peaks while kissing the remainder. If you were on foot at night and these peaks had each a fire beacon on its summit those lights alone would serve you well in tracing the vertical eastern edge of this cross for at least 80 miles!

But like all good workmen let's lean against this half-finished post for a few pages and ponder on a few things whilst taking a mug of tea.

Enter the guardians of the Grail

Now that we have seemingly established the eastern edge of the cross's upright, where is the opposite edge?

For this western line I was to trust in another inner 'tip off' which directed me to a village called Temple Sowerby and which, as a pure hunch, had me thinking of the Knights Templar who were rumoured by some to be the self-proclaimed guardians of the Grail. Anyway, continuing in the same carefree manner, I sent a second line through Temple Sowerby running it parallel to the previous line. It, too, ran nicely into the lamb's embrace, looking in good proportion to what I could already judge to be the width of the horizontal cross bar.

Indulging in a degree of self-congratulation, I settled again on Temple Sowerby and wondered if that hunch of it having a Knights Templar connection could hold water. At the time I didn't know that many places in Britain beginning with Temple were indeed sites of a former Knights Templar garrison or temple.

That said, I doubted whether there would be a Templar connection in this out-of-the-way spot, high as it is on this wilderness-sculpted Cross of Albion. But then again, if they really were the guardians of the Holy Grail, the cross wouldn't be a bad place to hang around, indeed the cross was their favoured insignia. I reached for a walker's guidebook on this area and found this village described in it. Imagine my surprise when I read that it has an ancient manor house by the name of Acorn Bank, which was once owned by the Templars - thus the 'Temple' in the village's name.

The mysterious mystic order of the Knights Templar, one-time hero protectors of medieval pilgrims upon their great and arduous journey from Europe to Jerusalem, were eventually persecuted and finally disbanded by order of the French King Philip IV. His motive? If asked, he would have told you that it was because of their heretical practices, but Philip also had a greedy eye on their wealth. Either way, by 1308 he had burnt many of them at the stake, by which time the manor house of Acorn Bank was, as were so many other Templar manors, taken over by the less secretive, and I guess poorer, Knights Hospitaller.

Now think back to the chapter on Pisces. Remember how edible acorns were believed to be the wisdom food from the Tree of Life and of which the Salmon of Knowledge ate. Add to this the Druids' belief that the cross on which Jesus was nailed was made of rough oak, which, to them, was synonymous with the Tree of Life and wisdom. So, suspecting that some Templar beliefs may have had groundings in Druidism, and because of the provocative spot occupied by Temple Sowerby, I could not help but wonder if those same knights knew exactly where they were constructing their acorn of a temple. Indeed, if that supposed title, 'Keepers of the Holy Grail' was true could one of the heretical secrets they died for be *this* secret, *this landscaped* Grail of Albion? Certainly one of their accused heresies was the worship of some awesome head (probably, as is surmised today, some strange rendition of the face of Christ) and if so, I wonder, if it was the one upon which lambs grazed and only four miles from their own front door! And as for their acorn bank of heretical knowledge - why! they chose to hang it on the branch of Albion's very own cross and oaken Tree of Life. So could provocatively placed, and provocatively named Acorn Bank be their sign to the effect that they knew too *this* heresy underfoot?

Today their old safe house has a beautiful garden, which is open to the public, where there are fragrances of 250 species of herbs and 20,000 specimens of daffodil or Lent lily. These, I believe, are planted on the oak bank beside a stream which, according to my maps, is fed by waters that all but pour out of what shall be the heart of the Lord of the Dance, the last giant on this grand tour. Again I wonder if those knights knew this topographical layout, and built their temple where they could dip a cup into that stream, from the bleeding heart of their saviour and drink of it as though it were wine - a Eucharist of the land. Let us also toy with that name Temple Sowerby. In 'Albion-speak', knowing that it is situated, not just on the cross, but upon the crucified Christ's own right shoulder, can it not be simply turned around now into the astonishingly apt **Temple by the Sower** - by Jesus the sower of the seeds of truth, of hope, of love, and of life. Simply gob-smacking isn't it!

Authors Bellamy and Quale, whom we met in the last chapter, stopped off here at Temple Sowerby, too, and seemed once more to become happily infected by the underlying spirit of the place, referring to its tranquillity as a *"modern day miniature Garden of Eden"*. How delighted those knights would be to know that their old garden is referred to in the same breath as that one of Eden - especially when they may have known theirs was under Albion's own 300-mile tall Tree of Life.

A return to Eden

Looking again at where Temple Sowerby stands, and having just read Bellamy and Quale's reference to the Garden of Eden, I could only smile at the sight of how a river Eden really does flow right past its door. But can you guess precisely where such a charmingly named water flows in relationship to Albion's great floor plan? Remarkably, it cascades down the cross for the best part of 40 miles as though watering its secret tree, growing as it is from out of Albion's paradise garden on earth. The poet in the land had laid another breathtaking gift at my feet! Indeed, so closely does this river follow my line of the cross's upright that, had I noticed it earlier, it and not Temple Sowerby might have prompted my pencil!

The poet Wordsworth also stood on the banks of this river and felt compelled to write, '*A name fetched from Paradise and rightfully borne*'. However, when we begin our walk around the body of Christ I'll show how this water is even more blessed than the poet suspected. But for a taster, hear Elaine Pagels in her book *The Gnostic Gospels* summarise a work attributed to the gnostic teacher Simon Magus, who suggests a mystical meaning for Paradise, that place where human life began. He wrote: "*Grant Paradise to be the womb; for Scripture teaches us that this is a true assumption when it says, 'I am He that formed thee in thy mother's womb. (Isaiah 44:2)* Pagels herself continues and clarifies, "*...Moses using allegory had declared Paradise to be the womb and Eden, the Placenta. The river that flows forth from Eden symbolises the navel which nourishes the fetus.*"

Is this mystic mumbo jumbo? Could be, but give Albion a chance to clarify some more. After cascading down the cross, Albion's river Eden seems to strive to become the visual placenta of the landscaped Christ, for just past the village of Great Musgrave this out-pouring of paradise is joined by one of its tributary streams, namely the Swindale Beck, which gives our Eden a visual extension curving to the east and directly into the town of Brough. Now if I tell you in advance that Brough will soon be seen as marking the very navel of this Cumbrian Christ, you will see Moses' strange allegory made topographically simple: the river Eden with that graphic assistance of the Swindale beck becomes the life-nourishing umbilical cord of the Christ. **The pictorial message on these mountains, therefore, is *not of him dying* on the cross but of being prepared to be instantly reborn while *in the same body*, by receiving, or winning, that nourishment of Christ Consciousness; which is why a phoenix blazes from his right hand. And which is why a fetus (Gemini) symbolises that Christ Consciousness on Albion's starry floorplan!**

For me, Albion's prophecy is encapsulated in just this one piece of magical land imagery; namely, we are all being invited back into Eden. Paradise *can* be found on earth by seeing through Golgotha's mystery, and before our journey through Albion's garden is done I hope Good Friday's mystery will be on its way to becoming no mystery at all. In the meantime do remember the imagery we've just seen and replay it when we are gathered upon his dark twin.

John too in his *Revelation* of the New Jerusalem was shown a water of life as being central to it:

"...a pure river of water of life, clear as crystal,
proceeding out of the throne of God and the Lamb."
REVELATION, Chapter 22 Verse 1

So in Albion's scheme of things, allow me to term the river Eden as a poetical water of life, pouring as it does over the branches of the Tree of Life? If so, notice from where, in that same scheme of things, Albion's water of life issues.

Although it pours from Cumbria's cross and Christ, note that this is still part and parcel of the lamb of Aries - so, can we further equate this station to *the throne of God and the lamb*? To do so is surely to tempt one to wonder whether England's bringing together of a river Eden and the Son of God, and placing them upon the lamb, is exactly the sight which shook John while at Patmos. Can we fail to be amazed at seeing such a scenario being set within a vast zodiacal floor plan, remembering that, in this same vision, John saw this New Jerusalem as having 12 gates. Provocative or what?

From a tree to a cross - to a mast?

While still leaning against the great gnarled and mystic trunk, where Adam himself might once have found cool shade, let us turn to ancient Greece to glean more evidence that many may have leant against this same tree, or cross, in the landscape.

I call then a well-known Greek hero into the witness box. Our questions to Jason will concern that golden fleece which inspired him and the flower of Greek manhood to embark upon their own Grail quest.

First of all, then, "Where did you eventually find that fleece?"

"I found it as foretold, nailed to an oak tree. The tree grew where the gods planted it, within the sacred wood of Ares."

"And what did you do with this fleece when you were safely back on board your vessel, the Argo (Albion's ark)? "

"I nailed it to the mast."

On the strength of these answers I propose to the jury that the sacred wood of *Ares* was the sacred wood of *Aries*, and that Jason's sacred oak upon which the fleece was hung is the very same Tree of Life which leans against the fleece of Albion's lamb of Aries.

Furthermore, look at the ground plan for Cancer, doesn't the cross also become the very mast of that all-enveloping ark - of course it does! Thus, in seeing Christ nailed to that mast where once Jason hung the golden fleece are we not witnessing two more myths flash in the mirror as one; one truth which shouts that the most wonderful prize in all the world is to be found hung upon that tree/cross/mast, a prize which, on Albion, has been pictorially summed up by the image of what we shall find later to be a dancing God-Man. OK, so a fleece is not a man, but, by God, how the imagery strives to blend as one when we kick around that other title of Jesus - the Lamb of God!

In Albion's amassing of mythology's truths, the Christ, the golden fleece, and the tree (or cross or mast) upon which both were historically hung, we surely see it all coalesce into the one ultimate and dancing prize for all men to attain to.

Beneath these heavy fruit-laden branches of Albion's Tree of Life, mast-head of this whole miracle, we'll witness many myths, legends, folklores, and even, dare I say, scriptures, all similarly coming together and making new and remarkable sense. Excitedly, we'll ask, if these islands have been visited, throughout the ages, by those few who have sought the ultimate fruits of knowledge? Amongst them, did the Sumerian hero Gilgamesh find his own Grail, his herb of life, here under the shade of this 300-mile tall tree, perhaps even where now herbs in an old knight's garden fill the air with the scent of thyme? Was it from this tree, too, that Perseus picked those golden apples of wisdom in the Garden of the Hesperides, here on the far western horizon where legend always said they were? There are many questing heroes, their destinations, however, could all be one and the same, always west and to the gardens of Albion's heaven on earth, to seek the truth behind their existence amongst its fields of stars. Madness I agree, but my how the land urges us nevertheless to enjoy the stupendous notion!

Those who know their astrology, of course,

will have been itching to remind me that *Ares* (as in the 'wood of') is another name for the god Mars and not related to the spelling of *Aries*. Quite right, but, by saying this, would they be turning a blind eye to the stubborn little fact that *Ares* or Mars just happens to be the ruler of the sign of Aries - indeed, he was looked upon as the protector of flocks! For me, to see that wood of Ares as being located within his own starry territory of Albion's lamb of Aries is surely not stretching the imagination too far. I rest my case.

Oh, and there's one more titbit I'd like to share whilst walking around Mars' wood: I found a delightful river pouring over the lamb's nose and carrying with it the charmed name of the river Aire; and whether Aire, Aries, or Ares who cannot smile?

From tree, to cross, to mast - and now to a sword?

As previously suggested in Sagittarius, could we equally see this same cross as a sword? Visually it certainly is not beyond the imagination to see its elongated proportions as so - the horizontal crossbar easily becoming the hilt.

But should you feel that a sword and a lamb rest uneasily together, let me take you back to what is perhaps the earliest interpretation of the zodiac. The Sumerians, in their table of *The Thirty Three Stars*, give to Aries the name of Gam. Incredibly it means 'scimitar' - a sword that was to protect the realm against the so-called *Seven Diabolic Spirits of the Storm*. Alongside this, it is also interesting to note that the emblem of the lamb carrying the cross, known since early Christian times as the Agnus Dei, was a treasured protective amulet against accidents and infectious diseases, but most of all against, wait for it... storms! Again, could it be that both are wrapped up in Albion's mast of the ark as a double talisman against the eventual coming of Scorpio, masked in a chaos of the elements?

I will further investigate this possible shape-shifting of cross into sword when we reach Cancer.

Back now to some high peak carpentry

So let's get back to work. Although a string of high peaks had been my guide for the down shaft of the cross, the horizontal bar was easily mapped out by roads and rivers. However, on this horizontal beam there was also an opportunity to obtain a similar result by using a peak and a tantalising place name. If you strike a line through both Cross Fell and Temple Sowerby you will have a reassuring piece of underpinning to the road and river version that follows.

The western arm (the right arm side of Jesus) starts at Langwathby at its top inner corner, and we can head either west with the A686 or do more or less the same on the river Eamont. This river then runs into Ullswater, that lake which at its furthest end magically bends a unique and liquid right angle to give this bar an almost perfect sharp corner. Do take a look at this lake's shape on the illustration and marvel as I did. On the end of this arm, south of Ullswater, there is a smaller lake with the intriguing name of Angle Tarn - *Angle Turn* I wonder? "Yes! Yes! Yes!" I hear from somewhere.

Out of Ullswater, the vertical end of the beam is helped on its way by another stream, the Goldrill, which leads the eye to the Roman-frequented peak at High Street.

Once at High Street follow the stream into Haweswater and note its own stab at creating corners. Flowing out of Haweswater, follow the watercourse east to Bampton. Here, using just a touch of imagination, continue directly northeast crossing over the M6 and picking up the country road to Morland, then onto Temple Sowerby and completion of this section of the plank.

We'll start the eastern arm on its upper edge on the A686 near the telecommunications mast. Proceed northeast past Hartside Cross and on through Alston, then take the country road to Ninebanks and Allendale Town, which is the furthest tip.

At Allendale continue to Cowshill on the river Allen. Once there, go back north on the A689 to Nenthead. Now it's across country to Garrigill where you must pick up the Pennine path to Cross Fell to complete the underside of this eastern arm and the entire construction of this cross of Albion.

THE CHRIST

Anticlimax

And so, after all the early morning gambling and testing of nerves, the cross seemed now well and truly hammered together - but was it a job well done?

I put my pen down. The day had been grey and the failing light of evening had already stolen into my studio without me noticing. Lolling back in my chair I should have been more than happy with the day's revelations, especially seeing that after all these years I was now at the top of Albion's clock - thus the miracle complete, my own work nearly finished, and the little boy's Christmas day fantasy an alive and kicking reality. And yet in that twilight I confess I was ill-content. Even after the wonderfully happy-go-lucky and typically Albion way in which the cross had finally grown into the scheme of things, bearing with it, as it did, all those lovely *Cross-by* name references as disarmingly obvious testimony to its presence, something still troubled me. I sat there a smouldering epitome of Doubting Thomas. Had my intuition served me correctly? Were those high points of Cross Fell and Rogan's Seat the right co-ordinates on which to pin the whole construction of the cross - no matter how the river Eden seemed to verify the same alignment? Indeed, it was that pronounced lean of the finished article that nagged at me - should it have not been totally upright?

God, how this cross continued to plague me. I shut the door on that creeping gloom and retreated downstairs for our evening meal, but a troubled mind ended it early for me and forced me back to my studio against all my wishes. Trudging heavily back up the stairs I was brokering a deal with myself to the effect that if, by the time sleep came, I had not banged together a better and more upright cross, I'd forget that I had ever seen one in the first place and would instead content myself with a cross-less lamb - just as the one at Glastonbury. I also accepted that if that should be the case, I would also have to acknowledge that my intuition had been faulty, a thought which I knew if it took root would sooner or later possibly strangle the whole project, forcing the whole silliness of it back into childhood's store of bright illusions. I *was* that fickle!

Then the shock of my life!

Back at my desk I was almost angry with that newly-drawn cross on the map - and remember, I never wanted its obvious Christian connotations in the first place!

As I've already mentioned, I guess the truth of it was that, for the first time, I was working to no fixed coastal profile and so felt terribly insecure - in truth, I felt I might be cobbling together things that didn't exist. The next three hours or so were going to make or break everything.

I gripped the ruler like a hammer and the pencil like a monstrous nail, as I thought to gag my childish self and let a more bullish and workman-like attitude dig out and bang together a different set of cross planks in a more upright fashion. I was ready to capitulate all to the ego. In this totally alien frame of mind I leaned over the map, little knowing that I was within seconds of the most amazing heart-banging, mind-dizzying moment of my life.

Tired and utterly disillusioned, I cast my eye to see if there was perhaps another line of mountain peaks that could suggest to me a more acceptably upright cross, maybe even backed up by a good motorway or two! As I rapidly scanned this way and that, however, my sight passed once more over the centre of the existing cross, and exactly where that cross-beam passed over the down timber **I glimpsed his face!**

From out of a seven-mile high piece of sparsely populated land between Temple Sowerby and Kirkoswald I was to be taught one final and glorious lesson in faith - this fickle Doubting Thomas was to come face to face with the living Christ! Yet all that first split-second glimpse had shown to me were his closed eyes, formed by a river, and that characteristic centre parting of his hair - a feature that hundreds of artists throughout the ages have, for some reason, felt compelled to illustrate. Nevertheless, upon these two scant pieces of visual intrigue, at the very crux of this cross, my eyes became locked like those of a hawk would be upon a young rabbit frolicking in a field of barley - I knew exactly who he was!

But guess what? As soon as I saw him I turned my eyes away in abject horror! The hawk unexpectedly peeled away even though he was hungry, and Peter-like I instantly denied the existence of him who was, albeit only in those two sparse features on the landscape, unmistakably shimmering off the map before me. In truth, I had never looked for him though I had many times sensed him, and so strongly of course in this area of the cross, but I never wanted him to appear in a full frontal graphic assault, for that would create insurmountable complications. If I had problems accepting the cross, well God help me now!

In those rushing, pulsing seconds when I averted my eyes from what I'd just glimpsed, all my old arguments and concerns relating to the appearance of the cross came bounding back, a delegation now swollen into a lynch mob! *"This is a zodiac!"* they yelled through every cell of me; every thought of me agreed: *"Albion does not belong to Christianity nor to any religion - you're tired, so he's not there, you didn't see him, but if you did, well then just bury him again!"*

Other thoughts also demanded attention, offering up more worrying theories: *"Surely this was me the artist, finally driven insane, too long in the solitary confinement of this mind-blowing landscape, I had now become lost amongst its beguiling lines and shapes, even seeing the face of the Christ where, in reality, there were only fields. The only faces abroad this night were probably those of a man walking his dog and a moon-faced owl watching him from a bell tower. For too long I had sought the Grail where it never was and now I was left shaking and perhaps even upon the verge of becoming mentally ill".*

Running scared, these were the thoughts that mobbed me in those shuddering first moments after those eyes of blue-lined running water had met mine. But above them all, thank God, came the laughter of that voice within. Through all the thunder-laden anxiety I felt inexplicable ripples of smiles born, it seemed, upon an unstoppable tide of rising happiness. I looked again at that tease of a face - it was still there, between the Grail guardian's manor house and Kirkoswald. I trembled with cold even though my room was warm. Out of the corner of my eye I watched it, hoping, I guess, that it would do me a favour and blend back into the map, but it didn't. Unwaveringly, it held its ground; I knew unsuspecting villagers must be lighting evening fires upon his brow, crows, perhaps in full knowledge of him, roosting in his hair. And me? Madman or not, I was struggling to

dam a brimming-up of tears.

Five minutes passed, and still the eternally patient face of the shepherd shone in mine and was growing in detail without me even leaning over to scrutinise it further. A pointed beard and the rest of his hair were coming into view via a sublime economy of line - it was like watching a photograph become second-by-second more detailed within its magical chemical bath, and *it was simply him* and *I was* experiencing the most trembling, scary, happiness I had ever felt. I also knew that if his streaming eyes opened they would only smile at my emotional plight and in their sparkle beckon me to go on. And so, with pounding heart, I picked up my pencil, now more like a feather than a nail, and applied it gently to the map. In seconds, his face positively flew into vision, but there was no time for me to stop to look at it, because my pencil went charging joyously on and, within moments, not only was that complete and haunting face bringing renewed and indescribable tears of mixed joy and fear to my eyes, **but the whole of his body had now appeared, hung so bewilderingly perfectly upon the alignment of the cross I had doubted!** Even today, and some seven years on, I still shiver at the magical memory of that evening, just two days before Good Friday - I will even upon my deathbed.

So, upon that evening of rampant doubt, and all within the space of ten minutes, the absolute truth of the correct co-ordinates of the cross had been hammered home to me in the most spectacular way possible, and of course they were exactly as already given to me. It seemed almost that, because I had not noticed the Christ, my unrest with its alignments was merely a way of getting me to return to it and open my eyes! Indeed, it was as if the land knew I'd need one last almighty and magical kick up the doubting backside to finally make me *really* believe in what I'd found, not only here, but throughout Britain. On that cross I had so doubted, the land had hung the Christ -

hung not just a touch to the right, nor to the left, nor a little too high nor too low, but staggeringly nailed bang where he should be, while simultaneously confirming that peculiar lean too!

Anatomically, too, his figure was perfectly married to the shape and angles of that cross. So precise was his bodily placement that Temple Sowerby and Cross Fell had become his own shoulders, for his body has been so realistically crafted that it sagged from his arms, and thus his shoulders were level with the horizontal beam's lower inside corners. Here were shoulders fit to cry on, and that *Temple by the Sower* I could now see was doing just that.

Just how long I sat there before him I don't know; it could have been an hour or just ten minutes - time had lost its hold on me. What I did know was I could see him crucified in perfect and harrowing reality on the cross I had strenuously fought against; my lack of trust answered by the great big laughing smile of the landscape. Like a Christmas morning long ago when I thought I had opened all the presents my parents had given me, the best gift of all was left until last. In hindsight, I can't help but wonder if the 'powers-that-be' knew all along that I'd lose my nerve when confronted with that cross and so kept back the presence of the Christ until my doubts were near to wrecking everything, and then let him reveal himself to me - the final image that calmly said "Be quiet, it is done" - Albion, in its entirety, now lay before me.

Breaking away from the bizarre mix of spell-binding bliss and shell-shocked fear that gripped me, I virtually leapt downstairs shouting to my wife Linda to come and see the extraordinary visitor. If I'm honest, I was still almost hoping that she might come and say that she was sorry but she couldn't see him and, even then, let me off that Christian hook. Instead, like me she stood speechless but filled, she said, with a great awe which made her tremble. If I had felt humble throughout the rediscovery of this great treasure, I now felt as though an entire satchel of minute sparkling gems had been showered like rain over my head and shoulders. I could only bow my head in the twinned agony and ecstasy and wonder "Why me?". I was overwhelmed and frightened too as the significance of this great zodiac had just grown beyond even my belief. I was in a turmoil of emotion, whilst the Christ hung before us in perfect and unwavering serenity.

Within the luxurious silence and calm which now descended on my studio where the presence of this beautiful visitor seemed himself to waft off the paper, I felt that my earlier fear of *"This is a zodiac and does not belong to Christendom alone"* was in a sense still true. Now, however, the same thought had not the fear factor. This great green Christ, I sensed, had grown beyond today's idea of Christianity, so much so, dare I say, that I believe his message to be a million times more beautiful than many of his followers of today already believe it is. Even in those first moments I could see now that the stars really did belong to this Christ, and rightly so, for did he not arrive 2000 years ago under one particularly bright one, and before me he had now returned within a firmament of billions on Albion's starry mirror. But here was no glorious advert for Christianity over every other religion, for the whole thing was now expanded beyond any classifications. This was confirmation only that here was a self-realised God-Man, a cognisant Lord of All, free now of all labels and spread-eagled amongst the stars of the universe - on earth! In him, the land is portraying the promise of a man perfected, a God-Man, his arms held open wide in exultation to the stars that are laid at his feet. *"Look, it is all yours, too - let me show you how to reclaim it through love and laughter."* I feel these are his words to all who would aspire to their true birthright - and today's

Christianity may have little to do with it!

But there was even still one more exquisite wonder to arrive on that reverberating evening a few days before Good Friday.

And the place of the Holy Grail was all but a midnight phone call away

Whilst still trembling from the discovery, I telephoned a good friend who was fully aware of my 'find'. Nervously, I shared with him the new wonder that lay on my desk and I remember that he fell unusually silent. Perhaps he, too, thought that I had now gone too far and, embarrassed, he didn't know what the hell to say. But, after a long silence, he asked me, in a tone of voice that seemed almost prompted by another, to look at the map again and see if there was any feature that would indicate a wound upon his side.

This was certainly not the response I had expected. I had not only found the cross, I had found the Christ upon it, yet here was someone asking me to now find a wound as well - I couldn't help myself asking with a wry smile "What do you want... blood?"

With the telephone in one hand I scanned his side for evidence of the spear's thrust, but there was not much of anything there, for this whole area of high northern England is so little populated that roads and villages are few and far between; the only features of note being nature's own works of moors, lakes, rivers, and mountains. Even these, not always named, leaving some parts of the map unmarked for miles except for contour lines - again, all the more remarkable for finding the Christ so succinctly scribed here. Nevertheless I looked as asked.

"No, there's nothing." I heard myself say, but then instantly corrected that with an "Oh my God...!" My eyes had just zeroed in on a high mountain peak on the land Christ's side, just below his heart, and my own heart was pounding as I quietly announced, "There's a

very prominent mountain peak called High Cup Nick." The voice on the phone answered, almost unsurprised: "Give me another name for a high cup" and I said: "The Grail!" Then he said: "And another word for a wound or cut? Good God, Graham, do you know what you've found?" Together we answered: "The wound and the Holy Grail into which it bled!" Silence engulfed us like giant motherly arms. It was midnight, a time when all sane people should properly be in their beds, but we two, in spirit, were hundreds of miles away high upon High Cup Nick. Above us, in the midnight air, on this zodiac clock's own midnight hour, the Holy cup was being filled with the wisdom of the stars - Christ's stars. Were we the only two people awake to see it?

We had no words left. The telephone line hummed expectantly, as each end hung in duplicated stillness. Instinctively I reached for Blake's *Jerusalem* and read, despite my trembling voice, in whispers across the wires: *"And did the Countenance Divine, Shine forth upon these clouded hills?"* Yes, said the tears that I think rolled down both our faces, for the disarming beauty of it was just all too much.

Truly, in the whole of this beautiful land poetry no other place is more worthy of his form than those majestic and clouded hills of Cumbria. On closing my eyes that night, I imagined looking down from a great height upon such a stunning portrayal, sprinkled as it was, to my inner sight, with moonlit flocks, and strewn with torn phosphorescent tufts of fleece-like mist, and I wondered if *it* knew that *I* knew. So, too, I wondered if the flocks knew, and the owls, and even if whether some shepherd had a lovely dream that night all because of what had returned into view beneath his bed. Fitfully I slept like a child waiting for Christmas morning, my bedroom festooned with magic, two thousand Christmas Eves shimmering in one because of the gift I had received so near to Easter Eve.

Next morning my friend came to see the

Christ and sat at my desk looking long at the face. Like a Thomas himself, he said he had come to touch the wound. It was as though we had witnessed his second coming and we spoke quietly - we usually cussing, bantering, and laughing pals reduced now to little boys lost. We also understood, too, that even the timing of the finding of that wound was seemingly designed for maximum emotional effect, for I would, of course, have found it the next day in my customary scrutinising of the fine details - but no, that mark of the Grail needed to follow the Christ by moments not hours.

Interestingly, when I did begin my scrutiny I could see that that incredibly wounded summit (according to my Ordnance Survey Landranger Map No: 91) is located upon the very tip of a veritable spear-head shaped piece of rising ground - the tightly packed contour lines brilliantly describing its pointed shape. Everything just kept on adding up to the fact that for some astounding reason, that afternoon at Golgotha was perfectly replicated here, and there was still even more astonishment yet to come!

Sickly icing?

Just before we add more finds to this marvellous body of evidence - an apology.

I apologise if this book has now become too much of an intimate and staccato diary whose last pages seem too full of sighs, wows and sights that are now pushing the bounds of believability just too far even for you, who have already soldiered on through hundreds upon hundreds of miles of sheer out-of-this-world stuff. Indeed, I am conscious that in pointing out this mountain Messiah, I may have, by the sheer enormity of him, in a sense, devalued all the previous giants you have patiently dug out with me. Perhaps in saying, "Look who I've found now!" I have heaped so much icing on the cake that I'm in danger of making you all thoroughly sick? I hope this

isn't the case, but I'll have to take that chance. I just pray that you read on, as the last full stop is not too many miles away, and then you can either believe or not. All I ask is that you look within your own heart for your answers to this beguiling phenomenon. Heaven knows how many others there will be determined to do your thinking for you. And if my literary romp has ultimately bored you I wouldn't mind if you ditched all the written stuff and kept just what the child and the artist saw, as I would beg that Albion should not sink or swim on the strength of the artist struggling to be a writer.

The most wonderful walk of all

Now I should here give those of you who'd rather skip all the map-reading stuff a chance of a short cut by sectioning off the following under the usual heading of 'Defining the body'. However, there are so many wonderful things to see on this particular hike that I know you wouldn't want to miss it!

Kirkoswald marks the crown of his head, and the top end of that distinct and classical centre-parting of the hair, while Glassonby marks where it begins on his forehead. And can we play briefly with that name Glassonby, as, in 'Albion speak', it turns into something like 'by the glass son' or 'by the son in the looking glass'. Glastonbury, too, may translate as a buried glass or mirror. Are these, then, special places where we can somehow see ourselves reflected?

Also, upon his forehead, is a circle of spectacular standing stones known as Long Meg and her Daughters - I wonder what earth forces are gathered there.

The rest of his hair is drawn by the country roads which curve around the outside of his head, from the right taking in Great Salkeld, Lazonby, Kirkoswald, Renwick and round to meet the A686 near Hartside Cross on the left side.

The facial line of his hair starts around

*Long Meg and
her Daughters*

Langwathby; then the country road goes to Glassonby, Gamblesby, and back up to Renwick. The right side of his face is drawn by the road from Langwathby to Skirwith on the bearded chin - Blencarn I'd say sits on its pointed tip. Now carry on to Kirkland, where we pick up the ancient pathway, the Maiden Way, to draw the left side of his beard and face as far up as Melmerby Fell. Here we leave the path and follow the natural lie of the land to Hartside Cross, which is almost at ear height on this left side of his face. Then carry on to Renwick and beyond, to Kirkoswald, and you will be back on the very top of his head.

In his incredibly clear eyes has his promise been stunningly kept?

Now to my favourite five miles of riverbank: surely we're meant to see his eyes brimming with tears, drawn as they are exclusively by an inspired ribbon of running water - thus he *must be ALIVE!* On the map this was the precious blue line that caught my eye in those first seconds of perceiving his face.

So pick up its course with me, spot the beginning of its artistry where it joins the river Eden just southwest of the village of Little Salkeld. Tracking it eastwards you can now follow its tell-tale bank into the gorgeously defined cup or gentle u-shape of his closed right eye. Ignorant of its blessed location, Hunsonby stands on the very edge of its closed eye-lid. From this eye, the river climbs just

enough to denote the top of the broad bridge of the nose at Broadmeadows. Thereafter the river spellbinds still further with another perfectly placed indent to give us the cup or crescent of the left eye, its shape aided by several unnamed streams and a narrow lane which ends at Meikle Awefell. The village of Melmerby is the pure teardrop in the corner of this eye and I must tell you that behind this particular name hides another from ages past which was Mael-muire, meaning *St Mary's Servant.* Brilliant!

Even more sublime land poetry twinkles out of this pair of watery blue eyes, and is encapsulated in the singing voice of this river's own name. Although it's a name that even I had to listen to more than once before its full and incredible significance dawned on me. However, once that name had penetrated my perception I could do no more than close my eyes in honour of this river's awesome part in Albion's passion play. It is a name in which is held and crystallised a moving eye witness account of those last moments high upon Golgotha. Indeed, in it we're invited to look through the very eyes of Jesus, and to see perhaps the last face Jesus himself laid eyes on before darkness engulfed that hill and the spirit of the earth fled to Cumbria to record, amongst topographical stars, every profound moment for people of another time to relive. Thus, the name remembered upon these eyes is Robberby Water, but with the evidence under foot now re-read as *by the robber!*

See for yourself! Was not Jesus on that day of days partnered by robbers on either side? And no, it's not coincidence - *it is* a beautifully eye-watering *FACT!* But then again, surely we are getting used to such magnificently disarming signposts on this fabulous journey where the wonders just keep on stacking up. Surely, this enchantingly named river has been chosen to remember that moment which perhaps moved Christ's own eyes to tears at the innocence of that robber's plea when he asked:

"Lord, remember me when thou comest into thy kingdom." to which Jesus replied: *"Verily I say unto thee, Today shalt thou be with me in paradise"*
LUKE 23, Verses 42-43

Incredibly then, that momentous promise of Jesus is thus seen to have been lovingly kept and recorded as another gem upon this miraculous landscape. See for yourself that **the robber *has* indeed been remembered forever in Albion's Paradise upon the very eyes of his Lord who saw him and held him in brotherly love.** The robber's innocent and faithful last wish *is* here recorded as granted. I believe this is not only another miracle within the miracle, but a pointer too that we all only need to innocently ask and *it shall* be given, passionately *knock and you will be welcomed into riches beyond your wildest dreams, whatever your background. *Remember this in the last few pages of this chapter.*

Upon the banks of these brilliant eyelids, and whether Christian, Hebrew, Buddhist, or anything else, see now a 2000-year-old moment from Golgotha astonishingly reanimated. Whatever your religion, what you can now see with your own eyes should be enough for you to know that God really is in everything, and everything must be, in some way, conscious of the fact, just as every religion based on love has ever said. No matter, either, where upon this globe you live, these times must surely be the most momentous ever to have drawn breath in. We, who are the damned robbers of life's holy vestments, are being shown perhaps the most wondrous thing ever seen by the eyes of ordinary men. Like he who partnered Jesus on the cross, we, too, for all our shared faults, are being shown that we can still make it into paradise, if only we can bring ourselves to believe in miracles again.

While trying to come to terms with this awesome realization, let us proceed.

From the bridge of his nose Sunnygill Beck flows down the centre of his face to delineate a nose line. I would say the tip of the nose is somewhere in the area of Ousby, or as I believe the locals pronounce it 'Ozzby', a pronunciation which has me rightly or wrongly toying with 'ooze' as in to exude moisture. So by the 'by the oozing'? As divine as this work of the land is, it is, however, innocently earthy - thank God!

Words from his own mouth

The mouth, although somewhat lost to view amid the beard, I would pin-point as being in the area of a tiny group of buildings, perhaps no more than those belonging to a single farmstead, on my map going by the name of Gill Bank. And if this is his mouth we should be delighted that a stream actually falls from it, especially when reading the following:

"Jesus said "He who will drink from my mouth will become like me. I myself shall become he, and the things that are hidden will be revealed to him."
THE GOSPEL OF THOMAS, Logion 108

Wounds from his crown?

Now take a look at possibly more revealing marks, found at the end of that previously mentioned lane which runs from Melmerby, in the corner of his left eye, to Meikle Awfell, an expanse of wild moorland or 'fell', on the left cheek bone and temple areas. And 'awful' indeed is the wounding here! Grab hold of the map (Ordnance Survey, Landranger 91) and, like me, gasp at the sight of those livid scars; like Thomas, touch them and marvel how another has named them Melmerby Low Scar, Melmerby High Scar and Hause-in-the-Scar. The first two names are given to two pronounced geological gashes of jagged rock outcrop, and which, as chance or divine intervention would have them, run in vertical stripes down the side of this Christ's head and tempting translation as the cuts or punctures made by the crown of thorns. And how close, too, they resemble those bloodstains on the Turin Shroud, even though they tell us that the cloth is a fake.

Once again, if this cluster of scars were on, say, his arm or chest, they would not be worth listing, but being so near to that circlet of thorns can we ignore them? Having said that, though, I haven't found, on any of my maps, a feature of the terrain that would suggest an actual crown of thorns, so I have not drawn it on the artwork. However, it must be said that maps do not show everything and if there is a crown to be found we may find evidence of it on site. For instance, ruined segments of an old dry-stone wall, or even a line of stunted thorn trees may hint at its presence. Whatever, I'm sure that I have not found all there is to be found of Albion - the rest I will leave for other hawks to find.

A wound taken on behalf of a brother?

Noticeable, too, is another 'named scar' that can clearly be seen just below Cross Fell on his left shoulder. Its name is Wild Boar Scar and perhaps a wound received from a single tooth of a barbed Roman scourging lash, which flicked over the shoulder and bit into the flesh there, and not unlike again the wounding as seen on the shroud.

On the other hand, however, perhaps we should take this particular geological wound of the land for its exact face value; if we do, it will open up wounds of two more who taught resurrection and regeneration. First, hear this from Frazer's *The Golden Bough*: "*Under the names of Osiris, Tammuz, Adonis, and Attis, the peoples of Egypt and Western Asia represented the yearly decay and revival of life, especially of the vegetable life, which they personified as a god who annually died and rose again from the dead. In name and detail*

the rites varied from place to place: in substance they were the same." So, guess what - two out of those four, Adonis and Attis, were killed by boars!

Other reflections of these same two (can I call them demi-Christs?) also flash across Cumbria's great green Christ. Attis, too, was born of a virgin and was said to have been a 'fair shepherd' beloved of Cybele, mother of the gods. His annual death and resurrection was, as is that of Christ, both mourned and celebrated in the spring, the season that abounds on this sign of Aries. And talking of Aries, we are told that the boar, which tusked Adonis to death, was really Ares or Mars in disguise - again in Aries we are in the astrological territory of that very god.

Reflections in reflections in reflections, would you not agree - layer upon layer of myth now all uncannily finding the same piece of common ground on which to gel into one fabulous picture of universal truth - this the amazing, recurring lesson of all Albion.

Continuing on our way, we'll begin his right arm at the shoulder where we find Culgaith. Here we need to take the unmarked road to join the A66, but as soon as we touch it we must walk straight over it, for we need to cut on through the Whinfell Forest to pick up the country road which then leads the eye over the M6 and on to Askham. Now let's go a little way south on the A6 or river Lowthe until another stream takes us west towards Martindale on the bent finger tips.

Proof even down to the placement of his fingers?

This whole hand and poignantly bent-back fingers are made by waterways joined to Ullswater, shown at their best on the map reproduced in *The Bartholomew Book of Cumbria* by John Parker, the scale being approximately five miles to the inch. On it you'll notice how the thumb also seems to have flopped inward behind the fingers; if so, this could be another poignant feature, because from modern-day medical analysis of victims of crucifixion it seems that when the nails were hammered into the wrists the median nerve was so damaged as to cause the thumb to actually snap into the palm. Could it be then that the land is here trying to record such minute detail?

Continuing this right arm, its underside is lined by a waterway that starts close to High Raise and curls into Haweswater and then on to Bampton on the elbow. Indeed, the underside edge of the cross bar draws the rest of the underarm to Morland. The stretched armpit is prescribed by the country road which heads southeast a short way to join the A66 to Appleby (by the apple?) on the right side of his chest. Apples, along with acorns and hazel nuts, are one of the three mythical fruits of the Tree of Life, that tree now transformed into the cross. Note, too, that minor road which leaves Appleby and in crossing the A66 seeks out Dufton; this and the Pennine Way footpath, I think, give him an indication of a breast line.

And a nail wound too?

On this right wrist, Loadpot Hill is an apparently uninteresting grassy summit, though for us who are learning to see differently, the ruins of a shooting lodge here may be a sign that blood has marked the spot! In the same area a place called Steel Knotts, or a stone circle known as The Dodd, may also mark where the nail was hammered home.

Now we go to the left arm, followed by a ramble down the left side of his body.

This shoulder starts at Cross Fell and arches around the Pennine Way path to pass Garrigill, then taking the country road to Nenthead. Still heading east, pick up the West Allen river and follow it northwards to Ninebanks at the top of his hand. Note, just below Ninebanks, a place called Carr Shield and a road from there

to Allendale Town, which again may be indicating another thumb, snapped inwards.

After Ninebanks go to Allendale Town before dropping southwards and along the eastern end of this horizontal bar to just past Cowshill, where we need to look out for the stream that will take us to the Burnhope reservoir and on to Burnhope Seat. Now head south following the county border to where it touches the river Tees and where just a final sprinkling of artistic licence will see us safely over the shortest route to the same county border by way of Mickle Fell, cutting out only the Cow Green reservoir. Follow this county border now all the way south to Tan Hill which draws his left side down to the back of his left thigh.

From Tan Hill it's back on the country road through Keld to Thwaite at the back of the left knee. A beautiful calf muscle is drawn by the road curving down to Askrigg, after which both the river Ure and a country road carry you south to meet another road which will take you to West Burton, roughly on the left heel, and then on to Waldon Head which marks the very tips of his toes.

Eden's magic

Now go back through West Burton and pick up the A684 north through Hawes on his right shin and then further on to where this road meets the B6259. We can now follow at our leisure the ingenious route set down by Mother Earth in her river Eden, for not only does it cascade down the cross but on its own sculpts virtually the entire right side of Christ minus the arm.

Locally this whole beautiful tourist trap of an area is known simply as Eden, and standing next to this cross/Tree of Life, seemingly another poetic masterstroke in its own right.

Not far to go now. Find the town of Brough and its ancient mound upon which the remains of a Norman Castle stand. This, as we have already found, is his navel, while the B6276 to the east and the country road west to Soulby (by the soul?) forms the top edge of his loincloth, its lower edge, I'd say, is outlined by the lane from Keld, on the rear of the left thigh, to Nateby, on the upper thigh of the right leg.

I think the lanes connecting Brough to Tan Hill along with the A685 until it meets up with the A66, hint at folds upon the same cloth.

And that wound? Once found you'll never forget where it is - you can see the spectacular High Cup Nick easily on his left side. Touch it, and you will have your fingers on the Grail!

I will leave two more highly significant bodily place names until we get close to the end of this chapter, as I'd like to end it on a giggle and a gasp!

The reason behind the lean of the cross and the number fourteen?

Hung upon the cross that I had vehemently doubted, his positioning was also final confirmation of its pronounced lean which had so bugged the draughtsman in me. The ancient Egyptians, though, may have given me an intriguing reason why it does lean so. Let me try it on you.

The Mother Goddess of Egypt was Isis. Her brother-husband Osiris, after being murdered by his evil brother Seth, became lord of the underworld, not as its evil overseer, but as a descended god of light who would forever after lead the dead back to life anew. In this same underground role, Osiris was also seen as a fertility god, who would, each year, push the golden grain up through the crust of the earth, fulfilling his role as their lord of resurrection and regeneration.

Regeneration and resurrection and their wondrous cycles and mysteries have long been at the core of many a mythological quest and religious foundation, and in Egypt they were celebrated on each New Year's Eve by the ceremonial raising of the so called *Djed Pillar*

of Osiris. This raising up of a symbolic pillar from its otherwise dead and horizontal position on the ground signified the continued energising and resurgence of the life forces promoted by Osiris. When that pillar became erect (sexual undertones?) so Osiris rose, too, triumphant over decay and darkness, perennial example to all men of the unbroken circle of never-ending life.

It was Isis who would symbolically aid in the raising of the djed (a word which meant 'durable and stable' or the 'backbone of Osiris') and while doing so she would sing to him who was her dead lover, raising him back to life: *"Come to thy house, come to thy house, thou pillar! Come to thy house beautiful bull, Lord of men, Beloved of women!"*

In Baring and Cashford's *The Myth of the Goddess* there is a lovely depiction of this rite that was painted on the walls in the temple of Seti 1, dating from 1300 BC. In this we see Isis and the pharaoh Seti in the process of raising the djed pillar. However, the artist very interestingly chose not to show the column fully erected, but rather still precariously slanting, seemingly halfway between life and death, light and dark. And tell me, doesn't that

slant look somewhat similar to the leaning of Albion's cross, which perhaps also speaks of our present position, balancing between the flames of the inverted phoenix and a spring lamb; and whether it falls back to a horizontal or 'dead' position or rises to symbolise 'life' could hold as much significance for us today as it did for the Egyptians.

And with such thoughts can you blame me for feeling that just below the green surface of Albion's own lord of resurrection, there, in the dark pungent peat, may be layered not only Attis and Adonis but now Osiris too? On the strength of evidence still to come, I'd even say that this particular god may indeed be but a few centimetres beneath him whose own backbone is against that pillar of peaks that form the very backbone of England.

Bemused by this proposed Egyptian influence lying under Albion's fields? Back on Scorpio we discovered that their Fields of the Blessed or underworld, was always envisaged to be in the far west. And knowing that Osiris was lord of that territory is it any wonder if we should find him so close to the surface here.

But also listen to this: Osiris met his end by being tricked into lying in a bejewelled casket, whereupon Seth seised his opportunity by having its lid instantly nailed down, and the coffin cast into the Nile. The evil deed, interestingly enough, was committed, we are told, when the sun was in the month of Scorpio. Significant? Anyway, distraught Isis eventually finds his body and goes about reviving it by magic. But Seth hears of this and has his brother's body butchered into 14 pieces, which he orders to be scattered throughout the land. Isis in the end finds all but one of those pieces and buries them where they were found - that 14th piece we shall rediscover in the chapter on the Dark Twin. For now, though, mull over that number 14 as I did when I first heard this myth recited to me one afternoon by my daughter Holly who had learnt it at school that day. Think of a landscape sown with 14

parts of a god, then think of the 14 once buried parts that for a fact make up Albion's own miraculous landscape!

Could there be anything in it? Before you answer weigh the above with two more snippets.

Robert Graves must have had his own suspicions about the transplanting of Egyptian myth onto British fields, suggesting in *The White Goddess* that the Welsh hero Gwyn *"...was a sort of Osiris and came to be identified with King Arthur."* Gwyn ap Nudd, let me tell you, was lord of the Celtic Annwn or Hades - so perhaps not only these two underworlds, but their lords too, could be not just 'sort of the same' but indeed one and the very same. Indeed, could Britain's brooding giants underfoot be the fundamental truth behind every other-world ever envisaged - that place where the secrets of life and death were to be found?

The second snippet I had put in my hand by my other daughter Morwenna; we were looking around a north Devon church and she handed me a small leaflet she'd picked up regarding its history. Alongside its own interesting history, however, was mentioned something else that I didn't know until then: namely that from Pilate's prison to the mount of Golgotha the exhausted Jesus dropped the cross 14 times, thus there are 14 so-called Stations of the Cross. And for a walker of Albion there just so happen to also be 14 pauses or stop-off points (counting Gemini's babe and griffin as two separate stops, along with another pause at the shock that awaits in the guise of the Dark Twin) from Libra's dove to Albion's own crowning glory!

"Pity then..." you might say *"...that Albion's tally-up wasn't 12 for that would have sat so prophetically with John's revelation in which he views that future paradise on earth."*

"...was there the Tree of Life, which bore twelve manner of fruits and yieldeth her fruits

every month: and the leaves of the tree were
for the healing of the nations."
REVELATION, Chapter 22, Verse 2

Yes, it would have been nice to have equated John's 12 wisdom fruits with just the basic 12 zodiacal giants of Albion, all scattered as they are around the trunk of Albion's own mighty Tree of Life; even their individual messages meant perhaps for the healing of all nations. Certainly, in John's words *"yielding her fruits every month"* there does seem allusion to a zodiacal time scale too - so what a pity that Albion's tally-up doesn't comply.

But wait! Let's re-read *Revelation,* but not this time the Bible's version; instead let's consult the Essene understanding of what John saw, translated here by Edmond Szekely in his *The Gospel of the Essenes* - and I might add, written with no apparent axe to grind as to 14 over 12:

"...stood The Tree of Life, which bore
fourteen *manner of fruits, and yielded her fruit to those who would eat of it, And the leaves of the fruit tree were for the healing of the nations."*

Let's toy, then, just for a second with the not-too-implausible notion that one or two of that mystic sect of the Essenes might have actually accompanied Jesus and his uncle Joseph to these shores (*see Pisces*) - then they'd have been in a very good position to know exactly how many fruits hung on the Tree of Life here! Interestingly, the theory that the young Jesus may have belonged to a branch of that sect is not a new one.

But we were talking of leaning pillars. So, even taking into account that the cross was once used as a device in nature worship, could this djed pillar really be overlaid upon Albion's cross for, no matter how intriguing their mutual slants, surely at the end of the day a pillar being one bar short of a cross will always

fall short of any valid comparison? On the face of it, this would seem a reasonable finishing argument against any worthwhile twinning of the two devices, until, that is, a little more research had the dust of ancient Egypt coughing up one last image of how they saw their pillar. It turns out that they sometimes portrayed it as a Tree of Life, and get this, a tree albeit with all its branches lopped off - all of them except one horizontal branch left at either side of the main trunk!

All are welcome!

Thus, all these teachers, heroes and gods, from Osiris to Attis and from Perseus to Perceval right through to him who may represent a part of them all, are remembered in this open-air temple of Albion, as catalysts to the development of man's climb back to the stars. This a temple devoid of any trappings that would identify it to any one religion, and even its portrayal of the Christ, whether you see him crowning the zodiac or poetically hung as the ultimate fruit upon the Tree of Life, is an image that I don't think any church in the land would be comfortable to hang behind their altar, even though he is their saviour. What a shame especially when earlier followers of Christ would have seen the beauty of such:

"He was nailed to a tree and he became the fruit of the knowledge of the Father. It did not, however, cause destruction because it was eaten, but to those who ate it gave cause to be glad in the discovery, and he discovered them in himself, and they discovered him in themselves."
THE GOSPEL OF TRUTH

No taboos, then, make the atmosphere tense in Albion's temple: a true open house of God. Step in and see that because it has no bejewelled crosses or heavy candlesticks to be stolen, it has no need of doors to bolt at dusk.

Welcome, whether you're Moslem or atheist - there are no ceremonies to make you uncomfortable. Its buttresses are the echoing cliffs, its ceiling a work of ever-changing art - by day sailing nimbus, by night the whirling constellations. Its congregation is dog roses, missel-thrushes, pike and April showers; its choir, wind through leaves and new-born babies' cries. And if there is a sermon to be heard here, it won't be a solemn one because I sense that the land might abhor any tool used to bow heads too low in order to consolidate the strength of hierarchies; you only have to look at Virgo's cancan to know that I am right! Thus if there is a sermon here, you are left to deduce it in the colour of a buttercup, hear it in the Friday night laughter of Liverpool girls out on the town, sense it in the gurgling of rain in gutters after a summer's night thunderstorm, and believe it in the burning tears of love falling at the side of a grave. This the bittersweet sermon of life.

There is no god
apart from poppies and the flying fish,
men singing songs, and women brushing
their hair in the sun.
The lovely things are god that has come to
pass, like Jesus came.
THE BODY OF GOD, D H Lawrence

So in this vast temple it is the image of this green Christ that must be its high altar. After all the other giants have been visited, as though like side chapels, so, all eyes are naturally drawn to this figure, the focal point where all the love and wisdom becomes amassed into one image of perfection. But remember, this altar, although shaped as the Christ, is first and foremost a vast expanse of hills and moorland; an altar through which worms tunnel, rabbits burrow and fishes glide; on which foxgloves root, men and women make love, snow drifts and buzzards roost with blood on their talons. Truly you are standing before an altar to all

creation, contained within the body that will at the end of this book transform into that of a dancing God-Man - but again turn all that into a stained glass window and neither church nor chapel, mosque or synagogue would touch it with a barge pole! Yet why - is it not all of God?

Reflect a long time on this open armed giant, but I repeat never ever stand before him and think solemnity is called for, for the first and last word from his lips will forever be "Live!" and to hear it is then to dance! Dance for the land wills us to see not death in that sag of his body, only the agony and ecstasy of a man drowning in the love of his parents met finally as one within him. There is in him, too, a pictorial promise that whatever we may commit against both this planet and fellow men we may still all find paradise if only, like that robber at Golgotha, we have the guts to ask sincerely for what we thought yesterday was impossible.

And finally one more giggle and a gasp!

Why! We are also invited to laugh our socks off before this highest altar. Hear the sound of one more place name, a name which, in fear of sounding flippant so near to the Christ, had stopped me from mentioning it earlier, though the innocence of it now urges me to stop being so bloody grown-up and to laugh it out loud - and so here goes: "Nateby"! There, I've said it.

So what's so damned funny about the good village of Nateby? Nothing at all on the face of it, indeed, it is anatomically perfectly correct, for Nateby rests on the upper right thigh of the Christ and with a tape measure would be no more than a few inches around from the area of the buttocks. My dictionary informs me that 'nates' is another word for buttocks, so, in other words, read cheeky Nateby as being *by the buttocks!*

No matter how poignant this pose of the Christ I find it reassuring to find honest-to-goodness smiles never far away for joy is what Albion is founded upon. And you know something else? I'm sure that Christ and the planet, right down to its molten core, laughs with us, thank God!

Now for that promised gasp, another 'Wow!', but typically Albion, one primed only to leave us smiling from ear to ear.

A sense of fun certainly seems to be the key that this landscape has provided within its green cunning so as to aid our unlocking of its riches. However, whether these riches will be of any lasting worth to you beyond that initial "Well, would you believe it", depends upon unlocking the door to that wise child *within* - a door, however, often barred by an ego fearful of change. But if that inner portal can be breached, one is then free to sound out those silly ideas which tease out of unsuspecting Temple Sowerby - *a temple by the sower*; ideas that can in that reflection of the robber in Christ's eyes instil into a northern stream magic beyond belief; than can on the ribcage of his 48 mile tall body note High Cup Nick and know it is beyond mere coincidence; and in cheeky Nateby know that God must be laughing with you! On the surface, silly ideas, and yet when taken *within* all potentially life enhancing via the new perception they can ignite. And should that inner door be perceived to be anywhere near the heart, then the following words may, in three paragraphs time, endorse three-fold my seemingly silly advice:

"All I say unto you, ask, and it shall be given you; seek and ye shall find; knock, and it shall be opened to you.'
LUKE, Chapter 11 Verse 9

Holding onto the above words and, here at the end of this station of the cross and the Christ, let's leave a lantern burning somewhere in the holy wilderness that has built this nature Christ so as to remind us that even at this midnight hour there is a light returning. So,

where should we leave the lantern; on his forehead by the looking glass (Glassonby) perhaps, or upon his Gill Bank lips? Or then again what better place than his heart? Let's go there and see.

First put an ear to the ground of his chest for the sign of a heartbeat. Did you hear that? Three magnificent beats, which seem in poetic tune with Luke - three places in a cluster where his heart should be and all three thumping out, "Knock here!"

Hear the first beat in the village called **Knock**, and no, I'm not joking! The second candidate, all but a few buildings huddled together, astonishingly sings out its own name of, wait for it, **Knock Cross!** And last, but certainly not least, is the 396-feet-tall **Knock Pike hill**, which out of the three, I'd say would be nearest to his heart. I'll leave the lantern here.

Knock three times upon your own heart and find the real miracle to be yourself. You are Albion and Albion is you, you're made of the same stuff, you are its Christ in waiting.

The wise teacher Silvanius, whose teachings were among those ancient texts found at Nag Hammadi, also advised; *"**Knock on yourself as upon a door** and walk upon yourself as a straight road. For if you walk on the road it is impossible for you to go astray... Open the door for yourself that you may know what is...Whatever you will open for yourself, you will open."*

It is now time to open this mountain door to the heart of the Christ for we must now pass through into the lamb's new dawn.

"Then said Jesus unto them again, Verily, verily, I say unto you, I am the door of the Sheep."
JOHN, Chapter 10 Verse 7

*Note: as well as my trusty Michelin Map No:402 that gave me my very first sight of Christ's face, I was also helped along the way

of this cross and Christ by the Ordnance Survey Landranger Maps 90/91 and their Travelmaster 5. John Parker's book 'Cumbria, A Guide to the Lake District and its County', carries a Bartholomew map of the area, which was also worth its weight in gold.

ARIES -
THE CROSS AND THE CHRIST

Just a segment here of what lies beneath the flow of Albion's Cross. And as if finally to relieve any remaining worries I had regarding its lean, the underlying Mind has sent down one solid river of Triassic Magnessian in almost the exact angle and position of the down shaft of the Cross. What is more, this magic flow is approximately six miles wide - and so too is the width of that shaft! Interesting too is that this same sediment appears nowhere else on the map!

Based upon Geological Map of the United Kingdom by permission of the British Geological Survey, IPR/26-11C

CHAPTER 13

ARIES
Part Two
• The Lamb •

★

*The thirteenth giant
along the way*

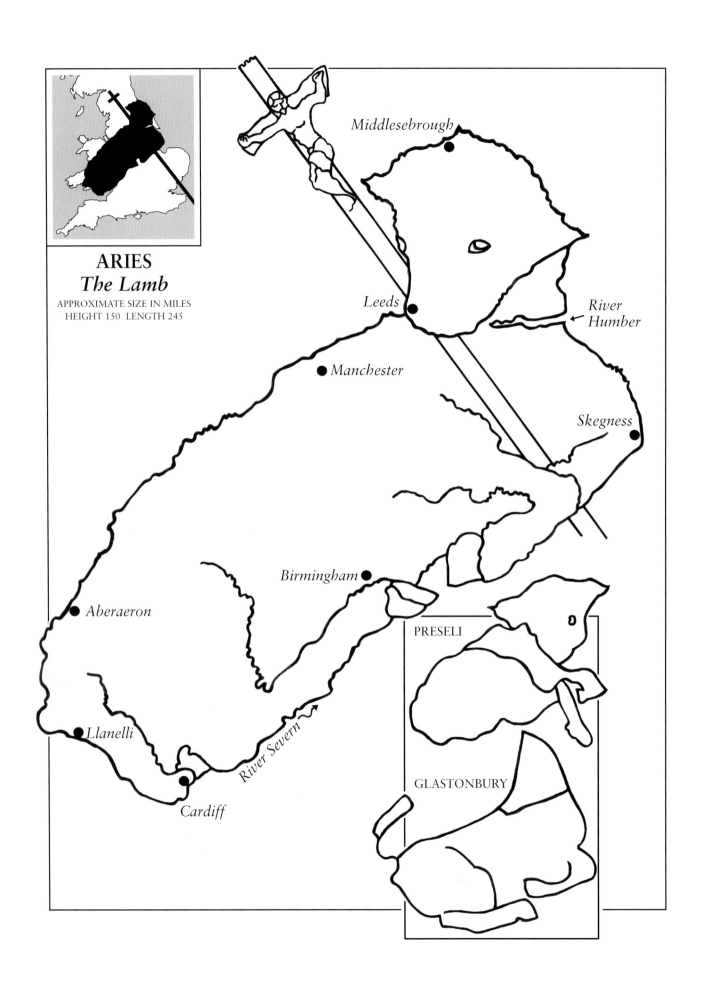

ARIES
The Lamb

APPROXIMATE SIZE IN MILES
HEIGHT 150 LENGTH 245

Middlesebrough

River
Humber

Leeds

Manchester

Skegness

Birmingham

Aberaeron

PRESELI

Llanelli

River Severn

GLASTONBURY

Cardiff

Stepping into the Dawn

And was the Holy Lamb of God
On England's pleasant pastures seen?

JERUSALEM, William Blake

GENERAL AREA: A RECLINING LAMB STRETCHING FROM THE NORTHEAST OF ENGLAND DOWN TO SOUTH WALES.

o I'd found the last zodiacal sign. The miracle was in place, for better or worse, my life from here on would be irrevocably changed.

For a start, I was an artist, but now I had to virtually abandon my colours and try to become a writer. Even if I could hack it on a word processor, would any publisher take a risk, not only on me, the unknown author, but on a manuscript that would seem to most more like the memoirs of a trip taken on the back of a magic mushroom or three.

But forgetting changes of career and publishers' rejection slips, how could I *not be affected* by the return of that lamb, that final piece of the miraculous puzzle? Whether I could learn to type or not, or whether anybody out there would ever take my discovery seriously, from that Friday afternoon onwards the world, the universe, and my own perception of my existence within its soup of sights, sounds, and feelings, were enchanted beyond anything I'd ever read in a fairy tale. To put it simply, *I was* changed because the world about me had changed, too, and I had no alternative but to buy my ticket to wherever this outrageous ramble would take me. Though I'd be a liar if I didn't say that behind my excitement lay concerns; I was a married

guy with children and wasn't delirious enough not to know that for me to go off into some magical blue yonder would be a massive financial risk. Luckily, my wife Linda believed I was not insane!

Anyway, after buying a word processor, the years of one-finger typing and ongoing research ticked by, and my personal Everest was slowly but surely being scaled. At times I climbed hundreds of feet per day under piercing blue skies, yet there were other days when I'd cling to ledges, where dwindling bank balance and the many worrying consequences of what I had found would have me wishing I'd never left base camp. However, one fine March morning I shouted, "Stuff the bank balance!" and agreed that for the writing up of Aries I would treat myself to renting a secluded cottage among the rolling, lamb-crying pastures of North Devon. After a quiet drive past banks of head-banging daffodils, beneath a blueness that only March can conjure up, I sat at the window of that cottage, high on the spring green back of Pisces.

Outside the window, Stravinsky's *Rite of Spring* was stabbing and leaping in everything. I could sense it in the frenzied slurping of new pink tongues on teats, and the thwack of the biting breeze through shivering catkins.

Everything was tremuolous to the change in the air, all was becoming re-energised. 'Expectancy' was the word to sum it up. And, though almost impossible to grasp, I was mindful too that if the fish upon which I now sat was for real, it too might be aware of its own forthcoming revelation, against all mankind's powers of reason. This was, though, dependent of course on either the bravery of some publisher I'd yet to find, or, as a last resort, publishing under my own steam. One way or another, the deal with myself was that I'd not rest until I'd birthed the whole wacky thing and presented it to the world; I could then return to my brushes and leave the world to make of it what it would.

Warm expectancy and the nearness of journey's end sank me down into the old-rose pattern of the armchair. I guess that, what with nearing the end of my writing, being tired after my 60-mile journey, and the sumptuous silence that washed that ancient, beamed room, I suddenly had a sincere wish to give myself up to the magic I'd been stalking for so long. I wanted to plunge into it and allow it to take me, the non-swimmer wherever it would. And guess what? I think I actually felt that mind, that force that had already proved it could hear man's myths and re-animate them gigantically upon the landscape, pick up my whim and welcome my leap into its current. So I played along with it.

I dipped a figurative toe down through the surface of the flag-stoned floor and into the scaly Piscean giant beneath, wanting nothing except perhaps to experience something of what I expected to be its inherent sense of timeless peace. But suddenly, and easy as sliding into a bath, I found that the toe had become a whole foot, then a leg and a moment after that the whole of me had gone down. Yet I had simultaneously felt a sense of being risen to a dizzying height; not only this, but I felt too that I was being condensed to the size of a pea whilst at the same time expanded beyond the rings of

Saturn! Why, if I went deeper and higher, and any smaller, but larger I may not even return. Though my eyes were closed, my fingers reassured me that I was still touching that cover of old roses, and yet the sensations going through me said I was not there. Suspended between being scared and yet mightily thrilled, I kept my eyes shut and held onto my uncharted space with short stabbing breaths, their sound and motion anchoring me to reality.

At such heights and depths I felt I should even stop clinging to these sensations and melt entirely within it all, in a sense becoming the water rather than the swimmer. So I let go of the arm of the chair.

My lowered, but heightened perception flew north, along puddle-filled furrows and bitterly cold streams to where, on this giant fish, they all tumble into the splintered spikes of its dorsal fins that agitate the exotic flow of the Gulf Stream. Although I was 20 miles or so away from that lapping current, I nevertheless basked in its Mexican warmth. The sensations were truly astonishing. I know we artists have grand imaginations, but these sights and feelings came in so fast, and with cinemascope grandeur, that it was all ravishingly light years ahead of my own model. But I was propelled on, breaths now hardly noticeable at all, still northwards through hundreds of miles of violet blue exhaust haze until I felt the vast presence of this lamb of Aries filling the width of England and Wales; though, in this heightened sense of perception, spread only across the width of my own shoulders.

Being then decimated, shrunk, and expanded over hundreds of miles, I was then for a desperately frightening, yet sensually sublime, moment or two the ochre pollen on every catkin from here to York. I felt my fish-tail swipe down at Land's End so many miles to the south behind me, but at the same time I was rising through the fleece and floorboards of the house where I was born so many miles away in the belly of Aries. There I was again; the wallpaper I had forgotten still brand new; mom and dad were 30 years old again and laughing. Centuries then must have been whooshing through me: flocks of voices, birds, weather systems, and a man with a hunting dog. I sucked in a torrent of sharp breaths; I gauged I was somehow defeating time but I was panicking; I was too far out of my ground; I was losing it. My hand again took hold of the arm of my chair, it was still there, and I began mentally to haul myself back for I knew my pen had no hope of making rational sense of what I saw and felt. Gulping more air, I bobbed, freezing cold, back into the room. By my watch, 45 minutes had passed, but it felt more like 10, and I told myself I must have nodded off. But I knew I hadn't; indeed, I'd felt more alive to my own existence than ever before. In truth I'd chickened out because I didn't understand. The magic was too beautiful and too fast for me to hang on to its shirt tails, and yet I knew too that it didn't need chasing, for it seemed there all the time, ready, willing, and waiting to be used - a workable magic.

Anyway, whatever that experience was, it dumped me back upon the shore of the everyday. I knew, though, I'd been nowhere but into a part of myself never really visited before, that part which never dies, the part which is at the nucleus of *everything, of you, of this gigantic earth fish, of the catkin, and of every moment that's ever been or will be. Nothing is dead or totally unaware, nothing is forgotten, and nothing is impossible when swimming in that tide.* And why shouldn't this land magic feel so intimate, when the wise have always said that *you are the land - the land is you.*

In your body is the mountain of Meru,
Surrounded by the seven continents.
There are streams too,
Lakes, mountains, plains,
And the gods of the various regions.
There are prophets there,
Monks and places of pilgrimage.

And above the ruling gods
There be stars, planets,
And the sun together with the moon;
And there are also the two cosmic powers,
The one that destroys and the one that creates;
And all the elements; ether,
Air and fire, water and earth.
Yes, all these things are within your body;
They exist in three worlds,
And all fulfil their ordered tasks
Around the mountain of Meru.
Only the one who knows this
Can become a true yogi.
Siva Samhita, Verses 1-5

As I threw another log into the stove I wondered what would happen if only we could give genuine credence to all this. What creative force would be ready and waiting to work with us? Perhaps herbs would need but a nod and a heartfelt smile to produce a cancer cure; by the same token if fishermen felt a sense of reverence and brotherhood to that vast and undulating liquid mind, would stocks be replenished and nets bulge like never before? If we could wholeheartedly ask forgiveness for causing that hole in the sky would it heal itself within a year? All creation may hang upon our every thought like we have never, ever guessed; its hand has ever reached out, offering us the opportunity of becoming joint creators of heaven on earth, but in slapping away that hand we have tilled only vast acres of wasteland.

I warned you that my pen would struggle, although maybe in its apparent naïvety, there might be a glint of something others may concur with and smile.

Drawing blanks

I had not, however, come to this cottage to dream away my time, so here's how I found the lamb.

As I've said, the lamb was the last zodiacal giant proper that I found and I believe that I was only able to see him when all the others had been revealed, as he, though the biggest of them all, was so well concealed, or perhaps I should say, lost to view. Until I had found him though, my 30 years in the piecing together of the jigsaw puzzle had, for all its novelties, resulted in a picture with three dirty great holes in it! The lack of Aries confirmed only that I'd found some freaky stunt of nature, and that's the way things drifted for maybe a year or two, and I was less frequently found staring at the atlas. But then again, how could I really let it go when I had found 11 out of the 12 signs of the zodiac, all virtual copies of those found at Glastonbury and Preseli? Either way, I thought, if it is to be doomed by the lack of a lamb, then at least 'spotting the giants in the map' would, if nothing else, be a lovely game to play with grandchildren one day. Why even Waddingtons might like to make it into a board game, albeit with one piece missing!

Those frustrating holes, by the way, stood in the eastern corner of South Wales, to the north of the The Wash, and the third (one day to surprise me with that Griffin) was what I'd thought as the 'nothingness' between Gemini and Aquarius. Three widely separated blank spots, not one giving the artist any help whatsoever, no matter how I turned the map this way and that, in search of a lamb or a ram.

It really did seem that disappointment was primed to be the only outcome and perhaps it was really time to label it all in Day-Glo pink 'A figment of the imagination!' However, the one thing that stopped me doing precisely that was that although I rated myself as a half decent artist with an imagination to match, there was, regarding Albion, always something definitely outside of me that seemed to govern my thought processes, something that was always one simple stroke of genius ahead of me, and I always hoped that it might finally take the wool from my eyes and show

me that last sign when it was good and ready. But who was I kidding? Those three gaps in question looked like they could defy even Picasso's genius in turning any of them into even the most abstract of lambs; so what chance did I stand!

The game really did seem to be up, yet only because I wasn't thinking! You see I was looking at those shapes *individually* and so had no idea that I was meant to be looking at those blanks as part of a whole, even though they were separated by 245 miles. Thank God Mary Caine made me see sense.

Mary had a little lamb...

...the last verse of which I knew went:

"And so the teacher turned it out, But still it lingered near, and waited patiently about, til Mary did appear".

Anyway, one day with time on my hands and Aries on my mind, I went back to my land giants' 'bible' and idly thumbed through more thoughts of Mary Caine. In her writings, she too pondered on the nature of Glastonbury's lamb. She had dug up a snippet she'd read in that anonymous and immensely intriguing *The High History of the Holy Grail*. In it Gawain, in search of the Grail, goes to what seems a very definite geographical location and which, according to Mary, seems most suggestive of the environs of Glastonbury's own giant lamb, of which the medieval chronicler says: *"The King of Wales was Lord of this Land."* Mary then goes on to mention that on Glastonbury's Aries there just so happens to be a hamlet called Walton, located upon the lamb's haunches, and a name that lends itself to be translated as *Welsh* or *Waellas Town*. So, with justification, she reasons that the *High History* must be referring to no other place than Somerset's lamb.

However, I've always had a sneaky

suspicion that some of the ancient writings that Caine and Maltwood have suggested as bearing coded reference to Glastonbury's secret may, on the contrary, be pointing a finger at the larger zodiac where Glastonbury, for all its splendid riches, is, as we now know, but the pupil in the eye of its mighty Pisces.

Nevertheless, Mary's intuitive spark that connected Wales to Aries suddenly shot through the ill-used vaults of my own mind and illuminated there what I needed to know. In a millisecond I was a stellar sheep dog trained only in sniffing out the constellation of Aries on the ground! Mary's theory had me reaching for my big old atlas with a zeal I hadn't had for a long time, and on page 31 my nose was against Wales with a vengeance!

Now if the king of Wales fancied claiming the haunches of Albion's Aries too, I excitedly thought, then these must be located in that only blank spot left in Wales, there in that south east corner... and if so his head must logically be in that other and opposite empty area above the head of Sagittarius! In another millisecond those two separated gaps clicked together and the almighty lamb of Albion bleated out, wagging his Welsh tail behind him!

Though why hadn't I spotted that now oh-so-obvious little giveaway ear sticking out of those wool-white cliffs of Flamborough Head? And just look at that woolly tail curled around Cardiff. I hadn't seen any of it, for the time obviously wasn't right. And whether that throwaway titbit of information in the *High History*, or the apparently Welsh labelling of the Somerset lamb's haunches have any grain of truth at all, they got me back on track; I had found the last zodiacal giant of Albion and I was spinning in my studio like a Dervish! Books were tumbling off shelves and papers flying up from my desk in my jubilant whirl. So, I'd got there in the end via a zany kind of logic, not, I felt, entirely mine, but then that's the way it had been for 30 years or more!

Defining the body

And this is where he's been hiding all along.

I will start at the tip of his left ear, which is located in the sympathetic whiteness of Flamborough Head's cliffs on the Yorkshire coast. From here we shall follow the coast north to draw the top of his woolly head, where the river Tees turns through Middlesbrough. Next we go along the A66 through Darlington and on until the A6108 forks off west to Richmond. After Richmond we travel to Marske and then to Grinton on the B6270, or there's a more natural line that defines the top of his right ear: just follow the river Swale.

From Grinton on the ear tip, we then go back southeast on the country road to Leyburn. Follow the River Ure past Masham but where the river makes a *ewe*-turn (sorry!). We'll then proceed on the country road to Kirkby Malzeard, then wind down to Risplith and beyond to Bishop Thornton, seeing, in the distance, Fountains Abbey on the lamb's eyebrow. Carry on heading south as though you are making for Hampsthwaite, but, just before, jump into the river Nidd and allow it to lead you to the A61 where we go south a little way to Killinghall. By doing this, we have just drawn the outside of the right eye.

Take the A61 through Harrogate and down to the urban sprawl of Leeds which is on the lamb's nose.

Sounds like Aries to me!

Hurry through Leeds by crossing the **river Aire (does its water sing of Aries? - wonderful isn't it!)** to Morley, Wakefield, and Ackworth where we now take the unnamed (on my map) tributary off the river Ouse. This waterway, along with a county boundary line, draws his chin eastwards to Goole and the river Ouse proper.

At Goole follow the river to where it points

at the M62 at Junction 37, then take the A614 to Holme-upon-Spalding Moor and beyond on the A613. Go through Driffield and Bridlington then follow the coastline back to that ear tip of Flamborough Head.

The eyes, by the way, can be approximately placed around Fountains Abbey, Bishop Thornton and Ripley for the right eye, whilst Whitwell-on-the-Hill, northeast of York, would be near enough to marking the left.

We shall now make our way down the neck starting from Bridlington. Down then to Kingston-upon-Hull on the A165, and cross the River Humber there to follow the east coast past Grimsby and around that Skegness corner to join the river Welland to Spalding. After this find Sleaford and take a direct route to Partney to complete that tucked-up left foreleg.

Start the right foreleg, also tucked up, at Spalding on its knee, where the river Glen will define the leg as far as Stamford. Once here it is back on the river Welland to Rockingham. After Rockingham take the A427 to Market Harborough and on to Lutterworth on the tip of its hoof. Then follow either the M1 or A426 to Leicester.

At Leicester take the A46 to Thurmaston and beyond to Rearsby, then the B674 to Twyford and back directly south to Market Harborough. This completes the entire hoof of that right foreleg.

Back now to Twyford with a view to going on to St Dalby and Melton Mowbray where either the B676 or river Wreake will carry us east to Colsterworth and then to Corby Glen. Once here we find again our friend the river Glen (west) provides us with the pleasing curve that brings us safely to Grantham and another river passage west via Harby, curling around into Cropwell Bishop, before running finally into Nottingham. Following the Trent to Derby will give us an excellent line for the back of the right foreleg - oh, and should I mention here that Derby County Football Club

are known as The Rams? Perhaps not.

Now it's on to Newmarket where the A17 and A16 will take us down to Spalding on the knee of this same leg and another meeting with the river Glen.

Part of the lamb's belly is easily drawn by the M69 from Leicester to Coventry. Coventry itself sits upon the rear hoof which curves slightly downward and which I will now describe.

From Coventry take the M6 to Harborough Magna on the tip of this hoof. Now pass through Rugby to Junction 1 of the M45; carry on over this roaring tarmac and try to follow the flow of the country roads and railway line to Leamington Spa on the rear of this same hoof. Once at Leamington, head the short distance to Warwick and the A46 back to Coventry and Junction 2 of the M6 to finish this rear hoof. The A45 in the centre gives the hoof its cloven appearance.

From Warwick we're now off southwestwards on the A46 to Stratford and going with the flow of the river Avon past Shakespeare's Hathaway Cottage to Evesham. Now take the A435 to Teddington, Cheltenham, and beyond to find the river Severn at Gloucester.

Flow out now along the Welsh side of the Severn, noting how Newport sits upon the joint of the back leg while Cardiff's sprawl forms the tip of the lamb's tail. From Cardiff follow the coastline to Swansea and Leo's leg; the lion lies down with the lamb here! At Swansea, though, cross overland for that swiping foreleg and then drop into the river Loughor on its other side where the coast of Carmarthen Bay will lead us around the top of the lamb's tail and into the river Twyi for we're going into Carmarthen itself.

At Carmarthen take the A484 and A486 with a view to joining the A487 at Synod Inn. Stay on the road until Aberaeron - it's still the A487 but with plenty of coastline, too, to where it touches the A494 near Dolgellau on

Virgo's nipple. Carry on down this same road to Mold where we need the A550 and A5117 to pick up the M56 north of Chester (which also lines Gemini's upper arm) to Junction 11. We now head through Warrington to Golborne on that babe's neck, taking the A580 east and picking up the M62 all the way to Morley at Junction 28 and the nose of the lamb south of Leeds. I said this sign was colossal!

We must now finish that rear leg by going back to Coventry on its hoof. From Coventry then, take the M6 to Junction 4 on the outskirts of Birmingham. Here we have a score of road alternatives to take us into a slight curve to where the M42 meets the M5 at Bromsgrove. We can either follow the boring M5 to Worcester or be different and take a barge along the Worcester and Birmingham Canal.

Once at Worcester we're heading for Great Malvern, then the B4218 and the A449 to Ross-on-Wye. Zig-zag with the river Wye itself to Hereford and the A40 to Ludlow. Beyond Ludlow, and just past the Craven Arms, take the A489 for Lydam and drop straight into Offa's Dyke west of Church Stoke for a well-earned rest, for that not only completes the line of the rear leg to where it joins the body, but also the lamb in its awesome entirety - phew!

The last shall come first

Purists will, of course, point out that, in modern zodiacs, Aries actually *starts* the yearly round rather than bringing up its rear, as it seems to do in Albion's out-of-sequence merry-go-round. But what a merry end it must promise, for the zodiac is a circle and thus the end becomes the new beginning. Just minutes after that midnight Son, the land is trying to assure us that no matter what the upheavals suggested by that grouping of fetus, scorpion, phoenix and Christ are, spring is seen to be just

around the corner - dawn *will* follow the chaos.

But don't take my word for it. According to Sesti, the star Alpha Arietis in ancient Mesopotamia was known as both Dilkar, which means '*She who announces the dawn*', and Dilgan meaning '*She who is the messenger of the dawn*'. When I also tell you that this particular star graces the actual head of the heavenly Aries, and that Aries is also supposed to rule the head in medical astrology, you may agree with me that this dawn must be closely allied to a newer way of thinking and perceiving. A change of heads is being called for!

And as for Aries bringing up the rear, you should know too that from 4000 to 2000 BC, when Stonehenge was in the building, Taurus was the accepted first sign of the zodiac while Aries was the last. So, in the fullness of time, the last becomes the first in the next turn of the wheel, and those today who see no hope at all may be the first to walk into the most wondrous spring ever to burgeon.

The lamb jumps over the ram

Those same astrological purists, however, may also want to question why the land has pushed out from its womb a reclining *lamb* when everyone knows it should be a *ram*. Well blame Mary Caine: she looked at Katherine Maltwood's ram figure and saw in it a paschal lamb trying to get out! But come on, who would choose a battering ram over a lamb as a symbol of spring? Seasonwise, Aries does indeed mark the start of spring in the month of March, and surely there can be no better sign than newborn lambs to mark it; certainly their leaping outside my March window jubilantly endorses that thought.

However, please forget what Mary and I think - it's time for you to read for yourself. You now need no one to work it out for you. See for yourself what the poetry in the land has demanded to birth amid both Somerset's pastures and Preseli's mountains, for both have reclining lambs, their legs tucked underneath them, and heads facing west. Surely we are now being presented with threefold evidence confirming that from Yorkshire down to south Wales it's a gentle lamb that's crying out for a new beginning - the ram's aggression has had its day. For good measure, see how the same land poet has chosen the greatest of the three to brandish that cross as a final "Yes!" to the lamb. Mary, I think you *are* vindicated!

On top of this, it is also fascinating to see that the distinctive reclining pose of all three lambs is exactly how the original images of the ram were drawn against its starry constellation in ancient times: Aries was always depicted *reclining and with a head that looked back*.

To add a little more spice to the possibility that we definitely have a lamb for Aries, I must again quote from *Mythic Astrology* where it says: *"It is to the Egyptians that we owe the sign of Aries, although in the beginning it was called a sheep as often as the ram."* Is this a softening of the ram's edges, perhaps?

Finally, and knowing that long before the Grail was deemed a Christian high cup its prototype was a bubbling cauldron, hear how the witch Medea once gave the ancient Greeks a demonstration of her own cauldron's amazing properties of renewal by submerging into its magic broth an old ram, whereupon, in moments, it climbed out again as a lamb! And so the lamb of Aries fills the Grail Ark of Albion from prow to stern with the same promise. However,

this time it may be a rejuvenated mankind, blessed with new eyes and insight, who will step out of whatever whirling turmoil our present blindness has set in motion. These happy few, in full mind blowing realization of their oneness with all creation, will not only note the buzzard spiralling upon a summer thermal, but will shiver in delight to be able to intimately share in that bird's own pleasure, indeed, to close one's eyes may be to simply *become* that buzzard in all but soul. Imagine too, via this new perception, to see a mountain spraying undreamt-of colours high into the ether, and then being spiritually able enough to go down to its roots and there share in its aeons-long sense of peace and place. And then to perhaps lean against an oak and find oneself not only feeling the rising of its sap as though it was in your own veins, but melting too into its storeroom of the thousands of tales of things that tree has registered, from yesterday's sermon of the bees to a dream caught from a shepherd's head that once lolled against its bark a full century ago.

Don't imagine, though, that this new dawn, this paradise on earth, will permit lazy living. There will be no mouths permanently full of grapes or bees without stings allowing fingers to poke into dripping hives. No, earth will still be earth; frosts will still bite noses; the foot-prints of the fox upon the fresh snow will still run parallel to the red-rose stains of his quarry; the wind will still bend trees and snap off their branches, no matter how fine a tale they may tell; and man will still return home most heartily hungry at the end of each day's endeavours to earn his crust, for life will always be gloriously bittersweet.

Time now, though, to take our berths aboard the ark.

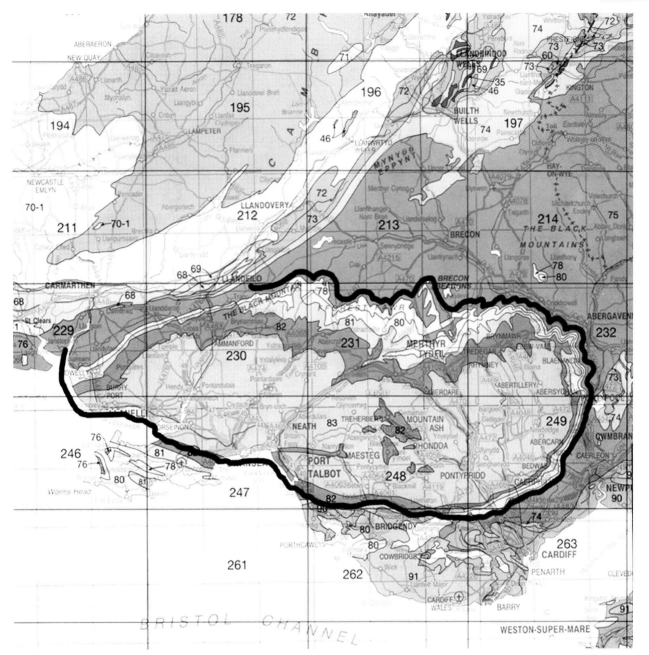

Based upon Geological Map of the United Kingdom by permission of the British Geological Survey, IPR/26-11C

ARIES
THE LAMB

The Lamb covers an enormous area of Britain and of course is cut through with all the sedimentary diversity of Albion. However, I must draw your attention to a charming piece of its anatomy; that of its tail down there in south east Wales. Here the Land has built a more perfect tail than the one the surface shows to us. See it curved and wonderfully woolly.

★

CHAPTER 14

CANCER

• *The Ark* •

Argo Navis - King Solomon's Miraculous Ship

★

The fourteenth giant along the way

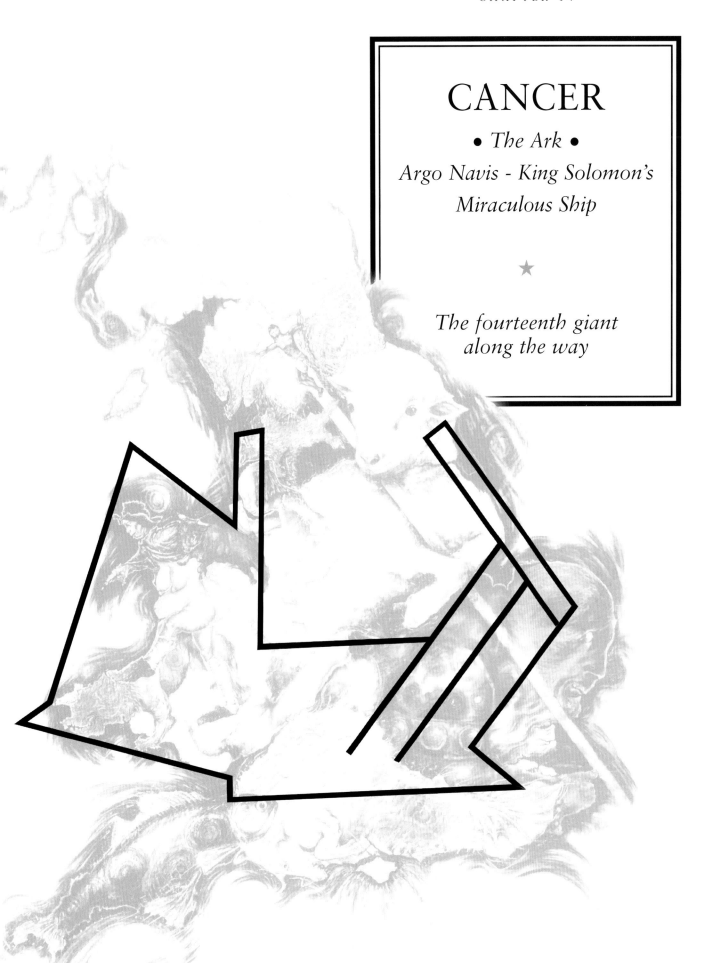

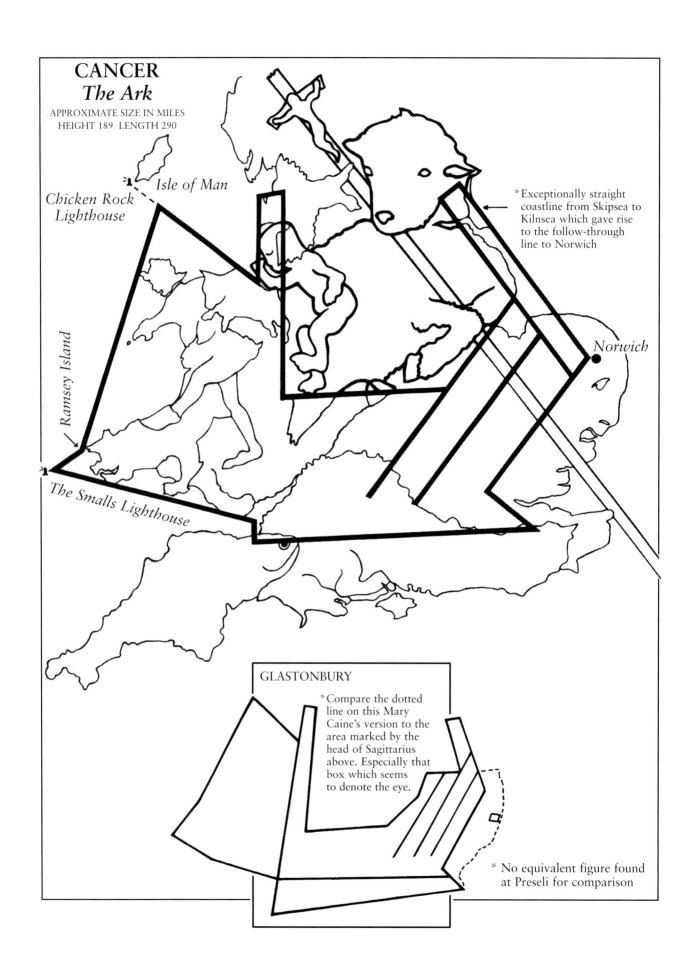

CANCER
The Ark

APPROXIMATE SIZE IN MILES
HEIGHT 189 LENGTH 290

Isle of Man

*Chicken Rock
Lighthouse*

Ramsey Island

The Smalls Lighthouse

*Exceptionally straight
coastline from Skipsea to
Kilnsea which gave rise
to the follow-through
line to Norwich

Norwich

GLASTONBURY

*Compare the dotted
line on this Mary
Caine's version to the
area marked by the
head of Sagittarius
above. Especially that
box which seems
to denote the eye.

* No equivalent figure found
at Preseli for comparison

From this starship could dangle a lifeline

And there came down from the mountain top to the sea Chiron, son of Philyra, and where the white surf broke he dipped his feet, and, often waving with his broad hand, cried out to them at their departure, "Good speed and a sorrowless home-return!"

THE ARGONAUTICA, Apollonius of Rhodes

GENERAL AREA:
THE ALL-EMBRACING OUTER EDGE OF THIS GREAT ZODIAC OF ALBION.

elcome aboard then, you metaphysical mariners! We are now upon the last of Albion's zodiac signs, that of Cancer's gigantic ark, although, throughout the bulk of our journey, we have been either rummaging in her holds or pacing her deck, for she encompasses many of the previous giants. Indeed, she is the strong bark cover that binds and protects the whole landscaped miracle. In her shape, we shall also discern the all-enfolding arms of the Great Mother, protective of her cargo of the song of life, at a time when men are turning deaf ears to the message, her arms becoming a lifeboat whose name may be as much Argo Navis as it is Cancer. Allow me to explain by telling you a little of this starship's background.

The original lifeboat

Not far away from where in the night sky the zodiacal crab snips, and in the region of the heavens that was once seen as the sea, sails the colossal star-studded ship that man, perhaps under the subliminal influence of God, built around the constellation of Argo Navis. And I cannot here resist including again that 1690 depiction of this same starship (as already illustrated in Sagittarius), because surely it's the sister ship to the one that enfolds Albion.

Notice that leaning mast and match it against Albion's own, though Albion's is made more wonderful still by the figure of the Christ nailed to it. *"But..."* you might say, *"...I've never once seen a depiction of an ark which has a mast, for the ark wasn't a sailing vessel as*

such but rather a 'stout tub' built only to ride out whatever the elements threw at it." - and I would agree. However, remember that this cross/mast of Albion is, in essence, the Tree of Life, and with that hear a legend preserved for us by Jacobus de Vorgaine in his *Aurea Lengenda*. The legend says that, prior to the great deluge, Noah actually dug up the Tree of Life, root and all, and took it with him aboard the ark.

Now try to visualise that 'tub' with the Tree of Life towering high above its deck - a mast by any other name? Though it signifies more than this, for that great tree rising above those tempestuous waves would have been a glowing sign of all that was preserved and enshrined within her vast hold - in a word *'life'*. Albion's own ark carries the very same. Why, even the Christ who is nailed to that tree is *alive* - see how his eyes are filled with river tears.

Remember too, from our findings under Sagittarius, that the earthly counterpart of this Argo Navis was constructed of wood from a 'talking oak', so is it any wonder that this ark of Albion should be attempting to speak to us now?

Another noteworthy pictorial comparison comes via a Roman representation of this same starship, chiselled on the globe of the heavens as held aloft by the giant Atlas in the

*Argo Navis,
from the
Farnese Atlas.*

magnificent Farnese statue. In my copy of this ship do note what looks like a *leaning mast/crucifix* - remember all my concerns regarding the leaning mast/cross of Albion?

Tradition says that this heavenly ark commemorates the first ship ever to sail, the one which carried Danaus and his daughters from Egypt to Rhodes and then to Argos. The Egyptians also believed it carried their Isis and Osiris during their own great deluge, a tale far older than the Bible's version. Likewise, in Hindu mythology, this same universal lifeboat arrived to save Isi and Iswara; while to the Greeks it was Jason himself who requisitioned it as his own Argo, nailing upon its mast that Grail-like prize of the Golden Fleece. And dare I suggest that Noah also had a turn at captaining her? Indeed I *do* dare, because whether in search of the ultimate prize of enlightenment, or in seeking the preservation of life at a time of global catastrophe, I propose that all those demi-gods and heroes had berths, and yes, even mystic re*births*, aboard this very down-to-earth Argo-come-ark of Britain, which, because of her fame, has been remembered in the night sky.

Can you blame me for these assumptions when also learning how two of Jason's original crew members, Castor and Pollux, seemingly retain their positions on the deck of Albion's own star-ship in the shapes of the Geminian child and its protector, the griffin - for via their earthly fame, Castor and Pollux are likewise remembered in the night sky as the starry twins of Gemini. Why, even that Jason and Noah tie-up gains extra credence when noting what nature has done to the Isle of Wight, and then hearing how Jason also released a dove to lead his Argo to the so-called Clashing Islands.

Thus I can't help wondering if Britain could prove to be the physical fact, and therefore the subconscious catalyst, for this fabled ship sailing into the Grail/Deluge dreams of so many cultures, albeit bearing many different names upon her fabulous prow. And if so, practical or what, an ark whose deck and holds are part of an actual living landscape - pasture for thousands of two-by-two species! An island vessel too big to be entirely engulfed, and one bearing the poetic truth of all Grails upon its mast - this a God-Man who we shall later find to be dancing off his cross in celebration of life without end.

Confronted by the possibility of that once mythic lifeboat now docking large as life into the face of this new millennium, and at such time when the seas are supposedly rising due to global warming, can any open-minded thinker afford to look away?

For myself, I see this vessel as like a gigantic crescent cup whose contents, if sipped and tasted correctly, could be tantamount to a sip from the Grail itself. Indeed, can I put it to you that the wisdom of the Grail was ever encoded into Britain's landscape, hence Joseph of Arimathea's symbolic gesture of bringing that wisdom filled cup of the Last Supper and, as some legends have it, burying it in the soil of Britain.

On that note, does another conundrum unravel itself?

Working to the same map?

If you have trouble seeing Albion's ark shape-shifting into the form of a cup, read something written by a man with a remarkably intriguing name, at least for us magic map readers - one Walter Map, chaplain and archdeacon of Henry II's Oxford.

Poor Map - experts feel that he was not the real author or translator of *The Queste del Saint Graal*, although testified as such in its text. However, it doesn't really matter because whoever did write the tale certainly gave us some most interesting and intimate details of the wonders to expect when in the presence of the Grail. We rummagers through marvels should have our curiosity further tweaked when hearing that the Grail was sometimes

small enough to carry whilst at other times it could swell to the size of a cathedral. *"So what's that got to do with Albion? He mentions a cathedral but nothing about it (whatever it is) swelling into a ship the size of Britain!"* you say - but allow me to return to this in a second or two. Before I do, your ears really should prick up when Map tells us that even the Christ himself would appear within it, sometimes crucified, sometimes as a baby, and at other times even appearing naked. So dare I try to translate what was in the mind of Map or whoever he was? Just try and stop me!

For instance, could that swelling to the size of a cathedral be an encoded riddle relating to the hundreds of square miles occupied by *this* star temple of Albion, enveloped as she is by a ship. I say this for the Church as an institution was traditionally likened to the so-called bark of St Peter, thus cathedral = Church = St Peter's bark or ship = Albion's landscaped star temple within an ark? And what grounds have I for asserting that this is correct? See how Map's three images of Christ are mapped out in this same temple-come-Grail vessel - see Gemini's Christ Child separated by but 50 miles from the Christ crucified, while as for him appearing naked - wait until the last chapter and I'll even show you this too!

Mary Caine also cites Map's intriguing account and naturally equates it with Glastonbury's own wonders. However, I must point out that although there is a Christ Child rising from out of the Somerset Levels, there is no cross and hence no crucified Christ to be seen, naked or otherwise. I therefore suggest that Walter Map's Grail clues are better interpreted when overlaid upon a far larger map.

Map also wrote of Sir Galahad's own experience of achieving the Grail, although not specifically recording exactly what the knight saw: *"Come forward servant of Jesus Christ, and look on that which you have so ardently desired to see."* Galahad drew near and looked into the holy vessel; only a glance, but from it a violent trembling instantly seized his mortal flesh at the contemplation of the spiritual mysteries whirling therein. The knight then with hands raised to heaven shouted: *"Thou hast granted my desire, for now I see revealed what tongue could not relate nor heart conceive"*.

Galahad, in seeing something so inconceivably beautiful, is said to have died on the spot in the agony and ecstasy of it all. May I be so bold as to suggest that what he saw might have been *this* staggering portrayal of Albion, somehow come more fabulously alive than even we can see now. In that dancing hologram perhaps the Christ Child transmuted amid phoenix sparks into the dancing God-Man who waits in the wings of Albion's last chapter. If so, I believe Galahad's death would have been no death as we know it. In the last few miles of this starship voyage we shall try to discern a little more of what might be its own encoded poetry, just as Galahad may have done when he sailed these same last few miles, in the so-called 'Miraculous Ship' which carried him, too, to the Grail. But more of that shortly.

Built upon amazing lines

So what name is on the prow of Albion's cathedral in a ship: Cancer? Argo Navis? Noah's ark? And what flag would she fly: Jewish? Christian? Egyptian? Hindu? Greek? It really doesn't matter what you call her or who first captained her, for this ship is, I think, code for the ultimate vessel of universal truth, which, at times, appeared to some as a cup, to those of earlier times, a cauldron, or even a severed head. To Walter Map it appeared as large as a cathedral in which the Christ alternated between being a child and a crucified man; but at times of great global peril it is *this* great ship that arrives, a lifeboat for dear life itself. Thus, this Grail vessel of Albion serves all mankind and carries, I fancy, wine pressed from truths gleaned by many faiths and cultures, and yet which, in its final distillation, is gloriously free of any one label, for the flag she sails under must be that of the entire universe - a single star would do.

In terms of shape, too, this vessel is built upon the lines of the constellations, for amazingly it is the outer extremities of the bodily contours of the other giants that give rise to her. We know already that her figurehead is the zodiac's own patron giant, Sagittarius, while Leo, Virgo, Taurus and Gemini's griffin provide the rest of the vessel's lines while, at the same time, being stowed away all ship-shape and secure within her holds as her own mystic cargo - a remarkably cunning piece of draftsmanship. But the figures that the shipbuilder decreed should be seated upon its deck must be the most precious of all its starry cargo: the hauntingly beautiful babe of Gemini and the lamb of Aries. The child is our potential of Christ Consciousness, while the lamb is the promise of the new dawn that will greet those who acquire that Consciousness. In a nut shell, the ultimate message of Albion is on that deck, visually cradled between that distinctly inwardly bent prow and stern, like arms endeavouring to cherish the babe as it sleeps upon the lamb's fleece. Indeed, to all intents and purposes, this ship could be built only to couch that child and lamb, so snugly do they slot into that deck area.

But what of the remaining signs, those who do not find either a secure place within her holds or an honoured place upon the deck? Astoundingly they are the *only* figures which could be excused from becoming part of that cargo; there to the south and cavorting quite naturally alongside the bows are the only two aquatic creatures of the zodiac: Pisces the fish following at the stern, while Capricorn the sea unicorn arches her back and prances in the swell of the ship's passage - logically creatures that no ark could contain or have any need to.

The only other free-ranging signs are, of course, those with wings: Libra's dove, seen skimming above the waves towards the ark, the phoenix scorching the air around the cross or mast, while the griffin, although allowing his head and beak to give us the line of a funny little stump of a stern mast, is also quite rightly excused to rise above the actual deck. So all three birds are free to fly outside the ark, although more than likely using her great mast as a roosting place when things get really rough!

Sitting on one's intellect for a moment, who cannot smile at such uncanny accuracy of placement? Again, it is all indelible evidence on the ground to the absolute 'intelligence' behind the forces that have created all this, for both our intellectual unease and childish delight, to hasten the death of one out-moded perception and to hurry along the birth of its bright new replacement. However, imagine if these giants had not been so arranged; imagine if the fish fitted into the scheme of things a lot further to the north, above the deck, say - a fish ridiculously out of water! Or that maybe one of those birds had been found cruelly caged below decks somewhere alongside a pitifully dried-out sea unicorn - the ground plan would be visibly flawed. But no, everything is miraculously where it should be in preparation for the storm.

Glaringly, though, the odd sign out in this so-logical layout is the scorpion. Banished from the ark to hover astern and above the babe's head like an ever-deepening weather system, gathering his fury about him into the meteorological upheaval that many environmentalists already believe to be imminent. This is nature's reaction to man being out of tune with her, and thus with himself. The natural law is perfect - we reap what we sow. Thus mankind around the planet may well have to reap a whirlwind propelled solely by our own ignorant anti-life doings. Scorpio is cast adrift and we should see this as

a reflection of our own imbalances, compacted and personified. It is us who are outside of the ark, outside of the laws of life and the universe.

That said, whatever the approaching mayhem holds in store, I sense that there is a life-line thrown out to all mankind from this gigantic lifeboat and we can unravel it within its cargo of constellations, those starry signposts which all good mariners have learned to read in order to find safe harbour.

OK, *a cleverly built ship - but where the hell has the crab gone?*

With so much talk of ships, some of you may well be asking what has become of Cancer's good old crab in all of this; so without further ado let's go crabbing.

When Katherine Maltwood discovered the Glastonbury zodiac she, too, found a ship where the crab should have been, though it was the astute Mary Caine who delved deeper and found that a ship, and more especially an ark, fulfilled Cancer's astrological characteristics far more expansively than even a crab could! My own research proved the same. Mary was also more than happy to name that ship Argo Navis. Starry attributes apart, though, my own artist's eye proposes that, in their basic shape, crabs and ships are not too dissimilar. Check out my comparative illustrations and see for yourself how mutually sympathetic their basic proportions are.

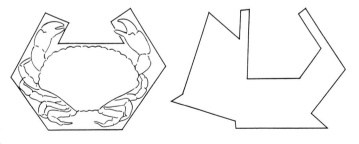

Shapes apart, let's also look at some equally surprising vessel-like astrological traits of those born under the sign of the crab.

In the book *Mythic Astrology,* authors Guttman and Johnson, although never for one moment suggesting the replacement of Cancer's crab by an ark, nevertheless convey to the reader some most vessel-like characteristics of Cancerian types in general. The authors also highlight a very strong mother/womb/baby link to this sign - and isn't a womb a protective vessel for an unborn child? Enlarging upon this, they refer to Cancer as being representative of the Great Mother herself and that typical Cancerians, along with expectant mothers the world over, have special requirements: *"...with such a strong relationship to the life-giving functions surrounding birth and the nurturing and care of the infant, it is no wonder that they demand a secure place to be."* And this too: *"...especially in ancient times the infants' and mothers' lives were extremely fragile and delicate, and anything that rocked the boat was considered dangerous, a cause for insecurity."*

I find it so very tempting to overlay the above with this secure Mother-ship of Albion, with that most delicate of all her cargo, the unborn Christ Child held, as it is, between Cancer's armoured and crab-like stern and prow arms. And there are further Cancerian attributes which link in so well with this womb-ark's protection of a young one: *"We also know that Cancer rules the breasts and womb in medical astrology, the two biological organs that exist to provide safe home and nourishment to the young infant."* So what finer home could that Geminian babe have, when Scorpio comes to rock the boat, than the Great Cancerian Mother herself transformed into an all enveloping and protective womb-ark - the ultimate Mother-ship - life's safe house when the elements swing out of kilter.

Neither is it surprising that this ark of Albion can be at first overlooked in that initial in-your-face rush of all the other giants, when we read another apparent trait of your typical crab: *"Because Cancer is so good at this*

merging process, the result is often a loss of personal identity. It can also result in a situation wherein Cancer is unaware of who and what it is carrying." Again it seems that Cancer slips so easily into the guise of this great landscaped ark.

The manger at its core

Cradling Gemini's babe as its most cherished passenger in those all-embracing arms, and remembering Cancer's apparent empathy with the womb, should Glastonbury's own ship bear similar motherly clues? Remarkably it does, and especially so because the rest of Glastonbury's giants are all individually spaced out in their circular merry-go-round order. In the case of Cancer's ship, however, Gemini's child has been taken out of that order and manoeuvred to sit upon the deck as its only cargo!

It seems that womb-boat theory is then doubly emphasised. That said, for all you crabs out there who perhaps find all this talk of protecting babies a bit too deep, let me try to convince you of your in-built motherly/protective instincts by taking you into the deep space at the heart of your own heavenly constellation. I found there something surprising just as I too was having a few second thoughts about all that baby stuff. In between two stars there, Gamma and Delta, are a smaller cluster of faintly glimmering stars and which are blessed with the name of, wait for it, the Manger! Thus there really is a manger/cradle at the heart of you - a crab turned into a rock-a-bye ark! Now do you get Cancer's land poetry - the hard shell of the crab lifts to reveal her inner secret - she is indeed a womb/manger, a Mother-ship wherein sleeps the Holy Child who is the fundamental token of her cargo. What is more, that same sleeping Christ Consciousness is carried at the centre of us all and the continuation of all life might again depend upon all of us allowing it to open its eyes upon an enchanting brave new world.

Unfortunately here on earth that reclusive cluster of the Manger has already been stripped of its enchantment and renamed the M44 - so what's new?

Taliesin knew it all along!

Taliesin or Merlin, however, may have known that cluster's real name. Cast your mind back to Virgo where we heard him confound his fellow bards with: "*I have been with my Lord in the manger of the ass*". Delta and Gamma, the two stars that sit either side of the Manager, are also named Asellus Australis and Asellus Borealis - in other words the asses! So, Taliesin's otherwise preposterous boast becomes a charming possibility - maybe he really did meet the boy Messiah in person in the Manger that is but part and parcel of the deck of *this* Cancerian ark of Albion! Or if not, perhaps the cunning bard was purely alluding to the fact that he had visited that Christ Child of hills and flowers, who has been rocked there for a million years. Either way, overlaid on Albion's map his teasing can now be seen in a fascinating new light.

Try code-breaking another seemingly absurd line from that old trickster: "*I have been in the firmament with Mary Magdalene.*" Re-read this alongside the legend of Joseph of Arimathea returning to Britain, after the crucifixion, with Mary Magdalene. According to George F Jowett, in his *The Drama of the Lost Disciples,* Mary was amongst that group who spent a short time here before taking the teachings to Marseilles in the south of France, where she ended her days. Thus, if Taliesin met her upon that visit here, of course he would have been at her side in the firmament of Albion!

The Glass Ship

Perhaps now feeling a little more comfortable with the idea of Cancer becoming a vessel, let's go back to talking about ships, especially one that Taliesin may once have navigated.

The artful make-up of Albion's ship, in allowing us to see through its sides and into its celestial cargo, gives us the impression that it's made of glass, and with that thought does another of his tall stories seem suddenly quite plausible? I ask this as in Taliesin's poem *The Spoils of Annwn* he tells that King Arthur himself once sailed aboard a glass ship, called *Prydwen*, which, according to Mary Caine, meant 'The Beauty of Cosmic Order'! But more to the point, we are told that he embarked upon a voyage to the underworld in search of the lost Cauldron of Inspiration, the property of Ceridwen/the Earth Mother (*see Virgo*). Upon its discovery, says the poem, man's lost self or wisdom would be recovered from the black hole of ignorance.

Armed with Albion's revelations, see that underworld as *this* recently discovered world under our feet. As you do, see right through another smokescreen! You *are*, in truth, looking through Arthur's glass ship - perhaps even the crystal clear Grail vessel itself, its contents surely the basic ingredients of Ceridwen's own inspirational cauldron brew. But let its contents cease their swirling and become a perfect, still, mirror surface, nature's own star-capturing looking glass. Use it, like any mirror, to see your own reflection, and see *your own face* superimposed upon that of the God-Man hung upon that cross/mast, and with the stars all laid down under what will become his *dancing* feet. Behold then *your own lost self!* The IMMORTAL you! The ETERNAL you! The RIGHTFUL you! You are seeing *your own* face shining out of that of the Christ, and the message must be that he is you and you are he!

Put simply, you will see yourself placed upon a pinnacle of stars - accept the fact that Jerusalem, this heaven set out on earth, has forever been laid at *your* feet.

Once more are we watching the mist of centuries clear? Was Arthur's voyage and search for this same treasure of the truth **on dry land**, his glass ship **this see-through ark full of star wisdom?** - just as it may have been Noah's, and Jason's, and all who ever sought to either protect or to partake of the ultimate journey of self revelation.

It seems the further we burrow into this miracle the more we learn that we are not the first to forage here. Sure, today we are seeing it at the absolute culmination of its loveliness and hopefully hearing its message sung more sweetly than at any other time. But even 2000 and more years ago I think the essence of its cargo was still percolating through this land powerful enough, even in that still embryonic state, to drag heroes and wise men from around the globe to hunt the ultimate within its baggage of marvels.

Does its cross/mast conceal a sword too?

With the shadow of Arthur once more flitting across our tracks, I think it's time to see if we can find Excalibur somewhere in these sparkling holds. Under the chapter of the Aquarian phoenix I sensed its fearsome cutting edge, perhaps being honed beneath one of those flaming lakes. It would not surprise me, though, if such a mighty blade were depicted in this cargo of lost truth, for although Excalibur shed blood, it was quintessentially a sword of the truth - the impetus behind Arthur's own striving for the establishment of a golden age.

So where shall we look first to catch a glimpse of this famous sword? Well, I suspect, as I did in Aries, its gigantic presence might be yet another poetic overlay upon that cross/mast - its edge already provocatively laid across the neck of Sagittarius. However, if this is true, we put our foot in a hornet's nest of implications when we are confronted by the

image of the Christ hammered upon its hilt! But think again. Because it is a blade of truth I warrant that its cutting edge must be the teachings of Christ himself. And doesn't the truth sometimes hurt?

Jesus predicted it so?

*"Think not that I am come to send peace
on earth: I came not to send peace,
but a sword.
For I am come to set a man at variance
against his father, and the daughter against
her mother, and the daughter-in-law against
her mother-in-law."*
MATTHEW Chapter 10, Verses 34 & 35

Is this why the earth has wrought him upon its own 300-mile long sword?

*Note: I recall that boyish looking statue of St George by the sculptor Alfred Gilbert, which is in the Prince Albert Memorial Chapel, Windsor. In the pose we are shown the patron saint of England having just vanquished the dragon and leaning against his sword with one hand raised in a Christ-like blessing. But pay special attention to the hilt of that sword, note upon it the Christ crucified!

The sword in the stone!

For those who can accept the possibility of Excalibur's truth-seeking blade being cast in Albion's bedrock, another new vista must instantly open out of this lush masterpiece. We can look upon this island of Albion as a richly ornamented scabbard for that sword, an island embossed with a picture of heaven on earth, the very state that Excalibur will always fight to bring about. And yet another scintillating prospect opens up - namely, are we now also witnessing the truth behind the legendary *Sword in the Stone*? If so, Arthur, when not much more than a child, and with

The figure of St. George on the Clarence Monument.
(Note hilt)

Taliesin's/Merlin's coaching, must have known what we know now and spiritually drew its secret out of the granite with a flourish and an innocent smile, so becoming the rightful wielder of its truth. Mighty warriors, for all their strength, couldn't draw it out of the rock; their ignorance just wouldn't allow it!

Has this always been the truth laughing behind the myth? If you believe so, spiritually pull this sword from out of Britain's stone as Arthur did, as countless nameless others surely have, though not by brute force but by the gentle hand of the innocent child within. You too can share in the joy, for you will now be a wielder of its truth - a champion of the land - a builder of heaven on earth! And as you do, watch another fairy tale take on solid matter to be looked at anew. For many, however, the absurd prospect will be agony to behold.

The most flabbergasting of early warning systems

So, Excalibur might be here for your taking, that's if you have courage enough to reach out and grasp a few more of its awesome implications. The Earth Mother, nature, the planet, whatever you wish to call her is, according to the evidence on the ground, about to set her house in order again. That will, I believe, require more rain, rising rivers, land slips, erosions, rising oceans, great movements of air across the face of the planet, flooding, forest fires, and seismic disturbance. Now, look at the cover and shiver as I did when collating the signs for such an ominous weather forecast.

We've already seen how the only two water-born creatures in this zodiac, Pisces and Capricorn, have been pointedly left outside the ark and placed in the waves alongside the bow. I wonder if in this uncannily accurate placement there is a warning that, in the event of massive flooding, these two creatures may, for a time, be partially submerged. If so, this picture would be animated to another astounding level of realism, albeit catastrophically so. Check out too what might be the additional warning cut into that figurehead: does that sword across its Sagittarian neck forecast that in that same flooding this head shall be physically cut off? Will water signify blood as it does in the already severed head of Virgo? Certainly the land at both the back of his neck and the place where the blade re-emerges at the throat is well known to be low-lying and flood prone. And as you shiver at this thought, remind yourself how, under Sagittarius, we discovered several mythological clues which also pointed to such a watery decapitation, not least the fact that the figurehead of Argo Navis was traditionally seen as being, at times, sliced off and separated from the main vessel.

So are you getting the alarming picture? If such a flood ever happened the consequences would be dreadful, but would we also have to admit that it was the most awesomely vivifying and final masterstroke to this whole prophetic picture? Those sea creatures at the side of the ark would take to the water and the ark would once more be seen to be riding out the flood, its figurehead beset by waves and seemingly lopped off, the myth animated beyond belief! Mythology, then, would be acting not only as a guide back to a better understanding of life but also as a vehicle of early warning.

The good news, however, and again according to the pictorial evidence on the ground, is that all these upheavals will pass: these are but the sword-thrusts which will mark the birth pangs of the new age, the age of Aquarius, age of the phoenix rising from out of fire and water. And as Noah knows, arks never sink!

Doom merchant?

OK, you've heard it all before. Countless prophets of doom who, several times a year it seems, somewhere on the globe, gather a devoted cult and ascend a mountain so as to ride out that day's predicted cataclysm at noon; and from what I've just put forward some of you will want to label me the same. Though before you do I would remind you that prophets usually base their warnings around *intimate* visions. I, therefore, am no prophet as my warnings are based on what this land is blatantly showing to *us all*. This rock-solid stuff of Albion being so colossally 'full-frontal' that it may be perceived by everyone the world over; so tangible that it can be stomped on, driven over, danced around on, picked up by the handful and made mud pies of, indeed so massively is it written that you may read it through a telescope while standing in the craters of the moon! This is no misty mountain-top visitation for my eyes only, for all men may now see and prophesy for themselves. There's no cult to join, and certainly no guide to follow up a mountain - because I'm staying where I am!

King Solomon's miraculous ship

Anyway, let's overlay another mystic ship over Albion's ark and see if it too is a nice fit. Let then the sword melt back into the cross and the cross into the mast of another mystic vessel, although one which also bore a mighty sword. Hear the wisdom of King Solomon, whose own 'miraculous ship' suddenly arrives out of nowhere and into the last few chapters of Walter Map's *Queste del Saint Graal*.

We are told in a fascinating passage how King Solomon hears the voice of the Holy Ghost which tells him that, in the far distant future, a glorious Virgin would be born to his lineage, "*...through whom man shall know great joy.*" The king then asks the voice if this lady would mark the end of his line, to which it replies: "*No, a man, himself a Virgin, shall be the last.*"

Note: the Queste casts that virgin male as Sir Galahad, the tale's Christ-like knight who achieves the Holy Grail.

On hearing this, Solomon had but one wish: he wished with all his heart that he could, in some way, send a gift through time to the last of his family line to let him know how he, Solomon, had had gracious word of his future relative's coming. What a lovely thought. Anyway, it was Solomon's wife who then advised him that a miraculous ship should be built of rot-proof wood, and inside it a mystic bed be constructed with an *"overhead crosspiece"* (symbolising the cross?) made from wood taken from the Tree of Life. On this bed would be placed the gift, the mighty sword of Solomon's father, King David, along with Solomon's own crown and a letter of greeting and explanation.

On the night this phenomenal ship was finished, angels alighted upon it and inscribed much wisdom on the blade, along with a warning painted on the side of the vessel that only those who had both faith and belief would be allowed to board her. The crewless ship draped in white silk then magically slid down into the sea and sped away into time to seek the last of Solomon's line. And yes, you've guessed it - I'm asking if this vessel too has slipped out of the mythic mist and docked in our time in the shape of Albion's own miraculous ark?

I think my question is reasonable for this land ship also happens to have, in the shape of Aries, a fine lambs-wool bed over which hovers the ultimate 'crosspiece' in the shape of the cross or Tree of Life, and which, in the blinking of an eye, becomes a sword lying across it.

In my Penguin Classic's explanatory notes to the *Queste del Saint Graal*, there is an interesting reference to that mysterious bed installed on Solomon's ship. We are told in the tale how on finding that marvellous vessel and having enough 'faith and belief' to climb aboard, Galahad falls asleep upon its mystic bed and awakes to see the city of Sarras, the heavenly Jerusalem (see following note). Now if that knight was aboard Albion's own ship things really do click nicely into place: he would have indeed awoken with heightened perception, insight suddenly sharpened to the point where he realised that all Britain was a reflection of that Jerusalem, built as it is upon a starry floor plan! Those Penguin notes certainly back me up, suggesting also that upon awakening he realised: *'Solomon's bed is the symbol of the ecstatic vision.'*

Note: in the Illustrated Encyclopaedia of Arthurian Legends, Ronan Coglan says this of Sarras: "It may be in Britain, but was also thought to have lain near Jerusalem." Right on both counts I'd say!

Another Penguin note may also prove to be significant: *'…the bed symbolises the perfect repose of death, which is to say Christ's death on the cross; therefore the bed is the altar on which that sacrifice is re-enacted.'* I say 'significant' for as we journey through the last two chapters of this book *'Christ's death upon the cross'* and that *'perfect repose of death'* may become decoded as meaning *no death at all*, only a perfect rebirth brought about by an ecstatic vision of the truth of oneself and the creation we are a part of.

For me, Solomon's miraculous ship *has* returned for all would-be-Galahads the world over to spiritually climb aboard and experience that perception which will strip away the mundane to reveal the God who resides in everything. Life will never be the same again! And who can't raise a smile to see just how cunningly this miraculous ship was sent through time, for how better to conceal it than under everyone's nose in the shape of an island the size of Britain - Britain, the time-capsuled wisdom of Solomon!

Sister tubs!

Don't ask how or why, but ever since the day I saw Katherine Maltwood's ship among those other shapes at Glastonbury, I just knew that the same would one day reveal itself via the outer edge of Britain. In fact, I was so cock-sure that the shape of a ship would eventually enfold all the other giants, that I did not even attempt to hammer its planks together until the lost lamb had been found. I just knew it was waiting until I'd found all the giants and needed a box to put them in! Yet even with all this assurance, I never guessed that once I'd drawn in the framework it would echo its Glastonbury sister-ship quite so precisely.

And so with hammer and nails in hand, and with the sky rapidly darkening, let's build our ark to the guidelines laid down by our Mother, the earth.

Clue number one had impressed itself on me since finding the lamb: that piece of coastline on the side of its neck which, owing to its unusual straightness, had refused to play any part in the lamb's otherwise curly contour. Indeed, when compared to the generally well-pitted coastline of the rest of Britain it really was an altogether odd stretch. I would even go so far as to say that it looked positively 'man-made', so for shipbuilding purposes exactly what I needed! Wanting more than one plank, however, I then quickly scanned the rest of Albion's coastline to see if there were any other straight edges, and yes, two other short stretches caught my eye; one stretch along Taurus's back had a most distinct angle to it, while the straight top of the griffin's head suggested a vertical.

OK, just three straight edges of coastline seemed scant encouragement for the finding of an enormous ship, but after being guided so sure-footedly over all the other giants, I didn't feel I was going to be short-changed now. Indeed, from my experience in finding the lamb I knew that the more unhelpful the initial prospects, the more 'gob-smacking' the final revelation might be. Not for the first or last time I felt that I was simply here to hold the pencil with an open mind and a tingling sense of expectation; in other words standard Albion procedure!

With mounting anticipation, and only minor palpitations, I then smoothed out my giant of a map and prepared to lay everything on the line again. As I did my mind filled with those memories of that shudderingly wonderful night when I found the Christ upon the cross, and, on cue, adrenalin began to course through me. I knew that, as on that weird and wonderful evening, here was another 'make or break' moment - if a ship *was* going to appear, it would begin to take shape within a few minutes or else not at all, anything longer and I would know that it was the artist in me trying to cobble something together. Yet rather than the panic which gripped my pencil on that evening of Easter week, it was confidence that buzzed through me - I just knew a ship was hiding here. So, with the obligatory deep breath, and pencil and ruler in hand, I prepared for a revelation on the strength of one or two dare-devil lines.

Without really thinking, I struck a hard and fast line down that stretch of straight coast alongside the lamb's neck *(1)*, from Skipsea to Kilnsea, and continued it south all the way

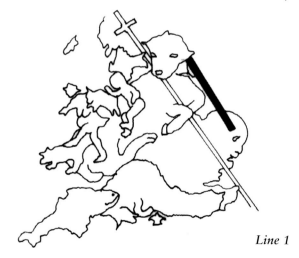

Line 1

down to Norwich on the head of Sagittarius. It was a furious start! I then noticed that the coast that goes from Skegness along the Wash to meet the river Welland was also something of a straight line, albeit a touch wriggly, but

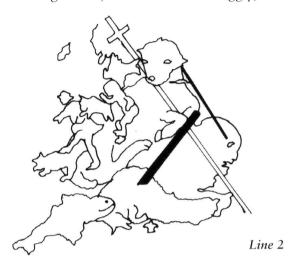

Line 2

what the heck, I blasted a line through its southwesterly pointing angle too *(2)*.

Just two cavalier strokes zapped upon the map of Britain, but I knew, even from that first line from Skipsea to Kilnsea, that I had been given a replica of that strangely backward leaning prow which is so evident a feature of Glastonbury's ark.

To bolster that all-important opening line I instinctively pencilled in another line in harmony with it, running at the same angle and

using Louth (around 10 miles inland) as its underpin *(3)*. True, there was no straight feature on the map to suggest this line, but that did not matter as it was purely an embellishment on my part to underline that Skipsea to Norwich angle, which on its own had already dictated the shape of the prow. And what a strange prow it was - but this was only the start, I knew that more impulsive strokes of the pencil would prove just as exciting. It was as though the QE2 was within moments of sailing right into my own studio and I was the little guy who'd got to get all the desks and pictures out of the way before they were smashed to smithereens! This ship had been away for too long and nothing, but nothing, was going to stop her docking right here and now. Elation waited with me on the quay. In short, I felt in wonderfully safe, if impatient, hands, especially so when I soon began to see that, in the case of this ark, some of its most vital rivets were going to be lit by lighthouses!

This 'lighthouse-guiding' insight was to come from my next line. Off I went to that straight, strong back of Taurus where I zipped a line along the river Dee from Chester to the Point of Ayr, continuing it right out into the Irish Sea *(4)*. This line seemed to seek out the very tip of the Isle of Man, even wanting to splice a path between the two lighthouses of

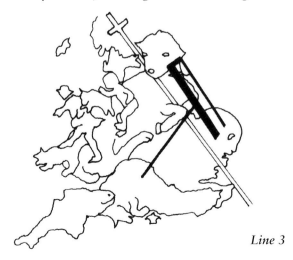

Line 3

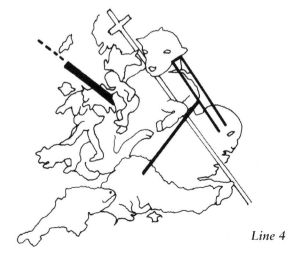

Line 4

Chicken Rock and the Calf of Man. But it was the angle of the line that really made me feel I was on a roll, so closely did it echo Glastonbury's own peculiar stern. Also, because I was sending straight lines along lengths of coastline (in effect, the outer edges of the giants themselves), I intuitively felt that, where no real straight coast was available, all I had to do was to either continue sending out lines that kissed the extremities of their outer silhouettes, or else link-up the last rocky outposts of Albion, and some of these lit by lighthouses, those guiding lamps to mariners.

Nice idea, but would it work? There was only one way to find out. I put my ruler on the twinkling tip of the brim of Virgo's hat, lit by the South Stack lighthouse, while to the south, the most western outpost of land I could see was Ramsey Island, just off the tip of Leo's crown, so I just connected these two *(5)*. I also continued it back northwards to touch that

Line 6

continued it to graze the Glamorgan coast and the lamb's tail *(7)*. The same line then hits the area around Weston-super-Mare, on the neck of Capricorn's wonder horse.

These carefree coast-kissing lines that were boxing in the 'cargo' and joining up a few prominent off-shore lighthouses, had given me

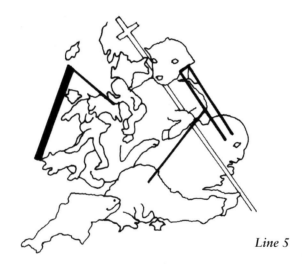

Line 5

earlier line I'd sent towards those Chicken Rock and Calf of Man lighthouses.

From Ramsey Island I sent out a line to another glittering rivet, the lighthouse on the rocks they call The Smalls *(6)*. Was there just a hint here of that slightly triangular tail-end that appears on the Glastonbury ship? From The Smalls I put another zodiac-clipping line east to touch against Stacks Rocks on Leo's chin and

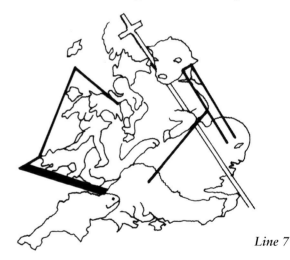

Line 7

a 'near-as-damn-it' copy of Glastonbury's ark. My ark was delightfully lit at crucial strategic points by lighthouses, glowing rivets that were surely becoming stars by any other name. Just as mountain peaks bearing imagined beacons had directed my straight lines in the making of the cross/mast, so these guiding lights were about to do the same in helping me build an ark! And how this procedure was already mirroring Glastonbury's version; even in just seven lines the two tubs were so much alike that I could happily have left my blueprint unfinished because it had, to my eye, already underlined the type of vessel the land wished to convey - proof too that whatever mind had fashioned Glastonbury's ark had been at work here too! Just look at those distinct angles both to the prow and stern, surely these are too damn similar to be coincidental, especially as we have in front us not everyone's idea of what an ark should look like.

And with little effort we can add another Glastonbury feature. Put a vertical line along the straight coast on the griffin's head from Lytham St Annes to Fleetwood and continue it

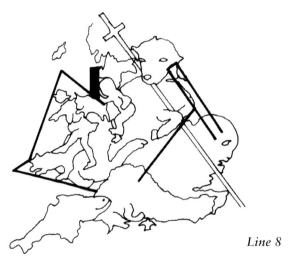

Line 8

back south until it touches the stern line at Queenferry on the river Dee *(8)*; see how it grazes the forehead of the infant Christ Child as though he's leaning against it. Now just cap this by running another line along the coast that slants from Fleetwood to Cockerham along the griffin's angled beak, which is also quite straight *(9)*. Just compare these few strokes of the pencil to Somerset's identical positioning of what looks like a rear mast, or a steering post perhaps. Whatever its use, it is unique to them both, so once more, same ship, same shipbuilder, however weird the lines.

Really a child with a ruler could now guess

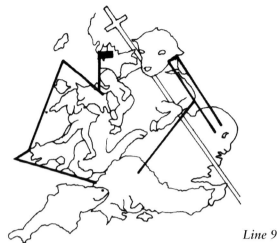

Line 9

the remaining lines of this vessel. I feel, though, that as with all the other giants, except the cross and Christ, and maybe the lamb too, the shape suggested by the coastline alone checks off so well against Glastonbury's template that one does not need to add another stroke to 'get the picture'. That said, and purely to please the draughtsman in me, I have dropped in the remaining lines at my own discretion, and thus without any prompts from the evidence on the ground; except that is for one beauty of a clue on the back of Sagittarius' head.

First of all, look at that little stern stump which I logically finished off by going inland from Cockerham to Junction 55 on the M6 and then running a line southwards *(10)*, in sympathy with what the coast had already

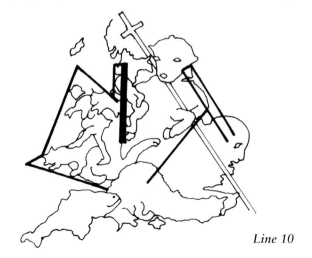

Line 10

dictated *(8)*. If continued, such a line takes us on route to Shrewsbury. If we wanted to complete this stern mast by taking the line already drawn along the griffin's head southwards, you'll see how Offa's Dyke also attempts to confirm the same line of thought.

We now go over to the other side of the country. Opposite to the line we've put along the inside of the Wash *(2)*, and a few miles further on into the back of the head of Sagittarius, you will come across those peculiar 17th-century man-made, drainage waterways designed to help prevent the Fens from flooding. You'll find these as diagonal slashes heading inland from around the Kings Lynn area, and known as Middle Level, Main Drain and Old and New Bedford Rivers, all of them just begging to be drawn through and continued south westwards. But more importantly their angles, seem to approve the angle earlier created by line *(2)*, thus giving us a nod and a wink that we've been on the right track! Though you have to smile at the possible evidence that man, who, in shaping the environment for his own needs, was also aiding and abetting the will of the land in not only helping the ark's figurehead to stay dry, but actually reaffirming that distinctly Glastonbury-styled prow.

Note: it's interesting to note that the lines drawn in the construction of Glastonbury's ark are also helped by drainage ditches, owing to the flood-prone flatlands which gave it its birth.

Incidentally, the waterway which I put my line through on Albion's prow was the Old Bedford *(11)*.

Then from Norwich, sitting prominently on the prow, I drew a line roughly at the same angle as before and found that London seemed to be attracting it *(12)*. At London, and for no other reason than to copy the Glastonbury design, I sent a line *(13)* southeast and running roughly with the M20 to where it would touch

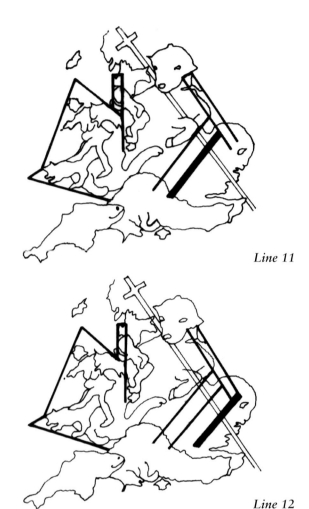

Line 11

Line 12

the keel line. This keel line seemed irresistibly drawn from Glastonbury via Stonehenge towards the Canterbury area *(14)*. To complete this feature, take the same line back west to Bridgewater, then directly north to Weston-super-Mare *(15)*. Interestingly, if you continue the line *(15)* northwards you will see that it's almost on line once more with Offa's Dyke and that funny little stern mast.

Lastly, I had a pure guess at a deck line. One option would be a line running horizontally from the corner of the Wash at Fosdyke to Uttoxeter on the Gemini babe's bottom, thus giving him a seat! The one shown on my line drawing, however, I ran horizontally through Kidderminster beneath the child's foot *(16)*. But I stress again that these 'guessed' lines are

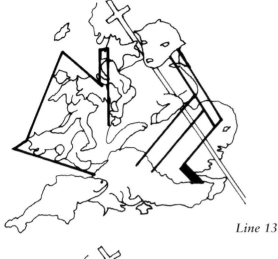

Line 13

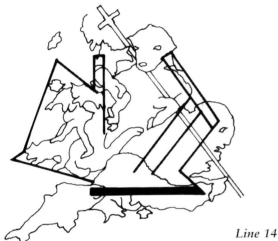

Line 14

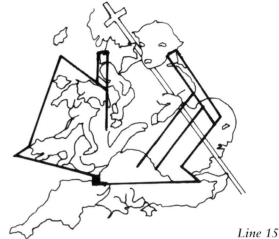

Line 15

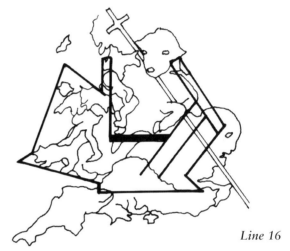

Line 16

totally immaterial, because long before these last strokes were made I think it obvious what was taking shape.

Looking now at the ark as a whole, notice again how its prime passengers are the babe and the lamb; just look at how snugly they sit within the cup of the vessel, the baby lying fast asleep upon the lamb's golden fleece while leaning so graphically against that rear mast, and at the same time delightfully using that strong back of Taurus as elbow support. While on the other side of the country we see the lamb also leaning, both for its own comfort and our smiles, on that otherwise awkward angle of the prow - both babe and lamb rocked in this vast floating cradle or manger and seemingly so befitting of Cancer's motherly and protective nature. Likewise, who can't be amazed at just how comfortably and lovingly the entire precious cargo has been stowed within her lines - initially to attract and delight the eye but then, and more importantly, to prompt urgent enquiry as to why.

Note: regarding the figurehead, neither Maltwood nor Caine mentions such a feature on Glastonbury's ark, but on Caine's illustration she has added a section to the prow that is not so straight cut as the rest of the vessel (see my copy at beginning of chapter). Looking at this, I can't help noting just how suggestive that shape (dotted on my copy) is to Albion's figurehead; indeed, she's indicated what seems to be an eye too!

Alike, but then again, mightily different

When drawn on the same scale as each other, the similarities of the giants from the Glastonbury, Preseli and Albion zodiacs beggar belief, and none more so than these sister ships; Don't you just love those sterns, nigh on exact replicas of each other and all the more amazing because the design of the stern is so very unusual; and as for the prows... well! What a pity that Preseli doesn't present a third ship for comparison.

However, it must never be forgotten that without Katherine Maltwood's discovery, Albion would still be lost, for without the guidance of its template I would have let that 11-year-old's glimpse of land giants remain a five-minute fantasy. That said, I must again remind you that there are nevertheless three vital differences between these two earth zodiacs. The first is that whilst the Glastonbury version is in correct sequence (a miracle in itself), it consequentially can sing of nothing more than the obvious: that the earth, of her own accord, can perform wonders way beyond our wildest dreams! Whereas Albion's out-of-sequence order seems to me to invite deeper thought. In Albion's new arrangement of star signs I gauge an invitation, no, a demand, that we regard them like characters from a sort of zodiacal alphabet, and therefore the next logical step would obviously be to try and *read* that new arrangement of constellations as a concise message, as we've been endeavouring to do - because frankly I don't believe they've been jumbled up purely to better shoehorn into the holds of the ark. In astrological terms, the actual positioning of the constellations, in conjunction with each other, has always been of the utmost importance in reaching a final reading of just what the heavens are trying to predict in any one formation.

The second difference is that the Glastonbury ark's *only* cargo is Gemini's child,

the rest of its signs keeping to their places in the normal zodiacal merry-go-round; whereas this Greater ark ingeniously holds within her, the entire family of star giants who in turn surrender their individual shapes to magically give rise to the all-embracing outer shape of the ark itself, while, at the same time, becoming its actual cargo. Only those signs which naturally feel more at home in either water or air have been freed from her holds - an arrangement which, for me, is an absolute masterstroke which graphically, symbolically, poetically and even logically shouts out that God and not 'wild coincidence' is its maker.

The third, and perhaps most important of all the differences, is the fact that there is no crucified Christ in Somerset and thus at the end of a journey around it no chance of witnessing that God-Man become animated as the Lord of the Dance, for that will be the magical finale at the end of our journey around Albion. In this difference alone, I believe that Glastonbury is lacking the last and most vital key of all, for the message that is primed to explode off Albion's cross will not so much unlock, but blow down, the door to a new age of perception, in a crescendo of visual celebration. For me, Glastonbury has always been the match and Albion the awaiting skyrocket!

But is Albion's ship built upon forbidden lines?

Having found our ark I'm now going to strip away its planks and see what makes up her skeletal structure, for there may be something more which the earth intends us to mull over at this unique time of seeing everything afresh.

Let's begin by taking another look at the mast. How do you see such a pole - 'rising from' or 'penetrating into' the main body or belly of the vessel? If seen as 'penetrating' the following should prove intriguing.

Cancer is, in astrological terms, adjudged to be ruled by the feminine moon, and the moon as a crescent lying on its back (akin to a bowl or boat) was once seen as being representative of the reclining body of the goddess herself, indeed remember how Cancer is also linked with her. Blake presumably knew this symbolism; in his own sublimely illustrated *Jerusalem*, Noah's ark appears as a crescent moon lying on its back on top of mountainous seas. The text to this same page is intertwined with naked females reclining in seductive poses, thus the mystic inference of the upturned crescent being symbolic of the body of the Mother is, I think, underlined.

Anyway, with such imagery in mind let's get down to brass tacks. Watch Albion's mast slip back into that 'phallic' Djed pillar of Osiris (see Aries); see it *penetrating* the deck of the cupped Cancerian ark, that upturned *crescent moon body of the goddess*, and as you do ask yourself if this configuration is not sensual poetry in itself - could it even be a coded rendering of the Sacred Marriage? Look at that strange backward leaning prow of Albion's ark, albeit cut in straight lines - does it not strive to curve a crescent? So, do we gain the impression that its feminine body is already inseminated, as all arks symbolically are, with the seed of all life?

In this glyph of two fertility symbols joined to make one there might be the pre-eminent law upon which this entire ark full of miracles is built, and that law must be *Love*. And just see what miracles have issued out of Britain's conjoined bedrock as a direct result. Moreover, if that's what happens when bedrock is so invigorated, imagine what would happen if this same marriage could be consummated within the fibre of a 'knowing' man! This will

My copy of Blake's Moon-ark

be the ecstatic proposition we shall face in the last few miles of this journey over stars.

But shall I now shatter this apparent symbol of divine intercourse by naming those two beautifully wedlocked symbols for what they really are today? So try grappling with the ramifications of those clashing religious symbols, the **Cross** and the **Crescent!**

Thousands of people over the centuries have perished wherever East has collided with West under those two banners. For some supporters of either device, the distrust of the other is so ingrained that it almost seems that the psychological wounds dealt out in the crusades have been genetically passed on, so who the hell is kidding whom in seeing the cross and crescent as a picture of wedded bliss!

Thankfully the land does see differently. Out of its union of those symbols which men would rather keep divided, has sparked a myriad of other working marriages which have not only caused 14 miracles to blossom out of supposedly dead stone, but also a symmetry that could be inherent of a poetic guidance wherein men and women may find a mirror in which they can perceive themselves to be God - that God which must now be proved to be aware within every atom of the creation. Thus talk with yourself within the dragonfly! Sing along with that part of you which is singing in the blackbird! And see in your neighbour's face your own.

Surely it is then an impassioned realization of Universal Oneness which constitutes the lifeline being dangled from Albion's lifeboat - but how many will even *want* to grasp such? What fundamentalist of either Christianity or Islam will be a picture of delight to see an ark, or anything else for that matter, built from their symbols linked as one? By the same token, what ordinary Joe will condescend to trying to appreciate that the ordinary beach pebble may have an awareness capable of knowing it has been momentarily chosen for casual inspection before being cast into the sea? And who'll give a toss to hear about what's on the cover of this book?

And Scorpio underlines the fact!

Scorpio's distancing of himself from the ark can only be in reflection of mankind's own distancing of himself from the harmonic workings of the creation, a distance now so great that it must constitute a real threat to the very continuance of life. Hence this message in an ark must have lain in wait, patiently preparing itself over aeons for a completion, and unveiling, timed to coincide with that generation who would be closest of all to pushing everything over the brink of no return. Ours!

Shown up then, in Scorpio's wayward station, could be generations worth of ignorance to the fact that everything affects everything, that all is interconnected and interactive to the point where, when a child steps on a mine in Africa, the vigour in the earth at that place recoils, and as a consequence a current of depression may leach into a household in Newcastle or New York; to have a fit of road-rage may be to become for weeks after, a magnet for the angry outbursts of others - and don't we already know now that when we fell a living, breathing, forest we in effect puncture our own lungs? Likewise, for the gardener to refrain from stomping on the caterpillar of a cabbage white butterfly, might be to change the heart of the hunter who had his sights trained on one of the last 70 Javan rhinos in existence; to show genuine compassion to the guy in the gutter may make a day in two weeks time the happiest you've

had for a long time, and yet for no apparent reason. And yes, I'm struggling to nail down something so nebulous and subtle that I'm in danger of bashing my thumb to pulp, but suffice to say, 'Like attracts like', and 'What goes round comes around', might in essence be a couple of truisms of more value than we ever realised.

In this ark's provocative fusing of the traditionally distanced cross and crescent in a loving embrace (and by inference all other man instigated segregations, including his own, not only from the rest of nature, but sometimes even from his fellow men) in order to build a safe house for the seed of life at a time of great upheaval, the message seems clear: Return to the ark, and rediscover that it is through the loving union of opposites that heaven materialises on earth. Perhaps the essence of the wisdom as contained in the Holy Grail itself amounts to no more than this.

Twaddle?

As for the zodiacal characters profiled in the coastlines of England, Wales and Northern Ireland - every atlas in the world backs the fact up! However, as regards all the stuff I've put to you in an attempt to translate what these giants in a landscape might imply, well, it must all remain pure speculation, no matter how the name place evidence on the ground has, in some cases, seemingly vindicated my admittedly wild theories.

I therefore concede that in a discovery like this it is easy to take flights of interpretive fantasy, and in my stripping away of the ark's outer planks, perhaps I have totally misread a cross and crescent configuration, and hence, all that stuff relating to the intercourse of opposites as being tantamount to all that the Grail itself contains, is indeed twaddle! And that's how the last few paragraphs began to weigh on me until, that is, I heard a guy called Wolfram shout across time: "Hang on a *moment - I may just have something to tease your speculation further as regards that cross joined to crescent theory".*

Wolfram's tease

Now this sounds as crazy as finding out that Albion's New Jerusalem is founded upon those warring symbols of cross and crescent, nevertheless it's a fact that even in the thick of the crusades a few followers of both banners really did put down their arms and embraced each other's beliefs. What is more, the two groups in question were the most fearsome fighters that each side possessed: the Shi'ite-formed Assassins and the Knights Templar. I hazard a guess that, like the results of their two symbols marrying in the foundations of Albion, the results of their exchanges of knowledge may have been wonderful, too. Certainly, upon their return to the West, some of these Templar warrior-monks were known to have become changed men, as the East had given them something that their own church had perhaps blacked out. Indeed, they may have acquired a whole new perception of their faith via this mix of East and West, and been given an insight, albeit heretical, which perhaps gave rise to that title of Guardians of the Grail that was to grow up around their enigmatic doings. As I've said before, there may be proof in the very placement of their 'Temple by the Sower' (see *Aries, Part One*) that they knew far more than anyone has yet imagined.

So, the consequences of the crusades were not all bad, just ask Wolfram von Eschenbach, author of *Parzival*, that most mystical of all Grail romances. It is known that he spent time in the Holy Land, and more than likely in the company of the Templars, gathering material that would form the backbone of his classic. I feel, though, that it was not so much the Templars' fighting prowess that he wanted to observe, but rather something gleaned from them that gave him the courage and conviction to write what could only have been at that time a most 'dodgy' first chapter. The tale itself, though brimming with rollicking adventure, carries between its lines a definite scent of the mysteries that transformed its pages into a veritable guide-book for all who sought the secret of the Grail.

At the height of the crusades, and amid all that anti-infidel zeal, Wolfram must have risked an outcry when beginning the story of the holiest of Christian quests with a chapter that tells of the marrying of a white western knight to a black eastern queen - lucky for us, he got away with it!

Briefly, he has the path to the Grail starting with a young knight, Gahmuret of Anjou, begging leave of his father the king to go to the East to seek adventure. Once there, he lends his brave heart and fighting skills to a besieged town held by a hard-pressed force of Moors, with, as Wolfram describes *"faces black as hell"*, although their oppressors were, like Gahmuret, the flower of Europe's finest 'white' knights! Upon entering the heathen town and seeing the dusky queen who ruled there, Gahmuret's thoughts are recorded: *"...although an infidel, a more affectionate spirit of womanliness had ever stolen over a woman's heart. Her modest ways were a pure baptism, as was the rain that fell on her - the flood descending from her eyes down to her sabled breast. Her pleasures in life were devotion to sorrow and grief's true doctrine."*

Cutting through the flowery waffle, Gahmuret had fallen head-over-heels in love with a woman who was, in my opinion, and I think as was Wolfram's intention, the Earth Mother made flesh - a living Black Madonna, no less. On the strength of his ardour, Gahmuret relieves the siege single-handed by jousting and defeating the knights of the besieging forces one by one, until no more stepped up to chance their arm. After this feat, carried out in full view of the Moorish township and its beautiful queen, he returns to her and they lie as husband and wife.

The whole underlying tone of initially warring black and white opposites coming together for some Grail-good in Wolfram's first chapter seals the virtual Yin and Yang 'way' for the remainder of the quest. This is even more pronounced when we read later that a son was born of this union of white knight and black queen and of whom it was said: "...pleased God to make a marvel of him for he was both black and white. The Queen fell to kissing his white spots time and time again". The name she gave to this obviously sacredly-balanced son was Feirefiz, which means 'pied', his skin Wolfram likened to a magpie. This bird is itself full of holy duality, and, contrary to modern belief, full of good omen, if perceived correctly. We must see its raven and dove amalgam as the positive/negative, Yin/Yang, Mother/Father polarities in flighted celebration - an animation of the Sacred Marriage.

*Note: with the magpie fluttering across our minds, I should also mention how the ancient Chinese saw a similar symbolic reunion of separated lovers, or shall we say the marriage of black/Yin to white/Yang. It seems that they allocated a day each year to celebrate the meeting of the Weaving Girl and the Herd Boy. These two mythological lovers were represented in the heavens by the stars Vega and Altair. However, the two were separated by the fast-flowing Milky Way and could only meet to embrace on one harmonious day of the year. This opportunity would arise by way of a magical bridge formed by living magpies, and the two would meet and embrace at its centre. On earth the Chinese would celebrate their coming together with a special meal, when poetry would be recited and the story of the separated lovers (holy opposites) retold.

But let's get back to Wolfram's tale. Gahmuret alas, wishing for more adventure, in time steals away from his queen and back to the greener pastures of the West, where eventually he is to sire the hero of the tale, Parzival or Perceval. Parzival becoming the achiever of that greatest of all prizes, although this honour he shares with his half brother, the Eastern Feirefiz, who would also grow to become a knight of wonder.

No finer 'Way to the Grail' has made its way down through the ages to us than Parzival - its prescribed course towards that ultimate cup also academically agreed as being sign-posted by astrological inference. In a sense it really is a 'Hitch Hiker's Guide to the Grail', and it gives me a smile to speculate that Albion could well be its map!

Gahmuret was, then, seemingly divinely inspired in his mission of uniting opposites and thereby creating from that loving mix someone who would be equipped to achieve the Grail. Interestingly too, and based only upon my earlier ripping away of the Ark's planking, Gahmuret was branded in the tale as such a 'rejoiner' for the benefit of all who could see beyond the commonplace. I say this as I'm tempted to believe that such 'branding' was Wolfram's intention in the heraldic device he had the knight wear, a device which to the unsuspecting readers of the past 700+ years would have sparked little or no reaction, for even Wolfram refers to this particular branding in apologetic terms: "...he had to bear this burdensome device, these Anchor signs, from land to land."

So, an anchor emblazoned his shield and vestments and also, I wouldn't mind betting, crowned his helm. But whether a 'burdensome device' or cunning signal will depend upon whether you are assessing all of this against Albion's map. So if you haven't seen the significance in Gahmuret's heraldic device yet, shut your eyes and visualise the structure of an anchor and why Wolfram might have chosen to set one upon the head of this 'all-unifying' knight at the very beginning of the trail towards the Grail. A switched-on inner child will, in an instant, decipher it as the masculine Christian cross/mast of Albion being once more joined to the upturned Islamic crescent/Mother moon-ark - surely the perfect configuration of any *anchor*! And what an apt shape to build an ark around too!

Or do I again read too much by suggesting that Gahmuret's livery bore a token, not only of the floor plan of both this ark and its cargo of a New Jerusalem, but also coded suggestion of the holy intercourse of Sky Father/Earth Mother that was behind it all: the sacred and sexual embrace of our parents brilliantly celebrated in a device which, to early Christians, was an emblem of hope and resurrection - the very stuff of the Grail!

Can you blame me then for putting an ear to Albion's astrological floor plan, and to what Wolfram might be saying, and hearing that the anchor might be shorthand for the hope of resurrection hinging upon the marrying of earth to heaven, man to woman; black to white; Yin to Yang; right to left; negative to positive; Christian to Muslim; Hindu to Buddhist and so on? If there is a code here, it must be saying that only in the observation and adherence to these basic laws of love and life can life on earth have any chance of surviving the chaos which, for generations, we have been brewing up via our manifold acts of ripping apart those same sacred marriages. Surely the miracle that is now singing out of Britain is the flower of such harmonic order, and mankind, in observing this, maybe being invited to join in with this same creative force so as to co-create a heaven over all the earth.

If so, did Wolfram learn of such twinning chemistry while sitting around clandestine campfires beside Templars and knights of Islam? I have absolutely no proof that this happened, nor even whether he, in his signing of Gahmuret with an anchor, was really saying that the cross and crescent were to be one day mystically united so as to unleash the Grail wisdom for all men to partake of.

Nevertheless, to hear that to the followers of the crescent, the divine female was seen as being represented by the crescent moon, certainly seems to give a nod and a wink towards my line of thought. This too from Malcolm Godwin's own research in his book *The Holy Grail* and regarding Mohammed's own daughter: *"She had once been known as the Mother of the Father, the Tree of Paradise, and the Red Moon Cow, which suckles the Earth. The name Fatima even signifies the Creatrix and her symbol, as the crescent moon, appears on Islamic flags."*

This also interested me: *"Both the Shi'ites and the mystical Sufis maintained that the feminine powers of sexuality held the world together. One of the finest Sufi poets, Farid, declared that true divinity was female and that Mecca was "the womb of the earth." The Shi'ites still await the Virgin Pairidaeza who will give birth to the Mahdi, the moon-(Ark)-guided Messiah and Saviour, known as the Desired Knight. The Shi'ites had formed the Assassins, the Islamic counterparts of the Templars, and had kept remarkably intimate links with their supposedly Christian rivals."* (My brackets)

Perhaps, of course, that Templar/Assassin intercourse was born out of nothing more than a mutual respect gained on the battlefield and went not much further than a brotherly 'high five' and a few drinks after hours, but Godwin is not on his own in suspecting that something more came out of their meetings: *"It is small wonder that 'heresies' began to spread throughout the Christian ranks, there to find their greatest expression within the mysterious accounts of the Grail."* None more so than Wolfram's, I'd say.

My earlier light-hearted suggestion of Albion being the map to Wolfram's Grail may also be not so silly after all: hear Godwin air what many have read in between the lines of *Parzival*: *"Astrology is Wolfram's major pre-occupation and he intersperses his adventures* with precise references to the zodiac, leading his reader from constellation to constellation as the plot progresses. As he takes us through each of the signs we discover just how well-crafted the architecture of his work really is. Each episode corresponds to the forces found within a particular sign. What we experience is the passage of a sun hero across the zodiac and the forces which come into play as he moves from one sign, or from one planetary configuration, to another."

Tell me then, is not Albion the most perfect stage for any would be sun/son hero to seek the ultimate? I reiterate that there may have been many who have, in full knowledge of their whereabouts, passed from one topographical constellation to another in an effort to harness these 12 wisdoms within the temple of their own being, and whether they were Christian, Muslim, Egyptian sun worshipper or a follower of the Goddess, I feel that, at the end of their journey, all preconceived notions and allegiances would have been melted down in this vast Grail cauldron of an ark. They would then return to their homelands knowing that the true God had no other name but *Love*, and love was everywhere and in everything.

Stein had no doubts - now neither have I!

Walter Johannes Stein, when writing his 1936 paper *King Arthur and the Problem of East and West*, would not have raised an eyebrow of disbelief at what seems Albion's organic promotion of a Christian/Islamic wedding. Even without the map of Albion before him, he sensed the eventual and unstoppable coming together of East and West as a holy law; but more bizarrely, he saw Britain as that reunion's likely catalyst! Here, after speaking of Gahmuret's marriage to that dark queen, he writes: "*With this, something of the deepest significance enters the Grail story. It shows us that the western man is brother of the eastern man, and that the eastern man can*

achieve his goal in no other way than with the help of the western. If this is a legend, it is at the same time a prophesy. For Britain stands today before the task of fulfilling the prophesy."

Uncannily far-sighted words (and for me pure goose-bump material!) which on Albion's Cancerian cross and crescent fields have found seemingly fertile ground on which to give hope of a full blossoming; if only Stein could have been here to witness it. And if only, when sifting through Guttman and Johnson's summing up of Cancer, my eyes had dropped on the following, my doubts in writing of what seemed an impossible interlocking of antagonistic symbols would never have materialised:

"*The Sun is at its moment of greatest power, while the sign itself is ruled by the Moon. Thus the symbols of Sun and Moon, masculine and feminine, re-united in one archetype. We may think of Cancer as the sign of the "mystic marriage," the union of alchemical opposites.*"

Bingo!

Ready to weigh anchor

Approaching the end of our journey, at least through the pages of this book, we then find ourselves spiritually gathered upon the creaking deck of this miraculous ark. The strengthening wind is ruffling our hair and the sea levels around the world are rising; even yesterday I read that according to NASA the ice sheet which blankets Greenland is, through global warming, melting at a rate of 50 billion tons of water a year. And yet, standing here shivering at this news, it amazes me to recall that when I first jumped aboard to begin my writing of this book I knew perhaps less than half of what this ark now contains (and nothing at all about melting ice caps), though I had faith enough in its wonders to embark upon this journey. Needless to say I do not regret the day I kissed the mundane goodbye and set sail for a new world of high enchantment, albeit without even leaving my room!

That said, some might suggest from my findings that any enchantment I have found is all part of a grand self-delusion, a whopper of a fairy story which, under the scrutiny of the real world, will turn into its customary vapours. However, the primary state of every atom of this creation is now 'enchanting' for me, and any vapours hanging around are more likely to be the smog which we have thrown up between us and the dazzling stuff which flickers in even the most unremarkable of everyday objects. It seems we prefer to dowse that magic in a dulling dust of familiarity and of eventual contempt - contempt that now allows us to grow human eggs in the flesh of mice, and feed pigs to pigs, with a clear conscious.

But whether delusion or dazzling discovery, it's certainly been a fabulous adventure for me, although it has not been all roses. Indeed, I would be a liar if I did not say that amongst the ecstatic fun and eyes full of astonished tears, there have been many moments when I have wished the whole thing would indeed vaporise and release me back into a normal life. Living with a burgeoning miracle on my wall has not been easy; it has, for the past seven years, been with me for the greater part of my every waking moment. For sure, it has been the most exhilarating seven years of my life; it has made me love my life, love all life, more than I ever knew was possible, filling every mundane nook and cranny of it with a wonder that not even the 11-year-old version of me could have imagined. And yet at times the vast truth of what I think I have stumbled over has been fit to break my back; it may still do for, 'enchantment' aside, the ramifications of it all are as terrible as they are sublime. Certainly the 'chicken' in me quakes in its boots at what he's let himself in for. But then I just stand back and

look at that picture on my wall, now on the cover of the book you hold, and remind myself of the absolute innocence of its almost perfectly programmed petal-by-petal unfurling, and then calmness descends in sumptuous folds like fat Motherly arms about that scared chicken. The burden, like Gahmuret's anchors, becomes a gift that even after these seven years still forces a genuine 'Wow!' out of me, and a refreshing of even the dullest of days.

You the reader, perhaps in the course of this book, have also I hope been through the mill of emotions, and many times have closed this book with its 'unbelievable' cover, wondering why you ever picked it up in the first place. I have asked you to chase my own intuitive shadows down either overgrown Celt-trodden tunnels of greenery, or through dusty Egyptian underworld passages, heavy with the disorientating images of things our ancestors deemed holy, but which we technological wizards have been told to look upon as interesting, but naïve. Perhaps, too, I have sometimes even lost the pair of us in hopeless thickets of madcap theory where even the most liberal mind cannot proceed further. If I have, I do not however apologise for, confronted by what our earth has done, no stone should be left unturned in looking for her reason.

I believe that every track we have cavorted or dragged our feet along has been in pursuit of a message that we *must* unravel and take to heart before the clock strikes midnight. We have every right to abandon today's mode of thinking which has, let's face it, taken us to what could be a terrible brink, and instead to seek out the ill-used tracks of the heart and psyche, prompted by this wondrous ark full of things too long out of sight and thus out of mind. An ark which has, seemingly, been born out of so many of our ancestors' own heart's desires and which, like Solomon's gift-bearing miraculous ship, has arrived out of this morning's mist; a gift from your ancestors who *knew*; a mother-ship bearing a message of love and life that, if heard, might ensure that we in turn will live long enough to pass on the same gift into the future.

With hindsight then, I hope you will come to see that all we have been through, madcap theories and all, were the obligatory trials and tribulations, that all who seek the thing that is truly worth the finding, have to pass through.

But now a confession

And so leaning against this prow I had every intention of wishing you all 'God speed' and leaving you to make of this whole thing what you will - yet, in so doing, knowing damn well that I was **selling you short!** I say this because at this point on our journey of exploration you would not have seen *all* of Jerusalem and for this intended 'con' your guide now drops his head and sincerely apologises.

Guilt forces me to prolong either your pain or pleasure on this journey by telling you that high above where I now lean in shame are nailed, along with the Christ you've seen, two more Christs, - indeed *triplets* are hung where I was going to leave you thinking there was but one. Moreover, the third one is I think **You**! I had, you see, with comparative ease, completely censored any sign of this additional discovery out of Albion's scheme of things, and for years had also done a pretty good job of erasing it from my own mind, too.

However, within a few days of putting the final full stop on this last chapter, the barricades I had flung up in front of what I knew was out there were finally smashed down by the child who had found it and who shouted out from the core of me: "How dare you censor Albion!" I felt disgusted with myself that I had even tried. Since then via some editorial backtracking I have endeavoured to warn you that something more was to come. Therefore, no matter how clumsily the following two chapters have been included, following my last-minute change of heart, I hope from them you will gauge something of the genuine fear which was my only reason for not wanting you to know more; fear which, I'm happy to say, has since been replaced by the greatest calm I have ever known.

So, in the next chapter, read what 'dread' tried to remove from this miracle and, thereby, rob both you and me of its fabulous finale.

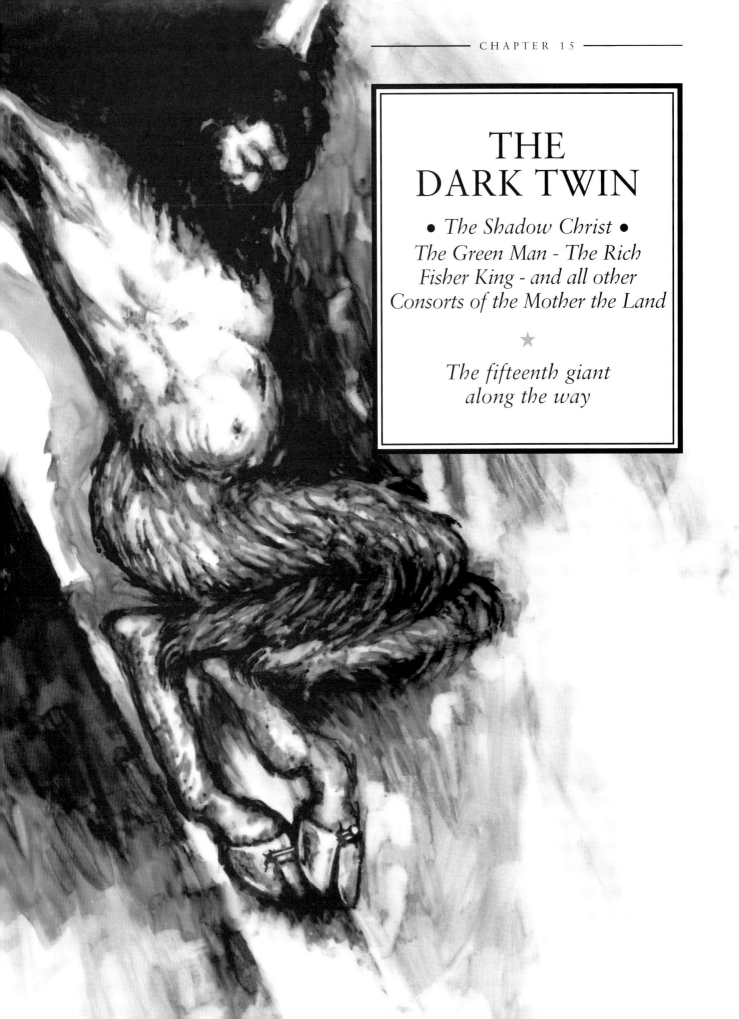

CHAPTER 15

THE DARK TWIN

• *The Shadow Christ* •
*The Green Man - The Rich
Fisher King - and all other
Consorts of the Mother the Land*

★

*The fifteenth giant
along the way*

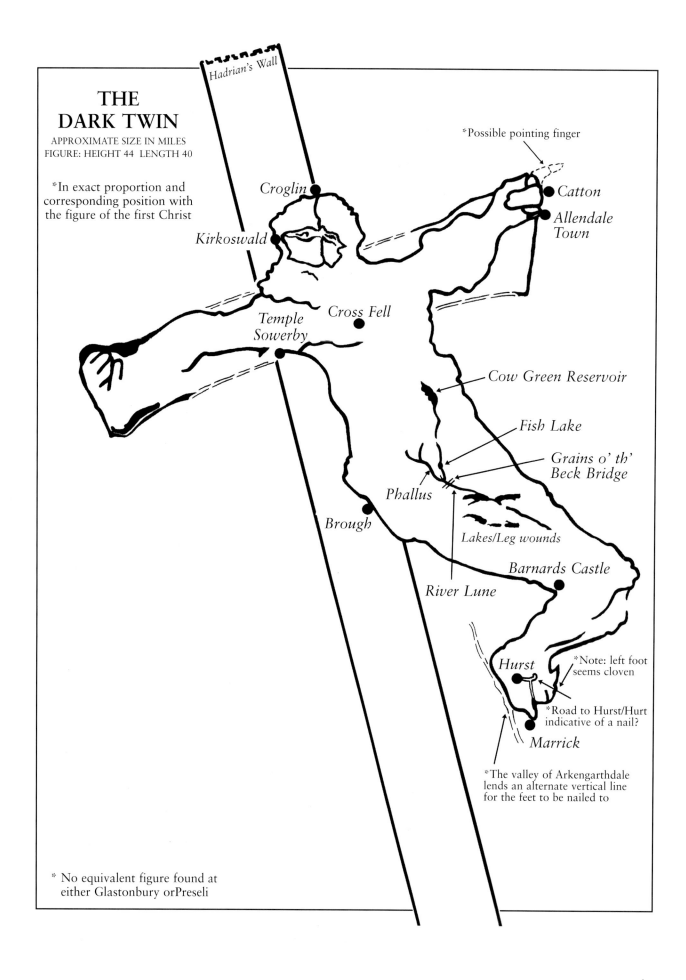

THE DARK TWIN

APPROXIMATE SIZE IN MILES
FIGURE: HEIGHT 44 LENGTH 40

*In exact proportion and
corresponding position with
the figure of the first Christ

Hadrian's Wall

*Possible pointing finger

Croglin

Catton

*Allendale
Town*

Kirkoswald

Cross Fell

*Temple
Sowerby*

Cow Green Reservoir

Fish Lake

*Grains o' th'
Beck Bridge*

Phallus

Lakes/Leg wounds

Brough

Barnards Castle

River Lune

Hurst

*Note: left foot
seems cloven

*Road to Hurst/Hurt
indicative of a nail?

Marrick

*The valley of Arkengarthdale
lends an alternate vertical line
for the feet to be nailed to

* No equivalent figure found at
either Glastonbury orPreseli

And I planned never to tell you of his existence!

Oak forests came and went with the hawks wing
Mountains rose and fell
He lay crucified with all his strength
On the earth

The Contender from the book CROW by Ted Hughes

GENERAL AREA:
ALTHOUGH NAILED TO THE SAME CROSS, AND INDEED SHARING THE SAME RIGHT HAND AS JESUS, THIS FIGURE IS HUNG SLIGHTLY MORE TO THE LEFT OR EAST. CROGLIN MARKS THE TOP OF HIS HEAD, WHILE THE SOLES OF HIS FEET REST AGAINST ARKENGARTHDALE.

Here follows an account of how I thought I was losing my mind one evening a few days before Good Friday. I was already awash with my 'Peter-like' rejections of the sight of that Jesus, hung so perfectly on Albion's cross, vehemently doubting that he was there. Like a drowning man, I lunged for something to save me from going under. I took a book from the shelf, knowing it contained a map to a different scale to the one I had in front of me.

You see, in John Parker's book *Cumbria, A Guide to the Lake District and its County* I needed urgent confirmation that I could *not* see that terrifying Christ, even though my pen had just charged around his very evident form! Imagine, then, my reeling senses when, not only did I watch this second map testify that Jesus was indeed crucified in Cumbria, but in the same sharp intake of breath had to declare that I could see what looked like *another* Christ nailed slightly to the left of him, yet hammered to that same damnable cross!

Yelling doubt scrambled my brain - I didn't know whether to laugh, cry, get bloody angry, or just grab a jacket and run and run through the drizzle until inevitable wheezing and familiar sights (traffic lights, couples out on the town, glowing shop fronts of Chinese take-aways) would bring me back to the real world, and hopefully to my senses. But the jacket stayed where it was, for the artist in me remained calm. Out of the corner of my enraptured mad eye I could see just how miraculously this second figure too was formed, overwhelming the magic of the land that seemed to join two Christs by the hip and even sharing the same right hand. Twins, for a fact, hung on Albion's cross - a cross now doubly confirmed.

I too hung spellbound, heart pounding, yet I was rooted to the spot; the rabbit in me wanting to bolt, while the artist wished only to wolf up the sight of it all. The rabbit's eye bulged, wanting to look anywhere but *there*, whilst the artist's was already greedily analysing what definitely *was there*. That more trained eyed, whether mad or not, was for the moment winning the tug of war.

I was struck, first and foremost, by the more athletic physique of the second figure, even his flowing mass of hair and beard seemed fuller. I sensed that, if freed from his nails, he would bound away like a leopard; indeed, there was a definite hint of lithe 'wildness' about him, whereas the first one I had spotted hung somehow calmer, almost serenely so.

The second major difference I saw was in the actual positioning of their respective bodies. It seemed that the great heaving chest of the second had thrust his whole frame towards a very definite left-facing posture, whereas the first, although facing more or less straight on, had, nevertheless, a body turned to the right. Even though my heart was still banging away, my Albion-trained intuition was quietly aiding my bewitched eye and calculating that if the first was purposefully turned to the right he might be representative of the Father's/white/positive/Yang side. His twin's turn to the left would presumably then signal a leaning towards the Mother's/black/negative/Yin - certainly his 'wilder' demeanour seemed to confirm my reasoning, along with what would turn out to be a plethora of place names to bolster his role.

Almost grudgingly I had to pronounce the first figure I'd found as Jesus, the Christ, but that second figure, and for all the above reasoning, just worried the crap out of me!

So guess what I did next? Insanity had already suggested itself to me, even in the split second when I first saw those blue river eyes of the first figure, but with apparently twin Christs now resurrected before me, amid a heady mix of rapture and downright panic, the rabbit in me now began to regain precedence. So, in the space of a couple of cold and calculating moments, I stealthily manoeuvred myself out of this agonizing corner by making it possible for me to forget that that second figure was even there.

The rabbit, you see, calculated that not only would that 'wilder' looking Christ confuse the whole picture, but would also, and this probably much nearer to the nub of my raging concerns, force me into another mountain of work. I would not only have more to write but would also have to fathom out what the hell he was doing here in the first place. All this, so near to what I thought was the end of my efforts in trying to put it all on a word processor, was a prospect that winded me as severely as a punch in the stomach. Sure, in stumbling over Albion I'd been on the trip of my life, and I felt truly privileged for the ride, but because I felt that it was imperative to let the world know of what was under our feet, along with a more practical need of putting bread back on the table after so long away from my work, I really did want to put the manuscript to bed. *So it was a blessing that I didn't know then that I would be fathoming and one-finger typing for another six years!*

But that was not all: because the sight of that second figure had frightened me even more than the first had, and because of his distinct 'wild' look, I attempted to square things up with my conscience (because, of course, I knew damn well he existed) by branding him the Anti-Christ, the devil himself. I honestly talked myself into the theory that if I was to unleash this hijacker of Jesus' cross he could perhaps put the entire miracle and message into jeopardy.

Thus, in now seeing myself as some guardian of the Grail, the dirty deal was done, and that threatened insanity seemed not nearly as serious as it had done but 30 minutes before. However, because of the remarkable phone call later that evening, which led to the finding of that Cumbrian Jesus' magnificent Grail wound (*see Aries, Part One*), I was left with no alternative but to write that first figure I had found into the whole scheme of things. I just hoped I could make a quick job of it!

"Once seen, never forgotten", however, is true of all Albion's giants, and so that shunned twin refused to disappear. Throughout the many months it took me to write the chapter on the first figure, the second one nagged me, eventually to the point where overwhelming guilt forced my eyes back to meet his. That guilt (although I was within days of putting what I thought would be again the last full stop to the manuscript) thundered: "**How dare you censor Albion!**" And so here, to the delight of the artist, I can now bring home the last and most wonderful black sheep of this House of Albion. Whether insane or not, I thank God that I'm coming clean, for with hindsight I can see that, without him, this whole miraculous mirror of Albion would be tragically dulled, to the point where you could not look at it and see yourself reflected back. And this is, I think, its final purpose.

Anti-Christ? No, rather just the Ante-Christ!

It's laughable now, but in initially branding him the Anti-Christ or devil I'd been making exactly the same sorry mistake that most of the so-called civilised world has been making for the last 2000 years. As we delve into how earlier cultures perceived (before the Church advised otherwise) the one who I now think shares Jesus' cross, we'll find him to be a vital component in the sacred balancing act that has always had the transmutation of a man into a self-aware God-Man as its ultimate aim. Therefore the land has rightfully hung him upon the same cross as Jesus, for I'm afraid to say that if I've read correctly Albion's near 50-mile-high replay of the passion, it seems that without him symbolically holding Jesus' hand upon that cross, Jesus himself may not have achieved that same exulted state of a God-Man, and would not have risen upon the third day as a Christ.

And why am I reluctant to say that? Well, it's surely already provocative enough of me to say that someone else is sharing Jesus' cross, whatever his name or reason for doing so; but to then have to warn you that when we later overlay this landscaped replay of the passion upon Golgotha's original we're going to have to struggle with the inference that *passion* indeed gripped that central cross and the figure on it. If I read it correctly, the land seems to be telling us that Jesus is playing bodily host to some divinely orchestrated act of mystical sexual intercourse between the male and female aspects of the one God; indeed, the Sacred Marriage is being consummated within him so that he can be reborn three days later as a Christ - heretically barking mad, or what!

Though I'll have to take my chances at the stake, if what I've read in this stunning 'take-2' of Golgotha is only 1% accurate, how can I now feel anything other than relieved that I finally mustered not so much courage, but more of that child-like sense of adventure and trust to accept that '*All's well*', as urged by Albion's own innocence in the soil. In doing so I've fetched this dusky Lord from out of the vaults of my own Christian-coached repression, because it's my belief now that that 1% means that here comes no Anti-Christ but rather the *ante or preceding* Christ, and is but the doorman to the knowledge of the Christ within *yourself*, however shocking his devil's foot may be - and believe me, the land *has* given him one of those too!

I admit, since setting foot upon Libra's dove, I have shown you preposterous things and asked you to accept them. And, for sure, things get no saner in what the land shows us upon the body of this Dark Twin. So be warned that in our unwrapping of his much-maligned body we shall expose layer upon layer of tabooed truth - truth that, because it puts the word sacred next to sexuality, is today generally shied away from as degenerative and pagan. And I confess that I once thought that way myself. Yet if these findings are seen in the context of how the land has innocently re-illustrated them, I think you may find little to morally balk at. Somewhere on the boundary of our collective unconscious these same findings might be answered by a warm and sympathetic resonance, for Albion's ship also lies there at anchor, and on it things taboo are rendered innocently beautiful - free of the dirt that fear, born out of ignorance, has periodically heaped upon them. These so-called taboos, that are now part of this ark's cargo, have been gathered from the collective endeavours of generations who searched for the truth of simply why we're here. These, the fruits of their findings, are now presented as provisions for us who might be sailing to the very brink of either extinction or the evolutionary leap of perception needed to avert that extinction.

All creation, I think, at this moment trembles upon our decision - shall we have sense of adventure enough to board this lifeboat and take up the keys left by the past, which just might unlock the door to a fabulous future; or shall we deny that such a miraculous earth ship has even docked right in our faces because to see it will be to constantly admit just how much we've got wrong in the way we view this planet and the lives we spend on it?

Those who do dare to look I know will also be adventurous enough to take a trip with me back to the first Good Friday, this in effort to detect what could be the chemistry of some monumental rite of sacred sexuality writhing within the breast of the crucified Jesus, in order to give birth to a Christ Child within him. But you must also be ready to come up against what might be a 2000-year-old fug of Christian propaganda, misconceptions and just plain fear which could have robbed us of the true wonder behind the crucifixion, and thus tarnished the gift of what life on earth was ever meant to be, according to this landscape - a gift few have ever fully unwrapped.

Setting our compass

Before we endeavour to allow the rightful shadow and twin of Jesus to both clear his name and re-educate us of the role he has in helping us achieve the realization of the divinity within ourselves, we must set our compass to what has been a recurring map reference throughout these hundreds of pictorial miles. In plain speaking, our way must be as much towards the black way as it is to the white; as much heading down the Motherly negative dark/left physical/nature track as it is to the Father's positive light/right spiritual path. And although I'm sure that to strike out on that road leading only to the light is to choose a safer route than heading solely along a darker course, I'm equally sure that Albion has been subtly hinting for miles that to aim only for the light might be to halve the treasure at our journey's end. Therefore I propose that to seek a neutralizing course down the *centre* of the two ways, having one foot in light/heaven, the other in dark/earth, is the 'Grail Way' that Albion has been promoting since the dove - a compass reading now emphatically endorsed by the land's pertinent nailing of seemingly perfect opposites upon the one cross.

Remember too that whilst on Albion's ark any old ingrained notions that all things black are possibly bad while all things white are generally good are faulty co-ordinates. Mother Nature built no evil as 'standard' into any of her black creatures, nor has she singled out her white creations as especially 'chosen'. Indeed, don't even take the word 'right' as a vote of approval, or 'negative' as somehow undesirable.

Hear two voices from the past vouchsafe pretty well the same:

"Light and darkness, life and death, right and left, are brothers of one another. They are inseparable. Because of this neither are the

good good, *nor the evil evil, nor is life life,*
nor death death."
THE GOSPEL OF PHILIP

"The Great Way is not difficult for those who
have no preferences. When love and hate
(good and evil) are both absent everything
becomes clear and undisguised. Make the
smallest distinction, however, and heaven and
earth are set infinitely apart".
Sosan, a Taoist Master

Trying to balance the mystic books

Having then set our compass as much to the dark as to the light, and because I'm asking you to put aside an almost genetically inherited set of basics for the supposed avoidance of trouble, a little reassurance wouldn't go amiss, especially since I know what's coming! Certainly I too had urgent need of some heavy reassurance before I had balls enough to 'go for broke' by owning up to this naked and cloven-footed hijacker of Christ's cross. And wouldn't this admission of mine be slightly less unpalatable, I thought, if I could show that, in the past, wiser men than I had also looked for a juxtaposition of opposites in order to balance the mystic books, so to speak, and who, upon seeing how the land has hung two upon *one* cross would have themselves shouted "Bingo"!

Because of my lack of knowledge in this area, I didn't hold out too much hope of coming across any tracks belonging to earlier hunters of a mystical Dark Twin to partner Jesus, though, without too much sniffing around, I surprisingly had the nod and a wink I needed to bolster my confidence in coming clean, as it seemed that there really were some who looked for Jesus' shadow in order to account for the divine balance they felt should be behind all things. It was nice, too, to find out that I wouldn't have been on my own come heretic-burning day!

A wink came from Mary Caine who

suggested in her own book that, for some of these mystic book-keepers, John the Baptist, the cousin of Jesus, had filled the slot of some essential opposite. John perhaps fitting the bill not only in his wilder, crying-in-the-wilderness, camel-hair-clothed, snacking-on-locusts character - but maybe he was also of a darker appearance than his cousin?

Complexions, hair colour, dress sense and rough manners apart, there was obviously some deeper reason running through the mystics' need of an opposite to partner Jesus, and being now schooled in Albion I naturally suspected that they, too, must have been working on the principle that the positive, Yang, or whiter orientated Jesus, must, as an esoteric law, be partnered by a counter balancing reflection of himself and biased towards the negative/black/Yin polarity. If so, I further began to wonder if such twin representatives of the fundamental forces of heaven/Father and earth/Mother would have been primed to somehow *mystically unite, a dissolving of one into the other, so as to promote some manifestation of absolute and balanced perfection - maybe even the ultimate figure of a Christ?* Either way, I took that furtive wink from John the Baptist via Mary Caine to be a tentative vote of approval for the interloper on Albion's cross.

Sure, the rabbit was turning mole again, and perhaps all this sounds to you like nothing more than another molehill of baseless speculation, and one that I'm attempting to build up into another Everest in an effort to give perfect reason for there being two figures nailed to Albion's single cross. Nevertheless, at this point I do have an advantage over you, for I'm basing all this on what I know is waiting at the end of our journey. The sight of the astonishingly animated finale that the land has been keeping up its green sleeve will speak for itself, saying that Jesus *had* to find such a twin, and clasp his hand, before he could truly experience himself as God. Furthermore, and still hoping that I'm reading the land correctly, I think Jesus may have instigated this particular part of his mission when he entered the wilderness where even the Bible says he met the devil. Devil, or his own symbolically cloven-footed dark/Yin brother from the 'underworld', not someone to be fearful of, but purely the representative of the holy animal, vegetable, mineral half of the being we all are.

So, even from the aforementioned wink, I was feeling reassured that the search of any mystic accountants was for the earthly or Motherly counterweight to him who had perhaps come to earth as the Father's emissary, and whose ultimate aim may have been to unite both Father and Mother within himself - to become the two made one - thus their true Son - a Christ no less. And I must keep stressing that this search was in no way for a twin of evil opposition, no matter how tempting to presume otherwise on the strength of the Church's way of seeing things.

My intuition, however, urges that I should add to this that anything which is deprived of its balancing other-half may become dis-eased to the point of becoming dangerous, evil even, and when Jesus went into the wilderness, that twin, perhaps already expelled from men's classification of what was holy, may indeed have been a wild and unbalanced man who needed his twin Jesus as much as Jesus needed him.

Note: regarding my theory of those two fundamental forces becoming one in Jesus - I accept the idea that all things, especially everything that is animated with life, may only exist because of this same essential union of Mother/Father. However, I think those old mystics may have sensed that only when man became fully aware of the divinity of both his material and spiritual identity, and by inviting those two fundamental male/female forces of the one God to consummate their sacred marriage within the core of his own bodily

temple, could he split the chrysalis husk of the old self and step out as a God-Man - a man still, but one who would thereafter intimately discover and commune with himself in all things.

But I needed more than the Baptist's wink and my own hunch of an ulterior motive for Jesus' stint in the wilderness - I needed it backed up by a more definite nod of approval. I needed hard-nosed written proof from antiquity that I was not on my own in suggesting Jesus had a symbolic twin, and I got what I needed from the author of the Gnostic *Gospel of Thomas*, who actually proclaimed himself, would you believe, to be Jesus' twin! Even his name, Didymos Judas Thomas, seems to have been doubly encoded with the same news, for in Greek Didymos means twin, while, in Aramaic, Thomas also means twin; thus the author's real name is Judas the twin! And are you thinking what I'm thinking? In the New Testament's casting of a Judas to play the negative role to Jesus (and who subsequently also got 'blackened' for his services) was there also hint of a symbolic twin? Indeed was there a very strong hint that Jesus actually *needed* his Judas, the Scorpio-like odd one out of the twelve, to help him reach his final goal, however painful the initial push?

Seemingly a twin for Jesus was not such an original idea after all - and boy was I glad!

Moles, though, have notoriously poor eyesight, I hear you say, and thus I accept again that some of the land's mystical small print on what's going on here may be beyond my reading capabilities. That said, this hanging of twins upon the same 300-mile-high cross was so utterly provocative that the bottom-line must be a proclamation that something phenomenally important happened over and above the Bible's telling of events on that first Good Friday. And, if we could understand this, it might not only enrich our lives, but may also be ultimately vital too to the well-being of the entire planet - for look, is not this poetic double-act being brandished like a flag high above the deck of Albion's life-preserving ark? Indeed, was the robber to Jesus' left, who went to paradise with him, representative of this same Dark Twin? In answer, Albion's own version of him will, at the end of our journey over this landscaped picture of paradise breathtakingly endorse the theory - however bizarre.

Though if you are already troubled by the way this chapter is going, or should I say, in the direction this Dark Twin is pointing us, I say be especially glad: here's how Judas the twin begins his own Gospel:

> And he said, "Whoever finds the interpretation of these sayings will not experience death." Jesus said, "Let him who seeks continue seeking until he finds. When he finds, he will become troubled. When he becomes troubled, he will be astonished, and he will rule over the all."

Needless to say, the more I delved, the less uneasy I became in owning up to this twin in Albion's passion in a landscape, even though I knew the more I defended his presence alongside Jesus, the more difficult it would be for many a Christian to accept. However, because of the sheer beauty of this whole zodiacal miracle, and its raising of Jesus to cap its summit, I knew that only some news of extreme value could be behind this raising of a twin to partner him upon the mast of the ark.

In another sense, however, one thing that I would discover in his make-up would remain to many as an anathema, no matter what his input to the rest of this landscaped message. You see, in that unobtrusive word *twin* there was still a concealment of the problem I'd had since the first moment I laid eyes upon him. Although he, at first glance, looked to be a virtual reversed mirror image of the figure to his right, he still radiated an aura of 'untamed wildness', and when I would later discover his left foot to be quite possibly **cloven** (unnerving confirmation of my initial fear of him!) I'm sure I really did hear the crack of Christian thunder and damnation above my head. A twin upon the same cross was iffy enough, even to me, but one with such a terrible foot meant I was saying that Lucifer was Jesus' brother!

How the hell was I going to justify what the innocent land had done? How did the land wish me to read this one's presence into the whole scheme of things - had I not already pointed a finger towards Scorpio as maybe harbouring a disgruntled Lucifer? Once more I needed the past to re-educate me; I was still troubled, but I hoped I'd end up wonderfully astonished.

The brother they never wanted us to know about

So I'd a Dark Twin on my hands, naked and with a devil's foot to boot! But hang on, was not his hoofed liability just an innocent sign to show us that he is of the great 'underworld', not hell, but purely the realm of the animal, vegetable and mineral, indeed, of all things solid enough to cast a natural and blameless shadow? Do all the accusations of evil heaped upon that accursed foot fog over the simple fact that he is but the representative of holy nature and as such, no one to be fearful of, but rather to be accepted as indeed our own twin - one half of our own duality?

Trying on ideas like this in an effort to alleviate my nervous twitch, I then went back to test-drive thoughts that had been motivated by our ancestors' reverence for the Mother's Son/lover, wherein I hoped to find more solace.

Briefly, the concept of the son who becomes the lover was, to our ancestors, a perfect vehicle upon which to illustrate the regenerative qualities of the life force. The goddess (signed by the moon) immaculately conceiving of a divine son who would grow with the rhythm of the seasons into her consort (the sun) and although perennially dying, yet resurrecting again at the advent of spring, he would, with the return of the corn, guarantee the eternal circle where life always follows death.

And the name they gave to this resurrecting son? Adonis, Aion, Attis, Bacchus, Dionysus, Mithras, Osiris, Tammuz and Xipe Totec may have been a few of the cover names given to his many global incarnations - certainly, all of these deities come across fundamentally as promoters of the concept of regeneration, and if regeneration is not a million miles away from resurrection, then all would have been somewhat Jesus-like too. However, because these laughing Mayday cavorters had flowers in their hair and inspired as holy an honouring of the earth and her cycles of fertility (as again did Jesus, although it seems all reference of this got edited out of the Bible) they were under Christianity's new broom swept out as degenerate. To the Church, the earth had roots in hell and anyone who saw differently was risking becoming the devil's own bedfellow; thus the whole lot of them were cast out as being but the masks of the one and ultimate demon.

Interesting name though, demon, derived, I discovered, from the Greek *daemon* and meaning nothing at all scary, but pertaining to *a divinity/super_natural_ being who was an intermediary (note - not barrier!) between man and God - also an inner or attendant spirit or inspiring force.*

Could we then look to this odd one on this cross, the one with the abominable foot, as a demon doorman - a guide or intermediary who will escort you through a leafy doorway into a hidden super-nature, discovering there that, if rivers and rocks can consciously shape a near 50-mile high Christ, then what wonders could you perform in collaboration with her, your Mother, the earth? And when Jesus ventured into the wilderness, was it to seek this shaggy-

legged guide or brother in order to experience exactly the same. Because that guide has since been branded by the ignorant as the ultimate demonic lord, our knowledge, kinship and love of the earth and her creatures have greatly diminished as a consequence. Could this be the reason the land has willed this cloven-footed one to hang hand-in-hand with Jesus on this Cumbrian cross?

Again, I am an artist desperately trying to read these bewildering pictures in a landscape, and of course I could be hopelessly off-target. However, appreciate that my strange theories are, for the most part, only based upon what others have previously discovered, believed or suspected. I have been permanently astonished to find that so much of what the earth has apparently depicted is but a gigantic graphic approval of many a hitherto unorthodox viewpoint.

For instance, and remembering my suggestion of Jesus in the wilderness seeking his holy animal other half in order to better know his relationship to the Great Mother, you may feel that my earlier snipe at the Bible's possible editing out of a Mother-earth-loving, environmentally-friendly Jesus has no foundation. Perhaps you just can't imagine Jesus actually referring to the 'Earth Mother' at all, let alone speaking words that would honour her holiness. If so, I would like you to read another of Edmond Szekely's translations of the ancient Aramaic texts which are claimed to quote Jesus' own words - unfortunately words that have no chance of making it into the Bible:

"…truly, no one can reach the Heavenly Father unless through the Earthly Mother."

Refreshing too these following lines. They were spoken 2000 years before the rainbow wagons of the New Age travellers-come-eco warriors hit the road and yet which could be from their own mouths:

He who doth destroy a tree
Hath cut off his own limbs.
Thus shall sing the Children of Light,
When the earth again shall be a garden:
Holy Tree, divine gift of the Law!
For the trees are our brothers,
And as our brothers,
We shall guard and love one another.

Hear too just how close some of those earth-loving pagan deities were to Jesus in terms of their birthdays and deaths, even though they were revered centuries before Jesus ever drew breath.

Take Dionysus - born in an ox stall! No, I didn't know that either, but when I did I couldn't help wondering if Jesus' own birth in similar surroundings was itself a starred gesture to the divinity of his physical or animal other half. Obviously, the editor of the scriptures didn't spot the code, so this lovely detail stayed in. However, some early Christians favoured another version of the nativity, which had it taking place in a cave. If it did, it would be the equally pagan Mithras who'd beat him to it this time; why, baby Mithras even had three shepherds to witness his birth too! Oh, and the date of Mithras' birthday? December 25th, of course!

These similarities are hard to ignore. They continue when we also learn that Adonis, Aion, and Dionysus all had virgins as mothers, while each one died around Easter time - a nexus now hammered home by Albion's emphatic placing of Jesus and this many-named nature deity on the same Cross; and what with their shared right hand being pierced with same binding nail I think we get the emphatic picture. Heavenly Jesus and this earthly twin were always meant to be read as one, and seen in the same divine light!

Simply, to my eye, the land is telling us that while we might have allowed the Father's son to speak of heaven and the spirit, we gagged his brother, the Mother's son/lover, and never

heard how equally divine was the earth and a life in the flesh. Indeed, until relatively recently, wild nature was deemed by the Church as something inherently bad unless beaten into some usable service. So is it any wonder that when men consider the earth as dross and the flesh not much better, there could only ever follow the environmental damage we have today, along with the piled up bodies from one 'ethnic cleansing' after another?

Nevertheless, I felt these thoughts and findings still only amounted to my first tampering with a lock, which, if I could pick it, could let me in on an even bigger reason why the land had seen fit to crucify the Green Man on the same cross as Jesus. My gut-feeling insisted that there was still more behind this than had yet dawned on me. As I sank into deeper thought, Golgotha began to present itself more and more as the real key. Golgotha and *two* upon *one* cross was urging me that here was a combination that could blow the barrier erected by the Church off its hinges!

How come? Well, Albion is essentially a zodiac ingeniously shoehorned into a Cancerian ark, and thus to have its mast crowned by, of all things, a re-rendering of Golgotha's non-astrological event, told me that even the stars had seen something extraordinary pass by unrecorded on that monumental afternoon of the first Good Friday. And, whatever it was must have been of universal significance because it has been replayed here with figures nearly 50 miles tall so that we can't miss it the second time around. Moreover, this being overlaid upon the very mast of the ark can only mean that we'll need to understand all that we've missed by the time the waters begin to rise.

I warn you again, however, that when we do attempt this second reading of the crucifixion with the evidence as nailed to the mast of this ark, something so astonishingly unheard of will be unveiled, something so challenging (yet for me so utterly enchanting) that I fear I might lose those readers who have hitherto stuck with me, even in my noting of buttocks at Nateby! But I hope not, for if the last chapter is to supply the fireworks, the resurrectional wonders surrounding Golgotha's passion, of which this present giant is shortly to sing, will supply the most perfect backdrop against which to see the sparkling crescendo of that final chapter.

In the meantime let me build up my case that this second figure on the cross *is* the Mother's own virile consort, proudly Yin in polarity, and thus 'blackened' to hell by those who didn't know the worth of Yin to Yang. I'll begin by pointing out the many blackened and sexually orientated, but entirely correct for this fertility god, place-name labels stuck upon him. Names that were put there by the many unsuspecting helpers of the Mother's grand design, confirming both his colour coding and role by the black and white evidence on the ground. We may then be in a better position to understand what might have been the inner ecstasy behind the outer agony of Jesus on that awesome afternoon at Golgotha, and also to thereafter look at our own metaphysically cloven foot and see no curse in it.

Time then to get closer, to feel your own twin's hot ox breath upon your neck - to smell upon him the Mother's anointing scents; from the moist vapours of dank, dark peat and the mysterious underskirt sniff of a fly agaric, to the sugary sweetness of the 20,000 daffodils that we'll find blooming within his Temple Sowerby armpit! Pick up from him, too, the rank stench of a decomposing badger lying in a roadside ditch, for he is as much death as he is life. This his paradoxical role from where the seed of misunderstanding has germinated, and which would grow on to bind him to his fate, for it has indeed become death which this Lord of the Underworld has been most associated with and thus cheaply condemned as evil. So, what a shame, for most of all he carries too, the hot musky odours of love's own mingled secretions; he, the unashamedly naked, sperm-spouting, life-promoting consort - one to whom death was just an ante-room to life again. Though carrying such a tabooed scent, I guess, brought further opportunity for the Church to taboo him to hell - along with the promoting of that life-insulting code of celibacy as the chain to keep him there!

First of all let's check off his markings of the dark and scary.

The Shadow Christ begins to speak for himself

I must stress that this high-peaked area of Britain, in which both crucified figures have arisen, is for the most part one of beautiful and wide-ranging wilderness. The choice of roads, lanes and place names from which to *concoct* (if that's what you think I've been up to since Libra) any picture are few and very far between; so to find one crucified Lord here in such astounding detail and with place name verification is for me a miracle in itself. But to find *two* figures side by side and upon the same cross still beggars my belief. But then I smile, for you should know by now that Albion defies any rule you care to throw at it.

And so because they told us to always aim *high*, awash as it is there in positively good white light, and to steer clear of the darkened and therefore negatively bad *below*, we branded the one holy and the other downright evil - one the incandescent highway to God, the other a pitch black alleyway leading only into the arms of the bogey man! So generations of us have been subconsciously programmed to think in this way. However, Albion is now suggesting that that divine high may not be as high as it could have been if one had first fathomed and embraced the equally divine low, thus, having already trod the body of him who equates to the light/Yang, let's see if this, his supposed twin, backs up my theory by aligning himself with the Dark and scary Yin!

Smile with me then as this wilderness, which clothes him, gives up his misconstrued identity. Smile especially at that dreadful place entangled in his overflowing beard, for in that matted coarseness find the once warning sign of Fiends Fell! See, too, Black Fell hanging among his tousled super-natural locks.

There may also be a dark warning behind a tiny hamlet's name, for Haresceugh is found nestling amongst the lashes of his left eye. Although perhaps not raising much of an eyebrow today, it may have caused suspicion to some early church father who would have known well enough that witch hares were especial fertility creatures of *her* who was wanton and him who was cloven, and so likewise tabooed the poor creature to hell too!

And yet how this fleet-footed creature still managed to tip-toe into the Christian calendar: to the Anglo Saxons the hare was sacred to Eostre, the spring goddess, who is now remembered in the name Easter. Know, also, that the 1246 spelling of Haresceugh will leave nothing to the imagination; it was the charming Harescock! Again, what an apt twinkle in the eye of the goddess' own spring consort!

If I have deduced correctly, it's also worth remembering that upon the left (Mother's side) eye of his brother, there is also intimation of the Mother hidden in the place name of Melmerby. This, I discovered, once meant 'Servant of Mary'; thus each twin has in his left/Yin eye a reflection of the Mother - the same Mother perhaps?

Before moving on from this suggestively winking eye, I must also tell you that there is another place-name relating to a hare upon this wild man. We find it on the wooded and thus delightfully bushy eyebrow of his right eye, in the shape of Nether Haresceugh. So we have snared two of Eostre's hares, remarkably one in each eye, and uncanny to say the least - or is it? For me, I see he has eyes only for his lover Eostre, bringing hope eternal for the continued fruitfulness of the earth. And because Eostre means Easter it's not only regeneration but also resurrection and rebirth that must be in the air if ever this twin opens his eyes.

"Speaking of eyes - how are his own eyes set upon the land; could they, just as his brother's, be carved by a river too, and if so is its name as significant as is that Robberby Water in forming the eyes of Jesus - or would that be far too much to hope for?" The answer is "no" - on Albion it wouldn't be hoping for too much, but allow me the luxury of teasing you for a few more lines before explaining.

A robber's mouth; a sniff of trouble; a wound full of Yin; a vein carrying black blood, and a scarecrow's head!

The jagged line of his mouth, perhaps showing a grimace of pain, is a 2.5 mile long track, which ominously ends in the bog of Melmerby Mire - and would we get into the mire if we listened to him? *"Yes!"* would say the Church. At the other end of the same track is the village of Melmerby (the same place that marks the left eye of Jesus, and which we know once meant *St. Mary's Servant*), so this Green Man must be telling us that above all else he speaks as the servant of the Mother - brilliant! What's more, out of this Melmerby corner of his mouth there runs a visual continuation of that Robberby Water which actually draws Jesus' eyes. So, besides saying that he is the servant of the Goddess, which as her consort he assuredly is, does this twin also speak through the mouth of that robber who was hung at Jesus' side and whom the Lord took with him to paradise? If so, then to my ear his full and relevant message must be: "I serve my Mother/my lover. I was poetically hung as the robber at Jesus' side, but was really his twin who accompanied him to Paradise. Without each other, neither of us could have made it."

Note too another couple of places with a sniff of something ever so slightly negative and foreboding hanging around them - check out the strangeness of Unthank and Gamblesby, both at the end of his nose. The Yin theme itself continues with Blackton Reservoir that lies like an open wound upon his right thigh, and by the Black Burn, which suggests a thick watery vein down his left arm. Then on the very crown of his head I catch sight of Scarrowmanwick Fell and maybe a hint of another man whose scary arms were outstretched on a pole - a crucified straw-stuffed scarecrow man perhaps?

Now a charred rib, and those eyes as 'all seeing' as Odin's own

We now have a couple of black birds which carry on the Yin thing and both prerequisite species of those who have dealings with the underworld: Crowdundle Beck gives him one charred rib, while best of all it's the tremendously meaningful stream known as the **Raven Beck** which draws and fills both his cupped and closed eyes with tears. So "Yes", this one's closed watery eyes are a remarkable copy of the way the Robberby Water formed Jesus's own closed eyes. Surely another resounding shout of "You'd better believe it!" to the fact that it is the intelligence of a super-nature rather than blind *coincidence* that is at work here.

I ask you, what are the chances of not only finding two Christs side by side and nailed to the very same cross, but both of them having perfectly cupped and closed eyes formed solely by running water? But, for me, more remarkable than this even are the actual names of the rivers involved, each name so damn pertinent to the one whose tears it carries. The By-the-Robber example being all too easy to uncover, whereas, although I was instantly happy that it was the coal black raven which colours the eyes of him who is the epitome of the Yin, a little further research into the bird brought rewards which had me whooping with delight, for no better bird could a Lord of the Underworld have to aid his sight. Let me explain.

The raven as a bird of mystic portent has been acknowledged ever since the Dreamtime. To the indigenous people of North America, the bird was even thought to carry the 'medicine of magic' to mankind from out of the Void, which is the Great Mystery - and surely I don't need to remind you that upon his death even King Arthur himself transformed into one. But it is in the Norse myths that the raven helps us travellers of Albion to see the full import of the eyes we're now looking into, for the raven's own mystic sight made them the virtual eyes of one-eyed Odin himself! Odin, *Underworld God of the Dead*, of poetry, of magic, and inspirer of the berserkers, those Viking warriors who'd wind themselves up to such frenzy that they could perform astonishing feats of wild daring during battle. *Odin, the raven-sighted god, who learnt the Secret of Secrets by hanging himself from the tree Yggdrasil, which overhung the universe.*

Ask yourself if we now see Odin's act of attaining knowledge spectacularly mirrored in this land picture of an 'Odin-eyed' Lord of the

Underworld, hung as he is upon Albion's own tree-come-cross, and which, in all truth, overhangs the universe in the shape of all these terrestrial constellations we have now unearthed. Shame I never had the guts to show him in the coloured artwork!

I find it eye-opening to see yet more overlapping of myth upon myth dance off this landscape, testifying how blind we have become to the wonder of a life on this thinking, listening, speaking, remembering, and what must be, ever-so-loving, earth.

The most ghastly, yet most beautifully telling, wound that man has ever had to feel into

Having then ticked off his *dark* and once-thought *scary* markings, let's discover why those raven eyes are full of tears (both happy and sad) by zeroing in upon a mark which it seems the earth wills us to see, just a moment after first noticing his crucified presence. I say this, as it took only a split second more after I first saw his great heaving form, to spot that gaping wound upon his side, indeed, a wound far more glaringly obvious than that High Cup Nick version on Jesus' side and which took that weird, though very wonderful, midnight phone call to make me see it.

Anyway, button up those coats and join me in the moonlight alongside this *dazzling* wound, this burnished sheet of white brilliance upon his left side. It is a lake of some two miles in length and beloved of fishermen for its wild trout; the local fishing rule states that no man may ever take more than twelve away in his basket. Its known name is the Cow Green Reservoir, the largest lake upon his body - its unknown designation is the Lance Wound (reflection of Jesus' own) of this, the Shadow Christ, or perhaps harder to take: the Green Man who as I write is being sawn to pieces, rooted up, genetically mutated, polluted by nuclear fall-out, river-poisoned, subjected to global warming, mad cow disease and a

punctured ozone layer. His wound, then, filled to the brim with the earth's own symbolic blood, is thus to be seen as the **glaring wound of the entire planet**, and one, let me tell you, that we've all had a hand in inflicting; from our double glazing's hardwood frames pillaged from another decimated rain forest, to the turning away of our famously blind eyes from the latest smashing of seal pups' heads upon the ice. And isn't that same blood-stained ice even now turning to slush, as a direct result, it is thought, of our appetite for burning fossil fuels - and yet we all carry on doing it anyway.

And yes, I could go on totting up the crimes we're daily committing against him, the times we've all jabbed that spear in his side ...but come on, you know all this already otherwise you'd not have followed me this deep into Albion! And because we're looking in a mirror, I also don't need to tell you either that this one's gash is reflected back on the self-inflicted, and life-disenchanting wound of *all* mankind.

Staring us in the face then, must be the *deep* wound of the Mother/material, just as High Cup Nick must logically be now viewed (because if *one* bleeds, then so too must the *other*) as the *high*-peaked wound of the Father/spiritual - that very peak a mere four miles horizontally west from where we stand - in *direct line* with this 70-foot deep gash! And I don't know about you, but as I look from one wound to the other I can only gasp in admiration at the amazing show of balance that nature has fetched from out of her own breast to brandish in our disbelieving faces. She couldn't be more forthright in her poetic plea that on this cross we see opposites in perfect harmony, even to the geographically high and low extent of their respective wounds. In this I see the repeated plea to acknowledge that the high spiritual is no greater than the deep, dense physical. Indeed, it must be complemented by it, otherwise a joint deterioration is set in motion.

Looking from one wound to the other, are

we also invited to symbolically take that Father's High Cup, placed high upon the summit of Jesus' High Cup Nick wound, and dunk it into *this* two-mile long 'Nick' of all nicks? I say yes!

Oh how these symbolic pieces begin to click together so poetically! Two Grail wounds; one black, one white, one high, one low, one to the west, the other to the east, and spiritually standing in the middle of the two, you are being invited to drink in your own divine joint nature, to drink in the mixture of the two and know yourself to be the one true God. So spin like a dervish of delight - the stars really have fallen down to worship at your feet - all is yours if only you can see through new eyes!

But then let your arms flop to your side and wipe any delight from your face, for the danger our planet is in must be horrendous for her to give birth to this achingly wonderful miracle from out of her crust, in images of our own mythological heritage, and surely in the hope that its near-universally-known pictorial tongue might be understood by as many folk as possible. Thus even in her death throws she presents to us, her murderers, a gift in the shape of the most wonderful opportunity any man has had in finding out the reason for our being here, and to know just how much we have always been loved by every rock and leaf of this creation. Perhaps it is also a first and last chance to realise that if what this land has done *is* testament to nature being a sensitive mirror of our every thought and deed, we might, even at this late hour, begin to heal both our own blindness and the planet's plight. If everything *is* so intrinsically and sensitively linked to us, the land might herself respond to our belated credence of her divinity as manifested in this miracle of Albion, and with the same force of love which must have given birth to this wonder in the first place, might begin joyfully to heal herself in a way, and at such a speed, that might yet take our breath away.

Am I mad, and you too, for coming this far

on an impossible journey? Could all this really be? Do we moles prod at fact? Have yesterday's interesting, but basically naïve, myths become today's sparkling chance to win through to a better tomorrow?

"But hang on," I hear some shout, *"that Cow Green Reservoir did not exist until 1960, thus your theory that we've been following the well trodden path of many previous hunters of the Grail comes somewhat unstuck. Previous hunters, upon reaching where we now stand, would have found no revelatory lake wound to freak them out on a similarly moonlit night a few thousand years ago!"*

"True enough, but only in part", would be my initial reply before adding: "You see, any Grail seekers who might have passed this way prior to anything that happened in those 'swinging 60s' would have freaked at the sight of a wound perhaps far more spectacular than even Cow Green by moonlight presents to us seekers of today. I say this for exactly where this reservoir now glints they would have seen something that must have been almost a minor miracle in itself - the so-called great watery *Wheel of the Tees*. I will let David Bellamy and Brendan Quale again from their book *England's Lost Wilderness* describe this natural wonder of Albion, now sadly submerged - the brackets being mine: *"Near the stone pile on the southwest side of the reservoir (Cow Green) you can stand and imagine where the great 'Wheel of the Tees' used to turn and turn again. This was not however a man-made wheel but a crescent of golden water where the river (Tees) turned in a great loop (Circle of Life?) as if savouring the magic and delight of the place before plunging headlong over..."*

Forgive me for the moment for stopping there, but what I'll tell you before I finish the above sentence is that the significance of where that fabulous loop of whirled water once plunged over (indeed where the waters of this replacement reservoir still fall) will make even us whoop a whoop that will have farm dogs barking for miles around! In the meantime, here's something that I hope may get you in the mood for that whoop - it's the intriguing significance behind that name Cow Green.

But who is the Green Cow?

There have been many cultures that have revered the Cow as a symbol of the Goddess' bounteous fertility - we are even told that Mohammed's own daughter Fatima was known as the Red Moon Cow who suckled the entire earth. Though we must return to Egypt to gain the full import of the name unsuspecting man has attached to the gouged-out wound of the Goddess' consort.

Standing upon the banks of this moonlit wound of a lake it is relevant to know that to the Egyptians their cow-horn-crowned Mother, Isis, just so happened to be known as both the milk-giving Cow Goddess and the Green Goddess - so don't blame me for looking at Cow Green with great expectations!

It is interesting too to note that the Green Cow's milk was linked in the Egyptian mind to the whiteness of the moon, which dribbled down from heaven to earth as the blessed rain. So, each river and stream was in turn seen as her running milk (a veritable water of life) for the suckling of all and the greening of the entire planet.

However, connecting this Cow Green wound to the Egyptian's Green Cow almost demands one to seek topographical mention of Osiris too, because these two were so inseparable - and boy will we find him close by! Before we unveil him though, we must meet another personification of the Great Goddess/Green Cow otherwise there's going to be big trouble!

So welcome back Ceridwen - and guess where I've found her cauldron?

As exciting as it is to suspect mention of Queen Isis upon English fields, there is one other lady whom we may not leave out of any Motherly doings that are local to Albion. How could she who is depicted so brazenly cavorting as Virgo not be somewhere in this picture of her own consort - how dare Isis try to take all the glory! So make way - here comes Albion's own Green Cow rushing down from the Welsh mountains to point out that she too is remembered in her consort's portentous wound - hail, then, Ceridwen, undisputed cackling hag-Goddess of Albion! And as she comes, all black rags and venom, remind yourself of her Cauldron of Inspiration, of rebirth, and of all knowledge, that very prototype of a Grail pot which we learnt of in our trip to Virgo; just to taste a finger tip's worth of its liquor was to be gifted in a flash with absolute wisdom.

She must be livid to see our small band gathered here like a gaggle of frozen little Gwions at her cauldron's lip, seeking a taste of all it holds.

"At the cauldron's lip did you say?" Sure thing!

I suggest the above name-play with confidence, as I believe her early Grail-like pot has now evolved into the shape of *this* Cow Green Reservoir wound of her Son/Lover, and in the symbolic sipping of its liquor, overlapped as it now is by blood, must be to drink in all the wisdom in the universe. Though I hear you counter: *"Here he goes, trying to cunningly manipulate another chunk of juicy mythology so as to fit in with his equally cunning artistry."* But, honestly, I'm not that clever, I'm just an avid adder-up of two and two. Listen, when Joseph of Arimathea held up the chalice that was used in the Last Supper to the side wound of Jesus, did he not inaugurate that blood and water spillage as containing vast wisdom, and fit to fill that more portable version of the Celts' cauldron?

Unconvinced, aren't you? I see the old girl eyeing the doubt in your face and she's sensing that she's going to make you bolt before you can dunk your own cup! So try this for size: the missing place-name I'd omitted from Bellamy and Quayle's earlier quote of where the swirling broth from that great Wheel of the Tees once plunged over (and which the contents of Cow Green's wound still spill headlong over to this day) is, wait for it, the **Cauldron Snout**, a boiling waterfall of both staggering beauty and now equally staggering portent!

God, how it all just keeps on uncannily falling into place - of all the names to put at the pouring lip of this Grail wound! And admit, with such transparent evidence like this on the ground, who needs to be cunning? Certainly this is one of the most enchanting pieces of earth poetry yet encountered upon Albion, and one where any further words would be an insult to its succinct verse.

The only thing I will do is to once more tip you off that when we come to the last chapter and see what the land has prepared as its final farewell, this same wound will sing even sweeter.

Before we leave this incredible place, and while the night is still wonderfully deep around us, let's just hang around amid the sound of the Cauldron Wound's mighty outpouring over that crag of a Snout, surely now the most sanctified of all Albion's waterfalls. While we immerse ourselves in the rush of sound, let's kick around these last words of Bellamy and Quayle before they too bid farewell to Cow Green with not the vaguest idea of the significance of where they sat, though compelled enough by something in the atmosphere to write down these words: *"Cow Green is a good place to sit and reflect on all the other sacred Cow Greens in the world today and on the wise management of the resources of this earth"*.

My, how the goosebumps rush up my neck, but let us be on our way.

In all his phallic glory!

As perfect in both look and symbolism as this Dark Son's wound is to the one received by Jesus at Golgotha, we must remember that we have here the consort of the Goddess, so we should not be surprised to find some show of his rampant virility to prove it - but let me build up to revealing it!

We now walk away from the beautiful wound of the Moon Maiden's lover; her pockmarked orb is still lighting our way past the frosted fleeces of sleeping lambs, our breath like a troop of silver phantoms; and the waters of the river Tees, freshly tumbled from over that cauldron's snout, chatter at our side, for both company and guidance.

As we go, and to introduce what comes next, we ought very briefly to remind ourselves just how close the moon and the Great Mother were seen to be in more sensitive times. Remember how those lunar cycles actually animated their Mother - when the crescent moon hung sickle-like they saw her in the guise of the maiden, whereas at the time of the full moon she was seen as being in full and pregnant motherhood. When a darkening moon came around they knew she had reverted to the old wise woman, now withdrawing her lantern of wisdom and fertility beneath her black shawl, though knowing that this same lunar cycle would return her to a maid once more.

Quickening our step, and taking with us that word *lunar* as a talisman, we're led southeasterly by this wound's outpouring, through the pass of the black-pillared rocks of the Falcon Clints that once, they say, echoed to the squeal of the Golden Eagle; today it's the call of the equally exciting Merlin Falcon that ricochets here. But the falcons are roosting, so carry only the sound of these chasing waters which, in the poetry of the land, are a rivulet of her lover's blood; a dribble of the Goddess' milky water of life; a spillage from the

Cauldron of Rebirth, sunken in the wound of the Shadow Christ.

Nothing phallic in that, you might say - but just wait and see where this same flow finally takes us!

Jump across this bleeding of the Tees so that we may continue south by one of its connecting side streams, the Merrygill Beck, a continuation of the bloodline we're following and which in this moonlight, and from the window of a passing 747, really does seem like milk running thinly down this wild man's abdomen. Along this ribbon we go, past Cronkley Fell, to where a forest of pubic hair would not be out of place, for we're now standing just above this consort's genitals.

Pity then, that there isn't a forest here. But hold on, Albion doesn't let us down, for where we stand the map has marked, in unusually large capital letters, the name LUNE FOREST - even though there's no forest to be seen! Now whether there once was a great forest here, or just another of those medieval tracts of relatively open hunting land, though nevertheless still termed as a forest, really doesn't concern us - what *should* interest us is whether there is a hint of a lunar link. Lunedale and Lune Moor certainly support this as they dapple like moonbeams the groin of him who is the Lunar Maid's springtime lover and my hunch that there *is* something going on here glows even brighter when placing that name LUNE above the head of a certain lady called Luned.

Take a heathery seat in this glittering nightscaped wilderness, pull your collar up, tuck your knees under your chin, and listen to a snippet from our wondrous past, which may yet return.

The fountain at the axis of the world

Alluring name, I thought - Luned - especially when I saw how temptingly the name smiled out of *Lune*dale. I had never heard of the name until I came across it in the *Mabinogion's* tale of *The Lady of the Fountain*, but when I did - oh, how it was to light up this twin's groin with all sorts of sexual innuendo!

It turns out that Luned was the handmaiden (perhaps even the personification of the Goddess herself) at a sacred and magical fountain, a veritable fountain of youth, and to drink from it, I'd guess, was a virtual Grail experience. Certainly, such rejuvenating fountains were once a widespread motif suggestive of some rarefied place where either great knowledge or some other life-enhancing experience could be had. However, the most celebrated of all these fountains was believed to be the one that cascaded at the very centre of the world, or the Axis Mundi, the ultimate fording place between earth and heaven - a magical time-defeating crossroads where all knowledge was focused and made accessible to all who sought it. So, to put a cup to its sweet waters was to achieve a state of paradisal bliss whilst still being very much alive. It's not surprising then that the finding of its location became a quest within its own right.

Listen to Malcolm Godwin pour more wonders upon this same location: *"The Grail itself is partially a manifestation of the Axis Mundi. It is the point from which all directions are established. This also applies to time, for as all directions flow from this point, so, at the centre, all times occur simultaneously. Thus it could be said to possess youth-restoring properties."*

When I read that, I looked at the whole of Albion and saw in its gathering and overlapping of so many nations' myths and legends how, in a sense, time really has found a place to stay young for ever. For this is the place where the golden fleece is *still* hung upon the Argo's mast; here where Ceridwen *still* chases little Gwion at the moment he shape-shifts into a single seed of grain; and just look at that sword in the stone, see how it too *still* waits here as a rock-solid truth -

waiting to be pulled out into the brilliance of another golden age. And in seeing all this, and more, I couldn't resist wondering if all Albion is indeed that axis of the world, the centre of some planetary consciousness, a highly aware focal point where the Mother's focused will has whirled together a miraculous fording place where heaven meets earth and golden myth finds a physical retelling. Moreover, and because of those Lune names dappling this apex of a miracle, could this high point of Albion's almost triangular floor plan have once spouted Luned's Grail fountain - here, upon the land's own Green Man, the eternal guarantor of virility, fertility, regeneration, rejuvenation and resurrection?

Difficult to answer, that one, and yet it gets easier when hearing that that ultimate fountain stood beneath the Tree of Life. Look where that Lune forest is in conjunction with the surrounding images of Albion; see it nestled alongside that great tree's very own trunk, that trunk of the cross - Albion's own Tree of Life!

You're probably itching to ask if, at the spot identified with the name LUNE, there is some sign of an actual fountain in memory perhaps of the Lady Luned's fountain. Well, if you're looking for a classical thing with water-spouting mermen and the like, and a scattering of coins in the bottom, the answer is no. I'd hazard a guess that if ever the Axis Mundi was located here, any 'fountain' might be just a front for a far more meaningful object. Therefore, there may well be a far more fabulous 'kind of' fountain near where LUNE marks the map, albeit one that disappeared from sight and mind after a certain King Amangons committed one of the most lamentable mythological crimes ever. Later we'll hear just what he did, but for now let's get really phallic - we, who are 'lunatics all' to the rest of the sleeping world, but, hey, I hope you're having as much fun as I am!

Revealed - one hell of a phallic fountain!

OK, we've been darting around his 40plus-mile-tall body and checked off those labels that show how often he's been branded dark and scary, but as he is the Lord of the Underworld, this is exactly what we'd expect. And we've just collected further evidence that seems to hint at a relationship with Luned, the handmaiden at one of those fountains of rejuvenation, perhaps even the most sought after one of all. Indeed, because of her name's possible lunar link, she may, herself, even be the personification of the moon-guided Goddess (his lover). But if any doubt still remains as to exactly whom we're hiking over, we'll now stop beating about his pubic bush and zero in upon the main attribute of any Lord of Fertility!

So, stamp some life into those cold feet and let's be on our wonderfully moonlit way again. The river Tees and Merrygill Beck have done their job by bringing us from his wound and into this pubic Lune forest. Now we need to pick up another stream which, although not quite connecting to the Merrygill, is but a few strides away from doing so, and to my eye it is still part of that side wound's poetic outpouring. Arngill Beck is this new guide's laughing name - laughing, for its flow has been blessed to draw the left side of this naked twin's phallus - and what a phallus, the best part of four miles long! Moreover, the amazing sign-posts placed upon it will whisk us thousands of miles, from Cumbria to Greece, and from Egypt to India, and so full of the past's poetic veneration of fertility and regeneration will these signs be that one will be hard-pressed not to see this land-craft as both celebration and endorsement of our ancestral know-how of a sacred sexuality.

Let's then take a closer look at this naked consort's phallus - not a satanically plotted insult to the loin-clothed Jesus at his side, but rather an innocent token to the glory of life.

Thus after describing the whole left or east side of his phallus, this cunning Arngill Beck finishes its artistry at its very tip, at which point it is perfectly met by another merry beck, called the Long Grain, which draws the right side of the phallus. At the tip the two becks then combine as one flow and trickle away like a stream of urine. However, to interpret that flow in that way would be a tragic oversight, especially after taking a closer look at what the map has to say.

Spread that map out in the moonlight and use a fingertip to reaffirm how the streams that led us to the tip of this phallus seem to be trying to keep turning the eye back to that Cow Green wound. The obvious conclusion, then, is that their merged flows are meant to be seen as part of that Grail wound's outpouring, and because this same water of life (moon milk of Isis) goes on to pour from the very tip of the phallus, surely the message the land is trying to convey is that, far from urine, this spurt from the phallus is a continuance of that wound's own rejuvenating cascade of wisdom. It must, then, be logically decoded as a veritable stream of life, indeed, an ejaculation of semen - and what better to spurt from the Lord of Fertility! *Indeed, what better fountain motif to grace the axis of the fertile earth!*

You may at this point be thinking, 'Of course he wants to see the flow as sperm to validate his theory that this figure is a Lord of Regeneration.' But you don't have to take my word for it. Allow the land to speak for itself.

Found - that missing bit of Osiris!

Alright, I'm saying that we're now gathered before the lunar-lit phallus of the many-named Lord of Regeneration from whom cascades the water of life - but you need more proof. Well, Egypt can supply it.

We've already heard how, after the murder of Osiris, which led to him becoming another regenerative Lord of the Underworld, he was found encased within a tree by his wife and sister Isis. We know she eventually frees and rejuvenates his body from this incarceration by her own magic, but only so that Seth, his brother and murderer, can order the body to be destroyed once and for all by having it butchered into 14 pieces and these scattered to all points of the compass. Distraught, Isis then searches for the dismembered parts of her beloved and, bit by bit, finds and buries them with dignity where they were found, marking each burial with a shrine. However, there was one part of Osiris she didn't find, for his penis had been swallowed by, of all things, a fish.

Note: Osiris was butchered into 14 pieces - so do remind yourself that Albion just so happens to have 14 stations (or shrines) that make up its own body of wisdom.

Curious fish food, a phallus, wouldn't you say? Wouldn't it have been more dramatic if, say, some lion had scoffed it? Curious or not, though, I'm going to show you just how such a threatening piranha comes within snapping distance of this dark twin's willy. If you look back along the Arngill Beck side of his phallus you'll see that in the course of its cunning work it actually runs in and out of a very conspicuous lake, for, not only does it nudge the very side of this phallus, but carries too the name **Fish Lake** - and what's more it even has a good go at shaping itself into one too!

Charming coincidence, that of all things it's a fish that nudges this landscaped phallus? Or are we being told that the memory of Osiris really is honoured in the shape of this once globally acknowledged consort beneath our feet? Then, when one finds a possible memory of his lover Isis reflecting back from that flashing mirror of a lake wound upon his side, I can only reply, "Coincidence? Do me a favour!"

I had earlier suspected that Osiris might lurk in the soil beneath the figure of Jesus, but I had been turning a blind eye to what must be his very own portrayal in this Dark Twin. But was Osiris ever mentioned as being especially dark? Well, "Yes" to that too. Baring and Cashford write that, not only was he known as the *Great Green Thing*, but also as the *Great Black Thing*!

Osiris is then found whole again, not below the first Christ, but paired alongside him, both counter-balanced teachers, who share the same cross and the same right hand - a union which, in the next chapter, will become dazzlingly animated.

Of course, I gratefully took the finding of a fish nipping the side of this Lord's phallus as another almighty clue from the past that I was on the track of no devil, but only the life-loving consort of the Goddess who, in one incarnation, was named Osiris. However, vindication of whose phallus I'd found continued to gush. Why, it became such a flood of disarmingly descriptive imagery, so innocently shot through with love and life, that I have now not the slightest qualm about summing it up as intensely holy, even though such topics of a sacred sexuality would never be spoken of from a Sunday pulpit. No matter, from the banks of this stream-sculpted phallus, and beneath the moon set against the procession of the zodiac, it'll sound just beautiful.

To hear more of this tabooed sermon we'll now take a short stroll along this Lord's silvered ejaculation.

A bridge back to the sanctity of love and life

Join me now by following the combined flow of those two phallus-sculpting becks as they race away from its tip, an ejaculation that we'll soon see speeds beneath a small bridge and whose name shall give massive authorisation to the role I've said this wild man is playing in Albion's scheme of things. Indeed, when I found it I knew once more that I'd found no anti-life demon, but a pro love 'n' life daemon/demon!

In your imagination, join me on this lonely moonlit bridge that spans this Lord's spermy flow. For me, it is the most enchanting bridge in all the world, which some either gloriously *knowing*, or wonderfully unaware, contributor to Albion's wonder work named for this day of magical revelations as the **Grains o' th' Beck Bridge**.

Granted, at first glance, there's not much to get excited about, but when allied to the poetry underfoot, and to what our ancestors once believed, I assure you that it'll begin to sing the most gorgeous affirmation of the divinity of the life force and the particular giant underfoot; a song that shall become an all-embracing symphony centred around the theme of sacred sexuality - music forbidden in the West for nigh on 2000 years.

As honoured spectators upon this balcony beneath the stars, and with the consort's seed spurting beneath us, prepare to watch the root of our ancestral belief ripen in a shock of corn gold light that the great Osiris will walk through. His appearance is not due to the hand of a multitude of Egyptian navvies shipped in for a busman's holiday, but solely to the worms working in unison with the rains; to glacial movements working in harmony with the plough; all at the behest of God as a sign that what was once believed of Osiris, and other corn deities, should be as sacred to us as it was to earlier peoples - their value to our understanding of the God in ourselves is as profound as the guidance left by Jesus himself.

What is more, you'll now be left in no doubt that in netting that phallus-gulping fish we have, via innocently collecting the 14 parts of Albion, made Osiris, Lord of the Underworld, whole again and ready to retake the microphone - though not to speak of death but of life! life! life!

Now we've made him whole again let's watch his grains of truth sprout golden!

Leaning over our Grains o' th' Beck balcony we will watch something reflect back off that silver semen stream that would have been as recognisably holy to the Celt as it would have been to the ancients of Egypt, Greece, India, and, for all I know, to the wise of many other cultures too.

The first image that flashes back comes when hearing how the women of ancient Greece would plant alongside the scattered grain miniature ceramic phalluses, in symbolic gesture of guaranteeing the fertility of the crop. From another glint, my suggestion that this stream is an allegory for the ejaculation of a nature god seems to receive a flashing confirmation - this time from India. Shiva, India's own god of fertility, himself unashamedly naked, would ejaculate his life-giving seed into that holy river Ganges to fertilise his bride, the earth. Alain Danielou in his book *The Phallus*, states that even today in some Hindu rites a sperm substitute is concocted and poured upon the soil in portrayal of such seeding of the Mother; this libation being made from *rainwater* mixed with rice *grains*.

Thus, if water + grains = the poetic sperm of the earth's lover, I say check out again where we stand. Before us a phallus, half-sculpted by the water craft of the Long *Grain* Beck, and then, for good measure, this same stream finally ejaculated from its creation by way of speeding beneath this bridge they call The *Grains* o' th' Beck, and I ask who can't be intrigued by it all? However, this same fertile poetry gets even easier to add up when we return to Osiris' Egypt - and so it should, seeing that he's lying before us! Get ready then to break the silence of this night with another whoop of delight that might even carry to the banks of the Nile!

The whoop begins to build up when we hear how each year, Osiris would be invoked to push the new wheat back up through the crust of the earth (his own body) from his realms in the underworld. Naturally enough, such regeneration of the land was correlated to the resurrection of the dead, who, like the sprouting grain, were seen as being guided back from out of the dark realms by Osiris. To guarantee this life anew, beautiful tokens of the ever-returning Osiris would be placed with the dead by their mourners.

Frazer's *The Golden Bough* mentions some lovely 'homemade' examples of such tomb offerings, and for me these are far more beautiful than any effigies of gold, for although worthless they were imbued with the poetically priceless potency to sprout life long after the tomb had been sealed.

However, the first example I'd like to mention was somewhat more sophisticated than the 'homemade' variety we'll hear of next. The tomb in question was that of a royal fan bearer and dated from 1500 BC. Inside, a linen-covered mattress was found onto which had been painted a life-size image of Osiris. And although the bed itself was doubtless wonderful, there was a greater beauty to come: within the reeded rib cage of that mattress, a damp vegetable mould had been packed and impregnated with *barley seeds*, which the archeologists could see had actually sprouted in the dark of the tomb in an attempt to break through the outer image of the god, in a splendid token of resurrection.

What a lovely gesture this was, although there is even more to fascinate us, standing, as we suspect, between this god's legs. Indeed, it seems that the earth is saying that in these simple poetic tokens of the ancient Egyptians there was something of profound and holy worth, and that life and the spirituality of those peoples who practised such beliefs bloomed the better for it.

Those smaller, homemade offerings, found in many other tombs of lesser stature, were made by again using dampened vegetable matter, and squeezed into the very basic shape of small green doll effigies of Osiris. These, too, were studded with *seeds of grain* in the hope that they would sprout after the tomb had been sealed. But best of all, guess where Frazer states these tokens of everlasting life were always placed in relation to the corpse? Answer, **between the legs**, indeed, the *exact and doubly grain-underlined location* where we now stand watching such ancient imagery burst new and golden before us!

To seal the whole scene before us as another series of interrelating myths made stunningly one and recorded in the landscape, let me now tell you the name of the stream which spurts from that phallus. This water that shoots beneath our feet upon this magical viewing platform of the Grains o' th' Beck bridge is the **River Lune** - ring a bell does it? It should do!

So come on down, Luned, handmaiden and probable personification of the Goddess at the Grail fountain of rejuvenation! And as the pennies drop, surely they stack up to the disarming fact that we could well be standing before the enchanting truth behind her fountain, in the shape of this moonlit and cascading phallus of Luned's consort! Add to this the observation that the River Lune is, in essence, Isis' moon milk falling from out of that cauldron or Grail side wound, and you're also witnessing in this ejaculation a visual continuance of those very same waters of life, of resurrection, of rebirth, along with all the wisdom that can make such a reality. Now tell me, what better source could there be to supply the fountain of eternal youth or indeed the phallus of the Lord of Regeneration!

Incredible isn't it - but even this isn't all. If Osiris really does account for a layer of this particular giant's make-up, and if you feel easy with his orgasm of grain-rich semen, then get this too: another name under which Isis was known was the *Lady of Bread*. So, who cannot see this Consort's grainy ejaculation as

having *her* **name written upon it** as clear as any DNA proof could give as to who we've found at the height of Albion's near pyramidal pile of stars! Indeed, if Luned herself was another name of the Mother, we can see double verification in that River Lune of whom this ejaculation is targeted for - the many-named Great Goddess!

When I also float upon these magically fertile waters Baring and Cashford's reference to Horus (the child born of Osiris and Isis) I think it really is message received and entirely understood: *"The new life in the grain is the child of them both."*

I find the seemingly phallic truth behind that ultimate fountain at the Axis Mundi divinely disarming! Here is no streak of devil's piss but the *'spurting to the glory of life everlasting'* seed of the land's Lover. As we look down from our little bridge, see how we are all reflected in it.

And does all this amount to some Eucharist of the land?

What with the Lady of Bread being written all over this Lord's grainy orgasm, which is linked via other streams directly to his side wound - are we now getting a picture which prompts further thoughts? The combined imagery of blood becoming a water of life, indeed a poetic wine, and this crucified Lord's sperm carrying the overlay of grain may be inviting us to share in some kind of Eucharist; is it an invitation to partake of his body of wisdom? Are we being urged to dip the Highest Cup into this stream and have it brimming over with the very same as Jesus offered to his disciples at the end of the Last Supper - a culmination of all the wisdom one needs to acquire a life eternal?

A few more pleasantly phallic findings

It's all so magical: the possibility of cups being filled, and we, standing at the tip of a fountain-like phallus, being poetically showered by such enthralling possibilities. So, glance to your right towards that twinkling light of a lonely farmhouse, once a wayside tavern that bore the same name as the bridge upon which we stand. At that time it would have been a watering place for all who thirsted in the wilderness, and how charmingly apt if once upon another time this place had been recognised as the delightful end of the quest for those who sought Luned's fountain.

With a beer on my mind I now flit back to that place name, Lunedale, and wonder if it cheekily remembers the once fabulous potency of *Luned's ale* that spurted from her lover, the rustic Christ in the landscape!

"Vulgar!" I still hear some cry, at my poetic suggestions of drinking from a phallus. To this I would only express sadness though, for you have obviously learned nothing from the innocence that is Albion.

Reading Albion is an art in its own right and I do not claim to have a degree in it. However, for anyone who may think that my reading of a phallus in the landscape is sure sign that I am indeed insane, my grin nevertheless remains. Indeed, it gives way to a schoolboy guffaw when my eyes drop just to the side of where I say it swings in the moonlight: the place name is Cocklake Side - and who, knowing what we know now, can't read that as *a lake by the side of the cock*?

But then the smile is wiped off my face

Joking apart, I firmly believe that the map's blatant overlapping of semen and grain might be far more than the simple endorsement of the wisdom behind ancient fertility beliefs. Certainly, we've already seen, under Virgo, how a sperm and any seed with its taproot are visually very much alike. Virgo's forceful pointing to that grain or sperm-shaped Bardsey Island has me wondering whether, in this whole grain-overlapping sperm riddle, there is

as much warning as there is celebration. I'm even more convinced that such is the case when seeing that this imagery has been provocatively hammered to the very mast of the life-preserving ark itself, and I wonder whether something I heard while pondering on this very point might be getting close to the nub of such a warning.

A friend of mine, who'd read a newspaper report, alerted me to the sickening news that an American company, involved in genetic research, had developed some new wonder-strain of wheat which it planned to market in third-world countries. However, the sting in the tail of this deal was that once the third-world farmer had harvested his new crop, he could not keep any of the seed back for replanting, for the cunning company involved had genetically 'doctored' the grain seed so that it would actually render itself totally infertile for another crop: the first grain seed ever to purposely terminate itself at the point of it turning gold. Thus the phallus of this Osiris in the landscape would, in the poetic mirror, spout no life, only impotent blanks!

Likewise, in our tampering with sperm in laboratory bottles, and the now not too far-fetched prospect of couples ordering up a Beethoven with blue eyes, there may be similar warnings that we are near to committing some profound and irreparable crime against the universal law of life - a final upsetting of the harmonies that make it all possible.

With thoughts like these, I think it's time we dug through into another layer of this giant's mythological character, where we may find ourselves paying a visit to a very sick man. Indeed, we may even find that in this sandwich of global consorts, the land has made this character the one at the top of the pile.

Hail the King!

We must now leave our wondrous little bridge of grain between the legs of Osiris by following its sacred under-flow away from the phallus. Luned's water of life (the River Lune) now leads us east and down to his thighs, where the horizon is showing the first hint of the radiance that heralds the dawn. Quickly now, for we *must* witness the last unfoldings of this twin's secrets amid the beautiful half light, that twilit 'inbetween time', when night and day, dark and light, embrace and hang in each other's arms as equals for a few fleeting moments just before either sunset or sunrise.

As we go, add up the simple face-value of the signs now coming into view upon the left thigh of the twilight world's own Lord. Start by considering this: if the lake of Cow Green is topographically assigned as a wound, surely it's logical to equate any other lakes upon his body as further wounds. If you agree, see how our guiding River Lune has just filled two more gashes in a line, those of Selset and Grassholme reservoirs. Notice, too, directly opposite us, upon the right thigh another row of wicked watery wounds: Balderhead, Blacton, and Hury are their own injurious names.

Note: Balder, by the way, was a Viking nature god, and so well-loved was he that, upon his murder, even the rocks cried!

So just who the heck is this giant underfoot? At first I said he was some symbolically wild John the Baptist, the down-to-earth/Yin cousin of a perhaps more heavenly or Yang-orientated Jesus, presumably to balance the mystic books. Then it was a conglomeration of an Osiris-Mithras-Dionysus-like consort/Son of the Mother that we had a strong body of evidence for. But then our eyes have to go and drop upon these terrible thigh wounds and have to concede that neither John, nor Osiris, nor any of those other corn gods, nor for that matter even Jesus himself, were reported to have suffered such distinctive wounding.

Albion is, however, a hall of mirrors and many myths from many cultures have

seemingly come here to reflect back as the one message they perhaps always were, and whenever I've met with a perplexing reflection shining back at me I've often found it helpful to return to Britain's own mythological heritage in the hope of finding a more focused decipherment. Accordingly then, let's go back to the medieval romances of the Grail to try to find a further ID for this now profusely bleeding man; these tales being so intimate to British soil and already an absolute boon in helping to translate much of this vast conundrum. And wouldn't it be good if we could start by finding someone within those homespun legends who was perhaps also underscored as the consort? Pushing our luck? Not at all!

Without further ado then, let's follow this scent of blood to the Grail's Rich Fisher King, for no one else in those romances bled quite like him! What's more, once we have pinned this slippery character down we're going to be within a whisker of achieving the Grail itself, for let me tell you that he was also that cup's guardian as it was known to materialise within the halls of his castle - thus find him, find the Grail! But hold your horses! That Grail-questing knight clever enough to have found the Fisher King's castle had then to ask a certain question of the king regarding the nature of his obviously mystical wounds - wounds which, although not life-threatening, bled incessantly for years. Indeed, to ask why those wounds bled so, would not only heal them but also healed the so-called surrounding wasteland - and don't let that obvious link of the health of the king/consort being synonymous with that of the land pass you by! The reward for the asker of that vital question, however, was the achieving of that Holy Cup, in short, self enlightenment.

Hence I think it's time we too began asking some searching questions of his wounds, and we'll begin by inquiring after what may have been their primary cause.

The great desecration

Buried in the human psyche there really does seem to flicker for some a sense, however nebulous, of a once paradisal time that came to an abrupt and cataclysmic end, triggered by some profound wrongdoing of mankind.

I've heard it said that some collective unconscious memory of the sinking of Atlantis could be the truth behind this twilit sense of loss, indeed, even the paradise found-and-lost story of Adam and Eve could itself be but the poetical flotsam and jetsam from the same catastrophe. Certainly, there are many tales from around the world that carry similar traces of some sunken golden age.

Perhaps from this same collective unconscious memory came those tales of when man lived in greater harmony with his surroundings, and nature responded by revealing sacred springs, wells and fountains. Again, anyone who drank from them would find that the veil that separated heaven and earth would dissolve - and I presume that that fountain in Luned's care was such a place. However, as quickly as Atlantis disappeared beneath the waves, so these fording places between heaven and earth also retreated beyond man's perception - and this in response to a terrible crime.

Enter now King Amangons, who I mentioned earlier.

It seems that these rarefied locations were all attended by the Earth Mother's own handmaidens, these, her personifications, being virgins and revered as such. But as is the way of men, there came along one day a certain King Amangons who had no such sense of sanctity or respect for either place or lady, and raped the first fountain maiden he found; a crime compounded by many other men who suddenly felt free to follow the king's example. We're told that the result of these defilements left the fountains dry, the wells rank and the maidens bleeding at every similar site. As a consequence the state of paradise shrank back from the fields like a tide that did not return. Almost overnight the earth lost a gleam of wonder that we of today cannot conceive of, and that which was left became known, by those who perceived the loss, as simply the Wasteland - the same place where we reside today. And boy, how we still fuel that ill-borne title!

Mirrored impotence

The rape of the handmaidens and the resulting gulf set between heaven and earth, man and consciousness of his own divinity, was also to be mirrored back upon him who, in the medieval author's mind, was at the time recognised as the king with the strongest affinity to the land herself, her consort no less. It was, therefore, unavoidable that the Rich Fisher King would receive a crippling wound whose bleeding could not be staunched. Understandably too, because the land had lost its vigour, the rumour was that this wound had been inflicted upon the consort's genitals (again very Osiris-like) and thus rendered him impotent.

But I reckon that wounding could have gone far deeper than even this.

Think about it: because man is also in essence *one* with the land, could the king's wound also reflect back upon all forthcoming generations until Amangons' crime could somehow be undone - the natural law of mirrors, I believe! If so, how we daily exacerbate this blighting two-way chain reaction by perpetuating Amangons' ignorance. And sure, although none of us literally bleed in sympathy with the Fisher King, I wonder if we mirror him in the leaking away of some essential perceptual skills, this dulling of our awareness, not only to our own divinity but to that same divinity which exists in all things around us; today that leakage might have become a torrent. Needless to say the blinder we get, the greater that torrent; the greater that torrent, the faster the undermining of the whole creation - and guess what, even that ongoing decline gets likewise reflected back in myriad ways upon us. Again, that law of mirrors!

Of course, the corn still comes through, swallows still return with warmer weather and folk still happily reproduce; why, our life spans are even getting longer! But in that perpetually repeated crime of Amangons I must also ask if a slow, seeping damage on a myriad levels has been set into almost unstoppable motion - are we, in fact, partying on borrowed time? I think many today sense the cracks under the pretty paper. Amangons' wrongdoing, I suspect, was but a mythological cloaking of the truer reason for the evaporation of paradise, more likely due to some mass turning away of mankind from the reverencing of the Mother Earth. And from this stemmed the general dulling of the perception that had hitherto seen wonders of which we, the inheritors and continuing propagators of the wasteland, are today unable to comprehend. But then I see Albion! Perhaps all is not lost.

Simply (and we've been suspecting this ever since Gemini, and certainly under Scorpio), the natural law may insist that what we give out is what we shall receive: mistreat the land, view it as a commodity, see no divinity in it, and not only does the land become dis-eased and unbalanced, but the perceiver does also; existence but a shadow of the gift it should have been. Therefore, and in true mirror-like fashion, the wound was, and still is, perhaps self-perpetuating throughout every aware atom of creation - and this replicated scarring forever spurred on by the blindness of generation after generation.

Anyway, the legends predicted that this wasting condition of both land and king (and, of course, mankind too) would continue until a time when that inquiring and perceptive Grail knight (and perhaps, ultimately, all mankind) would come and by his questions unblock the sacred fountains and springs. These questions, it was said, would simultaneously heal the Fisher King's wounds and free paradise to surge back into the perception of all those who thirsted, like a great tide cleansing and healing all that it overran, leaving everything re-enchanted.

Alas, the planet has been waiting so long for men and women *en masse* to ask the correct questions that not even the chroniclers of the Grail legends could conceive of the consequences. They couldn't imagine that our continued blindness to our relationship with nature would become so profound that the time would come when we could, without a moral care, turn our cattle into virtual carnivores by feeding them the carcasses of crushed sheep; could even feed pigs to pigs and chickens with their own shit and feathers - and then feed the lot to ourselves! These medieval chroniclers would also never have comprehended that such gross disharmonies could be committed that eventually they would cause a hole to be burnt out of the sky, through which the sun's rays would fall on the heads of folk and leave their skins blotched with cancers.

*Note: why even that name Amangons could well be itself but shorthand for **a man** - though representative of millions.*

Lifting the king's robes!

But I was speaking of the Fisher King's own wounds and we now need to lift his robes and take a peek at where exactly they are.

Now, if we see lakes as implying blood-filled wounds on this giant underfoot, that fish lake upon his phallus becomes an even clearer signpost to affirming, not only Osiris' own loss of potency, but also to that rumoured wounding of the Fisher King. Indeed, doesn't even the name of this particular wound (fish) more than hint at the actual name of the character nearest the top of this pile of consorts? But don't make your mind up just yet.

"*OK, but if lakes are wounds, what are those we've just found upon his thighs?*" - is the obvious next question. In answer, we're told that other reports of this king's grievous wounds placed them **upon his thighs!**

Can you believe it!

It seems then that we can't put a foot wrong upon this incredible body of evidence. We've got two accounts of the mythological maiming to the Fisher King; one says it was the genitals that took the blow, while the other, more curiously, points to his thighs; yet evidence of both *is* to be found both graphically and anatomically accurately reflected off Albion's land mirror. However, the gob-smacking evidence does not end here, for what if I told you of another rumour as to the manner of this king's injury, and, as unique as this new allegation may sound, I could also confirm its painful presence on the map as being bang on correct? The word on the streets had it that a piece of *iron* had somehow got lodged in his testicles/phallus/groin area, another obvious blighting of his virility.

Well, as amazing as it may seem, at the top of this Shadow Christ's right thigh, and a mere two miles from the tender area of his genitals (on this scale but a gnat's whisker away), there's a prominent high peak, the highest around, which is painfully emblazoned with the name of **Iron Band!**

If an 'iron band' had appeared on the head of Aries or the bare rump of Virgo, it would have meant absolutely 'zilch', yet lodged here in the groin area of this particular giant, it means plenty. It means we have lifted the green mantle of the land and caught the last elusive fish of Albion, the enigmatic Rich Fisher King, now established as another succulent slice of the whole gorgeously mythological sandwich which is Albion. Moreover, he must also be a pointer to the fact that here, near the end of our journey, the Grail, the essence of all we've

seen, is ready to materialise, but only if we can now ask nature, and in particular this communicative isle of Albion, all the right questions. By just looking at the map with new eyes those questions might already be forming.

And we must ask these questions before the zodiacal clock strikes twelve!

Curiosity, however, still urged me to ask "Why *iron?*" So I looked for help from Robert Bly's book *Iron John - A Book about Men*, a work plumbing the depths of the lost male psyche, and where I'd already found word of the above iron-related wound.

Bly goes on to point out that, in fairy stories, iron was usually associated with the imprisonment of men, whereas glass had the same effect upon women. He fascinated me further by quoting from the Brothers Grimm tale of *The Water of Life* in which a young man (Grail knight?) has to pass through many trials in his quest to bring back the water of life to heal his sick father (the Fisher King perhaps?). A princess then tells the lad where to find the fountain (to me all very Lady Luned-like) but advises that he must draw the water before the clock strikes 12 o'clock. Anyway, he accomplishes his task in the nick of time and with a bucket full of the precious water beats a retreat, but, so the story goes: "*...just as he was passing through the* **iron** *gate the clock struck 12 and the gate slammed with such force that it took off a piece of his heel.*"

Enthralled, though still none the wiser as to why iron, I sent my eye again roving around that phallus in the landscape. I was still wondering whether the truth behind those fabled waters of life was in the fountain-like spouting of the River Lune. What I found there would again defy coincidence. Just two miles downhill from that peak of Iron Band is a wayside marker with the absurdly rewarding name of **Swinging Gate!** Again, don't ask me what the hell it all means, for I am as breathless at the sight of its provocative entry into the scheme of things as that young man was to get through it on time! And who wouldn't be breathless after running two miles with a bucket of water?

But why do I throw in that *two miles* - for the brothers Grimm make no mention of distance? Well, it's also the distance from the tip of Albion's phallic fountain, from where the lad might have filled his bucket with the waters of life, to that Swinging Gate at the base of Iron Band. And he can only just have been on time, because this reanimated scene just so happens to be placed at the 12 o'clock high station on Albion's zodiacal clock! Uncanny isn't it?

I would dearly have loved to question those not-so-Grimm reapers of a field or two of Albion's gold. Or then again, were they too just unsuspecting helpers of Albion - recording what they thought was an original yarn, yet one being breathed out by a landscape in readiness for that time when the myth would be found to be land-sculpted into a gigantic truth? We'll never know of course, and what's more, we don't need to know - just enjoy!

Incredibly, we have accounted for all the Fisher King's mystic wounds, from genitals to thighs; all of them explicitly and accurately marked upon this Dark Twin as astonishing evidence of how he once showed himself to another age. Indeed, the wounds are so unique to that medieval version of the consort that, like dental records, one cannot fail to accurately identify the body from them. Though having said that, there is still that side wound to account for, and although I've found no mention of the Fisher King having suffered such an injury, what I did discover only added to my simmering fascination. You see, it's also recorded that the Fisher King received his wounds from the lance of Longinus, the very same one that the centurion used to pierce the side of Jesus while he hung upon the cross, and from where also poured blood and water.

My, how these twins share each other's pains!

Scotland's lake of learning?

While we are still gathered at the shore of these wound-like lakes, glinting upon the loins of this giant, how would you like to hear about a dream a Grail-questing knight once had, and wherein Jesus appears to wash himself in a lake which, wait for it, welled out of the loins of a king? Interested? So was I!

Before you hear it, here's a history lesson: did you know that Hadrian's Wall has not always marked the border between England and Scotland, and that the border was once the best part of 40 miles further into England? I didn't, but upon finding this out my first thoughts were that the bulk of these twins is upon previously Scottish soil, hitherto conspicuously left out of Albion's magic garden. Anyway, armed with this snippet, we can return to the dream as recorded by our old friend Walter Map in the *Queste del Saint Graal*.

According to Walter it was a certain highly-honoured Celydoine whom Christ sent to become the first Christian King of Scotland, and whom Sir Lancelot now sees (and I can only assume in gigantic topographical form) in a surreal Grail dream, this figure: *"...all set about by stars"* - those field-fallen ones of Albion, I wonder? And when reading the following who wouldn't start putting two and two together big-time: *"...a great lake which welled from out of his loins."*

Don't blame me for getting all hyper when reading things like this, especially when seeing that this particular giant that we're standing upon is a king stretched out on previously Scottish territory, and who is welling lakes aplenty from his loins; not to mention being all set about by stars to boot! Let's face it, these are not an everyday coupling of features! But let's hear the rest of that dream before you judge whether my excitement was warranted.

Lancelot then sees nine rivers flowing from out of this same lake and then: *"...a man came down from heaven, in outward sign and* feature like Our Lord. When he had come to the lake he washed his hands and feet in it and in the rivers one by one, and when he came to the ninth he washed his hands and feet and whole body."

The knight later relates the entire dream to a wise hermit who advises that this Scottish King Celydoine is: "...the son of Nascien, whom Our Lord sent to this land to confound and crush the unbelievers. This man was verily a servant of Jesus Christ and God's true knight. He knew as much as the philosophers, or more, about the course of the stars and planets and the laws that govern the firmament."

Mystically weird and wonderful for sure, but don't we moonlit ramblers feel on tremendously familiar ground again, especially when the wise hermit goes on: "He was a very lake of learning and of science in which the fisher after truth might find the principles and moving force of the divine ordinance."

Wow, is not all of this bewilderingly juicy when juxtaposed to what we see of this Dark Twin's body of evidence? And would a 'fisher after truth', standing upon this lake-sprinkled Fisher King realise the beautiful force that has created such a fabulously divine thing from out of the Ordnance Survey map of Britain?

It is also enticing to ask whether, when Jesus bathed in that lake's waters, it was a gesture, not only of the wisdom he gleaned from finding this giant in a landscape, but also a sign and seal that they were in truth reunited as the blood brothers they really were? If so, and if this Celydoine really was but a romantic front for the King of Nature we're journeying upon - you too can now go and bathe in the same!

*Note: one wonders if Jesus did find the Fisher King, whether he then, in a sense, took on the mantle of that Grail king. This would fit in with what is sometimes suggested in the Grail romances, namely that the Grail-achieving knight then took over the Fisher King's guardianship of the cup. So could Jesus himself be the ultimate Fisher King whom we must now all find? Intriguing, too, how the symbol of the fish was to become so associated with the Christ.

Find the place where Bran's head once was, and you might find the Fisher King in residence

Staying with 'lakes of learning', the following could also prove interesting for us now musing on the banks of one particular thigh wound.

Researchers into what could have been earlier sources of inspiration behind the Grail romances and their characters are pretty convinced that the Mabinogion supplied a lot of the detail. As far as the role of the Fisher King is concerned, it is felt that the giant Bran the Blessed (we met him under Sagittarius) might have been the prototype, Bran being not only a former keeper of the Grail in the shape of its earlier incarnation as the cauldron, but also receiver of an eventually fatal wound, albeit to his heel, the same as the boy received when passing through the swinging gate.

On face value, however, I always thought this tie-up a touch flimsy, but let's see what the land has to say about it.

Anyway, when Bran was dying from his battle wound (incidentally, received from the Irish/Scorpio!) he asked his loyal band of warriors to sever his head so that at least that part of him would, for a while after, magically continue to give verbal succour to his peoples. He asked them to carry his head to a small island called Gwales, where they alone would find a palace wherein time would stand still, and for a period a state of bliss would settle on this battle-weary group. Thus, Bran's own miraculously talking head became, for a time, a veritable replacement of the Cauldron of Inspiration, which had been destroyed in that same battle in Ireland, and Gwales was the place chosen to host this Grail-like experience.

"*So where is this Gwales?*" we ask. The thought is that it is the island of Grasholm off the Pembrokeshire coast, and you might be intrigued to know that, over 200 miles away to the northeast, one of this Fisher King's reservoir thigh wounds, now flashing in our faces, is called **Grassholme**! Why, we've even found Bran's cauldron, in the shape of that Great Wheel of the Tees, submerged but still present in this king's side wound! And, by the way, guess where Bran said he found that cauldron in the first place? *In a lake*! It had belonged to the gigantic mother and her son! Sorry for all these exclamation marks!

But that's not all the evidence that points to Bran's presence around this giant. In Welsh, the name Bran means either 'crow' or '*raven*'. Look over your shoulder then and into this wild twin's already raven-labelled eyes!

Suffice to say that where you find blood-stained Grassholme, the raven-eyed head of Raven Bran must also be near; and this is another sign that the cauldron/Grail quest must be at boiling point!

His mission half accomplished

If Jesus' gesture of washing in his giant twin's lake wound ever occurred (or is still to occur) Jesus could not have been more forthright in demonstrating that this twin was a blood-brother, one whom he had perhaps found again in the wilderness (a wilderness that may be partly allegorical of the disharmony ensuing from man's lost kinship to nature) and in doing so he had reconciled the high and low of his own dual nature. I think also that this washing, an act akin to Thomas' own touching into Jesus' wounds, could be encouragement for all to follow suit - to acknowledge the absolute truth of a Super-Nature, Albion's miracle being the sublime eternal proof of the divinity residing throughout the entire creation, and personified in this consort of the land.

When speculating upon Jesus having a need to find some wild side of his nature, like Thomas, I applied sharp and doubting brakes many times to what could have been my over-active intuition. It was, therefore, most comforting to find encouragement spoken by India's own Lord of Fertility, Shiva. I'd like to think that his words are spoken on behalf of all who are wrapped here in the land's green-blanketed amalgam of sons of the soil and that we should add more names to those already listed, so not only Shiva, but Hermes, Cernunnos, Enkidu, Priapus, Herne the Hunter and of course Pan, he from whom the word *panic* first sprang! All of these are lords of vegetation and good shepherds of the beasts, but most of all lovers of life itself. So hear all of them, through Shiva's voice, firing-up the artist (and calming down the rabbit!) with the confidence that his landscape-led eye is not so mad after all: "*I am Lord of the animals. It is not degenerate to recognise one's 'animal'. Only those who practise the rites of the brothers to the beasts, the 'pashupata', can surpass their animal nature.*" And, can I add on to the end of that: "*...and become truly gods on earth*" just as Jesus became.

Shiva thus underlines that, without first being united with the great underworld of nature, we may never really know how high we can fly. Through the intermediacy of nature, as this miracle of Albion surely shows, *is* the doorway to the buried God, not only in nature but deep within ourselves, and Jesus' washing in this giant's wound, albeit only in someone's dream, would seem to visually underwrite Shiva's advice.

I believe that Jesus' own efforts in acquiring the sense of his own holy wild other-half would have been the main object of his journey to this whole miracle in the landscape, or 'wilderness' if you like. Thus when Jesus either stepped out of that gaping mouth of Cetus the whale (*see Pisces*) or came dripping out of his wild twin's lake wound, he could have, under Shiva's guidance, grasped in spirit his brother's fur and feathered hand and in doing so became tinglingly aware that he was now brother and sister to every tree, fox and even stone. He could converse with hawk or wolf, or hang in sublime limbo within the preparation of sweet scents and blueness gathering within a bluebell bulb in February. And in this reconciliation with nature I believe he may have been halfway to becoming a dancing God-Man; in experiencing the holy depths, he had completed half of his mission in acquiring the consciousness of a Christ.

This same experience could now be open to us all. It is indeed a pity we didn't take up the offer when made so passionately two years prior to 1914's expansion of the wasteland, by James Stephens in his hauntingly beautiful piece of fiction-touching-upon-truth book *The Crock of Gold*.

Between the lines of this curious work, I feel this same wild son made a plea for us to face him and learn to truly love our existence. Alas the plea was all too soon answered by cries that stretched from the Somme to Hiroshima, and indeed ever since to the tune of men behaving like no animal ever could. And so I want to let Stephens' own voice of the pleading wilderness run free across these my own pages.

In the following piece it is devil-branded Pan who beseeches a shepherdess to acknowledge his innocent presence, and thus her own holy wild nature. If you listen hard enough, though, the same words can now be caught on the breeze, rolling out of his mouth of meadow flowers and mire which is Melmerby, and it's you he beseeches to look him in the raven eye and know yourself.

★ ★ ★ ★ ★

"I am afraid of you," said the girl.

"You fear me because my legs are shaggy like the legs of a goat. Look at them well, O Maiden, and know that they are indeed the legs of a beast and then you will not be afraid any more. Do you not love beasts? Surely you should love them, for they yearn to you humbly or fiercely, craving your hand upon their heads as I do. If I were not fashioned thus I would not come to you because I would not need you. Man is a god and a brute. He aspires to the stars with his head but his feet are contented in the grasses of the field, and when he forsakes the brute upon which he stands then there will be no more men and no more women and the immortal gods will blow this

world away like smoke."

"I don't know what you want me to do," said the girl.

"I want you to want me. I want you to forget right and wrong; to be happy as the beasts, as careless as the flowers and the birds. To live to the depths of your nature as well as to the heights. Truly there are stars in the heights and they will be a garland for your forehead. But the depths are equal to the heights. <u>*Wondrous deep are the depths, very fertile is the lowest deep. There are stars there also, brighter than the stars on high. The name of the heights is Wisdom and the name of the depths is Love. How shall they come together and be fruitful if you do not plunge deeply and fearlessly?*</u> *Wisdom is the spirit and the wings of the spirit, Love is the shaggy beast that goes down. Gallantly he dives, below thought, beyond Wisdom, to rise again as high above these as he had first descended. Wisdom is righteous and clean, but Love is unclean and holy. I sing of the beast and the descent: the great unclean purging itself in fire: the thought that is not born in the measure or the ice or the head, but in the feet and the hot blood and the pulse of fury.* **The Crown of Life is not lodged in the sun: the wise gods have buried it deeply where the thoughtful will not find it, nor the good: but the Gay Ones, the Adventurous Ones, the Careless Plungers, they will bring it to the wise and astonish them.** *All things are seen in the light - How shall we value that which is easy to see? But the precious things which are hidden, they will be more precious for our search: they will be beautiful with our sorrow: they will be noble because of our desire for them. Come away with me, Shepherd Girl, through the fields, and we will be careless and happy, and we will leave thought to find us when it can, for that is the duty of thought, and it is more anxious to discover us than we are to be found."*

So Caitilin Ni Murrachu arose and went with him through the fields, and she did not go *with him because of love, nor because his words had been understood by her, but only because he was naked and unashamed.*

★ ★ ★ ★ ★

I do not apologise for quoting that lengthy discourse between Pan and a young maiden for I feel its wisdom song, no matter where Stephens first heard its ravishing sound, is the quintessence of all that Albion beseeches.

Accept then that this twin, however you name him, is one half of *you* - accept and begin to reclaim the full and magical potential of your physical existence, your oneness with nature. Allow him now to take your left hand and lead you through *your* realm of an earthly paradise. Like a laughing child allow him to teach you again what shivering bliss it is to sensuously unwind as a fern frond in May time; to fly at the tip of an arrowhead flight of honking migratory geese against a massive autumnal sunset; or know what dreams bears have in their winter sleep - for such I think could be even *more* than half-way towards reclaiming the consciousness of a Christ.

Who then, after finally recognising the God in themselves, and existing in even the most minuscule particle of the creation, would allow an atomic test blast to turn the seabed to slop, an animal to be used in laboratory testing, or one gene to be manipulated with only 'good business' as the prime motivation behind doing so? I think it is maybe now imperative, due to the accelerating danger our protracted ignorance is placing the whole planet in, for all mankind to be ushered towards some whole new perception of our existence before it is too late; and for this cause, I think, Albion has arrived.

But coming back to Lancelot's dream, whether it has anything to do with Albion's ground plan or not, I still put it to you that the land's placement of Jesus and this cloven-footed fellow upon the same cross and, in particular, their sharing of that same right hand, is as forthright a gesture as any washing in wounds could be. I think this pairing on the cross is *meant* to be shocking and I think that the land is telling us that this mixing of the Yin and Yang at Golgotha culminated in some tumultuous and magnificent crescendo, resulting there and then in the metamorphosis of a man into a God-Man. Thus, contrary to what the Bible has told of that afternoon, it might have been that within Jesus was as much ecstasy as agony. Instead of his body slumped, there was a body somehow imperceptibly dancing throughout its every cell; and rather than a man dying, there was one being literally born again within that same body - though for heaven's sake please don't confuse this '*being born again*' with today's in-vogue Christian expression!

However, to follow through this theory, that I'm sure the land is willing us to accept before we reach the splendour of the gift it's got waiting for us at journey's end, we must become one of those 'careless plungers', earlier recommended by Pan himself, for the rational thinker has absolutely no chance of following where we go next.

Notes: legend has it that at the exact moment Jesus was supposed to have died upon the cross, Pan also died! This exciting snippet for us, contemplating Jesus and Pan upon the same cross stems from a tale about a seafarer off the coast of Italy who heard a voice exclaim at that moment when blackness engulfed Golgotha: "Tell them that Great Pan is dead!" - a shout that was followed by a global weeping.

It is interesting too that Hermes, previously mentioned in the list of blackened twins, was the god of thieves - so perhaps this is a further hint that the robber who went to paradise with Christ was all the time representative of a god, albeit of the underworld?

Building up to a colour-coded Metamorphosis

It was while I was upon my first mental visit to these thigh wounds, with the sun edging its way up to the horizon, and you, my fellow travellers, following with me a compass-reading *between* both black and white, that the following theory began to dawn on me. You see, for an artist it would sooner or later (especially with the mystic inference here of twins of opposite polarities becoming one) come down to colour and I was mentally going to mix black and white together and come up with a neutral grey. As I did, and as the glow from that rising sun began to mix its own light with the black of night, the word *twilight* rose into my mind like a smile, though insisting I explore the reason why.

Twilight - what an enchanting time of day it is - though more often than not it slips by unnoticed. And as one thought always leads to another, I then began wondering whether that yearning 'middle-light' could suggest, in Albion's poetical way, a meeting between the Motherly night and the Fatherly day, a mystic yet very visible twice-daily reminder of their wished-for mixing of fundamental polarities?

I then toyed with the thought of transferring that twice-daily condition of light, that tremulous pregnancy which gives birth to either night or day, onto these twins. As I did, up popped the crazy question as to whether in these overlapping twins' own merged polarities could be suggested the creation of a neutralizing or counter-balancing condition (symptomatic of that 'middle way') out of which a new Son/sun could rise - a God-Man no less? Or was insanity creeping in again?

Either way, with that thought came a bolt of instantaneous excitement. Was the sight of a Christ of Light sharing the same cross and right hand as his Dark Twin, promoting a balanced 'twilight' as another subtle clue to the mystic chemistry which may have been going on behind the scenes at Golgotha. And was this something which, although it passed unrecorded in the Bible, the land detected and recorded in so mighty a fashion for a time when all men would have to themselves face personal Golgothas, and thus have a need to know a truth to which they had been blind for too long?

Crazy, and yet again strangely pleasing, comforting even, the vibe I got back from such a palette of possibilities. I know it sounded stupid, childish, too damn simple to be taken seriously, but exactly that which had been my mainstay in finding the rest of this miracle! So I went with the flow, my inner eye mixing a poetically fizzing neutral grey where the twins overlapped each other, upon the high peaks of England. And as I did that, that counterbalancing light and all it stood for was to grow more magical still.

Twilight - what a magical ring the word has, and was that 'twi' in any way suggestive of 'two'? Did twilight actually mean two-lights? So, a new set of thoughts ran upon the shore of these lakes of learning, and I plunged my hand deep into an imaginary rucksack at my feet and pulled out a dictionary in search of a meaning as to where such flowing thoughts were now taking me.

Lighting an equally imaginary match the word 'twi' flickered off the page and confirmed my hunch - it really was an old English word for *two* and thus twilight really did mean two-lights! Another nice 'buzz' of Albion-reassurance tickled the back of my neck, but then I began to wish I hadn't bothered to scroll through what else the dictionary had to say about twilight itself: *'condition of imperfect knowledge, understanding etc'* - followed by: *'the twilight of the gods - destruction of the gods'* - *'and the world in conflict with the giants'.* Ouch - the match burnt my finger and went out.

Suddenly my thinking that twilight was brewing itself into some kind of key that would unlock a secret ulterior reason for dark and light to overlap upon the same cross, seemed now shaped only to open a Pandora's box of ill omen. I confess that I nearly didn't bother to read the very last listing of my dictionary's assassination of my daft hunch. Nevertheless, I mentally struck another match and in its flare got back the shivers of astonishment which were to race down this mad man's spine for a good hour afterwards, for it was to be another of those 'Albion moments' which not for the first time had come to save my backside just when 'doubt' looked like getting a big piece of it!

Anyway, that spellbinding last line said: ***'twilight sleep, a partial narcosis for dulling the pains of childbirth.'***

Rocket fuel or what, for an intuition that had for so long been journeying through pictures that possibly pertained to some ultimate birthing of an inner Christ Child, and which was now speeding after something that may have been left unsaid from that afternoon at Golgotha; a chase triggered purely by Albion's own black and white imagery, nailed like a challenge to its own masthead rendition of that passion. I was thus primed to ask whether twilight was, in Albion's picture sign-language, indicative of a half-alive, half-dead, limbo, some strange in-between state, experienced by Jesus on that cross, or later in the tomb. A state which was all the time cushioning what amounted to his own mystic birthing of that inner Christ Child/Christ Consciousness - a self-rebirthing, or if you like, *resurrection* by any other name! And yet, to an uninitiated eye, would the person going through such an inconceivable metamorphosis look, to all intents and purposes, as if they had slumped in death?

Were my thoughts inexcusably naïve, or was this really more of the same happy-go-lucky way of peeking just beyond the obvious and spying a wonder that had always been staring us in the face? Was this just another big helping of what had already torn away the veil from the miracle beneath my feet? Furthermore, if it was more of the same tripping-over of wonders, it would mean, dare I say, that **Jesus did not die on the Cross!**

Indeed, the land demanded me *to* dare. And I looked towards where it had already raised that 95-mile tall Geminian Christ Child, that token babe of our dormant, yet ever wanting to be reborn, inner Christ Consciousness. As I looked I couldn't help but smile when seeing again that that child carries *Liver*pool as its own sleeping smile. Why, even in Jesus' own landscaped depiction, his eyes are alive with running water, and I knew I wasn't being naïve.

I just knew the land was daring me to conclude that when Jesus hung upon that cross he was being accompanied by his underworld twin (again maybe in the shape of the robber at his side), and that, in that extraordinarily emphatic sharing of their right hands, there is the proof that we really did miss something very beautiful in that first performance of the Play of Passion. We missed understanding that within the birth of that God-Man was swirling some awesome embrace of Yin and Yang so profound that it was fit to birth a wonder-child, a Christ Child, within the fabric of a mere man.

Note: in drawing our attention to the robber as reflected in Jesus' eyes, might the land be telling us that Jesus became a Christ by virtue of **seeing and acknowledging his brother's value and divinity?*

Remember though, *brothers cannot by themselves conceive a child*, but they could create the perfect neutralizing condition of utmost harmony and balance into which the fundamental male and female aspects of the One God could meet within so as to copulate, conceive, and give birth to a wonder-child with eyes open and *looking out of the man* in all but three days.

Let's chase the idea some more.

Golgotha through new eyes

Wearing Albion's x-ray specs we've now jumped through the looking glass: it's 2000 years ago and we're looking up at Jesus. Eyes closed, he's slumped upon his nails. But in seeing just beyond the obvious, and with a map of northern England under our arm, let us dare to perceive that behind his outward agony there just may be an inner ecstasy - beneath that death-like pallor an expectant glow building from a *'twilight sleep, a partial narcosis for dulling the pains of childbirth'*?

Is he, via all the wisdom he has attained in his short but spectacular life, at the core of himself holding the hand of a twin in a mystic mixing of polarities, and creating an inner balance or twilight, a neutral bridge over which sundered lovers can meet and unite?

Then, staring with even wider eyes, can we accept that the scene is set for the Sky Father, the male aspect of the One God, to descend that cross to meet the Mother force which is itself ascending the cross from the holy depths of the planet? And where the vertical meets the horizontal do those two fundamental forces become rightfully one in a Sacred Marriage **within** the man who has offered himself, through his asking of all the right questions, to be their bridal chamber? In that inconceivable agony and ecstasy of that orgasmic fusion of lovers, too long separated by mankind's refusal of the divinity of his dual nature, we see that mere man, who gives them entry, becoming the ultimate product of that same holy union. In short, via his parents' mystic intercourse is he *rebirthing himself* as their *only* fully aware Son - one who would, upon the third day, venture out from that *womb* of a tomb as the *only* man in all the world who truly knew that not only is he is God, but so too is all else. A God-Man who, in mastering his one foot in heaven and the other on earth, could, according to his startled disciples, **and as adeptly as any spirit would,** pass through a locked door and appear within their room, yet at the same time **displaying the still open and warm wounds** of a physical and still very much alive man. Indeed, he was to ram home the point of his humanness by also showing those same amazed disciples that **he was as hungry as a horse by tucking-into their broiled fish supper to boot!**

Let us stay a little longer at the foot of the cross. While you stare on, notice that as the dance of those divine lovers is spiralling within him, his side is pierced for a reason, and perhaps not just to see if he was dead. For his blood must be so pulsating with that transformational and fundamentally neutralizing chemistry caused by the inner marriage, that providence needs it to spill into Joseph of Arimathea's Grail cup as a token for all men to thereafter drink of the same experience.

Indeed, even as you view those two rudely nailed planks that form the cross, be aware of the secret language of sexual union of which they may be singing. I'll let B Z Goldberg in his book *The Sacred Fire - The Story of Sex in Religion* translate: *"By further simplification it was enough to draw a vertical line to suggest the lingam and a horizontal one to signify the yoni, while the union of the two was represented by the cross."*

It seems, then, that Jesus hung exactly where the lines spelt **copulation!**

To sum up what we're watching, I put it to you that the perfectly balanced Yin and Yang swirling within the core of Jesus has created the partial and blissfully stilling twilit narcosis needed to withstand the orgasmic agony and ecstasy that would allow the inner Christ Child to be born out of pure love. This, then, rendered Jesus dead to all intents and purposes. He was taken into that *womb*-like tomb where some metamorphic chemistry would continue under the knowing eye of Joseph. Then, on the third day, the day of the sun/Son, he could rise

with reborn perception so boundless that he could, spirit-like, mix his atoms with a bolted door and enter a room full of shaking disciples, and yet, as a man, delight to share in their fish supper. Simply, he'd become a God-Man, a being who could know the best of both worlds, could know heaven while still on earth; he could love a woman and make a baby, and yet be able, too, to merge his atoms with Saturn's rings; could relish his supper and yet, while he was eating, know the mind of the mountain beyond the window. Not even the angel Gabriel himself could know such dualistic bliss!

At the height of that mystic intercourse within Jesus he would have literally become Father, Mother and Son. So hear Jesus in the Gnostic Apocryphon of John confirm this: *"John, John, why do you doubt and why are you afraid? …I am the one who is with you always. I am the Father; I am the Mother; I am the Son."*

And if sleeping upon the cross whilst going through some initiatory-like transformation sounds like more spin from yours truly to bolster my interpretation of Albion's cross, listen to Katherine Maltwood in her *Enchantments of Britain* discussing a form of initiation practised in ancient Egypt and India: *"The initiated adept, who had successfully passed through all the trials, was tied to a cross, **in deep sleep**, and allowed to remain in that state for three days and three nights, during which time his Spiritual Ego was said to confabulate with the gods, descend into Hades…"* She continues: *"At a certain hour the beam of the rising Sun struck full on the face of the entranced candidate, and like Hercules he was born again."*

Those words *'born again'* also have me remembering how in the chapter *Aries/Part One* we found how the river Eden, aided by the Swindale Beck, formed a navel connecting placenta and umbilical cord for that land Christ. Mightily intriguing in the context of all this birthing upon the cross stuff.

Nice not being alone

These thoughts, promoted by pictures in a landscape, may seem all weird and stark-raving heretical, and all too easy to write off as the ramblings of a mad man. I think I would have finally concluded the same if I had not, along this strange and challenging way, come across others who have periodically had courage enough to stand up and risk being labelled a crank, by sharing their intuitively-led thoughts. These thoughts so often mirrored my own and which I'd thought, until then, original to myself (triggered as they were solely by this miracle) and consequentially (because what the hell did I know) highly dodgy! And so, as all the above weirdness begs a little of your time in the hope of finding, against all the odds, a comfortable resonance somewhere within you, I ask you to also weigh alongside it a few more seemingly ridiculous theories. These were propounded by other 'carefree plungers'; so see for yourself how this land now gives even their ramblings a tangible vote of approval, and this especially exciting for us with improper thoughts of sex upon the cross!

Take for instance when, under Cancer, I first suggested sexual undertones in the capacity of the cross to become the mast of the ark, realising it could also be representative of the phallus of the male (sun) aspect of God penetrating the Mother's body of the crescent (moon)-shaped ark. Now take that eccentric theory, along with a mental picture of the new Son being poetically reborn upon this same cross-and-crescent floor plan of coupled opposites, and weigh it against these far-sighted words of another one-time hunter of the Grail - the late and still well respected Walter J. Stein: **"Christ unites sun and moon in the earth, and whoever can behold the union of the sun and moon in the earth, beholds the Holy Grail.** *The union will indeed only be fulfilled in the future; but Christ has by his sacrificial deed given a turn to world-evolution that shall lead to that event"*.

And still with thoughts that the cup-like lunar crescent of Albion's ark could be allegorical of the Mother's body, read this from Alain Danielou: *"In Persia, the moon was called Gaoeithra, the cup where the primal bull deposited his semen."* I find it fascinating that if topographical semen in the form of the River Lune is pouring downwards from this Dark Lord's phallus, it is also running down this same cross/mast/phallic Djed pillar towards that feminine cup/body of the ark! Need I also remind you that that same semen trail has the moon written all along it in its name of Lune/Luna! Indeed, boggle your mind still further by also tallying that Persian 'primal bull' way of seeing things with the fact that Osiris was himself seen as a bull. So, if Osiris is indeed one of the many masks of this Dark Twin see how that bull really is ejaculating into the very cup of the moon/ark!

Is this not a massive hint that some sacred sexuality was at work upon the cross, so powerful that it allowed a man to give birth to a poetic wonder-child within himself?

Further support might come from the Nag Hammadi's *Gospel of Philip*, especially so if we agree that in a sense, Jesus was, in his enfolding of the sundered lovers, presenting himself as their bridal chamber:

'If the woman had not separated from the man, she should not die with the man. His separation became the beginning of death.
Because of this Christ came to repair the separation which was from the beginning and again unite the two, and to give life to those who died as a result of the separation and unite them. But the woman is united to her husband in the bridal chamber. Indeed those who have united in the bridal chamber will no longer be separated.'

And this:

*'The Lord did everything in a mystery, a baptism and a chrism, and a eucharist, and a redemption and a **bridal chamber**.'*

Philip also states that anyone who would be initiated into such mysteries would be *'...no longer a Christian but a Christ.'*

Lastly, my thanks go to that pre-eminent scholar of mythology, Joseph Campbell, and his interviewer Bill Moyers in their book *The Power of Myth*. And as on many other occasions, I came across the following some time after formulating my translation of what I saw upon Albion's mapped-out cross. It was so comforting to all my theories regarding twilight, the neutral middle way, and the joining of opposites as pertaining to *The Experiencing of the Grail*. Here Campbell relates a little-known background to the Grail's coming down to earth: *"There's a very interesting statement about the origin of the Grail. One early writer says that the Grail was brought from heaven by the neutral angels. You see, during the war in heaven between God and Satan, between good and evil, some angelic hosts sided with Satan and some with God. The Grail was brought down through the middle by the neutral angels. It represents that spiritual path between pairs of opposites, between fear and desire, between good and evil."*

Towards the end of their discussion upon the Grail comes this exchange:

MOYERS: Is this what Thomas Mann meant when he talked about mankind being the noblest work because it joins nature to spirit?

CAMPBELL: Yes.

MOYERS: Nature and spirit are yearning for each other to meet in this experience. And the Grail that these romantic legends were searching for is the union once again of what

has been divided, the peace that comes from joining.

Tell me, don't you think these landscaped twins, one of the spirit and one of nature, and nailed to one cross, poetically and visually applaud every word of the above conversion? Thanks to these others then, I'm quietly confident that when the wheat is separated from the chaff of all I've dropped in your lap regarding this landscaped re-run of the crucifixion, there'll be enough good stuff left over to weigh with what the land has done to signal a *'Yes'*. Something extraordinary really must have gone on behind the scenes of that first Good Friday, revolving around a play of sacred sexuality - the almighty outcome of which was to not only give birth to a flesh and blood God-Man, but to also rubberstamp that long-held belief wherein the balancing of the Yin and Yang was central to the transmutation of the mundane into the magnificent. Indeed, what Albion has kept back as its final pictorial master stroke will, on its own account, rubberstamp the evidence, nearly 50 miles high, that *pied*, and thus *neutral*, was the inner chemistry that had Jesus dancing off the cross as a Christ. But please don't flip to that last chapter just yet!

*Note: just a passing thought here: if Osiris is wrapped up in the shape of this twin, there may also be the seed of a reason why this many named Lord of the Underworld ended up with a pair of devilish horns, for Osiris, as well as Isis, was known to have worn a horned crown! Also, because the landscape has willed that my suspected Osiris should share the same right hand as Christ, indeed the same nail, and because I mused on how a reborn Christ could perhaps commune with a wolf or condense the essence of himself into the bulb of a bluebell whilst still in the flesh, perhaps the following may add extra weight to this my idea of what true resurrection could be all about. It comes

from an ancient text inscribed in the tomb of the Egyptian prince Paheri:

Thou becomest a living soul.
Thou hast power over bread, water, and air.
Thou changest thyself into a phoenix or a swallow, a sparrowhawk or a heron, as thou desirest.
Thou livest anew and thy soul is not parted from thy body.

Defining the body

Time now to leave symbol and speculation behind and concentrate upon this most wonderfully tangible evidence underfoot - for what can't speak can't tell any lie.

My initial source of reference in the finding of this twin was the *Bartholomew* map as reproduced in John Parker's book *Cumbria, a Guide to the Lake District and its County*. However, this was to be greatly supplemented by the Ordnance Survey *Travelmaster 5* map of northern England, along with the OS *Landranger* series, numbers *86, 90* and *91*.

To begin with, find Croglin crowning the top of his great head, while Croglin Water single handedly outlines the left side of his tumbled hair, and most of the top of the head, until it meets that wonder water of the river Eden. That river then takes over to outline the cascading locks of the right side (just as it does for Jesus) down to his heaving shoulders. The connecting road between Renwick on his forehead and Croglin describes the distinctive, and Jesus-like, centre parting of his hair.

For the face-shaping inner hairline we'll start from Kirkoswald, heading to nearby High Bankhill and onwards to Renwick where we'll be aiming to take the lane out to Outhwaite. Once there we'll need the footpath that will take us to the forest, (this also fills in as his left eyebrow), and where we'll branch left in the hope of picking up the Loo Gill. If we then head along its bank in a southeasterly direction, we should come across a well-defined track, which crosses its flow. This, if we follow it to the right, will lead us into the lane which, in drawing his jaw, tumbles us south and eventually into the busy A686. Head south on this but only until you spot the lane on the right, which will take us along the top of his moustache, past Hazel Rigg and onto the tip of his nose at a point just south of Unthank.

Returning to Kirkoswald, his hair will frame the right side of his face. Leave the village at its southern end and take the lane to the left that should bring you alongside some castle ruins. Here we pick up a footpath that will take us all the way down to Glassonbybeck; then a better quality lane should have us marching into Glassonby itself. Once here we just follow the upper edge of his moustache to Gamblesby just beneath his nose.

To complete the beard's outer shape it's best to start from Langwathby on the right shoulder, into which the river Eden has already tumbled his hair. From Langwathby run a little east along the shoulder on the A686, turning off southwards to Ousby, as this village, I'd say, sits upon his beard's pointed tip. Unfortunately there is no visible line to complete the left side of the beard; that said, the whole head is so well defined that virtually no imagination is needed to fill in where the line of his beard should go. However, perhaps beyond the scope of my maps there may be some subtle feature of the landscape, maybe even a dry-stone wall, which could denote the missing line.

His nose is far easier to spot. From Renwick on his forehead just follow south the direct route to Unthank. Keep on going and you'll see the same lane will bend round into Gamblesby and give that nose a lovely hooked end. Carry on through Gamblesby and you're again following the upper edge of his moustache to Glassonby. As for the mouth, we've already seen how that track south of Gamblesby, which connects Melmerby Mire back to the village of Melmerby, denotes its grimace.

And now those closed raven eyes. East of Kirkoswald we can pick up the Raven Beck subtly describing the closed cup of the right eye before it flows over the bridge of the Renwick to the Unthank nose line in an effort to do the same for the left eye too. It must be pointed out, though, that this section, which runs through Haresceugh, could well be a feeder stream to that Raven Beck and perhaps may even bear a different name. That said, that blue line still conspires with the Raven Beck to present a very decent pair of cupped eyes. The lane that connects Ravenbridge Mill (nearly in the corner of this left eye) to Haresceugh and beyond to Selah also provides very good back-up to the work of the stream in denoting the left eye. Indeed, I'd say that lanes could, in their own right, do a half decent job in describing both closed eyes: begin at Kirkoswald and just truck on down the lane which heads eastwards through Howscales, thereafter crossing that nose line as an even narrower lane-come-track, which, if you follow to its end, will have you eventually upon Skelling Moor. However, nothing beats what the Raven Beck does and all it stands for!

Groucho's own!

Oh, and I nearly forgot a lovely pair of Groucho eyebrows; ever so charmingly shaped by two horizontal strips of perfectly placed woodland. Over the right eye it's the wood surrounding Nether Haresceugh, while the left one is raised just north of Haresceugh proper.

Now that the face is complete we'll trace the shoulders and the tops of both outstretched arms. Starting with the right, the main A592 and its easterly flow into the A686 etches its upper contour - the same line having already delineated the top edge of the cross'

horizontal beam. His right hand is, as you know, Jesus' own, while the arm's lower contour is precisely that which denoted the top edge of Jesus'. Superb economy of line or what!

The A686 describes the top of the left arm as far as the turn off to the village of Catton. After Catton it's Allendale Town we want, all the time drawing the knuckles of this left hand. Now we need the unmarked lanes to head us back west, passing through Carr Shield and Coalceugh, before crossing over the A689 into Nenthead and Garrigill that nestles in the armpit.

Just an observation here: the lanes around Catton lend themselves to the shaping of a forefinger, pointing to either Hexham or a place called Low Gate, or indeed some other spot well beyond these two. Whether or not there is any significance in this, I don't know.

Going back to Garrigill in the armpit (sorry Garrigill!) it's now southwards down the left side of his body, admirably drawn by the B6277 through Teesdale to Middleton-in-Teesdale, thereafter picking up first the B6282 and then the B6279 on the wounded left thigh as we head to Staindrop and the top of his bent knee. Now curve southwest around it on the B6274 to Winston, or if you'd prefer a meander along some tranquil waterways you could do almost precisely what the road has just done - even sailing into Ovington where we're due next.

From Ovington we go to Hutton Magna, Newsham on the shin, and continue over Barningham Moor by still following the only road it's possible to take all the way along the top of this left foot into Marske, where toes *should* be - I'll come back to this.

Anyway, go right on through Marske for it's Fremington we want on the side of the right foot, around about the position of its little toe. However, once there, let's just backtrack slightly by going back out of Fremington some two miles to Marrick. If you follow the same lane through that village it'll have you completing a potato-like shape back again to Fremington, which at the same time, describes the finest big toe in all Albion, Marrick being its nail! This veritable cartoon of a big toe is especially apparent on the Ordnance Survey *Travelmaster* 5 map.

That terrible foot!

But that big cartoon of a toe then almost forces one to look back at the left foot (which seems nailed upon top of the right). As one does, you realise what might be the message, for the left markedly lacks a similar toe, moreover, one becomes aware that it has no toes at all and is instead *wonderfully cloven*. This club of a foot is pointedly cleft by the track that goes from Marske to Skelton and eventually to a dead end; a stream also cuts the same course.

So one foot (the left/Mother's Yin side) rightfully cloven and thus caked in primordial mud, this an emphatic reminder of man's brotherhood with the beasts of the fields. One foot in heaven, the other in earth, is again shown as the true pedigree of us all. But also get a load of this, especially if one of the many masks of this Darker Twin is Dionysus, or if you're thinking *"Why only one foot cloven?"*

"Come hither, Dionysus, to thy holy temple by the sea; come with the graces to thy temple, rushing with thy bull's foot, O goodly bull, O goodly bull!"

This, according to Frazer, was how the women of Elis hailed him - and do note that 'bull's foot' is in the singular!

In Hurst find the hurt

We start again at Fremington and head northwestwards to draw the underside of his more human right foot, sculpted by the <u>Ark</u>le Beck that flows along <u>Ark</u>engarthdale. If his foot is nailed against this straight edge, surely we're being told the name of the ship whose mast must bear him!

The Ordnance Survey *Travelmaster 5* map asks another highly intriguing question of these feet, and we get to the point of it by following a track from Marrick to Hurst that outlines the top of the right foot, and actually separates this right foot from the left hoof. Anyway, in following this otherwise straight wilderness track from Marrick you'll notice that it's capped as though by a short 'T' bar, its left arm ending in Hurst, while going right leads to nowhere but a complete dead end. In doing so it surprises by throwing a tiny, and what seems on the map to be entirely needless right angle. So why that bent back bit? I don't know, but oh how it tempts the eye to see it as the bent-over head of a crude nail - and if you hit that nail on the head does that place name of Hurst hide the *hurt*? Too true, *for Hurst is exactly where such a crucifixion nail would bite*! *See line drawing.

Leaving the feet (or foot and hoof) on we go now to Langthwaite upon the heel. Just beyond here it's back northeast through The Slang to join the A66, thereby completing the calf muscle of his right leg. This same once well-flogged road of Rome's legions will take us northwest to Brough at the beginning of the buttock.

After Brough, and not long after passing the village of Warcop on your left, we shall branch off this highway by taking a right to Hilton upon quieter lanes. Then we pass through Murton, Dufton, and Knock before picking up the stream that runs out of the Crowdundle Beck to Newbiggin, again being pulled to that magnet of **Temple Sowerby** which nestles in this particular giant's right armpit. This same spot on his brother marks the top of the right shoulder. So rest awhile here amid the underarm scent of the Green

Man, a perfume from Temple Sowerby's 20,000 daffodils and Lent lilies!

Carry on now by following the upper contour of Jesus' right arm, as this cunningly denotes the under arm of his twin. Thus is completed their shared right hand and nail.

Heart of Hearts

So that leaves only the place of his heart - and what a heart, here at Cross Fell, aptly the highest point of his entire high-peaked frame; this same place already having been such a boon in helping me earlier to find the co-ordinates of the cross itself. This mount is an admirable marker for the great thumping heart of the Mother's Son and consort, especially so with the Ordnance Survey Landranger map number *91* in your hand, for see how it's even *heart-shaped* too! One mile is its pumping width and befittingly described by Bellamy and Quayle as the epicentre of England's last great wilderness - yet again, well said, sirs! *See following line drawing.

His heart must have been even wilder some 1500 years ago when it was said St Paulinus scaled its height in order to drive out the demons who had made it their stronghold - all wonderfully evocative of him whose heart it is! Having cleaned up the joint, the saint then raised a cross upon the spot to mark the coming of Christianity to this apex of Albion. But, I ask, was he, by this gesture, being used to proclaim this twin as holy after all, or was he sign-posting this same place as the lynchpin of Albion's colossal cross beneath? Either way, thanks too to St Paulinus.

More powerful land poetry comes with the news that from this same high fell the mighty river Tees has its birth, thereafter trickling like a rivulet of blood down this giant's chest to fill that Cow Green reservoir wound upon his side - thus his Grail wound is visibly filled from his own heart's blood.

Marks of further approval

To complete our check list of the eponymous clues that identify exactly whom we're treading on, I would like to add a few extra last-minute giveaways that may also be useful in the final

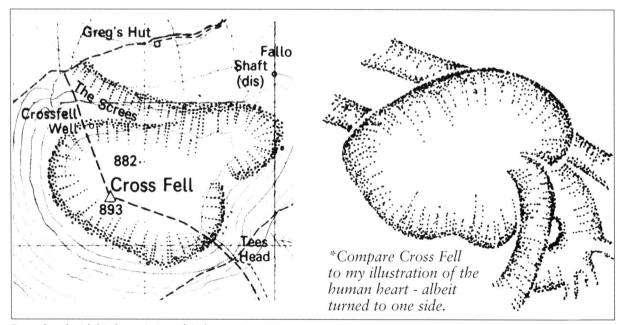

*Compare Cross Fell to my illustration of the human heart - albeit turned to one side.

reckoning of both his character and role.

First of all, note North Stainmore, South Stainmore, Stainmore Common and Stainmore Forest, for all are gathered in the area where his thigh wounds are visually weeping trickles of blood in the shape of many streams and thus poetically 'staining' the entire area. Historically, too, blood stains this area, for it was here that the battle raged wherein the last of the Viking kings in England was dispatched to Valhalla; his name, Eric Bloodaxe.

Another sign, and one which we have already found on the body of Jesus, perhaps now needs reappraisal seeing that it also falls upon this his pagan reflection. Wild Boar Scar, that geological tear upon the shoulder of Jesus, which had us wondering if the memory of those old gods of rejuvenation, Attis and Adonis - both killed by wild boars - was being recorded here, alluding perhaps that they too lay in the multi-mythological layers beneath the Christ. However, this scar falls far more dangerously on his twin, being but one inch away from his heart! It seems to me then that the presence of Attis and Adonis, corn gods both, is validated and that they are here exactly where they should be - within the wrappings of this the Darker Lord!

So why isn't this twin shown upon the cover?

In Christendom, and so for the best part of 2000 years, this twin has been condemned as evil, though ironically, and thanks to the medieval stonemasons he has still gained entrance into many a church under the guise of the Green Man - often up there amongst the rafters and gleefully spewing oak and hawthorn over the heads of congregations! It's a pity then that I had not the guts of those masons, for my artwork bears no trace of him.

You see, I completed the coloured artwork at the time when I was happy to con myself that he wasn't there, and although I guess I could have painted him in once I'd come to my senses, I nevertheless decided that I wouldn't, for in my own ignorant banishment of him that 2000 years worth of misunderstanding and downright fear is succinctly underlined.

So let that blank space remain, a challenge to each individual to reinstate him into the gap within their own lives, and in so doing re-acknowledge their own holy cloven foot. Indeed let that blank space, instigated by my own fear, serve as a reminder for all time of the beauty that fear and ignorance can repress.

Fearlessly then, we go into the last mile of our journey.

***Note:** why, if I earlier placed Lucifer, or a dis-eased faction of the negative force, in Scorpio, do I now also pinpoint him on the cross? In answer, I feel that, in Scorpio's banishment from the main body of the zodiac, the land is illustrating just how dangerous it is for us to create, albeit ignorantly, divisions and imbalances in our lives and environment, for they will be reflected back upon us time after time. Whereas in his portrayal upon the cross, we see how, rather than dividing, if we join and rebalance we may know paradise on earth.*

CHAPTER 16

YOU!...
THE LORD OF THE DANCE

• *The Twins made One* •
and dancing

★

*The sixteenth giant
along the way*

YOU!...
THE LORD
OF
THE DANCE

The Twins made One -
as they are positioned
upon the Earth

APPROXIMATE SIZE IN MILES
FIGURE: HEIGHT 50 WIDTH 40

Cross Fell
The Heart

Cow Green Reservoir

Iron Band

*Ordnance Survey contour lines
(Landranger Series - 91) appear to
perfectly describe a penis shape
around the area of Beldoo Moss.

The outline itself is primarily
created by both a fold and the
outer edge of the loin cloth of the
first Christ.

Maiden
Castle

River Greta

* No equivalent figure found at
either Glastonbury orPreseli

The Miracle within the Miracle

I danced in the morning
when the world was begun,
And I danced in the moon
And the stars and the sun;
And I came down from heaven
And I danced on the earth;
At Bethlehem
I had my birth.

Chorus:
Dance then, wherever you may be,
I am the Lord of the Dance, said he,
And I'll lead you all wherever you may be,
And I'll lead you all in the dance, said he.

LORD OF THE DANCE, Sidney Carter

For God's sake tell me you see him too! Four legs become two; four arms become two; **twins become *one*** and giving the impression of actually **dancing off the cross** - surely a portrayal of an arms-outstretched, legs-jigging, **God-Man!**
And I ask you, could this, that is for me Albion's most stunning surprise of all, be any more graphically emphatic in what must be its spectacularly animated assertion of the fact that Jesus *did not die upon the cross*?

★ ★ ★ ★ ★

Though I didn't see this dancing one until several weeks into my chapter upon the Dark Twin - a task that had become so gruelling that I had decided, for an afternoon at least, to shut down the Mac and do what I did best - put on my artist's cap and carry out the black and white line drawing of that troublesome twin, to the same scale as the illustration I'd already done of the Jesus at his side.

The illustration itself was simple enough to carry out, and because I was working upon clear drafting film it was equally simple for me to overlap the completed drawing accurately to that of the Christ at his side; indeed, just as they appear on the landscape. Without the roads, place names and contour lines, I could see far more clearly than the map had hitherto shown me of how they shared that same cross.

Anyway, as I slid those two pieces of film together, my running battle in trying to unravel not only why another shared Jesus' cross, but also the whys and wherefores behind this whole discovery became, from that moment on, more like a stroll in the park! Why? Well, when those two figures overlapped, as the land has positioned them to do, my artist's eye (and I hope your eye too) saw in a flash the mini-miracle that had apparently been primed to cap the greater miracle that was all Albion. I saw in a split second the pair of them fuse and dance off that cross as one - a spontaneous piece of magically ignited animation which could only be spelling out **JOY**, as the final outcome of what this whole vast conundrum was prophesying, no matter what upheavals might occur in the interim. Indeed, in this masterstroke of a finale, the land had made any further fathoming from me utterly needless. Simply, I felt there was no need for any further gruelling inner debate as to whether I was right to come clean in admitting that I knew Jesus shared his cross with another - and whether that interloper was cloven footed or not!

God, how I thumped the air and sent myself violently revolving in my chair - papers flew about me; war was over; and for me was there dancing going on throughout every street of Britain!

In my sliding of those two figures together, the map had turned my fear of a dark opposite sharing Jesus' cross into a joyous whoop of sudden understanding. It had in one simple folded inkblot-like piece of cunning made Jesus jig off that cross in what could only be a pictogram of an unshackled God-Man, a Lord of the Dance. For me this was a crowning capstone glyph wherein the oh-so-simple visual mechanics that fire its animation, this arising from the land's canny overlapping of twins of opposite polarities, must speak a near timeless and universal tongue. It was a dance-encoded symbol, which whether found upon the ceiling of an ancient tomb, or cut into a rock face upon Mars, could only ever translate as *rapture out of balanced union.*

Moreover, how could I not see in this same dazzling show of exaltation that we, the masses, might be being allowed to see something of that Yin and Yang chemistry which might have been behind Jesus' Golgotha transformation of man into Christ? And in this an invitation for us all to somehow poetically share in the same wonder, though now without need of the nails, for Jesus paid that price. Certainly, if you doubted my suggestions in the previous chapter of seeing Jesus as not dying on the cross, surely here is our planet's own

emphatic backing-up of my heresy: no man is slumped on its 300-mile-high cross, but a 40plus-mile-tall rendering of a very much alive-and-kicking messiah! But do take note that without that twin at his side to supply those extra limbs, his harmoniously pied dance of delight, and the jubilant statement contained in it, would simply not happen.

"And we remembered what the ancients said - that at all times the God of Duality is at work within the cosmos, measuring out its cycles of millions of years, enumerating the stars:
The God of Duality is at work,
Creator of men,
mirror which illumines things,
Mother of the gods, father of the gods,
the old god
spread out on the navel of the earth
within the circle of turquoise
He who dwells in the waters...
He who dwells in the clouds,
The old god, he who inhabits the shadows of the land of the dead,
The lord of fire and time."

Taken from HEAVEN'S MIRROR
by Graham Hancock; the poem,
Florentine Codex, cited by him from
THE SECRET OF THE INCAS

But forgetting all the mystical this, that, and the other, can you imagine a more hopeful picture to mark both the end of our extraordinary journey and what must be the potential future of mankind, than Albion's own Lord of Duality, this God-Man *spread out on the navel of the earth* - Britain, and dancing off the mast of the *turquoise* encircled ark of life? The constellations are spread out at his feet, not in subjugation to him, but, in their underlying zodiacal message, they are supplying the firm foundations for those same joyful steps. Surely, the keys are there in their zodiacal imagery to unlock a perception that will allow all of us finally to free ourselves from those many life-dulling shackles of our own making, and to dance to the full potential of our existence; a dance that will, it seems, have the whole universe as its partner. The only thing that could trip us now is our ego's fear of having to bow to anything that makes a mockery of its rules of what can and can't be. We mustn't sneer at the fact that the mountain *is* as aware as the shaman always told us it was, or that our thoughts are alive enough to not only affect others around us, but also the environment for both good and evil. And how the ego will baulk at such a theory!

In typing the above, however, a shuddering reminder shoots through me of how close fear was to preventing me from ever showing him who represents the dark, and so robbing Albion of its magnificently dancing finale. Indeed, one look at my coloured artwork tells how close I came to doing just that, there is no Dark Twin there and therefore absolutely *no chance* of the means to ignite that slumped Lord to dance; and yet perhaps in the context of this whole story even my fear-instigated omission was, and is, part of the overall message.

But you may think that a portrayal of Jesus 'partying' at Golgotha rather only caps my own madness. Though, surprisingly, even this, my final picture of heresy, isn't original!

This final laughing outburst of the land speaks so succinctly for itself that for me to endeavour to further boil it down would be an insult to both *it* and, I hope, *you.* So, beyond me pointing out this dancer's own body of evidence on the ground, it really is now *over to you!* That said, and before we put our noses to the map for the last time, let us bolster the artist's sanity just a little more!

Of course, this sight of a Christ made up of two separate individuals, and that resulting figure showing all the signs of enjoying a good knees-up on the cross, must seem very much against the biblical version of events surrounding Golgotha. However it comforts me no end to say that I was to later find out that the land and I aren't the first to suggest Jesus advocating two into one as some mystic goal, nor indeed, that he took part in jollifications in the final few hours leading up to, and including, his crucifixion.

Hear first Thomas, that self-proclaimed twin of Jesus, repeat what Jesus said to him regarding two made one and the wonders that might ensue:

"Jesus said 'When you make the two one, you will become the sons of man, and when you say 'Mountain, move away', it will move away."
GOSPEL OF THOMAS

How about this, too - I found it in Elaine Pagel's *The Gnostic Gospels*; in discussing the variations of the Genesis story concerning the creation of man she brings to light a very interesting Greek account: "...*that suggested to Rabbi Samuel bar Nachman, influenced by Plat's myth of androgyny, that when the holy one first created mankind, he created him with two faces, two sets of genitals, four arms and legs, back to back...*"

Weird, but is that not the very likeness of this dancer on Albion's cross?

And what about the jollifications going on anywhere near the crucifixion? From the same Nag Hammadi sands that gave us Thomas the twin's gospel, we have *The Apocalypse of Peter* in which Peter, grimacing at the sight of his friend being crucified, is suddenly stunned to see Jesus laughing where, but a moment sooner, he thought he saw him writhing in agony:

*"...who is this one, **glad** and **laughing** on the tree? And is it another one whose feet and hands they are striking?'* Jesus replies: *"...He*

whom you saw being glad and laughing above the cross, he is the Living Jesus."

Best of all though, check out this scene: it's set in the Garden of Gethsemane, the evening before the crucifixion, where there is a Jesus seemingly worlds apart from the Jesus described in the Bible's account. This comes from the Gnostic text entitled *The Acts of John*.

See through John's eyes, a Jesus not sorrowing to death or sweating blood but with *a song in his heart*, even though this was within a few moments of Judas pointing him out. I can't help thinking that this stemmed from his knowledge that he was near to becoming the living, singing, dancing Grail. Certainly, whatever the reason for Jesus' happiness it made him want to sing and dance!

"...he assembled us all, and said, 'Before I am delivered to them, let us sing a hymn to the Father, and so go to meet what lies before us.' So he told us to form a circle, holding one another's hands, and himself stood in the middle..."

Jesus instructed his disciples to *"Answer Amen to me"* almost as a chorus, and began to teach them this incredibly beautiful song of the dance:

"To the universe belongs the dancer."
'Amen.'
He who does not dance does not know what happens - 'Amen'...
Now if you follow my dance, see yourself in me who am speaking... You who dance, consider what I do, for yours is
This passion of Man which I am to suffer.
For you could by no means have understood what you suffer
unless to you as Logos I had been sent by the Father ...
Learn how to suffer and you shall be able not to suffer."

John continues:

"After the Lord had danced with us,
my beloved,
he went out to suffer."

Wow! Can you believe this extraordinary scene - Jesus DANCING with his disciples in the Garden of Gethsemane and with Judas and the Romans on their way? Of course *you can* - because the land has now recorded him as doing exactly that! And could Jesus' words of *"To the universe belongs the dancer"* be anywhere better illustrated than at this point, which is the culmination of our journey through the landscaped constellations? Wonderful!

I tell you, when I found the above passage, and it was a long time after I'd slid those two pieces of drafting film together, I received the final shove to see this whole extraordinary project through. Until then, and even with all these giants daily laughing and making faces at me from behind the weather forecaster's back, and that dancer himself shouting out that *"Everything's gonna be fine"*, the rabbit in me still wanted to do a runner from the consequences of it all - consequences not unlike the following: Pope Leo the Great condemned the above *Acts of John* as: *"...an hotbed of manifold perversity, which should not only be forbidden, but entirely destroyed and burned with fire."* Thank God that a flame never scorched the edge of its pages otherwise we travellers couldn't, with I hope growing understanding, have experienced the thrill of reading it alongside what our earth has done.

To aid that understanding a tad more, hear a final few lines from John's condemned book. We find him now fled from the ringing hammer blows at Golgotha and hiding in a cave at Gethsemane; suddenly a vision of the Christ appears before him saying:

"John, for the people below... I am being

crucified and pierced with lances... and given
vinegar and gall to drink.
But to you I am speaking, and listen to
what I speak."

Christ then reveals to John a vision of a 'Cross of Light' and continues:

"I have suffered none of the things which they will say of me; even that suffering which I showed to you and to the rest **in my dance**, *I will that it be called a* **mystery**."

Can we dare hope that that 'mystery' is now no more? As put forward in the previous chapter, was he in his enfolding of the sundered lovers within the bridal chamber made of himself, writhing only in the agony and ecstasy of a passion that was climaxing around that inner sacred marriage, and from where his own inner Christ Child of expanded perception was to be birthed on the third day within Joseph's tomb/womb - hence this picture of rapture upon the cross?

Staying with dancing, but changing religions, I'd just like to supplement this image of a dancing God by pointing out the purely pictorial similarity between what the land is showing and the traditional depiction of Shiva. You may recall we've already suspected Shiva too as being within the wrappings of the darker twin. And yes, I accept that naked Shiva has but two legs, but please do note those four arms!

Surely to see one's God dancing, whether you're Christian, Moslem, Hindu or whatever, must be the ultimate picture of hope.

So, trusting that I no longer need fathom why we're presented with the spectacle of a pointedly pied man dancing off the cross, it leaves us only to free-wheel around what the map says of this, the last giant of Albion.

His body of evidence

How gorgeously simple, and yet with what terrifically ebullient results, four arms magically become fused as two, and four legs likewise. These new limbs no more nailed to the cross, but seemingly freed to dance in a starburst exclamation of joy and what must be *"Welcome to a mystery unveiled!"*.

Their amalgamated torso looks proportionately convincing resting on those new legs, though I'd concede that the two arms fused out of four, when compared to the weight of the rest of the body, do look somewhat too bulky. Nevertheless, after coming this far around Albion, I hope you'll agree that the object of its message in this make-up of a triplet (perhaps somehow significant, too, of the *three* crosses at Golgotha?) is as ingeniously sculpted as it is crystal clear to understand - bulky arms or no. In short, *we get the picture!*

But putting our noses back to the ground let's, for the last time, allow the map and man's own uncanny naming of places to give the final fillip of life to this wonder man. I confess that within a few minutes of finding him, manifest to the artist's eye as he was, I still urgently needed to know if, at ground level too, there were any reassuring hints to back him up. After all these miles I should have known that I wasn't to be disappointed.

Heart of hearts and a cup full of Yin and Yang

Obviously, in the overlapping of the twins in order to give rise to their triplet brother, they sacrifice themselves. However, some interesting things happen in the process. Cross Fell, that perfectly geologically sculpted heart-shaped heart of the Dark Twin, for instance, becomes in this same melting process, the perfectly placed heart of this triplet; while the Cow Green Reservoir side wound becomes his equally well-positioned Grail wound. And isn't it beautifully significant, too, that this dancer, born as he is out of a marriage of black and white, can only be bleeding *pied* blood. So, to put that high cup to that cauldron of a wound's outpouring will be to now have a cup brimming over with both Yin and Yang - a spillage that only a perfectly balanced God-Man *could* bleed. Indeed, his lifeblood can be essentially no different in its two basic ingredients to that which must have swirled within the Celt's Cauldron of Inspiration and Rebirth before it and its properties, in the mythological scheme of things, became synthesised within the Christ's spear wound - an evolution now so concisely illustrated by this land poetry.

And that abominable foot stays!

Shifting our attention to this dancer's left foot, we'll see how its fusion from out of the two of the darker twin still leaves it befittingly cloven. Although this dancer is still a God-Man, he does not shirk his animal and earthly lineage, but proclaims it holy, and I'm sure that half the compulsion and impetus that drives his jig comes from honouring that lineage.

For those with keen eyes, however, you'll notice that I've changed slightly the silhouette of this fusion of right and left feet compared to the shape they made when separate and belonging to the Dark Twin. Prompted only by intuition, then, leave Marske (at the tip of that cloven left foot), by taking a lane left as though making for the A6108. However, just before making that connection take instead the river Swale west and around into Fremington on the

sole - previously upon the sole of this twin's right foot. This procedure makes for one big club of a foot for our dancer to stomp with, and one which now gets cloven by the joint efforts of that track to Hurst (which previously separated the right from the left) and a stream that touches the track, before flowing on to splice this foot between Marske and Marrick - thence running into that defining river Swale.

The Ordnance Survey *Travelmaster* map 5 shows this shaping very well.

Incidentally, could it be that the track to Hurst (Hurst Moor conspicuously dominates the centre ground of this fused foot), which, in the previous chapter, led our thoughts to the HURT received from a crucifixion nail, also points to the equal hurt which has, for ages, been piled upon this whole subject of a cloven foot?

Either way, here is no loathsome hoof of a destructive Lucifer, but a purely innocent token of the holy left and Mother's side, that half of the divine duality that shall always give us our divine (not derogatory!) kinship with the beasts and the land. Why, even the whole left leg of this dancer seems, in its slightly more 'bumpy' silhouette, to be suggestive of being perhaps shaggy too, when compared to the slightly sleeker right that materialised from the fusion of Jesus' legs.

In the final analysis, though, the lesson we should take from the shape of both dancing feet is that one foot is in tune with heaven's music of the spheres, and the other with earth's glorious mud. As such, it is tuned to the deeper sounds of bodhrans, didgeridoos, choruses of frogs and a cow's belly-deep moo resonating upon a cold and frosty morning. Thus *both* feet are in paradise!

Same feet, but a brand new phallus!

On seeing how the vigour of his dance had opened his legs wide apart, I couldn't help but wonder if the land had conjured another phallus there. If it hadn't, the placement of the one belonging to the Dark Twin would mean that this triplet would have a penis dangling from his left hip - not so clever!

But the land hasn't missed a trick - with admirable economy of line, the phallus of the dancer takes its shape from two distinct lines already given away in the hitherto nondescript shape created between a fold and the outer edge of that loin cloth as worn by Jesus. However when this shape is seen again after the overlapping of his twin, it perfectly lends itself to what the land seemingly had in mind all along. Having said that, when I first caught sight of its possibility, I still couldn't resist investigating the area at closer quarters in the hope of finding a loophole by which to save myself from yet more sexually-tabooed deep water. However, I was soon smiling at more than enough delightful evidence on the ground to underline what I *knew* just had to be there - for how could a dancing Lord of Life be minus that seed-head which signifies love and life's continuance?

Its outer shape is described on the right side by the county border line between Cumbria and Durham, although to get rid of what looks like a nasty carbuncle we must, from half way between Round Hill and Beldoo Hill, take a straighter route; while the old Roman road, now tarmacked as the A66, does a good, unbroken job of outlining its left side. And as I've already said, within and around these two defining lines were enough name-dropped hints, along with some exquisitely penis-enhancing contours of the land itself, to convince me that I was not indulging myself in some end-of-journey wishful thinking in order to round off the whole thing without a flaw.

Just before sharing these phallic embellishments with you, however, I'd like to point out that for all his show of maleness, *hermaphrodite*, in my opinion, must be his truer gender, for he is, as are all Albion's giants whatever their appearance, constructed totally of femininity - the matter of him, from his ribs of rock to his skin of grass, being all of the material Mother. This important point I think we've already heard intimated in the previous chapter by Jesus himself, as the poetic make-up of a man who has come to know himself as God - hear it a second time from the *Apocryphon of John*:

*"John, John, why do you doubt and why are you afraid? ...I am the one who is with you always. **I am the Father; I am the Mother; I am the Son.**"*

OK, let's take a closer look at how I think men have dotted the area of this phallus with sexual nudges and winks.

Zero in firstly upon the glans itself, wonderfully bulbous and made so by the curving and climbing contours of windswept Beldoo Moss; a feature particularly noticeable upon the Ordnance Survey *Landranger* map 91. And doesn't *Bel* have a charming ring to it, especially when finding it here on this paramount symbol of fertility; Bel, being once a god of these shores, while Belili was the name given to the Earth Mother long before a masculine Bel was ever conceived of. So take your pick, for either Bel wouldn't be out of place in ringing at the end of this swinging phallus!

The Mother's interest in this glans does not end there, though. Indeed, she leaves us in no doubt whatsoever of her claims to it when she has had someone name a Roman fort upon that same phallic head as **Maiden Castle** - seat of the Mother? I say no more!

Another puckish grin I find flitting around Plucka Hill, prominently placed upon its shaft, and which mischievously goads me into rhyming it with that four letter slang word for sexual intercourse; though even when I looked up *pluck* in the dictionary the grin remained when seeing *pull at*, *twitch*, *tug* and *snatch* attached to it! But if this my sheepish hunch is correct there'd be not one jot of smuttiness in it, just more of that innocence which, once upon a time, allowed girls to dance around the phallic maypole in celebration of procreation throughout all nature. Only the advent of Christian piety, with its relegation of women, and promotion of unnatural celibacy within its own ranks, turned that innocent happiness of being a sparkling procreative part of life's wonder into something indecent. The celebration of sexuality was then sent scurrying underground where imbalance and evil (evil - the word *live* turned back-to-front as an affront!) was ever eager to turn that which was holy and beautiful into something to be almost ashamed of, and thus a breeding ground for abuse.

True, sexuality and the Church aren't as troublesome a pair as they used to be, but those earlier scars, along with a degree of uncertainty in looking upon sex as a holy act, I think still lurk in the background.

Certainly, we have much innocence to reclaim, and Plucka Hill may or may not hold an old smiling trace of it.

Not actually upon this phallus, but stationed right at its tip, is a single stone pillar set conspicuously all alone in a sea of wide, open wilderness and known as Rey Cross, for once at its top it carried a Celt-like wheel-cross, the spot marks where they say the Viking king Eric Bloodaxe met his end. Even more interesting, though, is the fact that this same stump was believed to have once marked the border between England and Scotland - thus placing everything but the legs of this dancing amalgamation on previously Scottish soil.

But let's tinker with that name Rey. Historians say that it stems from the Norse word *Hreyrr*, meaning *boundary*; but for me, and again rightly or wrongly, I hear in it one of the many names men have given the goddess, that of Rhea, Earth Mother to the ancient Greeks. If so, what a statement that old stone would make in her name, standing as it does

right there at the spurting tip of the dancer's phallus.

"Spurting, did you say - suggesting that this dancer, like the Dark Twin, is also ejaculating?"

Well, it certainly seems that way, for this phallus also spurts a river, and would you believe, bears another female Greek name! Not only this, but along its flow someone has dropped a virtual plethora of suggestive names which fuel sexual innuendo.

Anyway, this dancer's own spurt of life begins as a stream falling from the very tip of his phallus, again nameless on my maps, although after a short stretch it runs into the stronger flow of the river Greta which gurgles past my suspiciously Grecian Rhea/Rey Cross. Because I was in 'suspicious name mode' I was soon looking into the background of that name made famous by the screen goddess, Garbo.

Intriguingly, I found it derived from the Greek name Margaret, meaning *pearl* - and was I being excessively fancy free when I instantly linked that pearl with sperm? Answer - *"more than likely"*, for perhaps I was again looking for any excuse to have this dancing God-Man ejaculating sperm rather than urinating over Albion! But allow my dictionary to stimulate that fancy of mine with these seductive references to the pearl: '*a precious thing, dewdrop, tear, pearl drops, reduce barley to small pearly grains*', not forgetting '*Mother of Pearl*' and '*Pearl Fisher*'.

You still might think this is poetic licence being pushed to the implausible limits, but that dictionary definition allowed me at least to feel more confident in marrying pearl to sperm; and don't the words **barley/small pearly grains** bring back all that barley/grain/sperm imagery we found spurting from between the legs of that Dark Twin while we stood upon that *Grains' o' th' Beck* bridge?

However, place that river Greta just a few miles to the left or right of where God has willed it to flow on this dancer, and its background meaning would amount to absolutely zilch! Likewise, if his phallus spouted, say, the nearby Deepdale Beck or Ay Gill, it would be but *urine* pouring from him, for there'd be nothing in those names to suggest otherwise. In such a way the magically paced style of this land poetry has many times presented itself since page one. I have always found the visual shape first, before being thrilled by some uncanny place-name verification of that shape's existence, sometimes many months, even years, later. This disarming magic leaves me to surmise that behind this same delightful post-dating of clues there must indeed be a most fun-loving Intelligence.

But there was even more post-dating here, more pieces of cloth left upon twigs, to lead me through the deep dark forest to what can only be our lost inheritance of the love that flows beneath our feet.

So what with pearly grains perhaps intimating droplets of sperm, I then let my eye wander on down the line of this ejaculated river Greta until, in this wilderness of no names, five place names suddenly sprouted along a three-mile stretch of its waters, nodding in approval of the line of thought I was then tracking - and all carrying the odd word *Spital*; Spital Ings, Old Spital, Spital, Spital Park and Spital Grange. Needless to say, *Spital* had me again reaching for the *Oxford English Dictionary* where it was listed as a variant of the word *spittle* as in 'to **spit**' or 'to **eject** saliva' - nudge! nudge! wink! wink!

Could it be that in this God-Man's spurting of spittle-shiny pearls, dewdrops, pearl drops, barley reduced to small pearly grains, we are being abundantly showered with pearls of extraordinary poetic wisdom. And if so, could the most fundamental part of their worth be, not only to underline the absolute jewel-like divinity of all life, but also to rain down upon us a warning that in our protracted blindness to that divinity all around us, we are upon the

verge of committing some irreparable damage to it all - hence this almighty landscaped shout?

Undoubtedly, from the above, and those signs already mentioned concerning the blighting of the consort's fertility, together with the way in which even Virgo herself is strenuously pointing to the sperm/grain-shaped Bardsey Island, our attention is assuredly being pulled to something of such gravity, with an obvious life-force link, that the continuance of not only humanity, but all life from dragonflies to daffodils, may rest upon our urgent understanding of this the earth's pictorial scream.

However, if you feel that in my references to the symbolism of spittle and sperm I am pushing my luck even further, allow me to call Thomas Hardy to maybe say a word in my defence.

In one passage of his classic *Tess of the D'Urbervilles*, I feel Hardy used the same sensuous innuendo that this landscape is employing when he has the love-sick Tess wistfully wandering through summer's luxuriant undergrowth, erotically linking the secret scents and secretions oozing out of the greenery and its minute inhabitants with those exchanged between a man and women entwined in sexual intercourse.

From the introduction of the *Penguin Classic* version of Tess, A Alvarez picks up on this same passage: *"The intense eroticism of the writing - more erotic, I think, than the full frontal attacks we are used to today - is not in the people but in the detail of the scene: the sound of Angel's harp, with its stark quality like that of nudity', the 'damp', 'rank', 'juicy' undergrowth through which Tess moves 'stealthily as a cat', 'gathering <u>cuckoo-spittle on her skirts</u> ...staining her hands with thistle milk and slug slime, and rubbing off upon her naked arms sticky blights which... made madder stains on her skin'. It is as though the vegetation itself contained all the secret smells and juices of the act of physical passion.*

Hardy's version of the paradise garden was closer to Gauguin's than to that of the Book of Genesis".

Fooling around with Plucka and Rhea, along with innuendoes of a Maiden (Castle) sitting upon a phallus, semen-like pearls and cuckoo-spittle apart, this phallus belonging to a dancer in a paradise garden still has one more mark by which to prove earth's intent, and one that, even in this picture of celebration, is warning too.

Cast your mind back to that baneful piece of iron which was said to be lodged in the genitals of the Fisher King, and which not only blighted his role as consort to the Mother, but which also instigated the withdrawal of paradise and its replacement by the wasteland. Remember then how we found evidence of this exact wound in that mount named Iron Band, lodged, not in the genitals themselves, but close by in the top of that darker Lord's thigh, and how, due to this uncanny find, we then had, I think, every right to suspect the one beneath our feet as having once worn the mask of that Fisher King.

Well, we can now go one better even than that, although in doing so we'll again find that this dancer, as splendidly hopeful as his presence at the top of Albion's starry pile suggests, signifies *only the potential* perfection of us all, and thus in no sense a guarantee that we're all gonna make it - for let me tell you that that same blighting Iron Band is, on this the triplet, plunged not *near* his genitals but smack bang at the base of his phallus! In this, I feel, remains some warning revolving around not only our, but all nature's, future ability to healthily reproduce.

Note: just before we close the map, one last, and I think charming, observation. The Knights Templar, who we found had built their Temple Sowerby retreat upon Jesus' shoulder (now upon the upper right arm of this dancer) were known to have chosen Psalm 67 as an important chant in their chapter services - the psalm begins with: "God be merciful to us, and bless us; And cause his face to shine upon us; Selah!" So smile when seeing that upon the side of the face of the Dark Twin, and thus now upon the head of this dancer, is a tiny place called **Selah** so, as I have suggested earlier, did the Templars know this landscaped face, too?*

Time now to see yourself in the mirror

The urge to muse long upon these terrifyingly beautiful acres of Albion will, I hope, be irresistible for you, but for me I feel these giants demand more, even some eventual poetic melting of us into them and they into us, and this especially so in the case of this consummate dancer. So, since we're already gathered upon this figure, why not, for the fun of it, indulge me one last time by simply turning your back and letting yourself fall backwards, arms and legs spread-eagled, into the mirror as a falling starburst body of delight, which will have you perfectly slotted into the shape of this God-Man.

Caught within his mountainous arms, and with constellations both below and above you, and his heart become your own, shut your eyes and imagine yourself being one with the land, with all Albion; one with all the planet and thus with the entire universe, and as you expand, so feel that neutralizing twilight, that perfectly-balanced state of no-time at all, wrapping you as snugly as swaddling clothes. *You are* now the awaited axis between heaven and earth; *you* the meaningful magpie between the raven and the dove; *you* the connecting bridge between sundered lovers, indeed, *you* the very bridal chamber wherein they'll entwine as one.

Feel your sensory roots go down and tangle with the roots of the Tree of Life upon which you hang like Odin did in his seeking of the Secret of Secrets - go down deep so that you can climb as high - realise you're now 40 miles tall and yet, at the same time, infinitely tiny; your own God-aware atoms tuned to those which twin you to the equally God-aware molecules that form the iridescent strands of a spider's web, for in such contraction you might paradoxically have the chance of catapulted expansion to the very stars and beyond.

As massive as you are then, be aware of the life going on upon you; that vixen trotting down your arm, stolen chicken in her mouth; on your chest a shepherd climbing the stairs to bed; while hundreds of miles to the south feel the bullet of a London to Scotland express train hurtling towards you, a string of amber lights rushing out of Sagittarius' illuminated capital of a heart. Feel, too, the rushing in your veins of this land's every stream and river - some still welcoming a few of the last returning salmon, while others, seconding the warning buried in your groin, are flushing so much filth that not even a newt could make it a home. And what are you breathing - is that the taste of Sellafield's noxious outpouring carried but some 40 miles or so on a westerly breeze?

Gauge then your own health by the health of this giant in the landscape.

Expanding your awareness still further, look down now upon the rest of your star-giant kin, see them in your mind's eye laid out in their chronological placements to your own, which is at 12 o'clock high. Sense their full gargantuan splendour: there blazing from your right hand, a phoenix, and there a little further south that unborn child, sleeping Liverpool lights its face. Below that babe, and south of a bull's bellow, observe with a great big grin that child's Mother, your Mother, breasts a-swinging and cocking legs more than 60 miles long to the same tune that drives your own dance. Then way, way down at the base of the pictorial pyramid which *you* cap, mark the frothing tides of the English Channel where a milk-white unicorn dips her broken horn - what does it mean to you? See there, too, the dove homing in, time-frozen in her act of returning to Noah's ark; and above her to the east that almighty brine-blasted head that groans and rises from vast slumbers - it's he who is Sagittarius, Noah, on another day, and figurehead of the ark itself, where you yourself are spread-eagled like a star on its giddying 300-miles-tall mast - *you*, held up as the ultimate, though possibly most threatened, masterpiece within this ark, full of forgotten wonders.

Perceive and feel yourself within all of this; make it intimate to you; look over your shoulder, and if you see Scorpio, isolated as a picture of man's own isolation from nature and the recognition of the divinity therein, it's this artist's belief (admittedly no guru!) that held out to you are the keys to the Kingdom of Heaven on earth - and I say grasp them and take what's always been yours before it's too late.

And if, after all, we are nothing but dreamers...

...we're in the best of company! I have always intended to bring our journey to a close with a song, the one which I've found myself humming or whistling on many occasions throughout this walk through the stars; it being so wonderfully apt and written by him who was perhaps England's greatest dreamer of all time. Though how I wished he were still around to see this song of his made physical by the land, which inspired it in the first place. Why, even upon his death bed, they say, William Blake sang like a lark, as though there in the London heart of Sagittarius he beheld Jerusalem like a spring sap returning through the grimy streets below his window; a sap that was even then giving birth to an almighty Lamb of Aries from the west to the east coast and strongly answering his question: *"And was the holy lamb of God on England's pleasant pastures seen?"* Likewise in Cumbria, was there another massive 'YES' to his *"And did*

The Dance of Albion, William Blake. ©The British Museum

the countenance Divine shine forth upon our clouded hills?" - and that countenance just so happening to belong to a naked and arms-outstretched dancing God-Man, *exactly how Blake had painted the personification of the psyche of Albion upon some future day of global celebration!*

Indeed, before I write down the full verses of that farewell song I should like the last picture in this book to be one of Blake's, for the one mentioned above remarkably mirrors the land's own farewell masterpiece - why, he even entitled it *The Dance of Albion!* And when you see it, tell me it's not a watercolour depiction of what we see now rendered in rock over 40 miles tall! Look at it, and tell me Blake didn't see in spiritual vision something of what I'm here presenting as rock-solid fact!

The only thing different in Blake's rendition of the dancer is the omission of that cloven left foot, although there just so happens to be a worm conspicuously placed beneath that human left foot, which art historian Robert Lister in his book *The Paintings of William Blake* recommends we see as a symbol of *darkness* - and that will do for me!

Blake's *Jerusalem*, then, is the song I'd like to end on, as we're lying on our backs at the apex of a miracle, and what finer place to sing it than upon this dancer's heart of Cross Fell - aptly the highest point of his entire form. And can I seal the magic of the moment by letting a hedgehog (and no, that isn't a typing error!) sing it to us, while Albion's most famed king of all reclines at our side in the gathering dawn twilight.

Thus I invite the author T H White, who was another glorious dreamer, and who perhaps got closest of all to sniffing out the real character of Arthur, to lead us into this very special rendering of *Jerusalem*, because, for me, he has that hedgehog do a goose-pimply good job of it, and far more moving than any massed orchestra and raucous audience at a BBC 'Last Night of the Proms' could do.

White sets the scene near the end of his *Book of Merlyn*, where an aged King Arthur has just climbed a high peak beneath a massive moon to have one last look over his realm. It's the evening of his own Gethsemane, as the next day brings the withering clash of arms upon that fatal field of Camlann - and the old king knew it.

With him on this high vantage point is his friend the hedgehog who, having been touched by Merlyn's magic, had a fine, if delightfully 'country bumpkin' grasp of the English language.

So there they are; and here we are with them; the king and the hedgehog scanning the sleeping realm they loved with all their hearts, and I would beg of you, even if you do not read the whole book, to read White's short chapter in its entirety, for in this beautiful passage some of the rustic down-to-earth magic of Albion oozes through, each paragraph a lilting simple prayer to the honest-to-goodness strivings of man in his effort to use the spirit that resides in simple British fields as a springboard to a finer realization of what a gift it is to live a life on earth - indeed a springboard eventually back to the stars from whence we all came. And, in my opinion, White, Arthur, and that gifted hedgehog come oh so close to guessing that the stars were all the time beneath that same moonlit coverlet of fields.

Space, however, will only allow me to start from where Arthur with, I sense, an emotional lump in his throat, senses he is but a few hours away from the end of his own journey, and so takes his last long look at the landscape whereon he had wished to build a golden age founded upon a Round Table of stars.

Enter, then, Arthur's friend the hedgehog, seeming to me to be innocently speaking on behalf of the land in professing her never-ending love and patience in waiting for humankind to realise the true wonder of their being. Anyway, the creature senses the brimming eyes of his king and offers to sing him a song to give him heart to believe that all his strivings to bring about that golden time would eventually not be in vain:

"*Dost tha mind as how us used for to sing to 'un?*"

"*I minds 'un well. 'Twas Rustic Bridge, and Genevieve*
and... and..."

"*Home Sweet Home.*"
The king quite suddenly bowed his head.
"*Shall us sing 'un for 'ee agean, Majesty mun?*"

He could only nod.

The hedgehog stood in the moonlight, assuming the proper attitude for song. He planted his feet squarely, folded his hands on his stomach, fixed his eye upon a distant object. Then, in his clear country tenor, he sang for the King of England about Home Sweet Home.

The silly, simple music died away - but not silly in the moonlight, not on a mountain of your realm. The hedgehog shuffled, coughed, was wishful for something more. But the king was speechless.

"*Majesty,*" *he mentioned shyly,* "*us gotter fresh 'un.*"

There was no reply.

"*When us knowed as you was acoming, us larned a fresh 'un. 'Twas for thy welcome, like. Us larned it off of that there Mearn.*"

"*Sing it,*" *gasped the old man. He had stretched his bones upon the heather, because it was all too much.*

And there, upon the height of England, in a good pronunciation because he had learned it carefully from Merlyn, to Parry's music from the future, with his sword of twigs in one grey hand and a chariot of mouldy leaves, the hedgehog stood to build Jerusalem: and meant it.

And did those feet in ancient time
Walk upon England's mountains green?
And was the holy lamb of God
On England's pleasant pastures seen?

And did the countenance Divine
Shine forth upon our clouded hills?
And was Jerusalem built here
Among these dark Satanic Mills?

Bring me my Bow of burning gold:
Bring me my Arrows of desire:
Bring me my spear: O clouds unfold!
Bring me my Chariot of fire.
I will not cease from Mental Fight.
Nor shall my sword sleep in my hand
'Til we have built Jerusalem
In England's green and pleasant land.

And again, what better '*height of England*' than *this* high Cross Fell heart of this dancing figure - from where just 20 miles to the north (*see Aquarius*), Arthur would be brought to that probable site of Camlann, and where his golden age came to an end in his possible failure to accept Mordred/Scorpio for better or worse as part of that Round Table of stars.

In my opinion then, we are privileged to be living at this time when dreams (maybe T H White's included) really are becoming beautiful realities - even a very far-fetched one about a Jerusalem rising out of England's green and pleasant land, for I say **Behold Jerusalem - it has arrived!** Though I think it's never been away.

★ ★ ★ ★ ★

But like that hedgehog I myself cough and wish for something more to end on - and it comes out like this: at the end of the day, and when all is said and done, it really does not matter whether or not my many intuitional soundings throughout this book, from signs of flood to a new reading of events at Golgotha, are bang on target or hopelessly astray.

Therefore don't worry too much whether Arviragus was the truth behind Arthur, or for that matter whether Arthur ever existed at all! The same goes for whether or not Taliesin was Merlin; if Jason did or didn't find that golden fleece hanging on Albion's Tree of Life; or whether that Cow Green Reservoir has sod-all to do with Isis. "Poo Poo" to high heaven too, if you like, my hunch that in the *High History of the Holy Grail* that hermit might have caught visionary sight of Sellafield's nuclear reactor a thousand or two years before its time, and likened it to that forever-burning castle (*see Aquarius*) where from the '*end of the world*' would receive its initial trigger. Your sniggers may well be all that such a hunch deserves. I certainly wouldn't give a damn. And as for the theory of global warming and rising seas, who knows for sure whether it's for real or just plain scare-mongering which will itself raise sniggers in the future.

I also hasten to add that it will not spell disaster to what the land has done if Jesus never once set foot in Britain, nor even if his purely inland portrayal in Cumbria is nothing but the product of my imagination. Nor, for that matter, would it be ruinous to my discovery if Jesus, as some historians claim, never even existed. But if you feel in your heart that Jesus did exist in the flesh, but that my re-reading of those events surrounding the crucifixion was an exercise in naïvety, then I will not argue with you. Here, at the end of this wacky walkabout, the only thing that I *can* honestly tell you without a shadow of doubt is that the appearance of 12 zodiacal signs, plus a griffin, sea-carved into Britain and Northern Ireland's coastline, and these being virtual template copies of those 12 zodiacal giants that bulge the landscape around Glastonbury, not to mention that group in the Preseli mountains, **IS A MIND BOGGLING FACT** - and I think that that alone is enough for any of us to struggle with!

Dismantle every one of my bolted-on revelations and Albion will still stand, because it's in those *coastal*-cut shapes alone, and these cross-referenced to what Katherine Maltwood found in Somerset, where you'll find the fundamental evidence that a miracle has taken place within these British Isles, a phenomenon written so bloody massively that even from outer space a man may now look down and see heaven reflected upon earth. I call it a living vision of a New Jerusalem, a foundational springboard to a newer outlook of our existence - but you can go call it what you will because it's *your* gigantic baby now!

What I'm trying to ram home, as I pack my bag, is that what Britain's coastline, along with Glastonbury's fields and Preseli's mountains, have to say between them is all that's needed to prove that a miracle *has* taken place beneath our noses, and one that does not count on any of my intuitional embellishments for its credibility. So, I would rather you tossed this entire book of mine away than let its many inland dilemmas vex you; but I hope you'd just keep the single 'shout' of the coast as featured upon its cover, for in that outer tracery is sea-pounded every second the inescapable truth that God, the Cosmic Mind, call it whatever you like, is trying to catch our eye for some almighty reason. The physical reality of its work is neither enhanced nor dented one jot by this artist's many leaps into areas, whether history, religion or mythology, where he is many leagues out of his depth.

Simply, this baby has now a gigantic life of its own, indeed, I repeat that it's *your* baby now. But whether or not you disown this wondrous child left on your doorstep (and I say again that it's on *your* doorstep whether you live in Sheffield, Shanghai, Seattle or Sidney!) do note this: it will from this day onwards never ever go away unless nature herself wishes once more to take it back, on account that we're not fit to nurture such a treasure. Such an act would leave us blind to at least 50% of the true glory of an earthly existence on this miraculous and holy third jewel from the sun.

So what should we do with earth's screaming
bundle upon our doorsteps?

"Ask and it shall be given you;
seek and you shall find;
knock and it shall be opened to you."
MATTHEW, Chapter 7 Verse 7

Farewell.
New Year's Eve 2000.

Last but not least - a plea

Many of you (myself included), having seen the magic in the map, will,
I'm sure, be drawn to visit these giants physically as well as
spiritually, and, in particular, to experience the locations of some of their
most potent features. For instance, who wouldn't, knowing what we know
now, like to stand quietly at Jesus' High Cup Nick wound or dip a hand into
that Cow Green wound of his twin? Or maybe, if you're a Gemini, wouldn't
you just love to feel in person something of Liverpool's deep secret; or as a
Sagittarian to look into Eye! And I wouldn't blame others for wanting to do
nothing but sit quietly within that sperm/grain shape of Bardsey Island and
relive Gwion's metamorphosis into rainbow-browed Taliesin, knowing that
the 120-mile-tall goddess reaches out to pluck you up as she did him! Why,
you could even happily allow her to swallow you as she did Gwion by
trekking down her throat and into her belly, before flowing with that river
Dovey out to a poetical rebirth.

Without doubt, this landscape is now alive with the most magical places in
which to stand with eyes freshly opened. What is more, I know the spirit of
whatever place you visit with that new perception will, in return, welcome
your awareness.

Having said all that, I must make a plea to you that no matter where you
stand on these giants, and no matter how tempting it may be to take a small
stone or some other keepsake, or even leave your own offering or mark there,
please let the temptation go. Do not even disturb a blade of grass, if you can
help it, for, if you love this land and accept its own awareness, I hope you
sense too that to take or leave anything would be a crime - every stick, leaf,
and stone knows where it is; it is one with the giant below it.

So if you do come, please, please let it all be.

Bibliography

The Acorn Book of Birthing the Cosmic Child
Published by The Acorn Centre, Shepton Mallet.

ASHE, Geoffrey
The Landscape of King Arthur
Grange Books, 1992

BEAUMONT, Comyns
Britain - The Key to World History
Rider & Company Ltd.

BARING, Anne & CASHFORD, Jules
The Myth of the Goddess
BCA, 1991

BAUVAL, Robert & GILBERT, Adrian
The Orion Mystery
Mandarin, 1994

BELLAMY, David & QUALE, Brendan
England's Last Wilderness
Michael Joseph Ltd, 1989

BLAKE, William
Jerusalem
Facsimile Edition. The Tate Gallery Publications, 1991

BLY, Robert
Iron John
Element, 1990

BULFINCH, Thomas
The Golden Age of Myth and Legend
George G Harrap & Ltd

CAINE, Mary
The Glastonbury Zodiac
Published by Mary Caine, Kingston, Surrey. 1978

COWPER POWYS, John
A Glastonbury Romance
Picador - Pan Books Ltd, 1975

DANIELOU, Alain
The Phallus
Inner Traditions International, Vermont, 1995

von ESCHENBACH, Wolfram
Parzival
Penguin Books, 1969

EVANS, Sebastian - Translator
The High History of the Holy Grail
James Clarke & Co.

FABRICIUS, Johannes
Alchemy
Rosenkilde & Bagger, Copenhagen, 1976

FAIRBURN, Neil
A Traveller's Guide to the Kingdoms of Arthur
Evans Bros, 1983

FRAZER, Sir James George
The Golden Bough
Macmillan & Co Ltd, 1929

GAD, Dr Irene
Tarot and Individuation
Nicholas-Hays Inc, Maine, 1994

GODWIN, Malcolm
The Holy Grail
Bloomsbury, 1994

GOLDBERG, B Z
The Sacred Fire - The Story of Sex in Religion
Jarrolds, 1931

GRAVES, Robert
The White Goddess
Faber & Faber, 1961

GUEST, Lady Charlotte - Translator
The Mabinogion
Facsimile Edition. John Jones, Cardiff, 1977

GUTTMAN, Ariel & JOHNSON, Kenneth
Mythic Astrology
Llewellyn Publishers, MN 55164-0383, 1993

HANNCOCK, Graham & FAIIA, Santha
Heavens Mirror
Michael Joseph, 1998

HARDY, Thomas
Tess of the d'Urbervilles
Introduction by A. Alvarez
Penguin Books, 1985

HUGHES, Ted
Crow
Faber and Faber, 1974

JOWETT, George F
The Drama of the Lost Disciples
Covenant Publishing, 1961

JUNG, C G - Translated by HULL, R F C
Psychology and Alchemy
Routledge & Kegan Paul, 1974

LAWRENCE, D H
Selected Poems
Penguin Books, 1960

LISTER, Raymond
The Paintings of William Blake
The Press Syndicate of the University of Cambridge,
1986

MALTWOOD, Katherine
A Guide to Glastonbury's Temple of the Stars
James Clarke & Co Ltd, 1964
      and -
Enchantments of Britain
James Clark & Co, 1982

MANN, A T & LYLE, Jane
Sacred Sexuality
Element, 1995

MATARASSO, P M - Translator
The Quest of the Holy Grail - (Queste del San Graal)
Penguin Books, 1969

MATTHEWS, Caitlin & John
The Encyclopaedia of Celtic Wisdom
Element, 1994

MATTHEWS, John
The Grail Tradition
Element, 1990

MEREZHKOVSKY, Dmitri
The Secret of the West
Jonathan Cape, 1936

MILLER, Hamish & BROADHURST, Paul
The Sun and the Serpent
Pendragon Press, 1989

PAGELS, Elaine
The Gnostic Gospels
Penguin Books, 1979

PARKER, John
*Cumbria - A Guide to the Lake District and
its County*
Bartholomew, 1977

ROBERTS, Anthony - Editor
Glastonbury - Ancient Avalon, New Jerusalem
Rider & Co, 1977

ROBINSON, James M - General Editor
The Nag Hammadi Library
Harper, San Francisco, 1990

Siva Samhita
The Oriental Book Reprint Cooperation, 1975

SESTI, Giuseppe Maria
The Glorious Constellations
Harry N Abrams Pub, New York, 1991

SHEPARD, Odell
The Lore of the Unicorn
Senate Editions, 1996

SPENCE, Lewis
The Mysteries of Britain
Newcastle Publishing Co Inc, California, 1993

STEIN, Walter Johannes
The Death of Merlin
Floris Books, 1989

STEPHENS, James
The Crock of Gold
Macmillan & Co Ltd, 1953

SZEKELY, Edmond Bordeaux - Translator
The Gospel of the Essenes
and -
The Gospel of Peace of Jesus Christ
The C W Daniel Co Ltd, 1993

TENNYSON, Alfred, Lord
The Complete Works
Macmillan, 1902

WILLIAMS, Prof. Mary - Editor
Glastonbury & Britain, a Study in Patterns
Research into Lost Knowledge Organisation, 1990

WILLS, Pauline & GIMBLE, Theo
Sixteen Steps to Health & Energy
Quantum, 1992

WRIGHT, Dudley
Druidism
E P Publishing, 1974

Maps used

Bartholomew map as printed in John Parker's book
Cumbria, a Guide to the Lake District and its County.
*Listed above

Institute of Geological Sciences
Geological Map of the UK (South) 3rd Edition, 1979
Published by Ordnance Survey

Michelin - Road maps of Great Britain
Sheet numbers: *402* (1992), *403* (1993), *404* (1991),
and of Ireland: *405* (1993/94)

Ordnance Survey - Landranger Series
Sheet numbers: *86, 90, 91*

Ordnance Survey - Travelmaster Series
Sheet number: *5*

Ordnance Survey - Outdoor Leisure Series
Sheet number: *28*

The Readers Digest Great World Atlas
Readers Digest Assoc, 1961